WELCOME TO THE BALLROOM

no.2 | TOMO TAKEUCHI

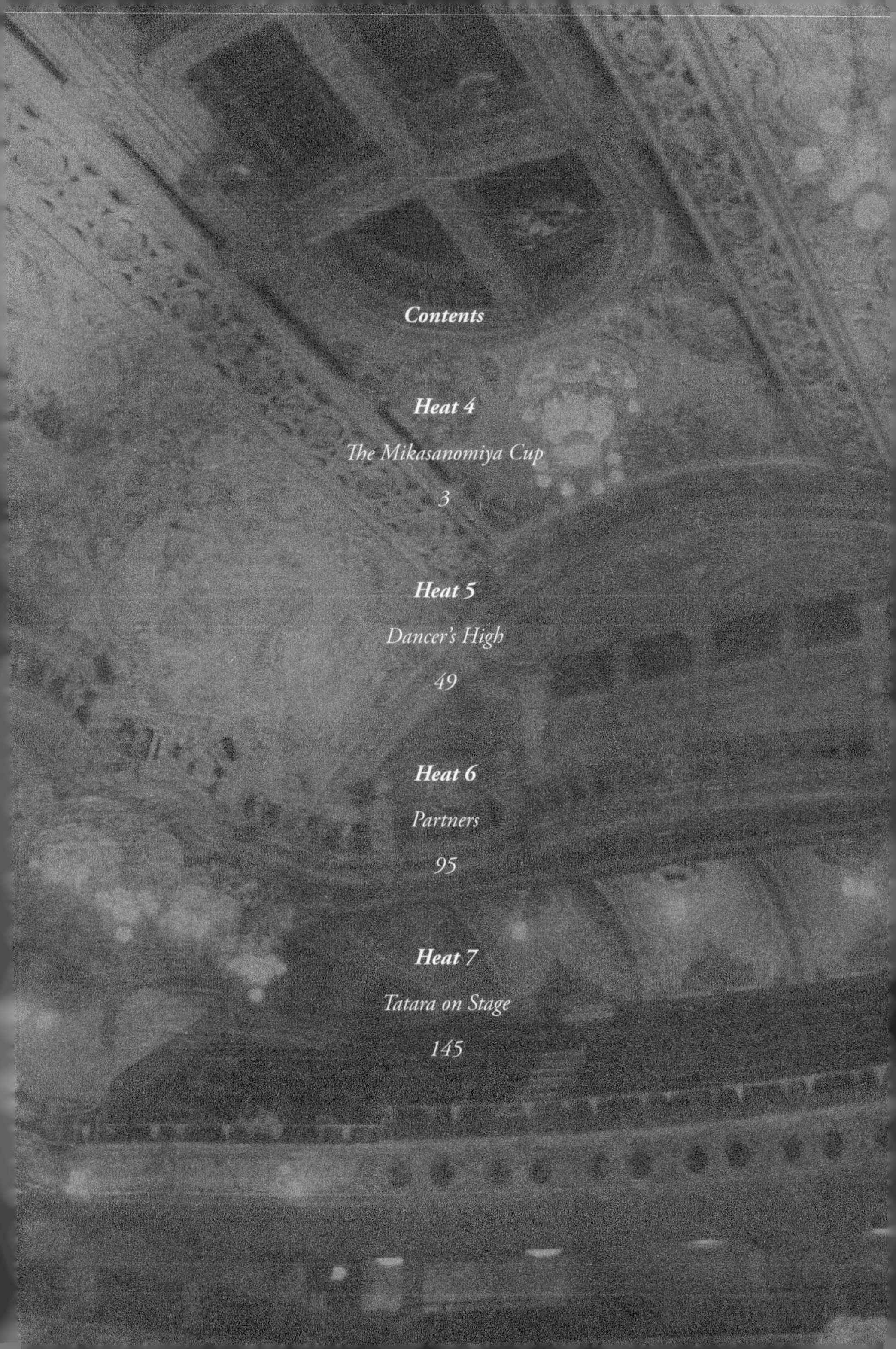

Contents

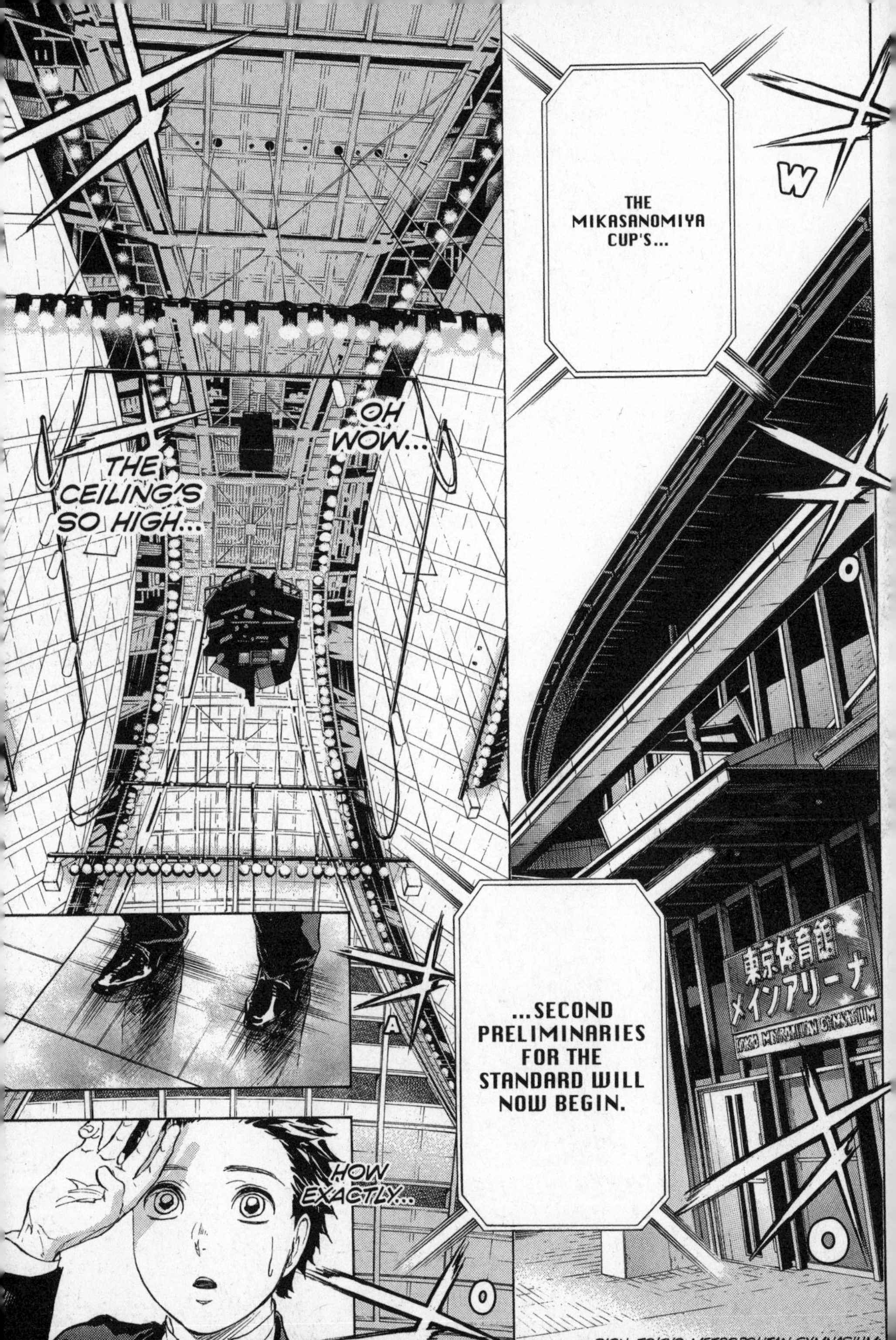
THE MIKASANOMIYA CUP'S...
W
東京体育館
メインアリーナ
O
...SECOND PRELIMINARIES FOR THE STANDARD WILL NOW BEGIN.
O
OH WOW...
THE CEILING'S SO HIGH...
A
HOW EXACTLY...
O
SIGN: TOKYO METROPOLITAN GYMNASIUM; MAIN ARENA

Heat 4
The Mikasanomiya Cup

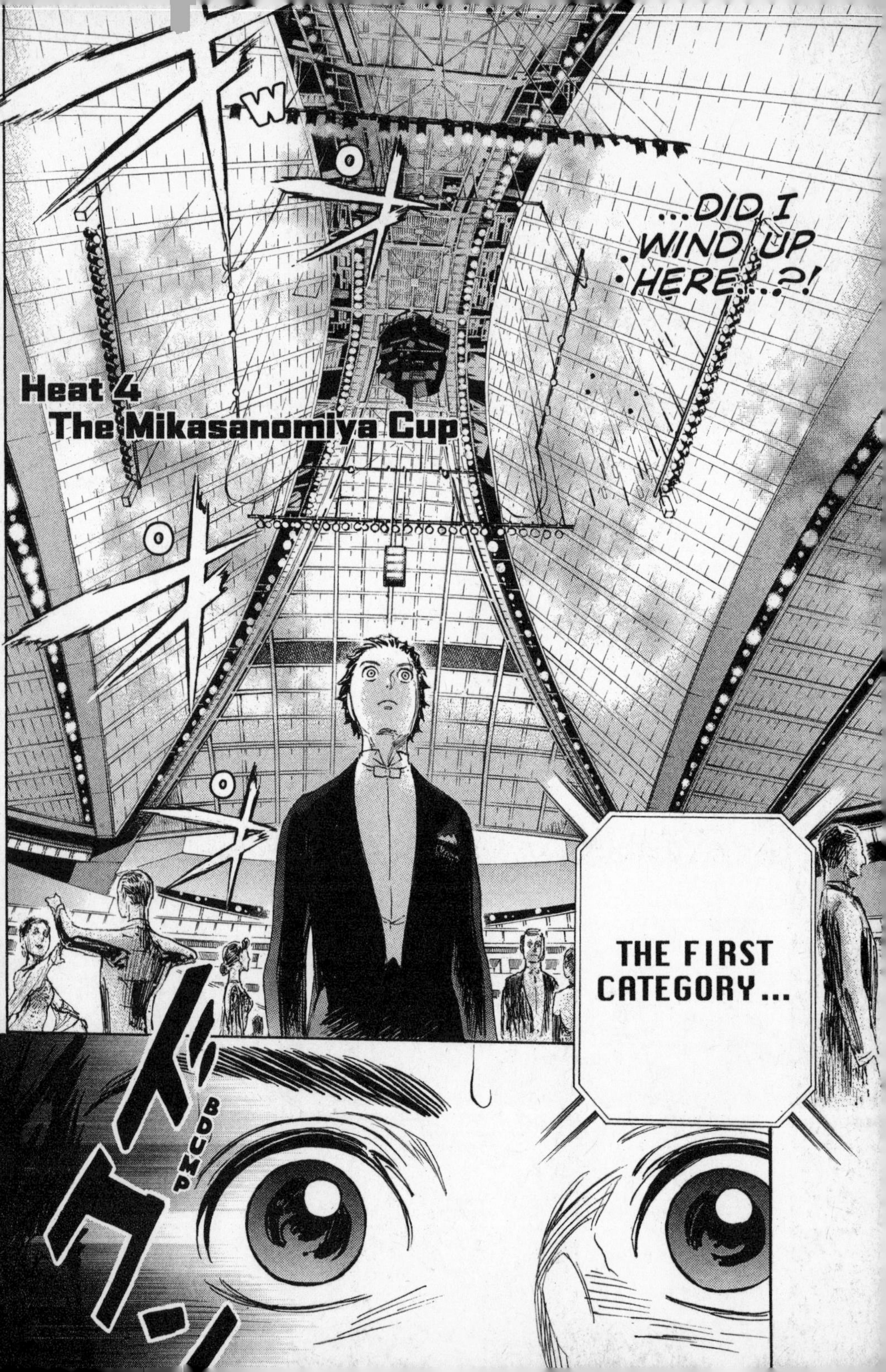
...DID I WIND UP HERE...?!
W
O
O
O
THE FIRST CATEGORY...
BDUMP

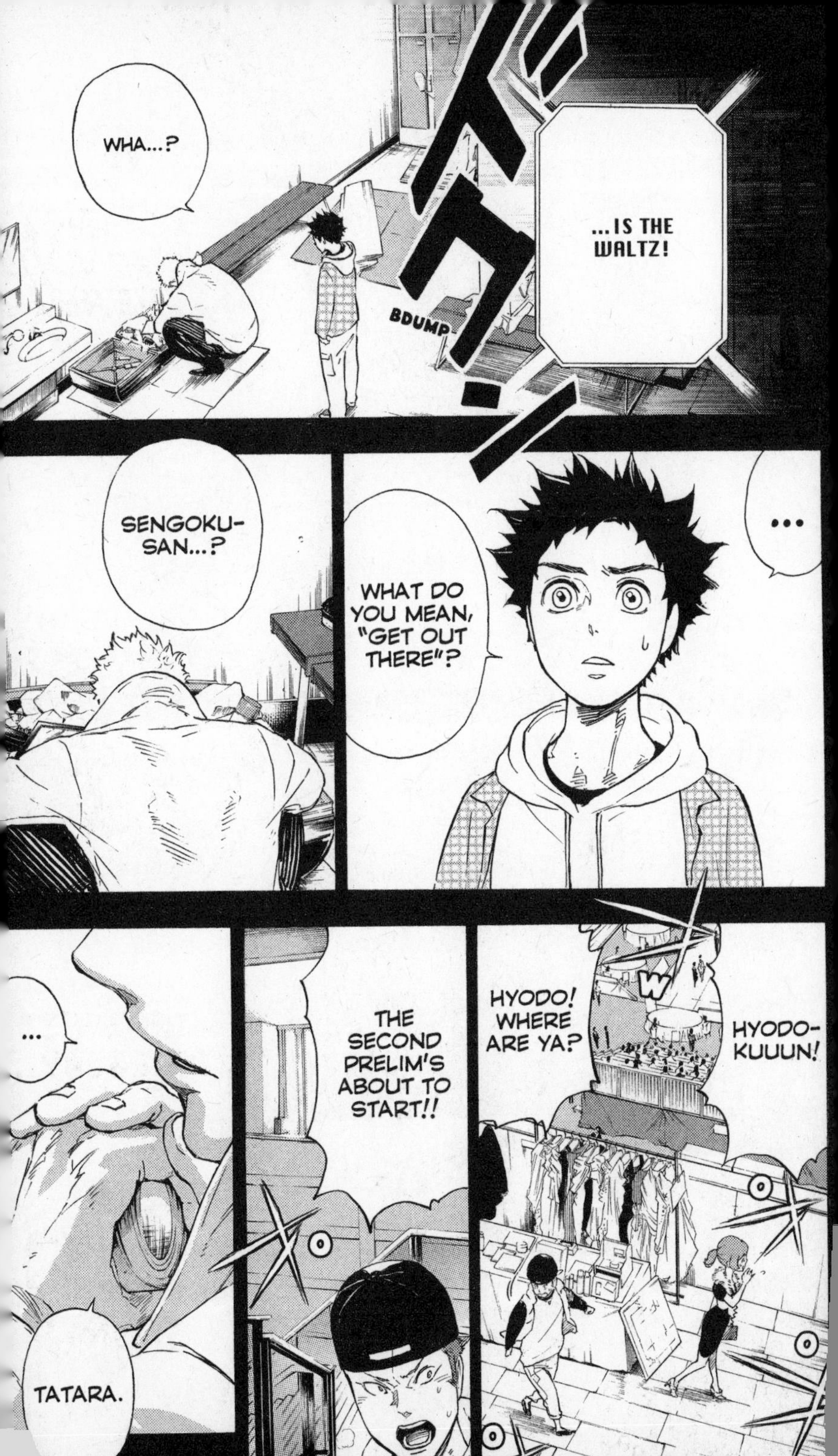
...IS THE WALTZ!
BDUMP
WHA...?
...
WHAT DO YOU MEAN, "GET OUT THERE"?
SENGOKU-SAN...?
HYODO-KUUUN!
W
HYODO! WHERE ARE YA?
THE SECOND PRELIM'S ABOUT TO START!!
...
TATARA.

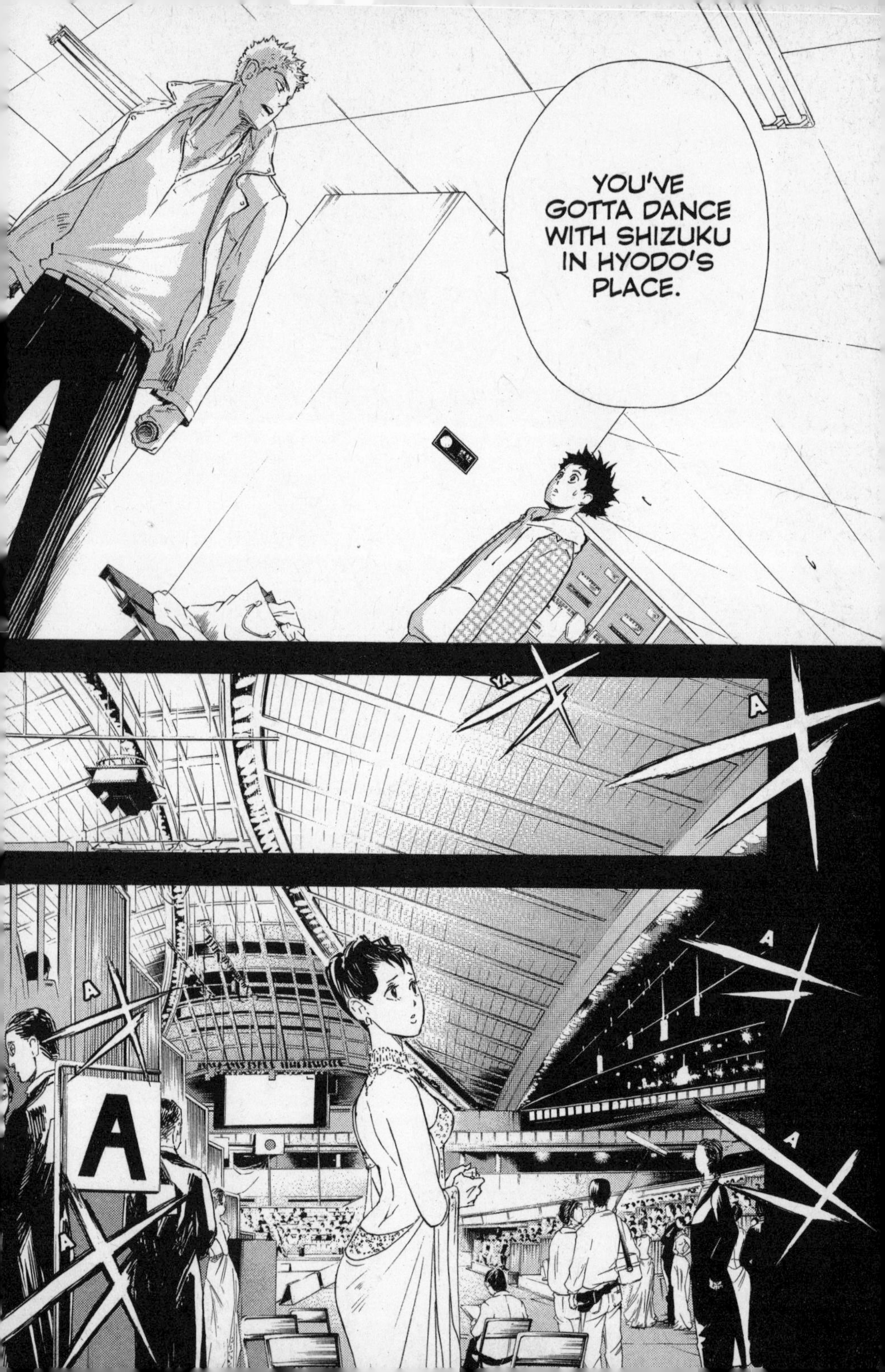
YOU'VE GOTTA DANCE WITH SHIZUKU IN HYODO'S PLACE.
A
YA
A
A
A
A
A
A

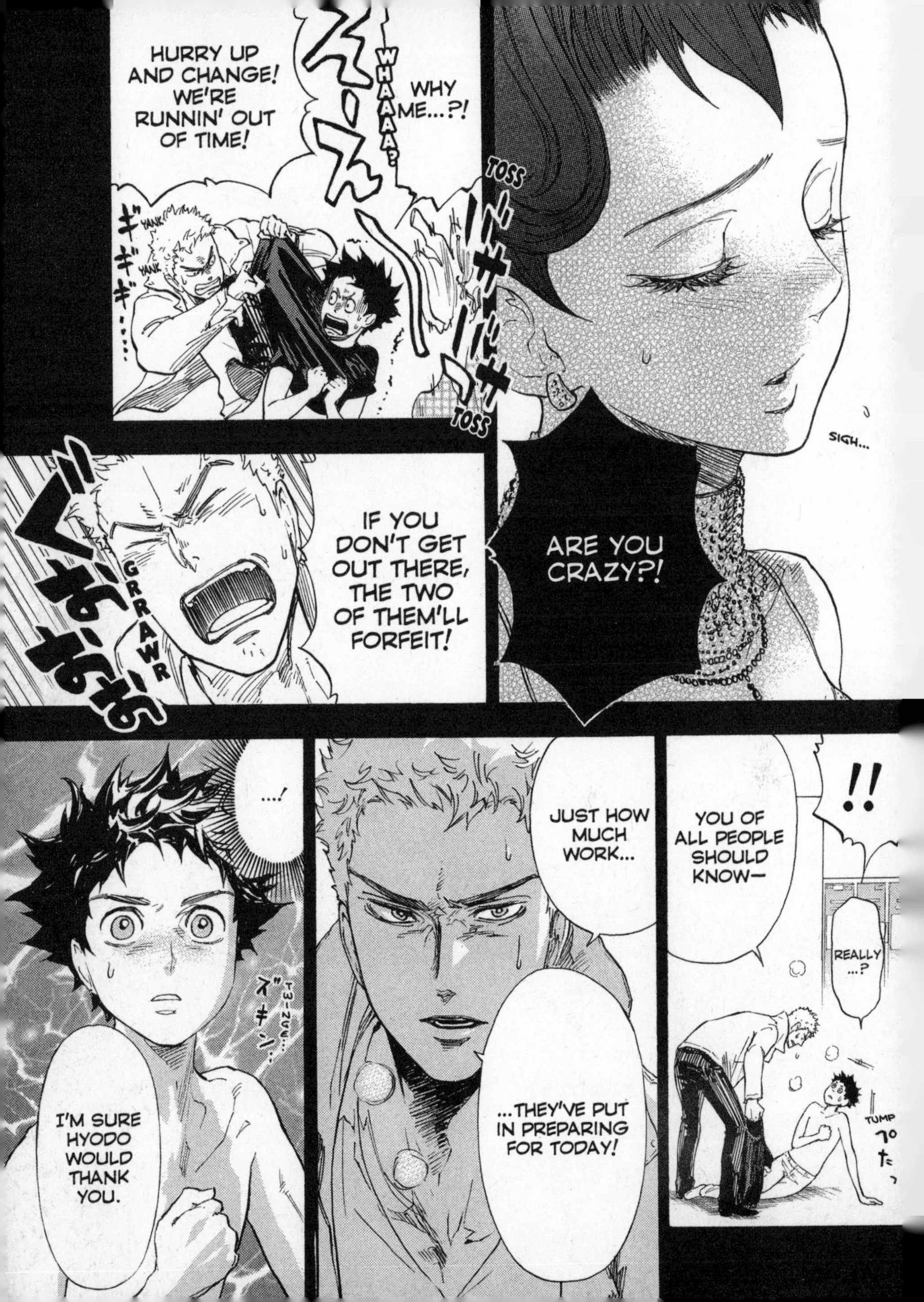
SIGH...
ARE YOU CRAZY?!
WHAAAA?
WHY ME...?!
TOSS
TOSS
HURRY UP AND CHANGE! WE'RE RUNNIN' OUT OF TIME!
YANK
YANK
GRRAWR
IF YOU DON'T GET OUT THERE, THE TWO OF THEM'LL FORFEIT!
!!
YOU OF ALL PEOPLE SHOULD KNOW—
REALLY ...?
TUMP
JUST HOW MUCH WORK...
...THEY'VE PUT IN PREPARING FOR TODAY!
...!
TWINGE...
I'M SURE HYODO WOULD THANK YOU.

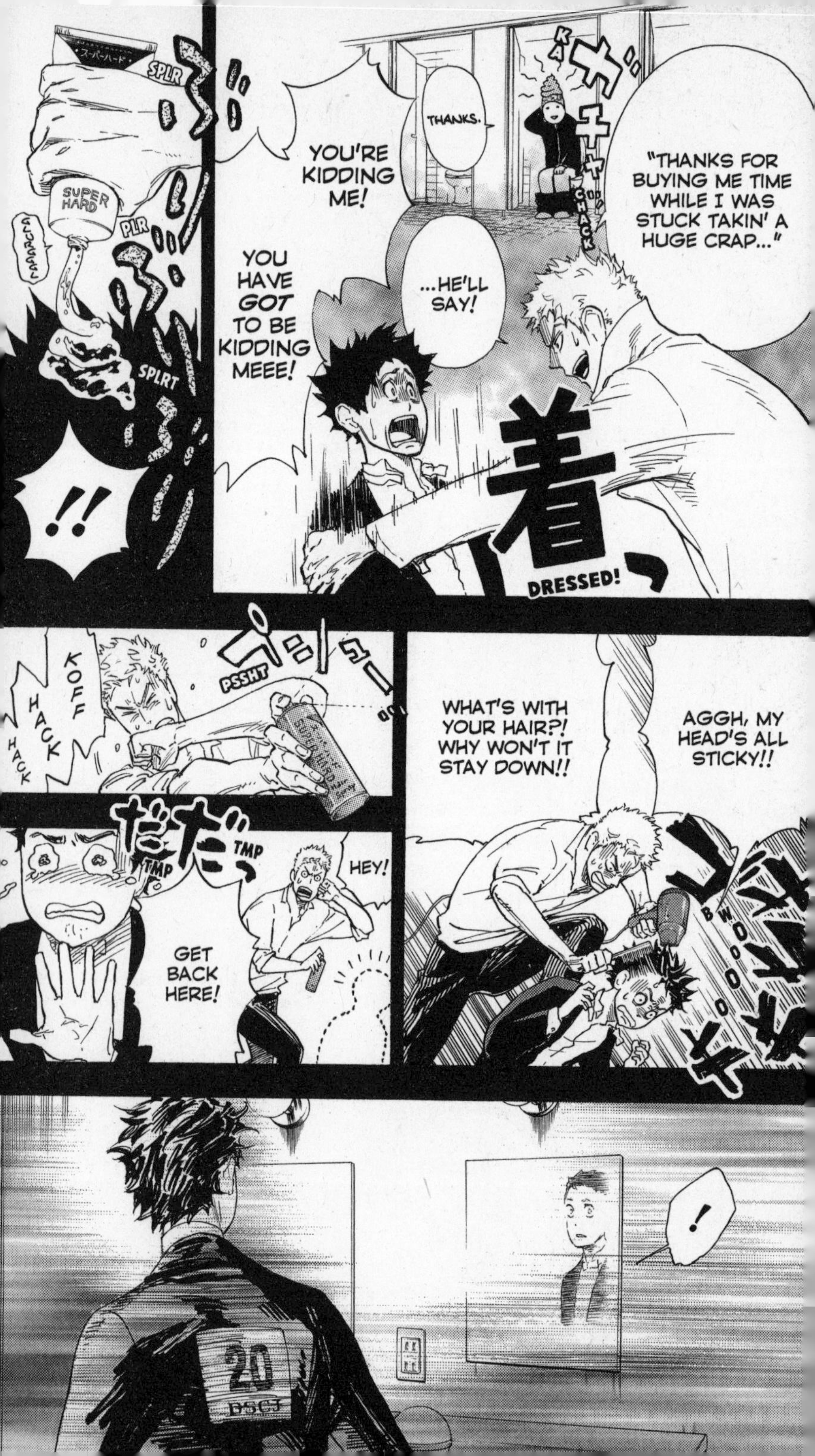
KA
"THANKS FOR BUYING ME TIME WHILE I WAS STUCK TAKIN' A HUGE CRAP..."
THANKS.
CHACK
YOU'RE KIDDING ME!
...HE'LL SAY!
YOU HAVE GOT TO BE KIDDING MEEE!
着
DRESSED!
スーパーハード
SPLR
SUPER HARD
PLR
SPLRT
!!
AGGH, MY HEAD'S ALL STICKY!!
WHAT'S WITH YOUR HAIR?! WHY WON'T IT STAY DOWN!!
BWOOOOO
PSSHT
KOFF
HACK
HACK
HEY!
TMP
TMP
GET BACK HERE!
!
20

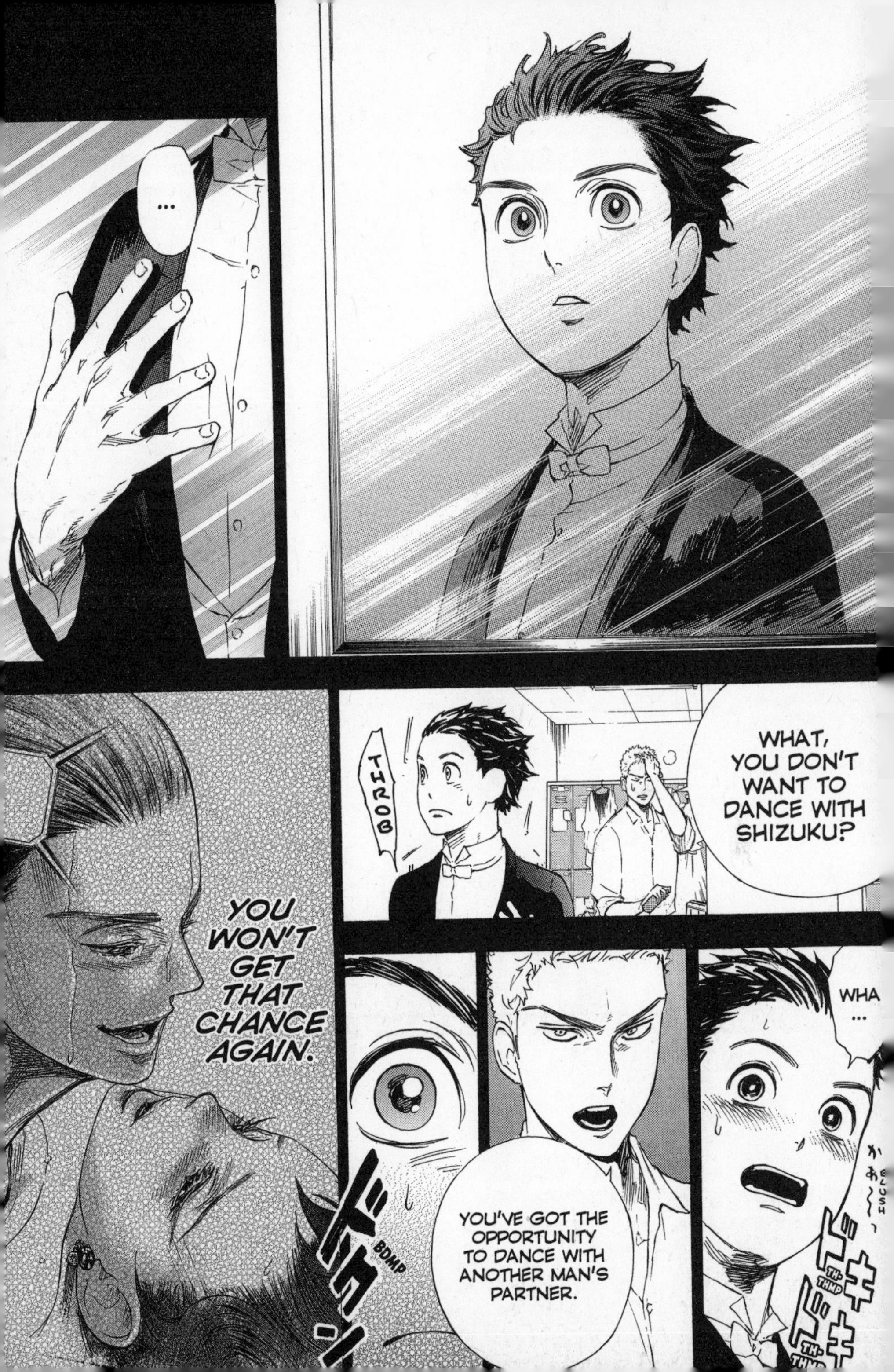
...
THROB
WHAT, YOU DON'T WANT TO DANCE WITH SHIZUKU?
WHA...
BLUSH
TH-THMP
TH-THMP
YOU'VE GOT THE OPPORTUNITY TO DANCE WITH ANOTHER MAN'S PARTNER.
BDMP
YOU WON'T GET THAT CHANCE AGAIN.

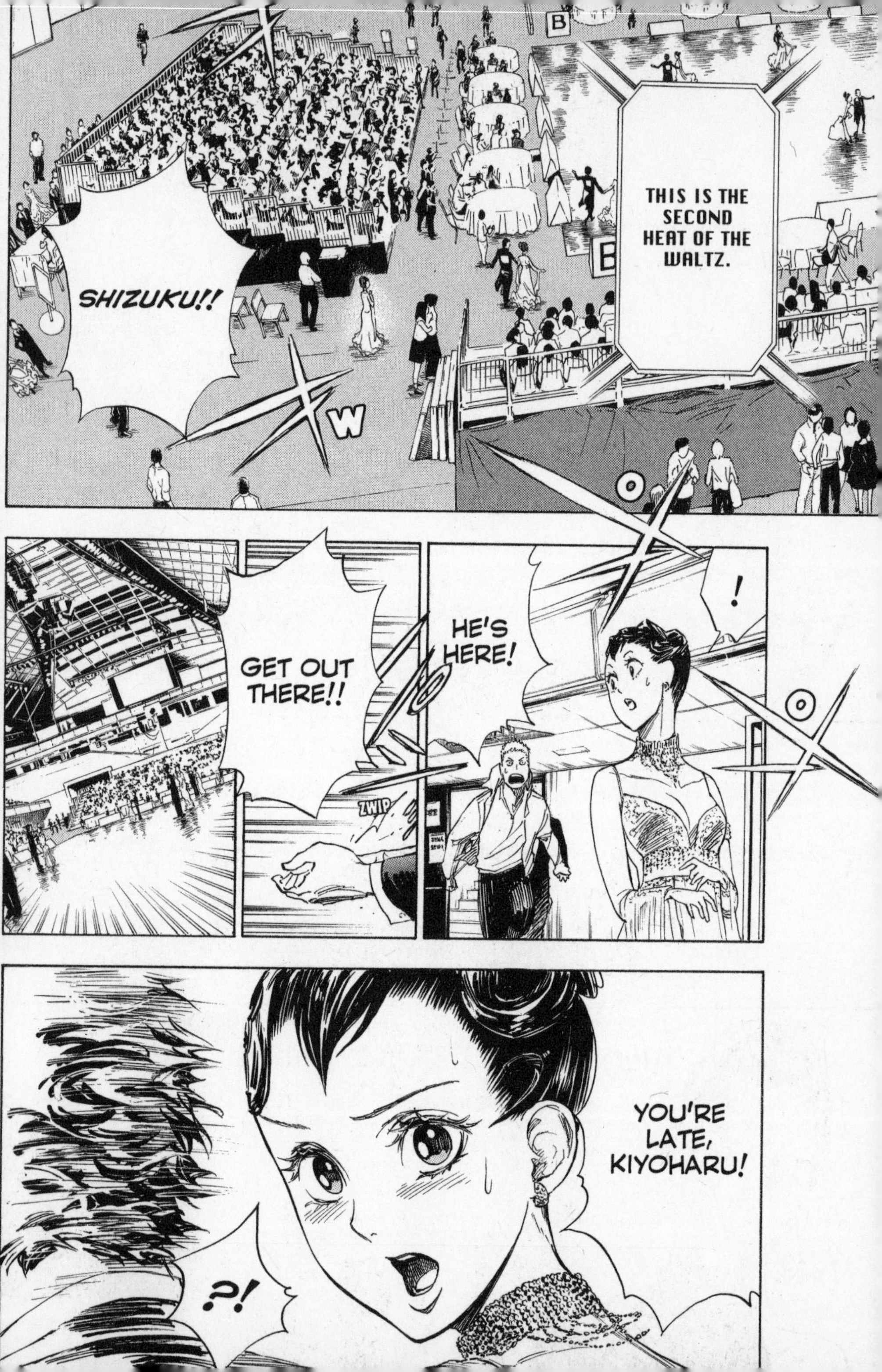
THIS IS THE SECOND HEAT OF THE WALTZ.
O
W
SHIZUKU!!
O
!
HE'S HERE!
O
GET OUT THERE!!
ZWIP
YOU'RE LATE, KIYOHARU!
?!

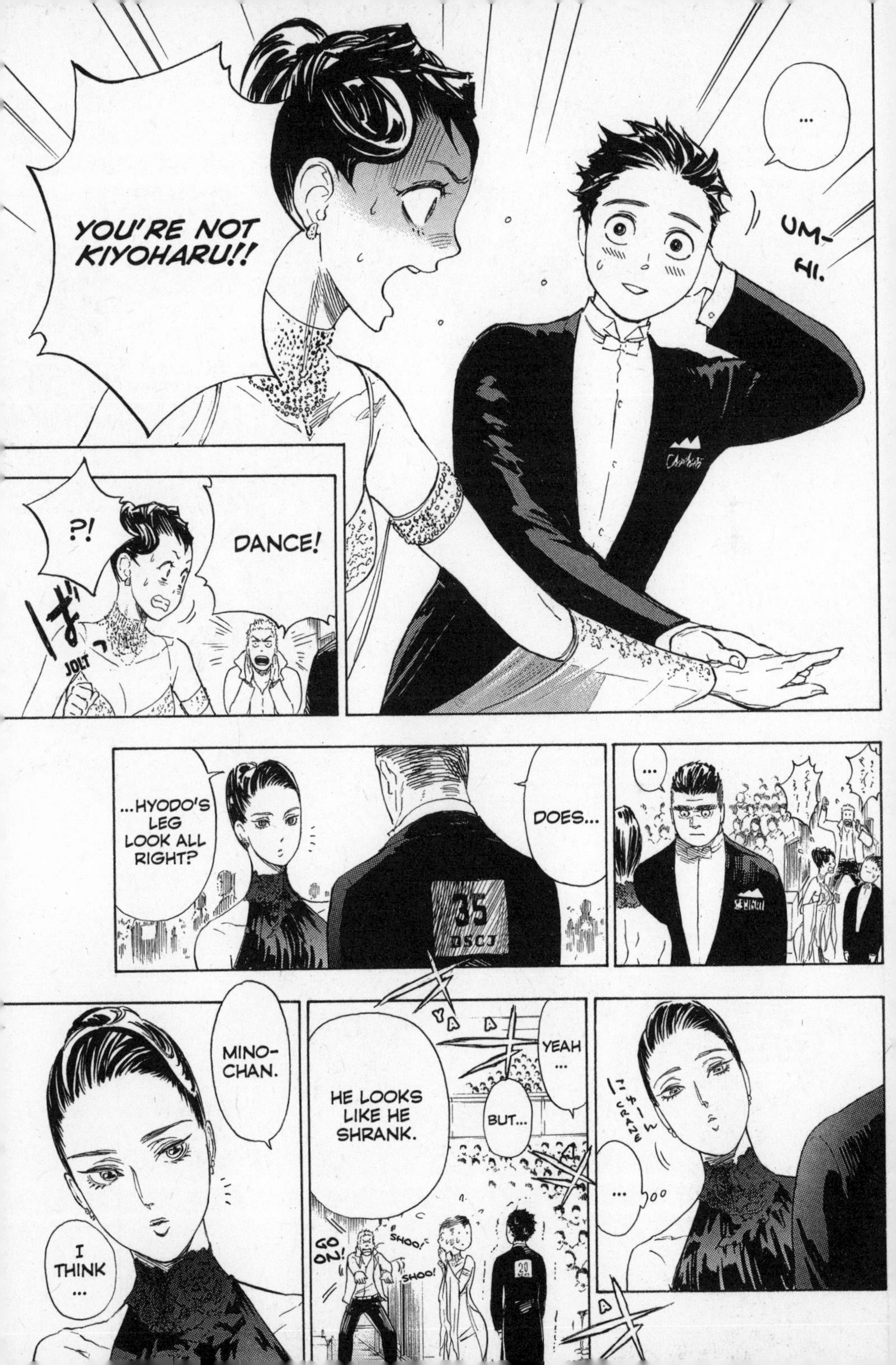
...
UM-HI.
YOU'RE NOT KIYOHARU!!
DANCE!
?!
JOLT
...
DOES...
...HYODO'S LEG LOOK ALL RIGHT?
CRANE
...
YEAH ...
BUT...
HE LOOKS LIKE HE SHRANK.
SHOO!
SHOO!
GO ON!
MINO-CHAN.
I THINK ...

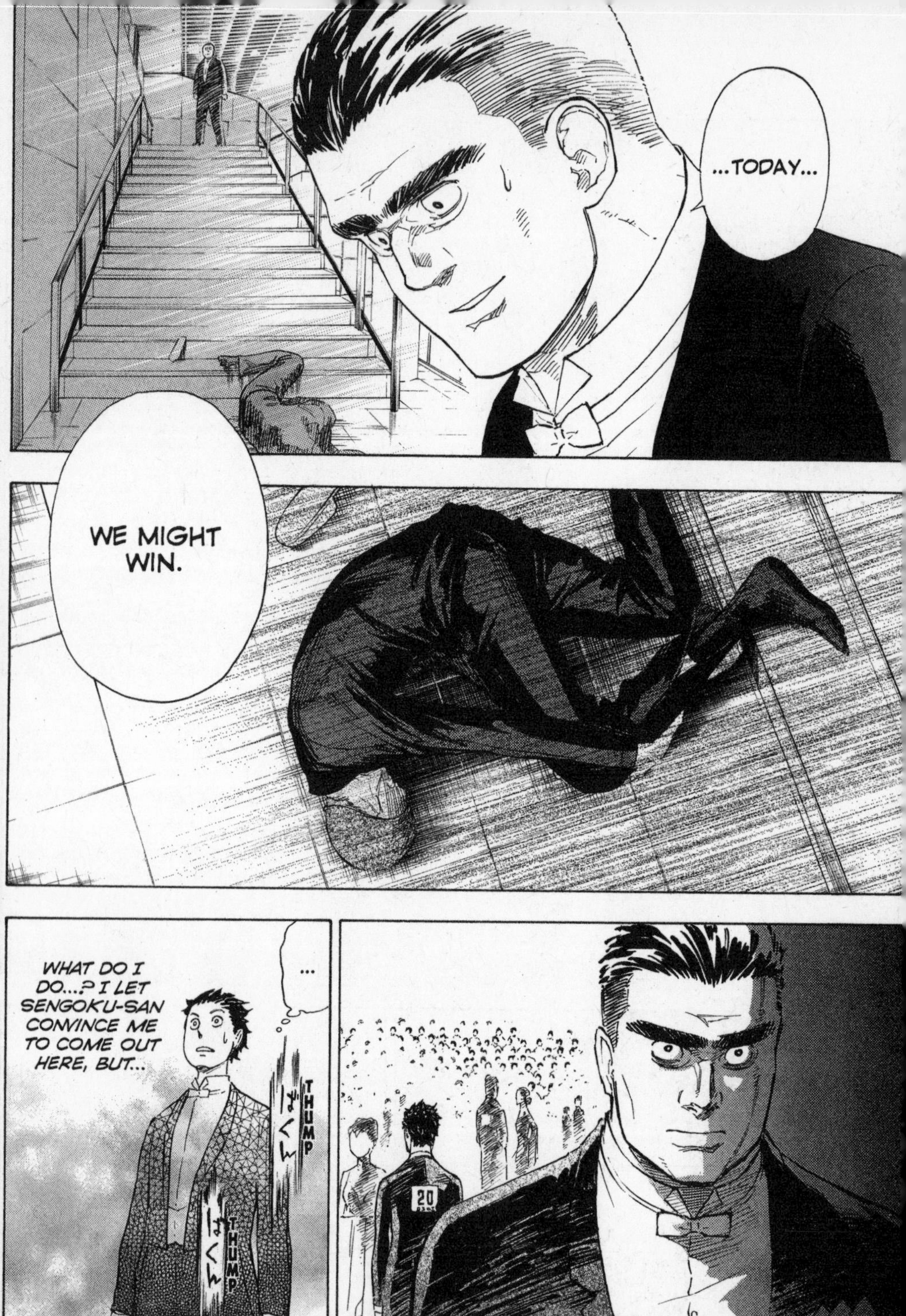
...TODAY...
WE MIGHT WIN.
...
WHAT DO I DO...? I LET SENGOKU-SAN CONVINCE ME TO COME OUT HERE, BUT...
ばくん THUMP
ばくん THUMP

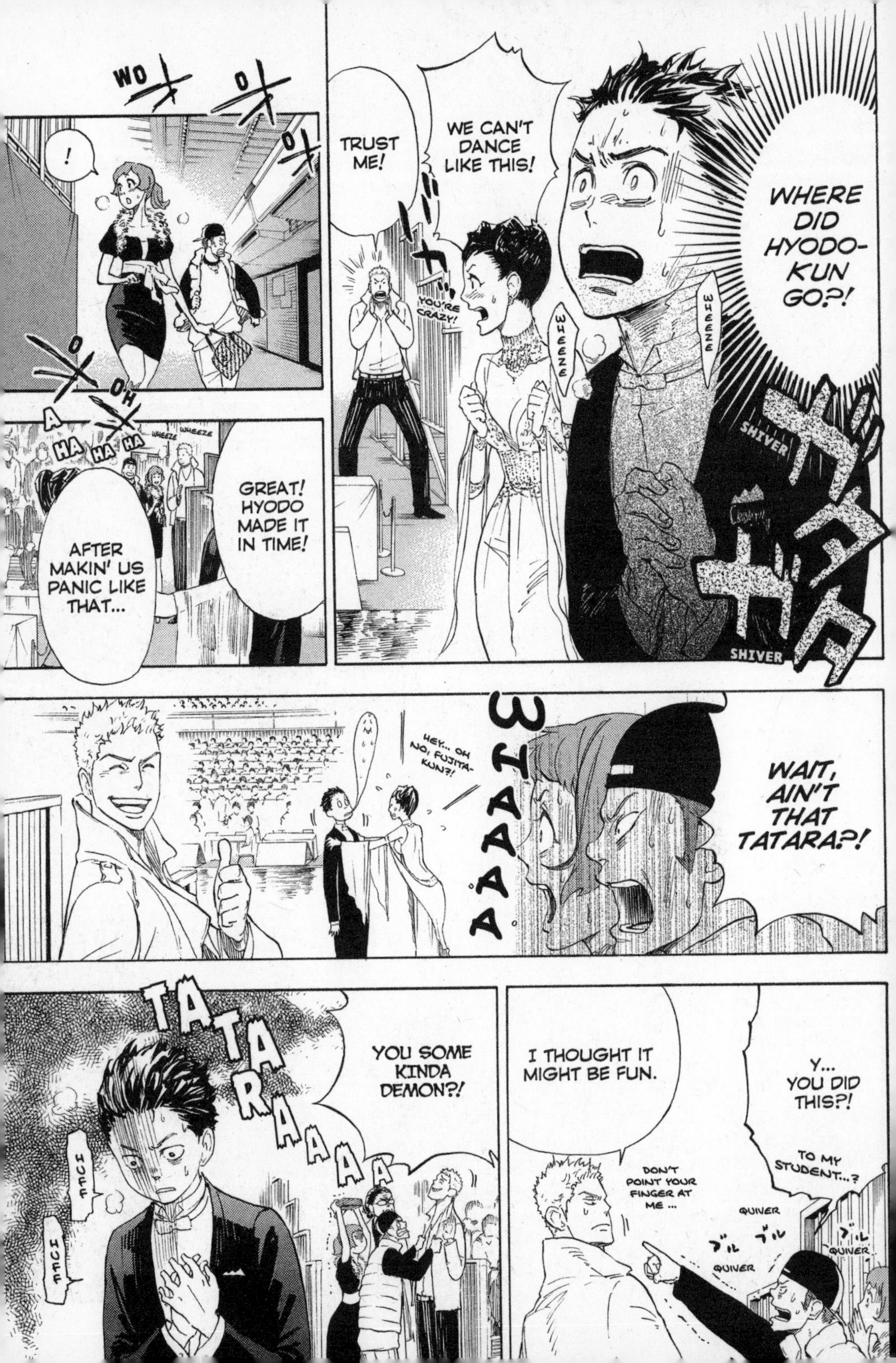
WHERE DID HYODO-KUN GO?!
WHEEZE
SHIVER
SHIVER
WE CAN'T DANCE LIKE THIS!
TRUST ME!
WHEEZE
YOU'RE CRAZY!
WO O O
!
GREAT! HYODO MADE IT IN TIME!
AFTER MAKIN' US PANIC LIKE THAT...
WHEEZE WHEEZE
O OH
A HA HA HA
WAIT, AIN'T THAT TATARA?!
HEY... OH NO, FUJITA-KUN?!
Y... YOU DID THIS?!
TO MY STUDENT...?
I THOUGHT IT MIGHT BE FUN.
DON'T POINT YOUR FINGER AT ME ...
QUIVER
QUIVER
QUIVER
YOU SOME KINDA DEMON?!
TATARAAAAA
HUFF
HUFF

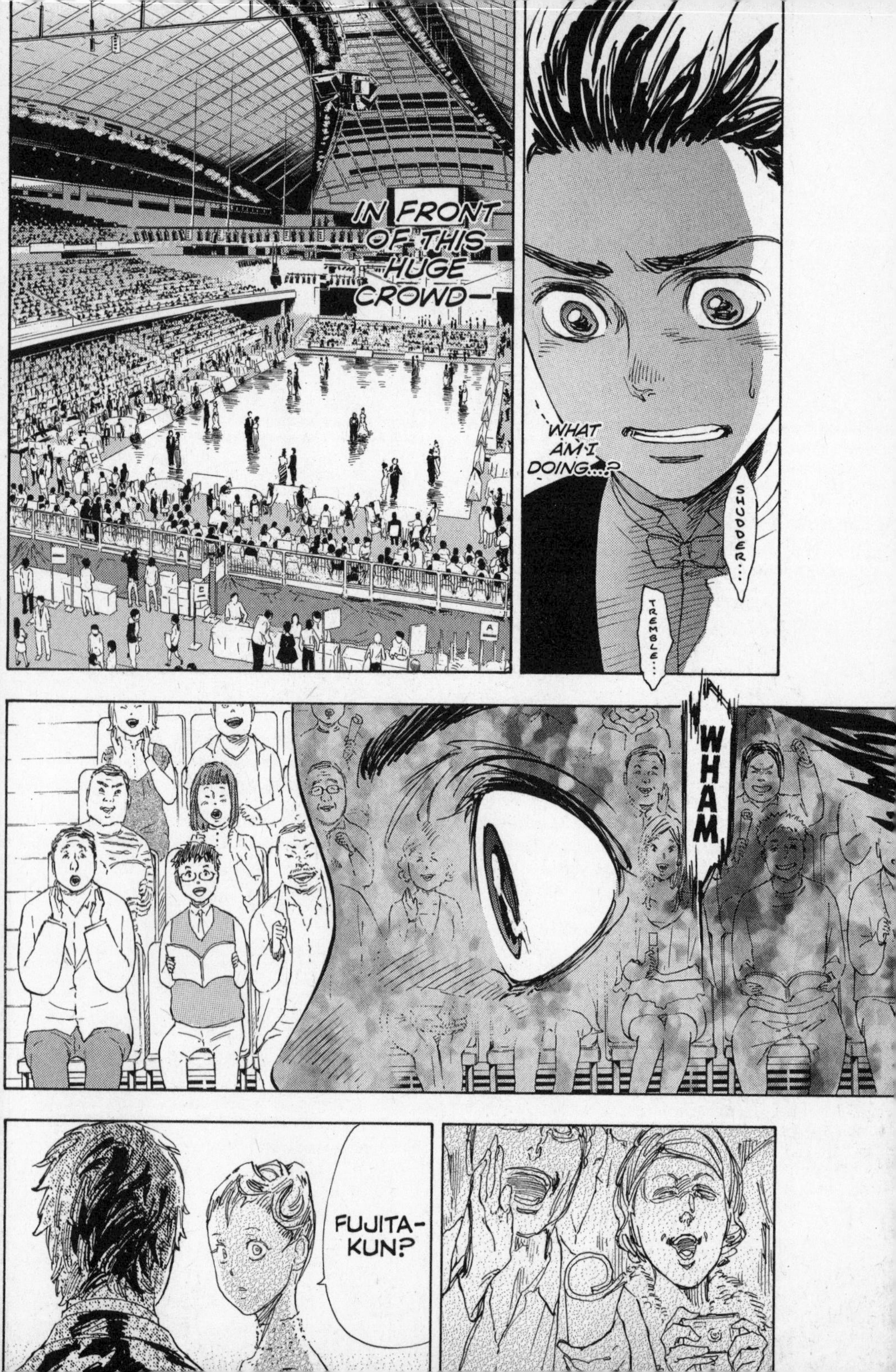
WHAT AM I DOING...?
SHUDDER...
TREMBLE...
IN FRONT OF THIS HUGE CROWD—
WHAM
FUJITA-KUN?

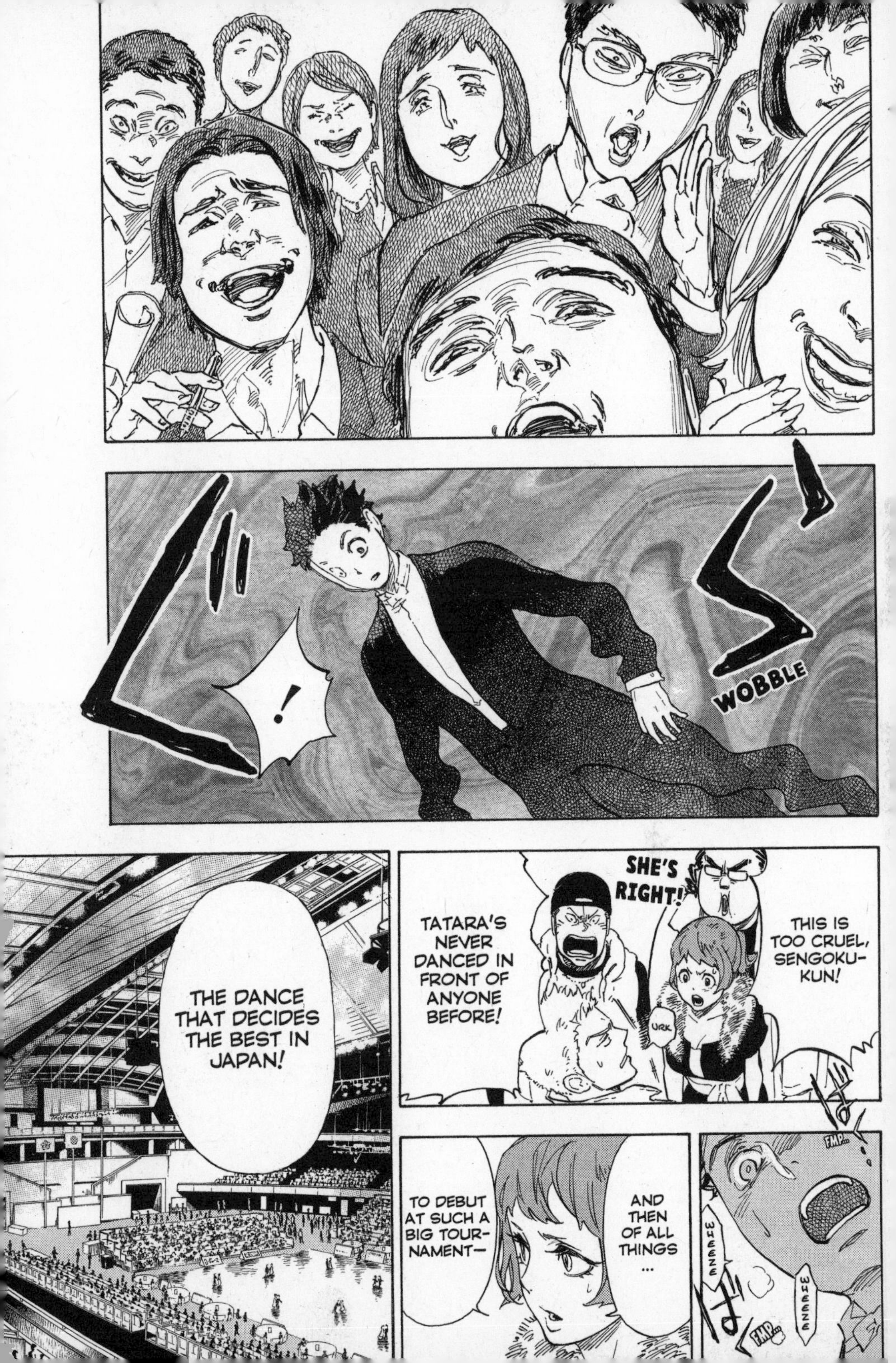

!
WOBBLE
THIS IS TOO CRUEL, SENGOKU-KUN!
SHE'S RIGHT!
TATARA'S NEVER DANCED IN FRONT OF ANYONE BEFORE!
URK
FMP...
WHEEZE
WHEEZE
FMP...
AND THEN OF ALL THINGS ...
TO DEBUT AT SUCH A BIG TOURNAMENT—
THE DANCE THAT DECIDES THE BEST IN JAPAN!

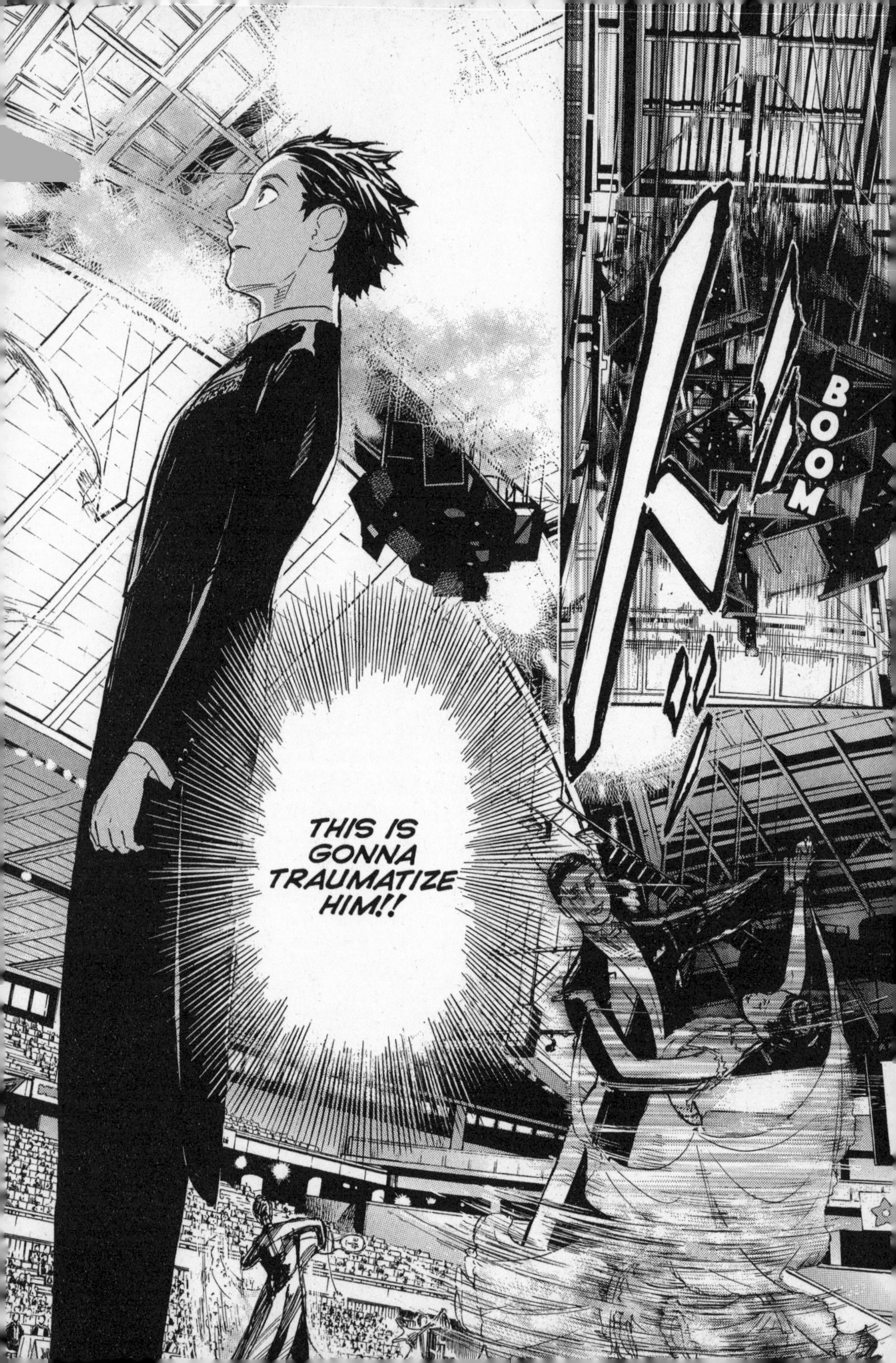
BOOM
THIS IS GONNA TRAUMATIZE HIM!!

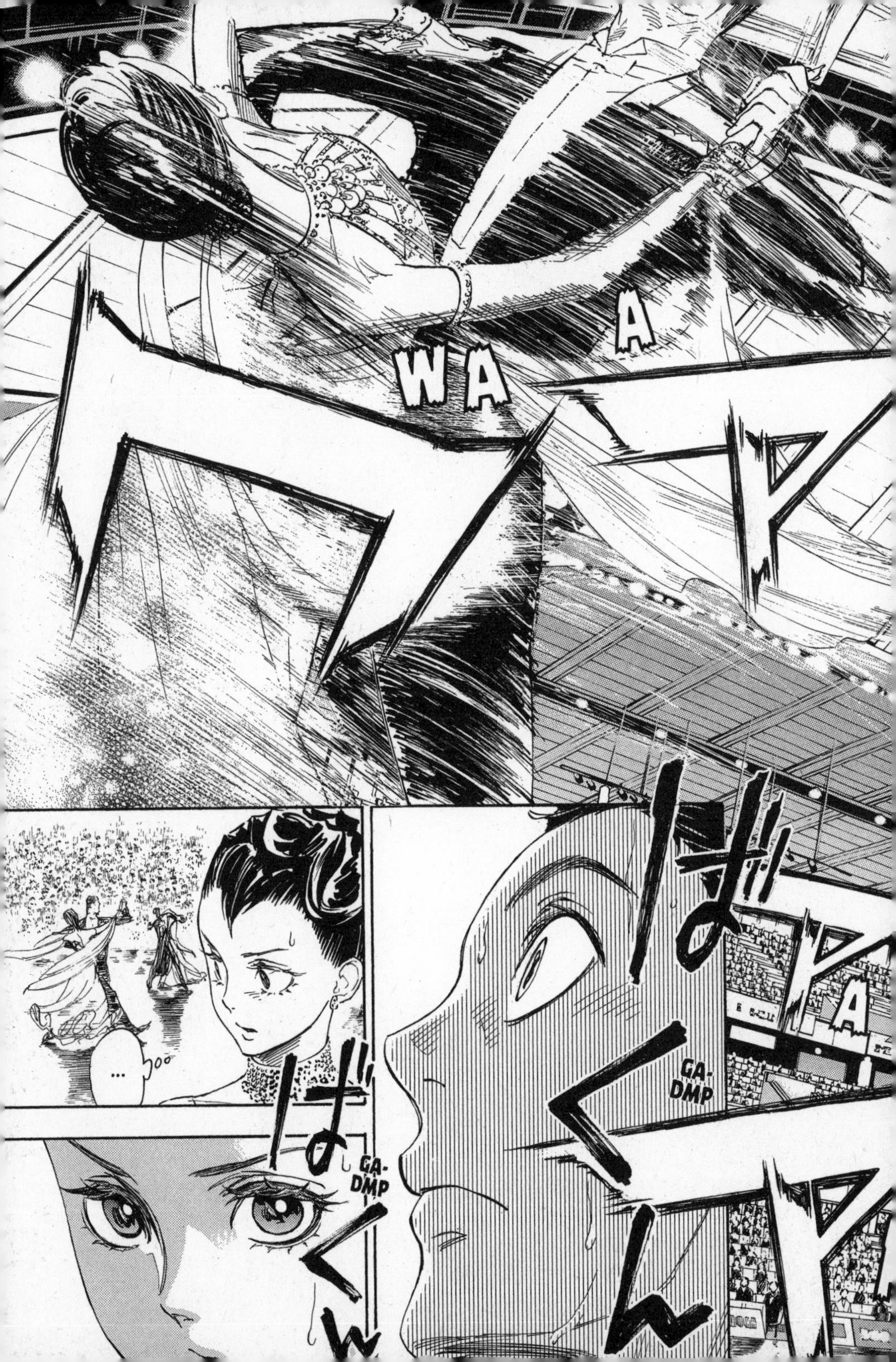

ワア
WA
A
ばくん
GA-
DMP
...
ばくん
GA-
DMP

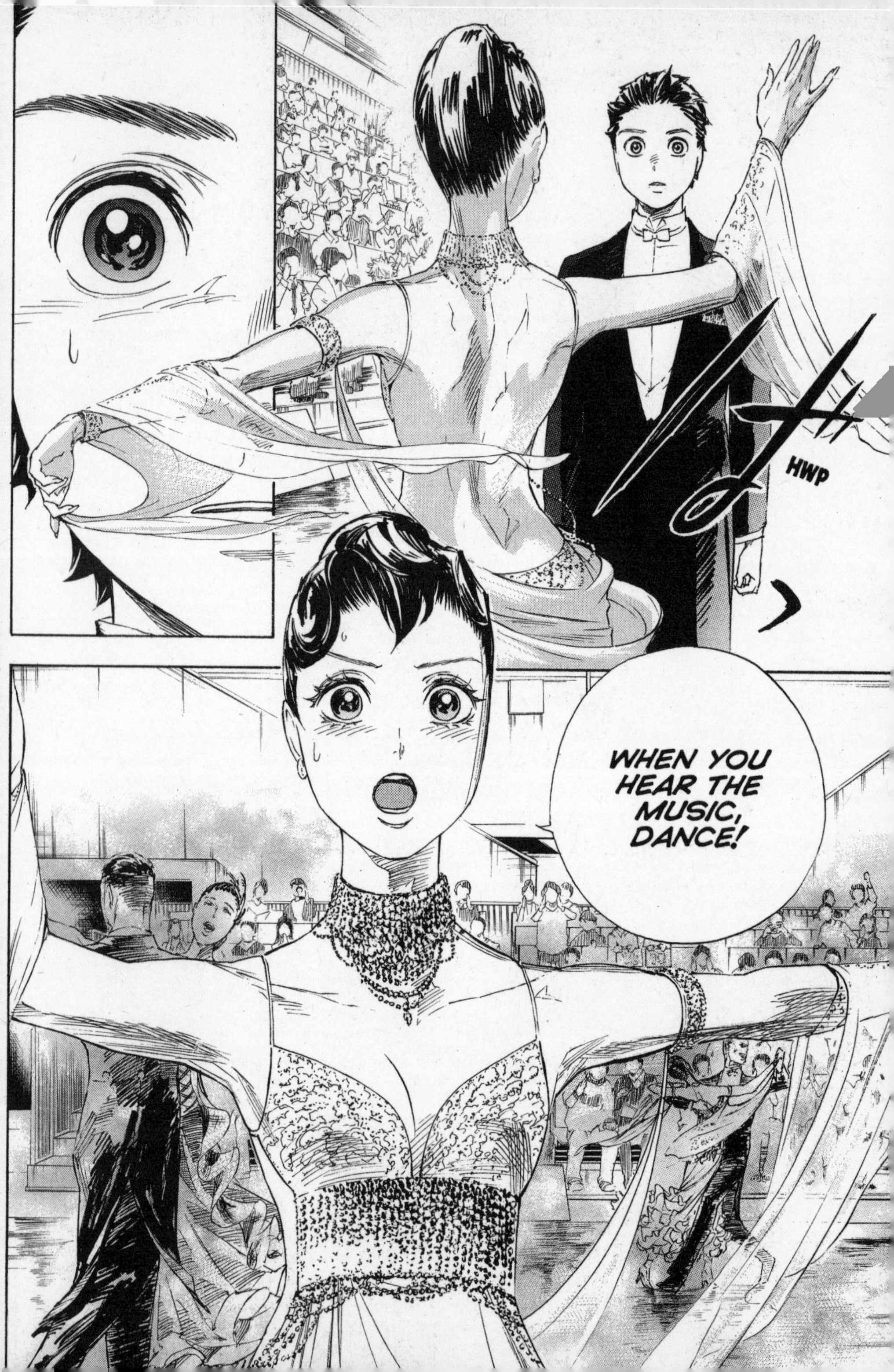
HWP
WHEN YOU HEAR THE MUSIC, DANCE!

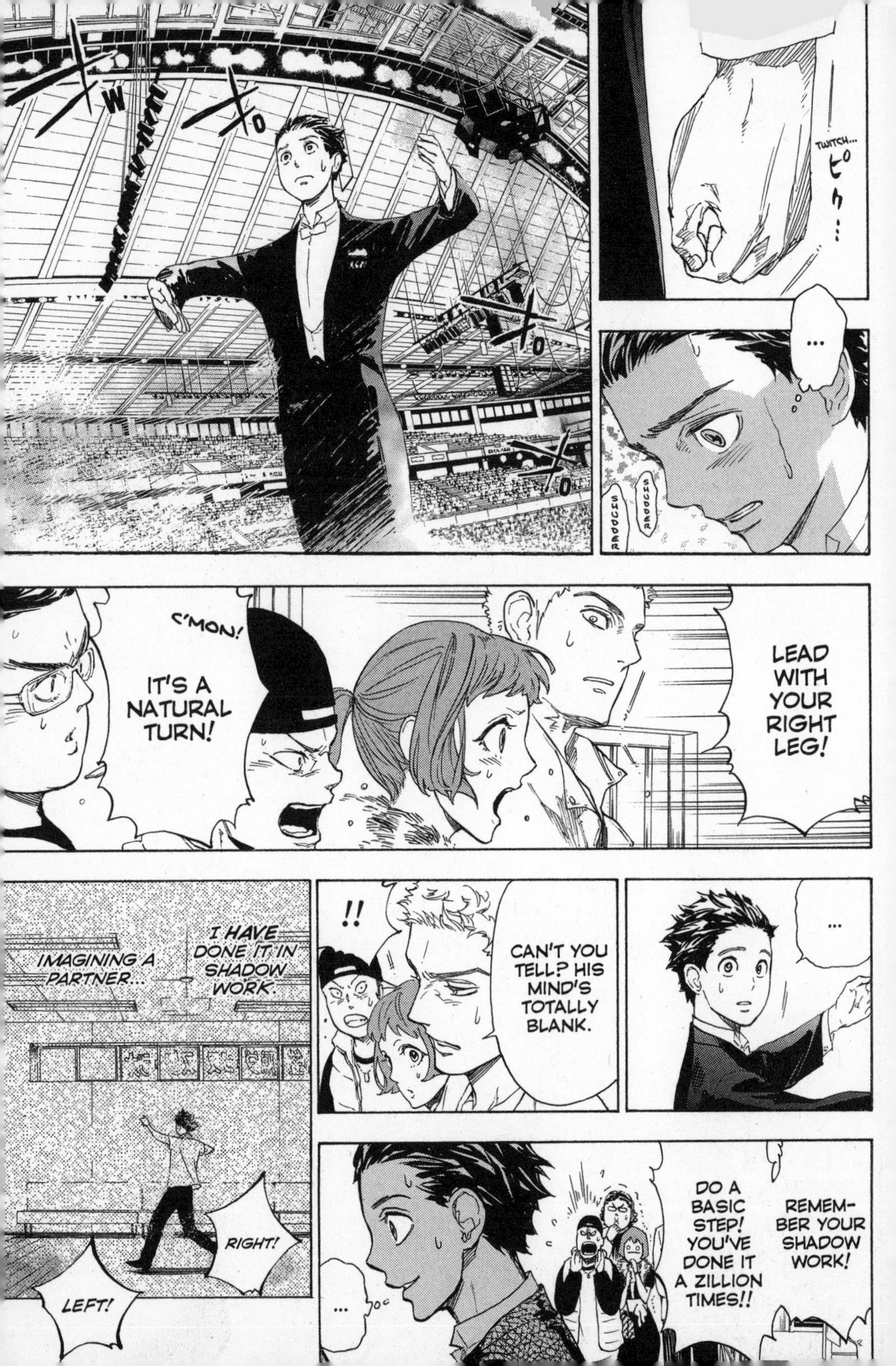

TWITCH... ピク…
...
SHUDDER
SHUDDER
LEAD WITH YOUR RIGHT LEG!
C'MON!
IT'S A NATURAL TURN!
...
CAN'T YOU TELL? HIS MIND'S TOTALLY BLANK.
!!
REMEM-BER YOUR SHADOW WORK!
DO A BASIC STEP! YOU'VE DONE IT A ZILLION TIMES!!
...
I HAVE DONE IT IN SHADOW WORK.
IMAGINING A PARTNER...
RIGHT!
LEFT!

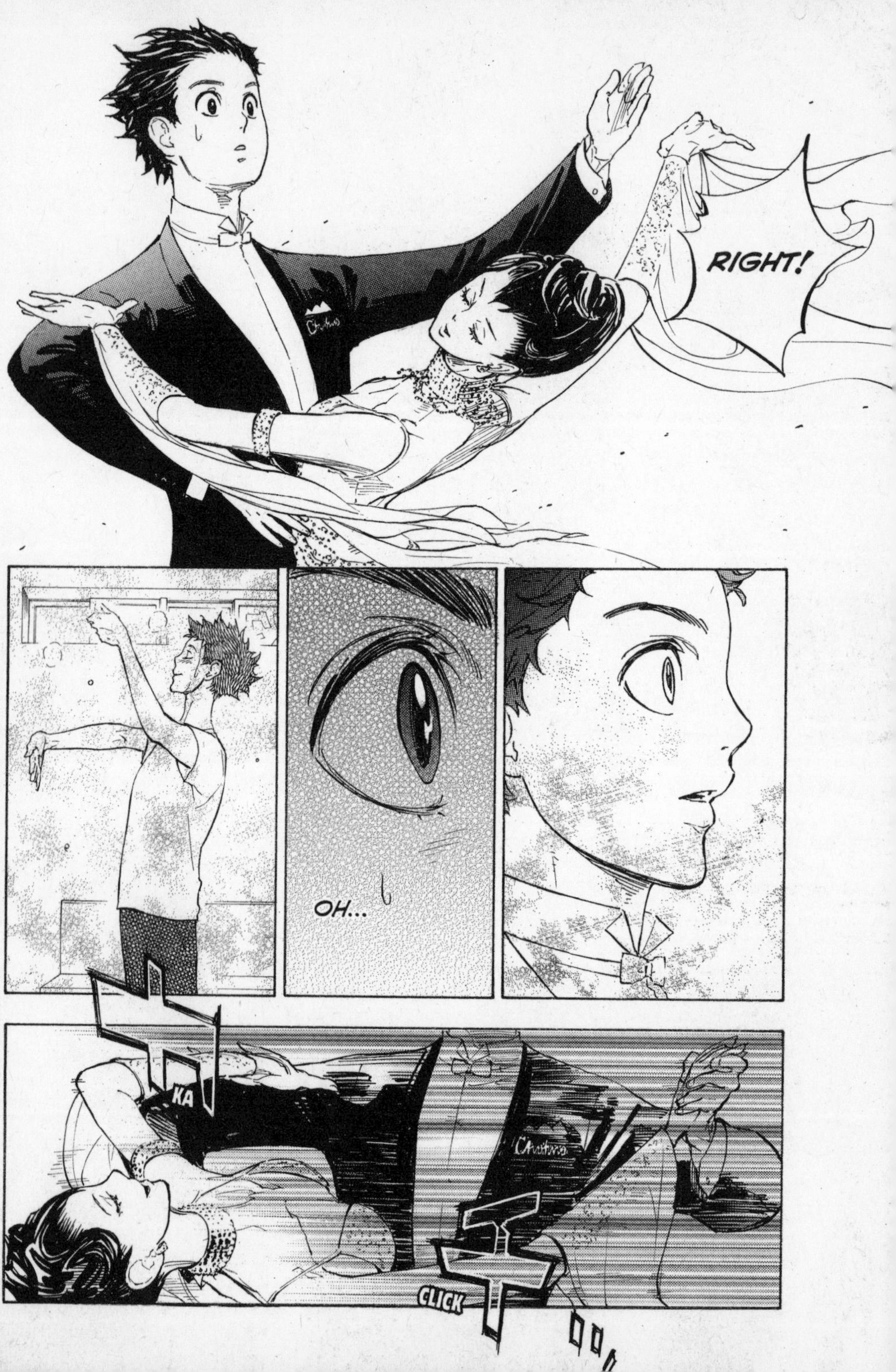
RIGHT!
OH...
KA
CLICK

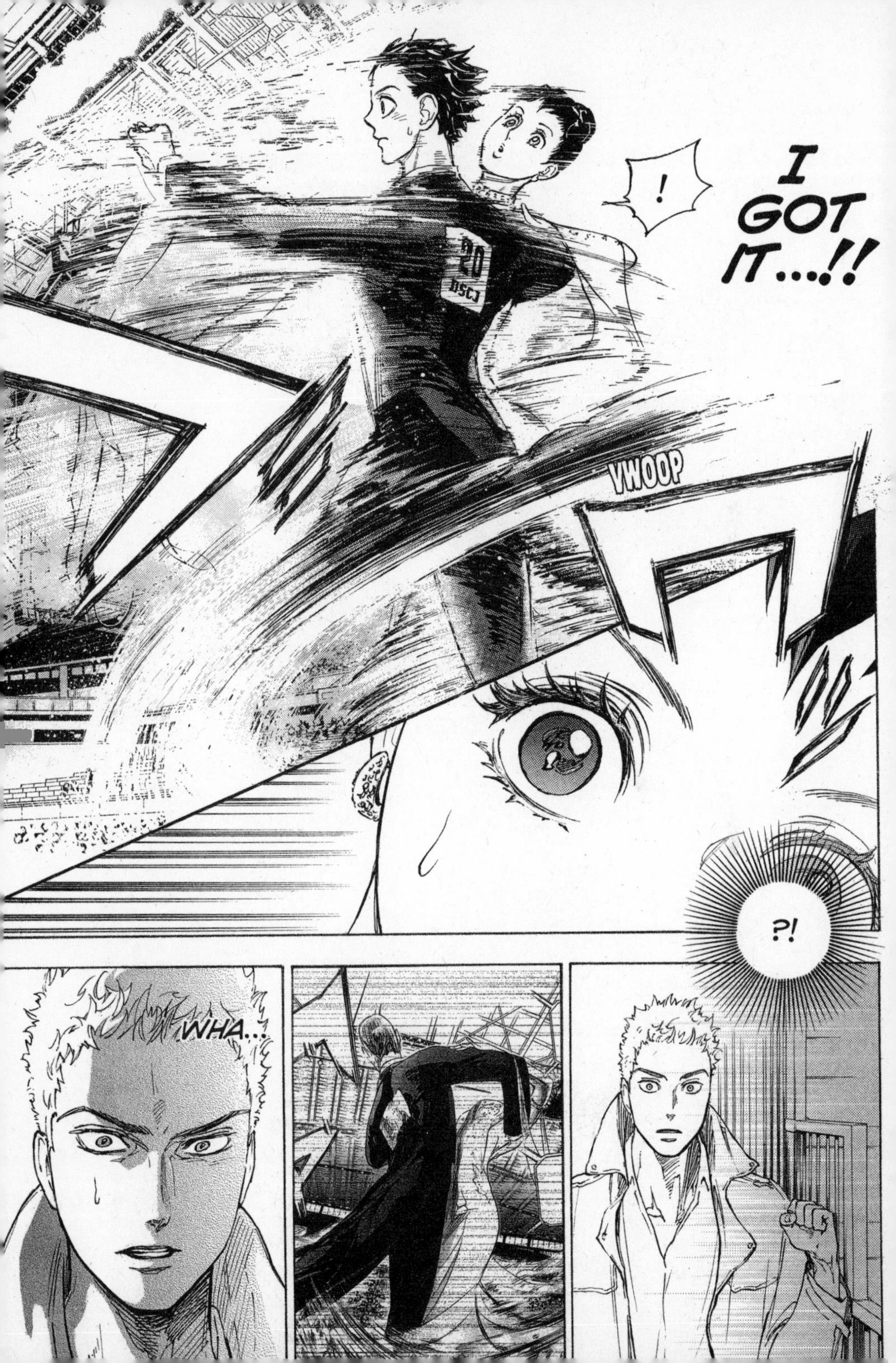
I GOT IT...!!
!
20
DSCJ
VWOOP
?!
WHA...

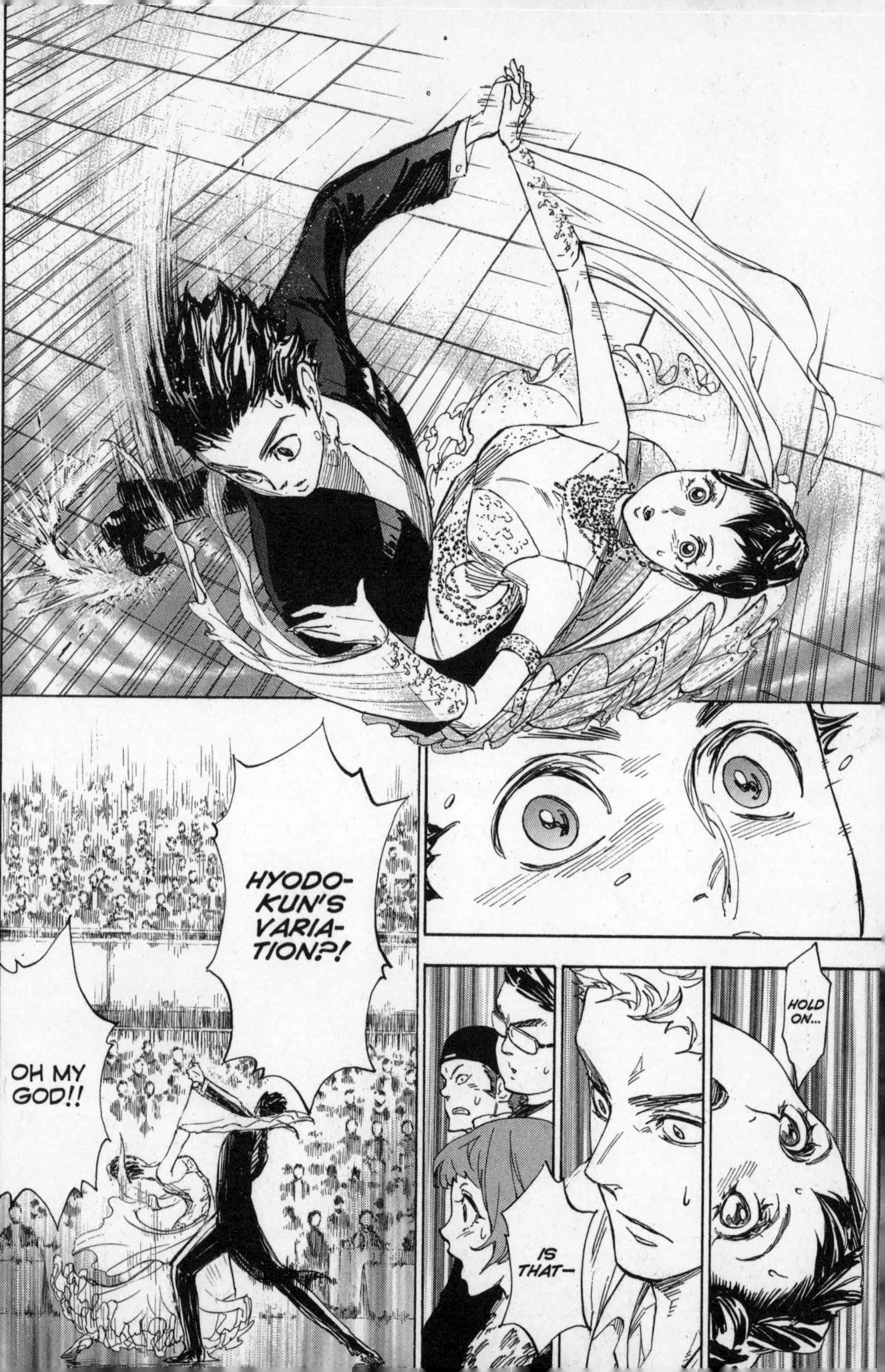
HOLD ON...
IS THAT—
HYODO-KUN'S VARIATION?!
OH MY GOD!!

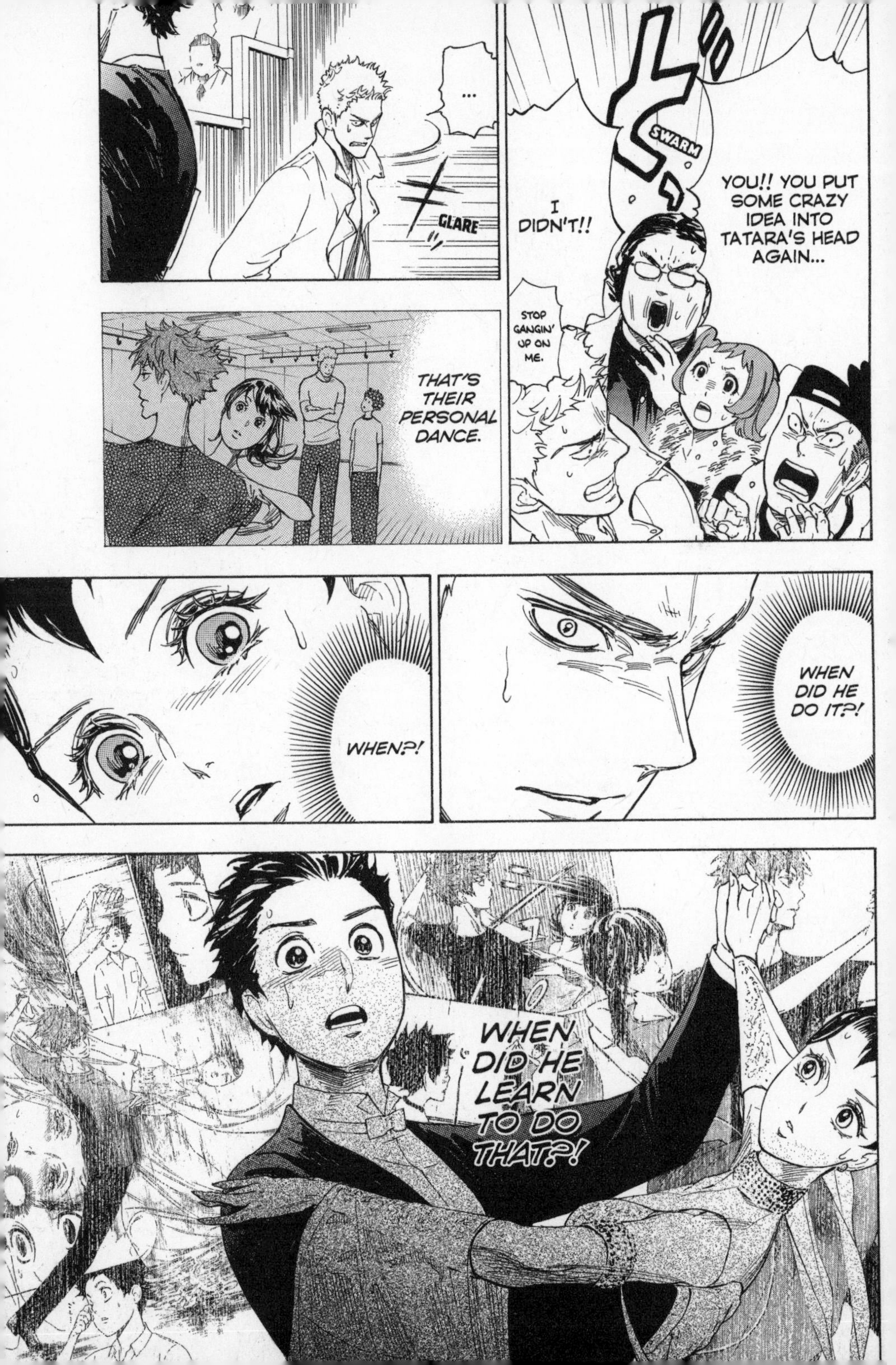
SWARM
YOU!! YOU PUT SOME CRAZY IDEA INTO TATARA'S HEAD AGAIN...
I DIDN'T!!
STOP GANGIN' UP ON ME.
...
GLARE
THAT'S THEIR PERSONAL DANCE.
WHEN DID HE DO IT?!
WHEN?!
WHEN DID HE LEARN TO DO THAT?!

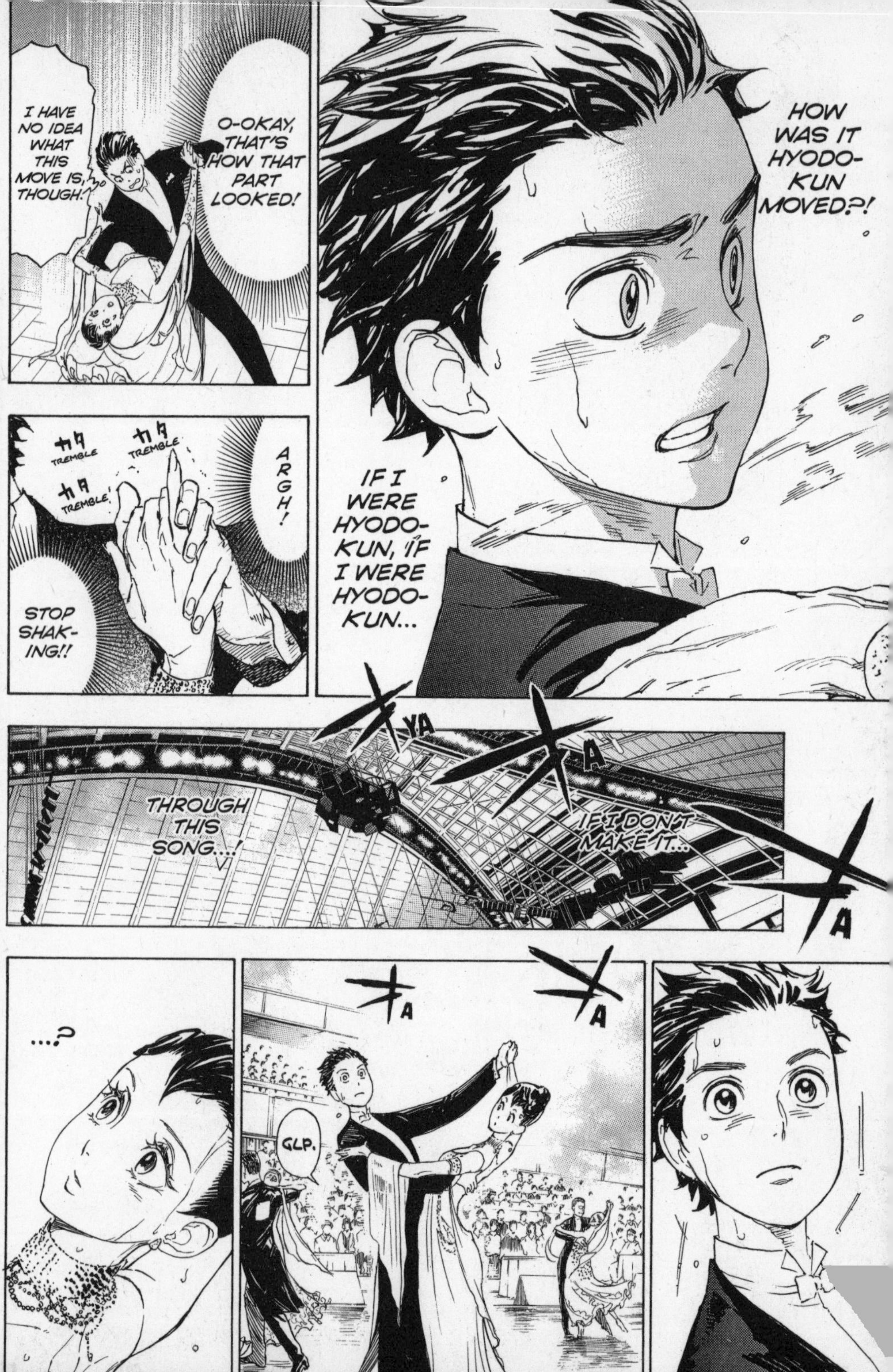
HOW WAS IT HYODO-KUN MOVED?!
IF I WERE HYODO-KUN, IF I WERE HYODO-KUN...
O-OKAY, THAT'S HOW THAT PART LOOKED!
I HAVE NO IDEA WHAT THIS MOVE IS, THOUGH!
ARGH!
カタ TREMBLE
カタ TREMBLE
カタ TREMBLE
STOP SHAKING!!
YA
A
A
IF I DON'T MAKE IT...
THROUGH THIS SONG...!
A
A
GLP.
...?

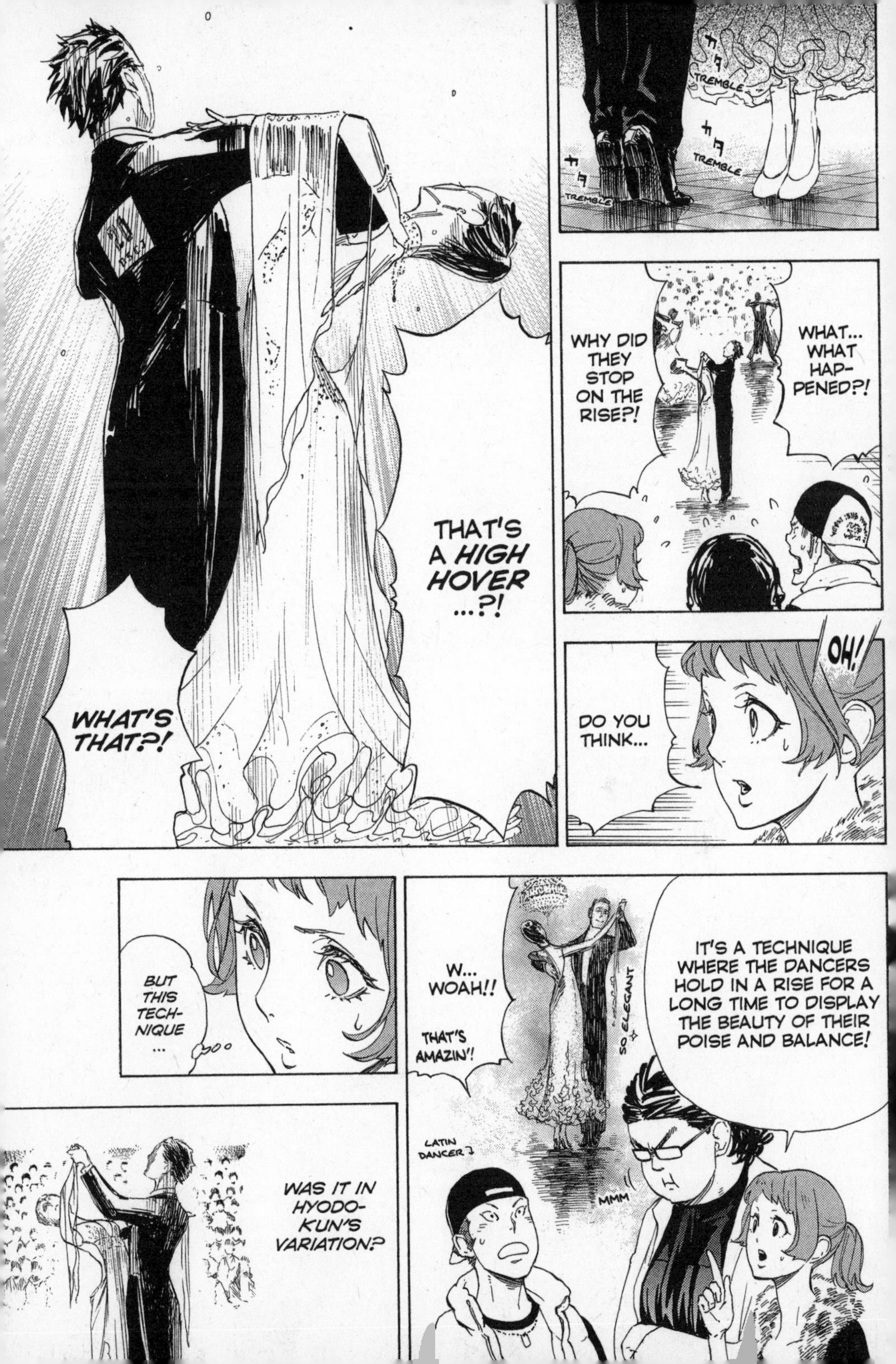
TREMBLE
TREMBLE
TREMBLE
WHAT... WHAT HAP-PENED?!
WHY DID THEY STOP ON THE RISE?!
OH!
DO YOU THINK...
THAT'S A *HIGH HOVER* ...?!
WHAT'S THAT?!
IT'S A TECHNIQUE WHERE THE DANCERS HOLD IN A RISE FOR A LONG TIME TO DISPLAY THE BEAUTY OF THEIR POISE AND BALANCE!
SO ELEGANT
W... WOAH!!
THAT'S AMAZIN'!
LATIN DANCER
MMM
BUT THIS TECH-NIQUE ...
WAS IT IN HYODO-KUN'S VARIATION?

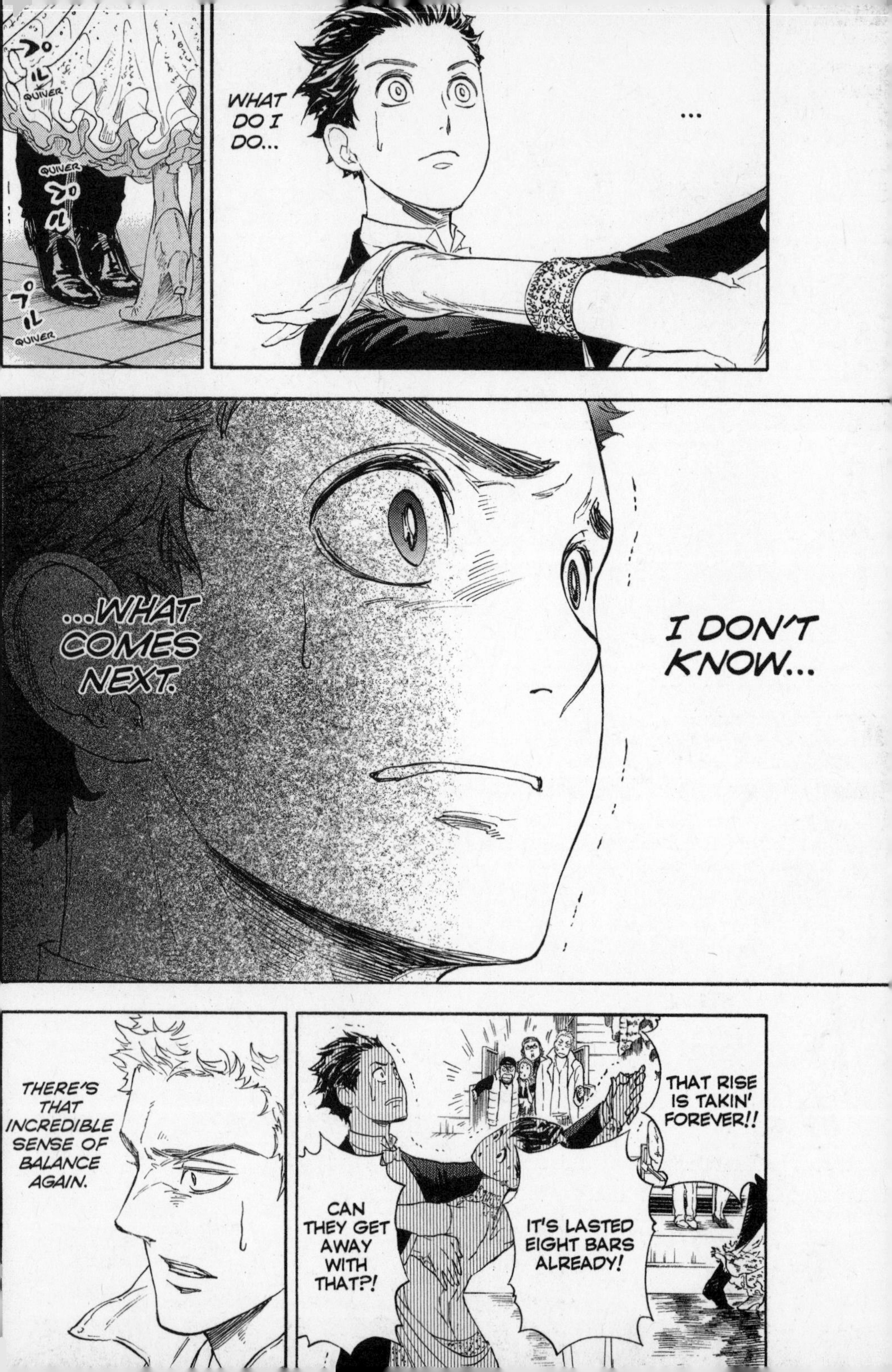
...
WHAT DO I DO...
QUIVER
QUIVER
QUIVER
I DON'T KNOW...
...WHAT COMES NEXT.
THAT RISE IS TAKIN' FOREVER!!
IT'S LASTED EIGHT BARS ALREADY!
CAN THEY GET AWAY WITH THAT?!
THERE'S THAT INCREDIBLE SENSE OF BALANCE AGAIN.

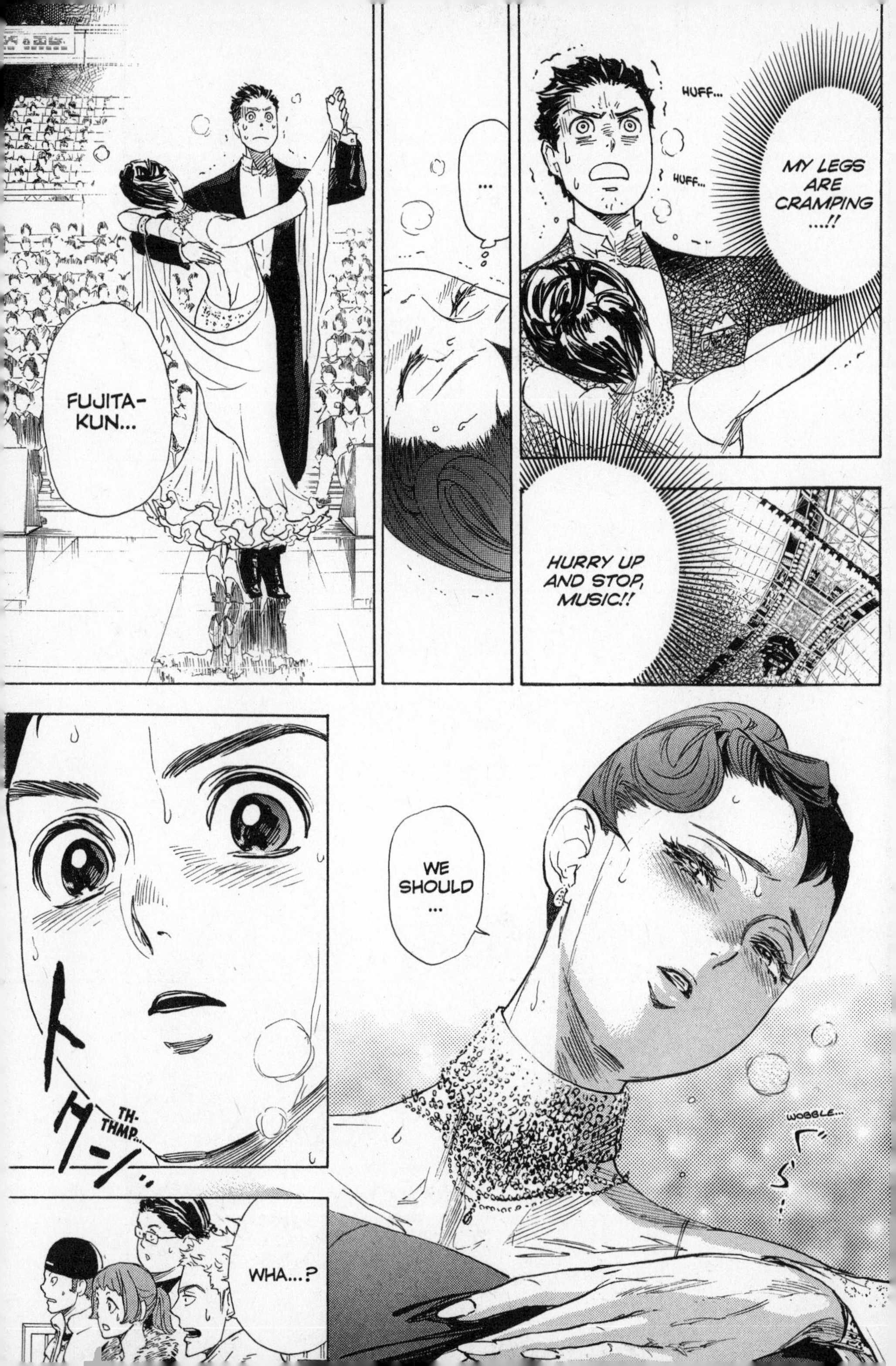
HUFF...
HUFF...
MY LEGS ARE CRAMPING ...!!
HURRY UP AND STOP, MUSIC!!
...
FUJITA-KUN...
WE SHOULD ...
WOBBLE...
トクン
TH-THMP...
WHA...?

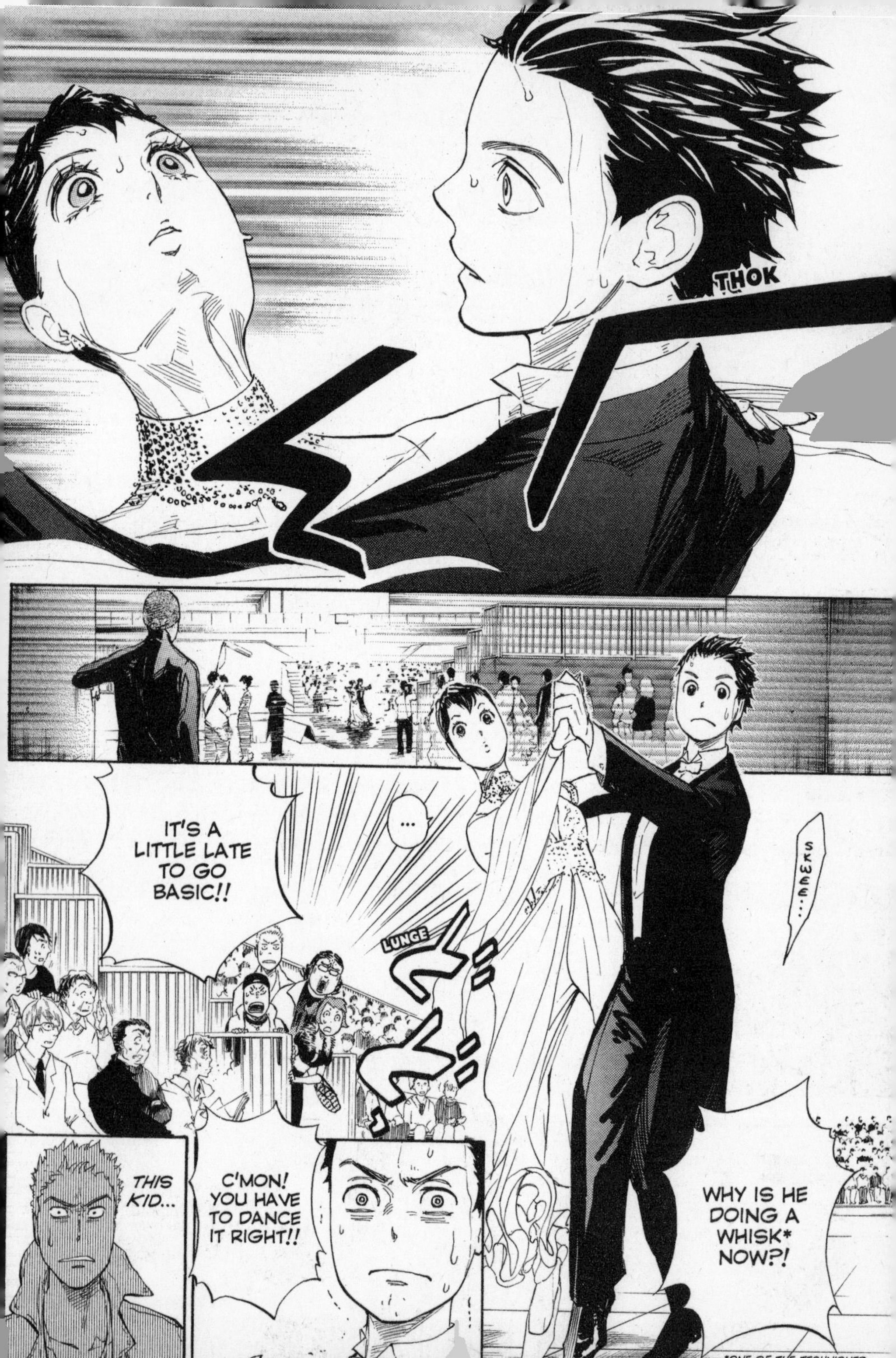
THOK
SKWEE...
...
LUNGE
IT'S A LITTLE LATE TO GO BASIC!!
WHY IS HE DOING A WHISK* NOW?!
C'MON! YOU HAVE TO DANCE IT RIGHT!!
THIS KID...

*ONE OF THE TECHNIQUES

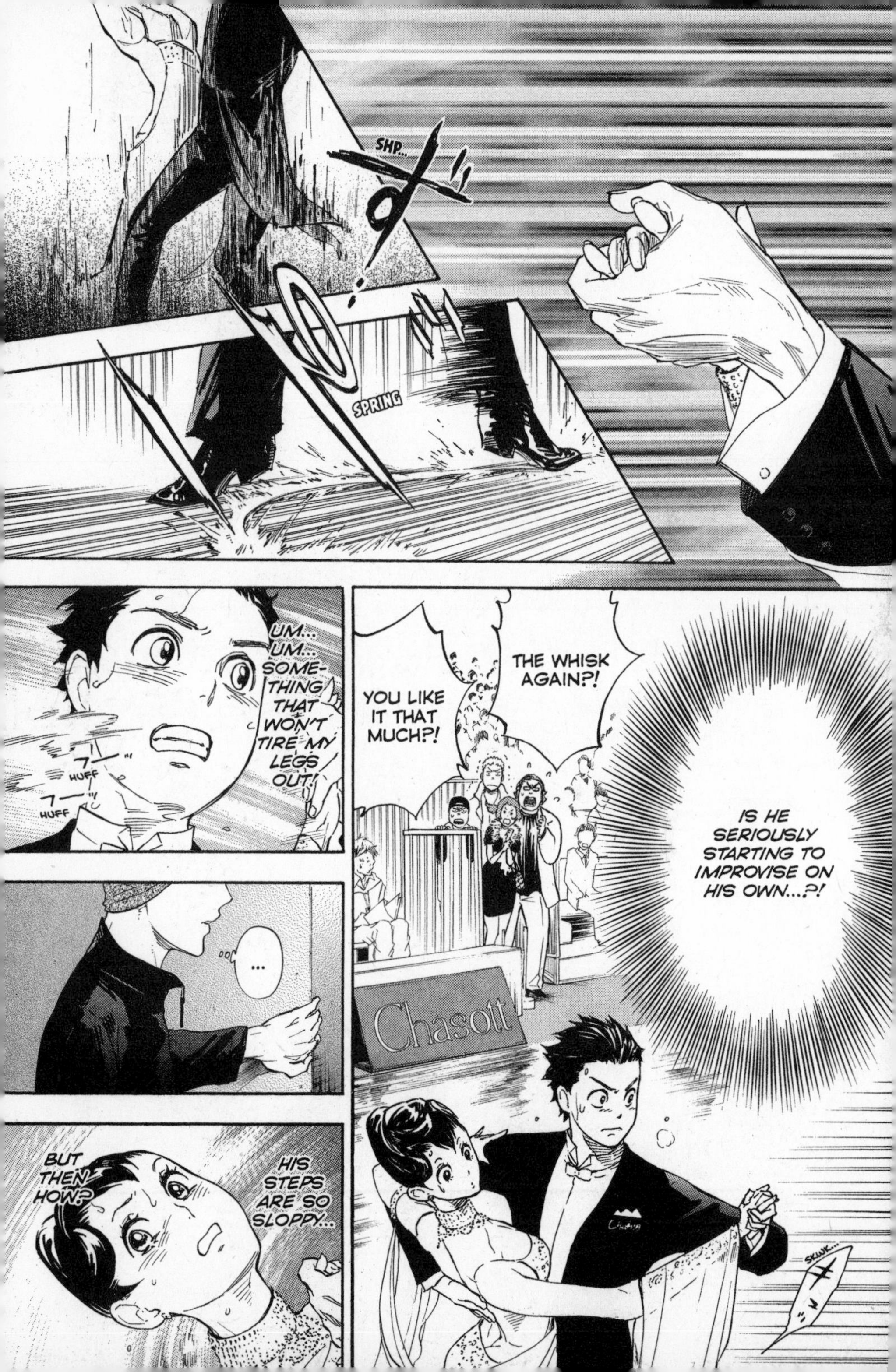
SHP...
SPRING
THE WHISK AGAIN?!
YOU LIKE IT THAT MUCH?!
IS HE SERIOUSLY STARTING TO IMPROVISE ON HIS OWN...?!
Chasott
SKWK...
UM... UM... SOMETHING THAT WON'T TIRE MY LEGS OUT!
HUFF
HUFF
...
HIS STEPS ARE SO SLOPPY...
BUT THEN HOW?

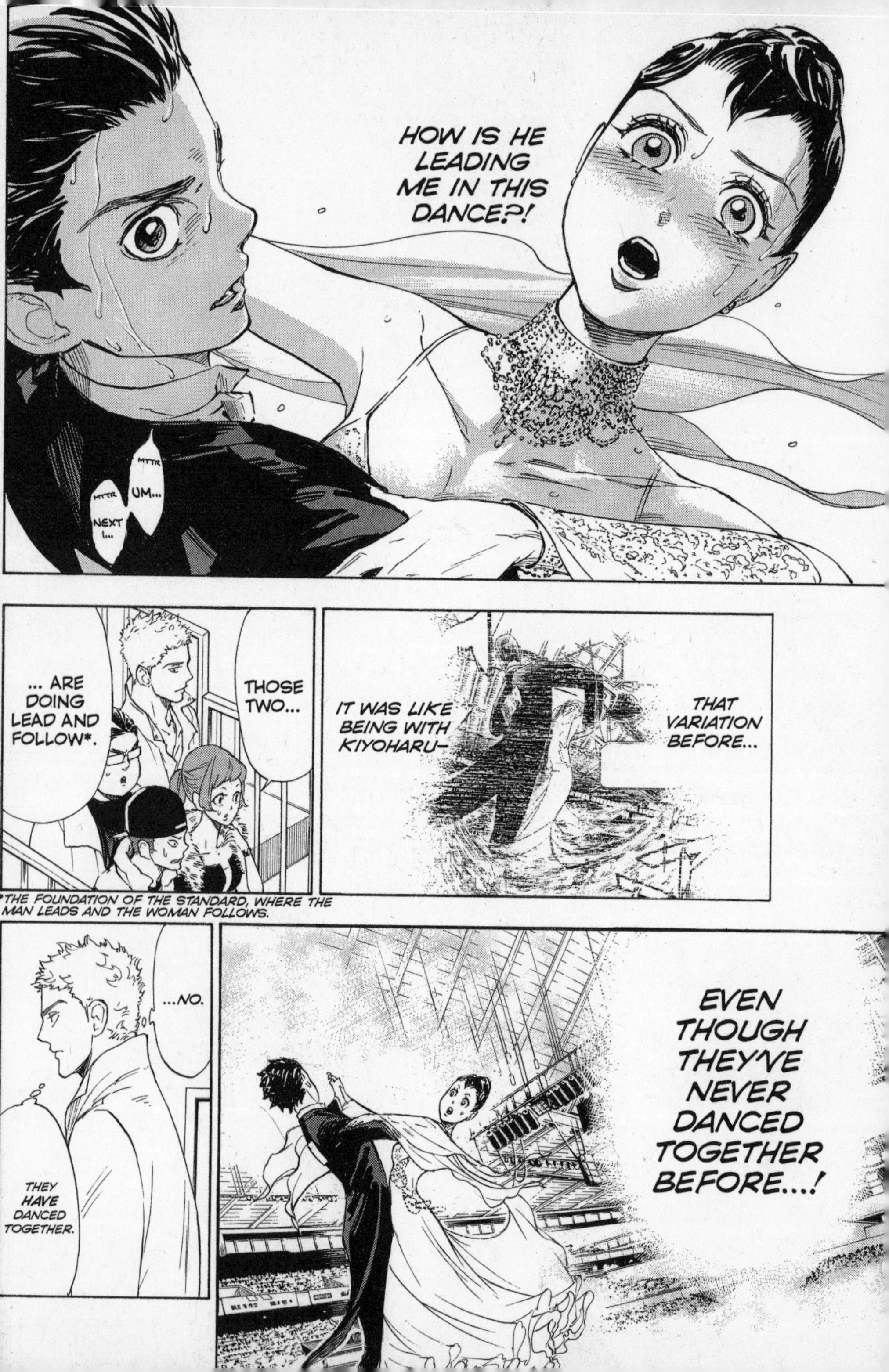
HOW IS HE LEADING ME IN THIS DANCE?!
MTTR
UM...
MTTR
NEXT I...
THAT VARIATION BEFORE...
IT WAS LIKE BEING WITH KIYOHARU–
THOSE TWO...
... ARE DOING LEAD AND FOLLOW*.
EVEN THOUGH THEY'VE NEVER DANCED TOGETHER BEFORE...!
...NO.
THEY HAVE DANCED TOGETHER.

*THE FOUNDATION OF THE STANDARD, WHERE THE MAN LEADS AND THE WOMAN FOLLOWS.

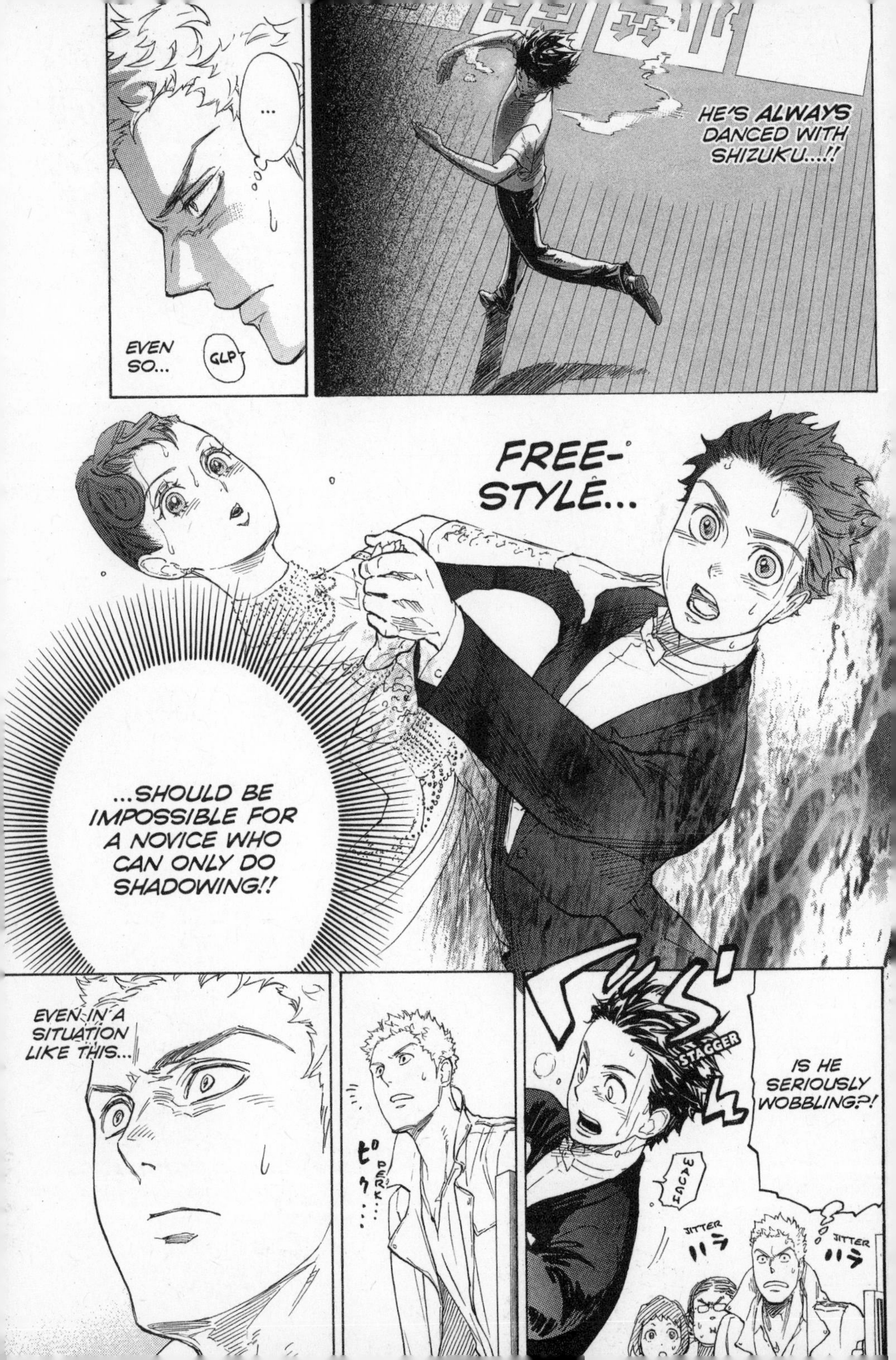
HE'S ALWAYS DANCED WITH SHIZUKU...!!
...
EVEN SO...
GLP
FREE-STYLE...
...SHOULD BE IMPOSSIBLE FOR A NOVICE WHO CAN ONLY DO SHADOWING!!
STAGGER
IS HE SERIOUSLY WOBBLING?!
JITTER
JITTER
PERK...
EVEN IN A SITUATION LIKE THIS...

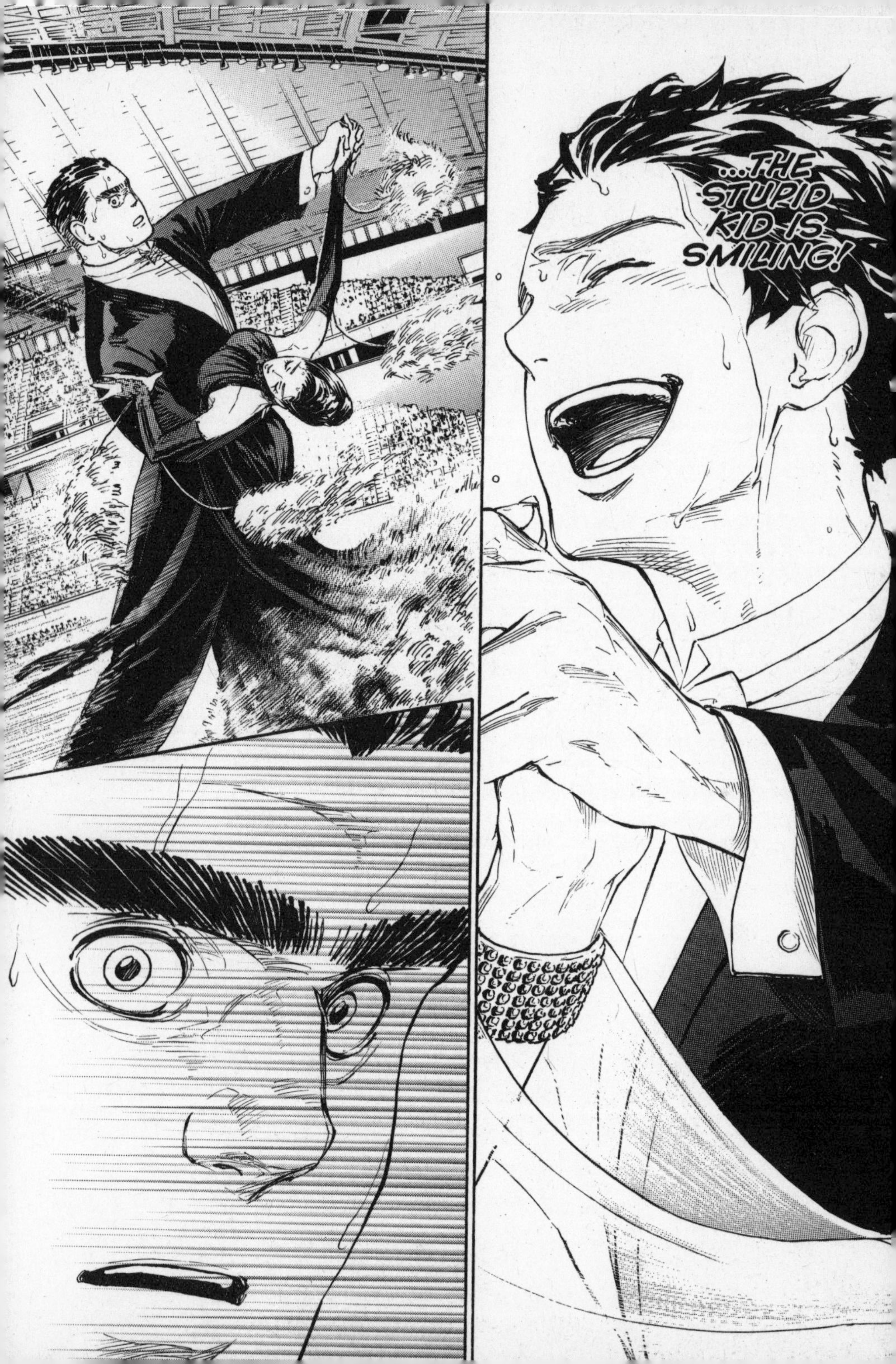
...THE STUPID KID IS SMILING!

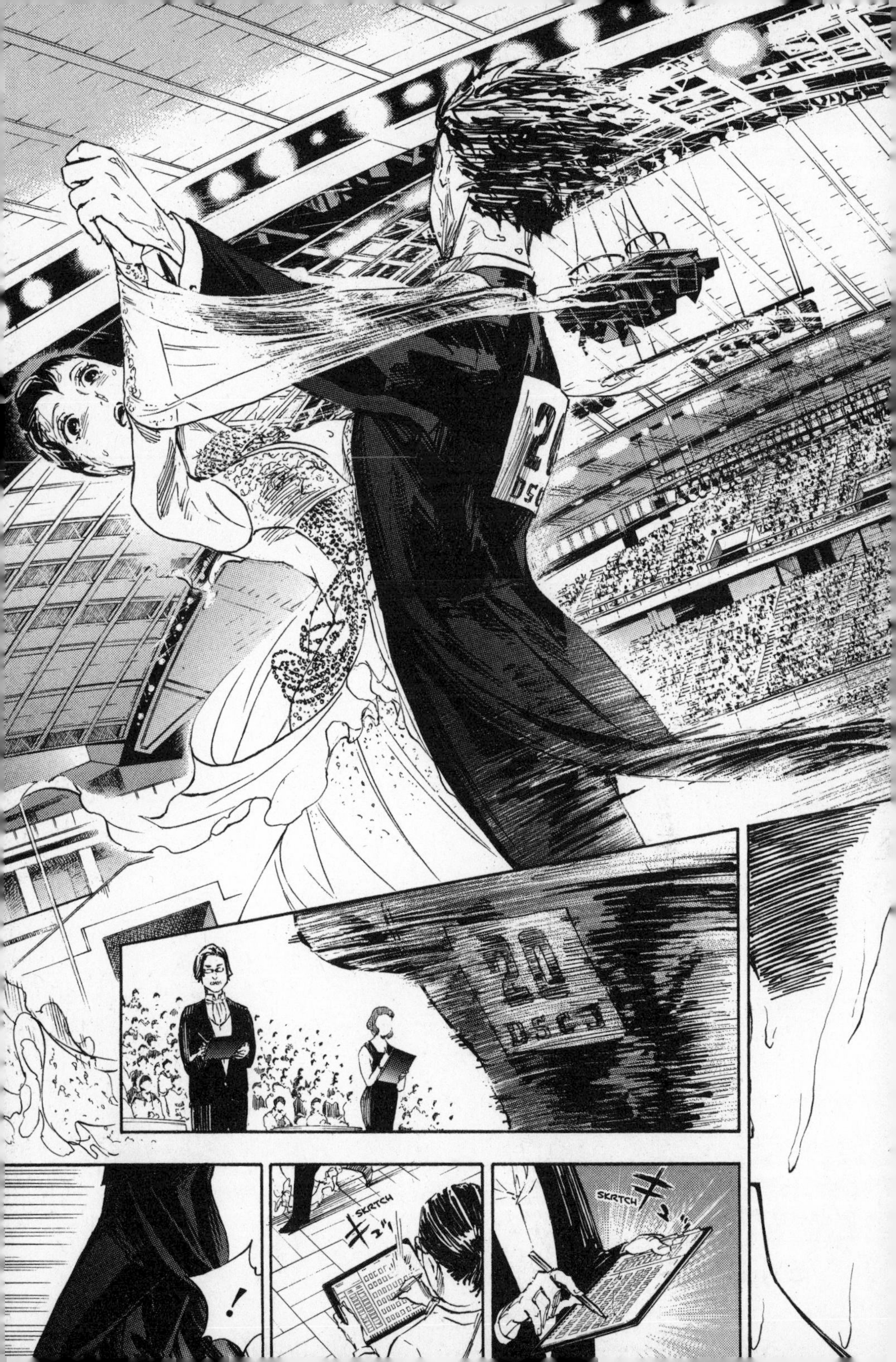
20
D.S.C.J
SKRTCH
SKRTCH
!

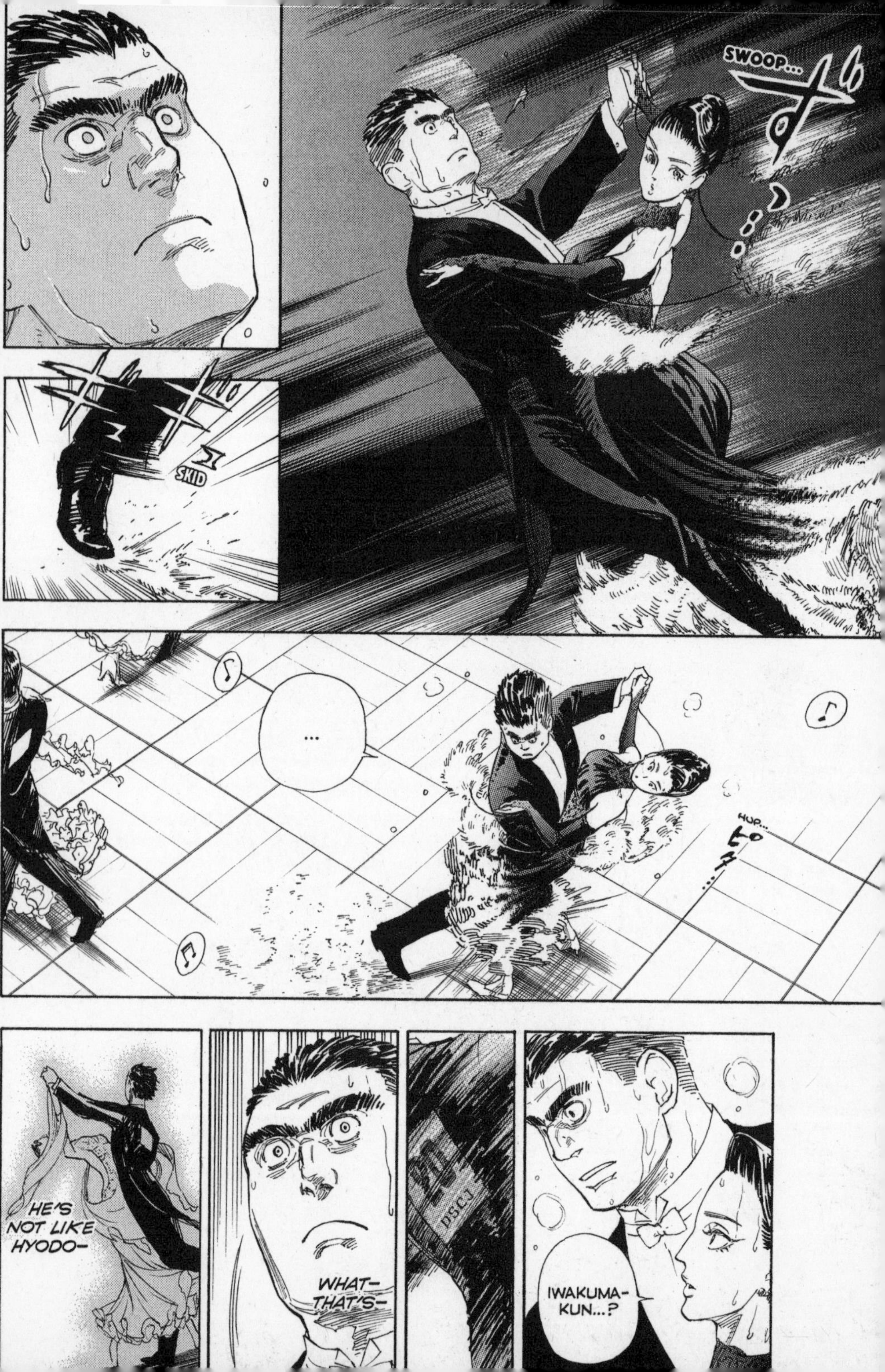
SWOOP...
SKID
...
HUP...
IWAKUMA-KUN...?
DSCJ
WHAT— THAT'S—
HE'S NOT LIKE HYODO—

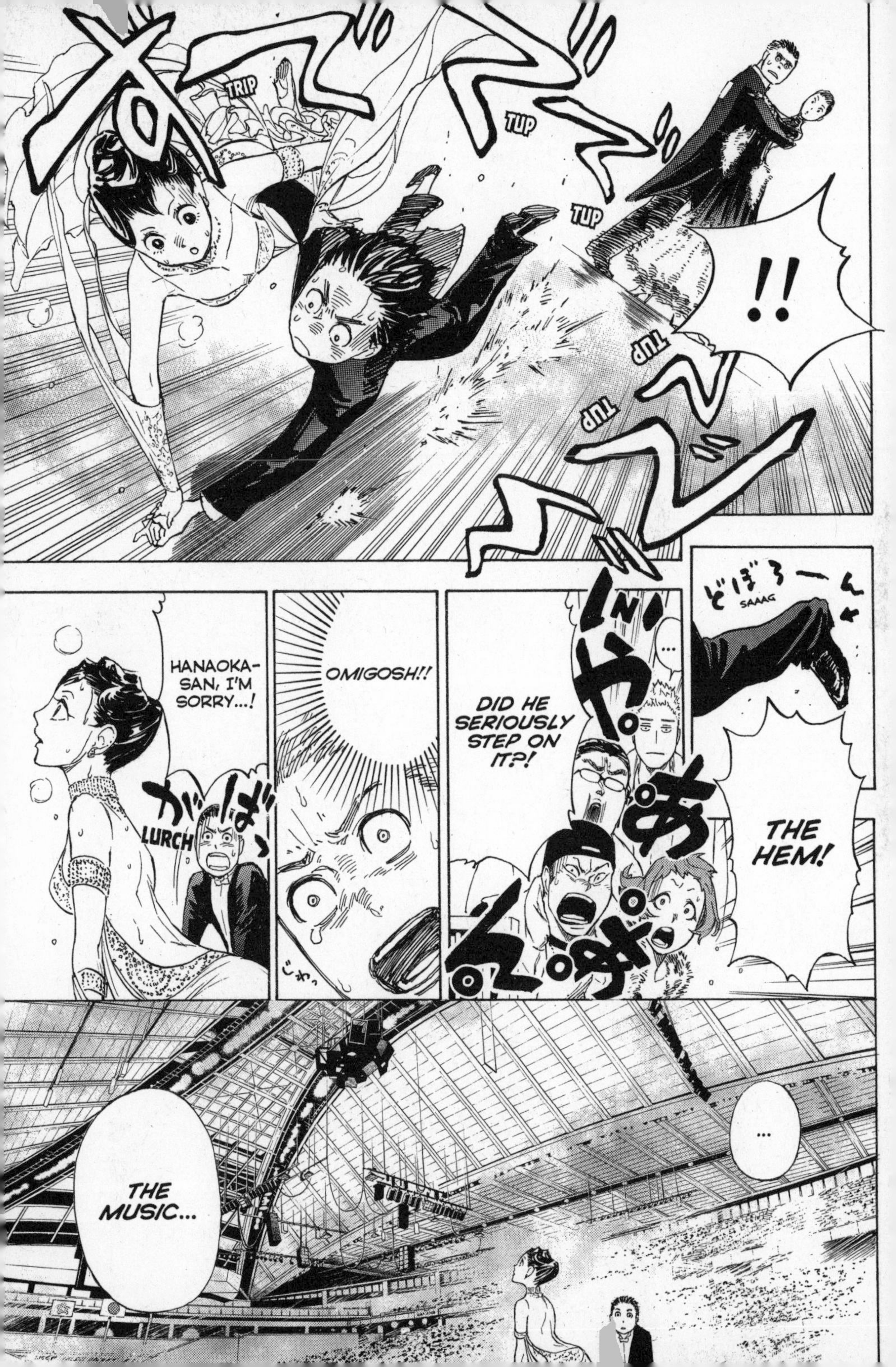
!!
TUP
TUP
TUP
TUP
TRIP
どぼろーん
SAAAG
THE HEM!
...
DID HE SERIOUSLY STEP ON IT?!
OMIGOSH!!
じわっ
HANAOKA-SAN, I'M SORRY...!
LURCH
...
THE MUSIC...

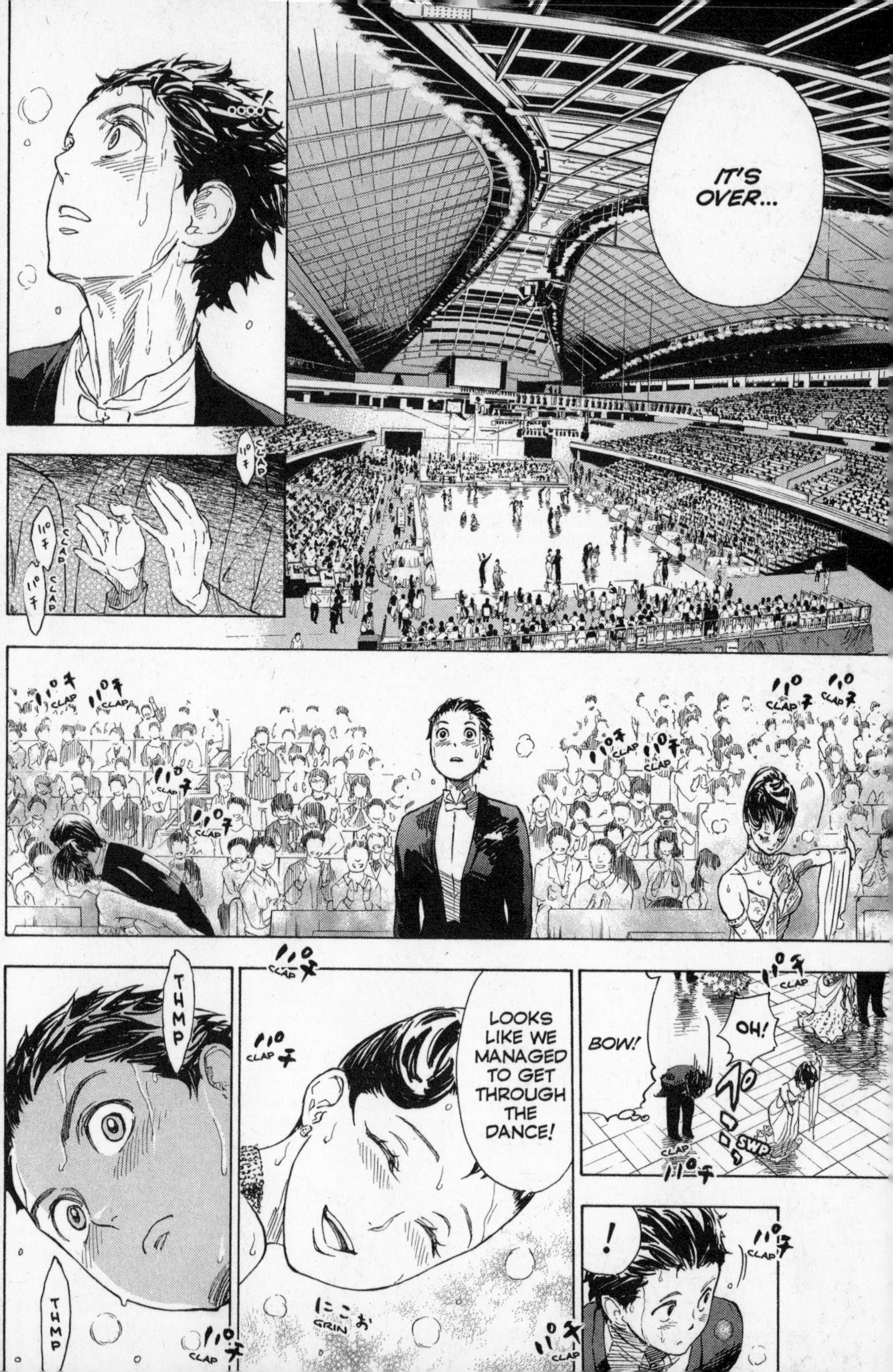

IT'S OVER...
!
CLAP
CLAP
CLAP
CLAP
CLAP
CLAP
CLAP
CLAP
CLAP
CLAP
CLAP
CLAP
CLAP
OH!
BOW!
SWP
CLAP
CLAP
LOOKS LIKE WE MANAGED TO GET THROUGH THE DANCE!
CLAP
GRIN
CLAP
!
CLAP
CLAP
THMP
THMP
CLAP

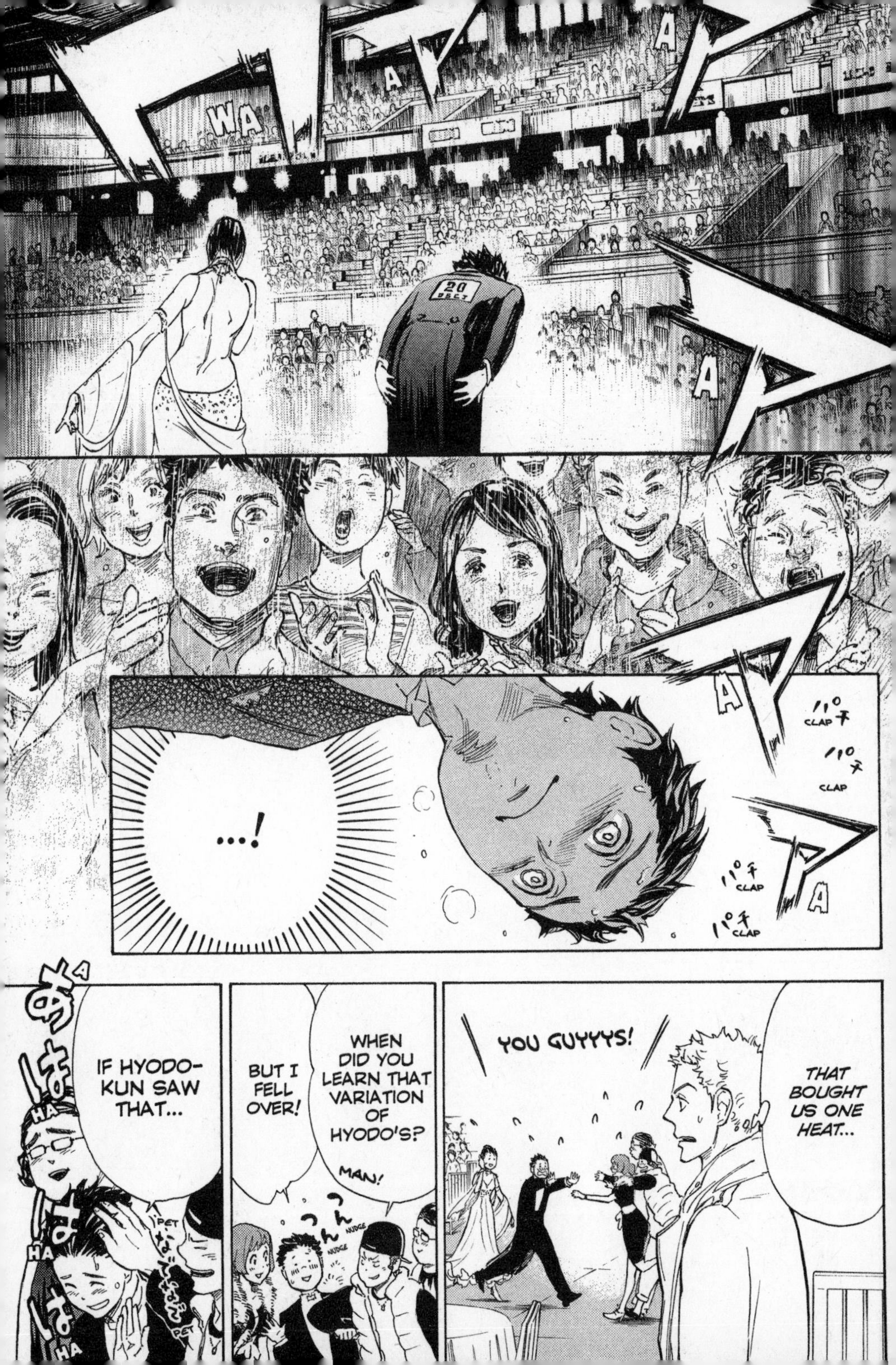
WA
A
A
A
A
A
A
CLAP
CLAP
...!
CLAP
CLAP
THAT BOUGHT US ONE HEAT...
YOU GUYYYS!
WHEN DID YOU LEARN THAT VARIATION OF HYODO'S?
MAN!
BUT I FELL OVER!
NUDGE
NUDGE
IF HYODO-KUN SAW THAT...
PET
PET
A
HA
HA
HA
HA

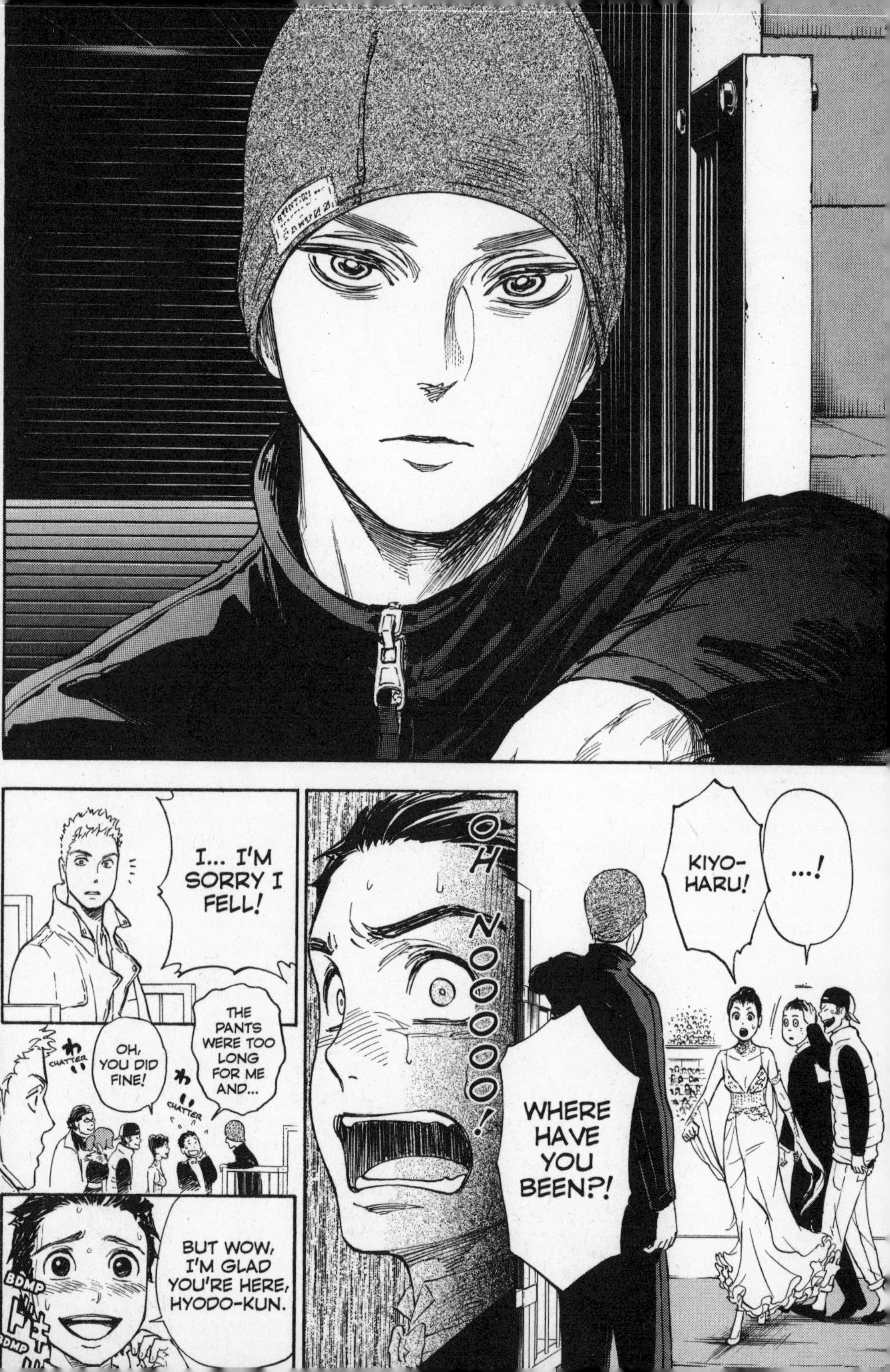
...!
KIYO-HARU!
WHERE HAVE YOU BEEN?!
OHNOOOOOO!
I... I'M SORRY I FELL!
THE PANTS WERE TOO LONG FOR ME AND...
CHATTER
OH, YOU DID FINE!
CHATTER
BUT WOW, I'M GLAD YOU'RE HERE, HYODO-KUN.
BDMP
BDMP

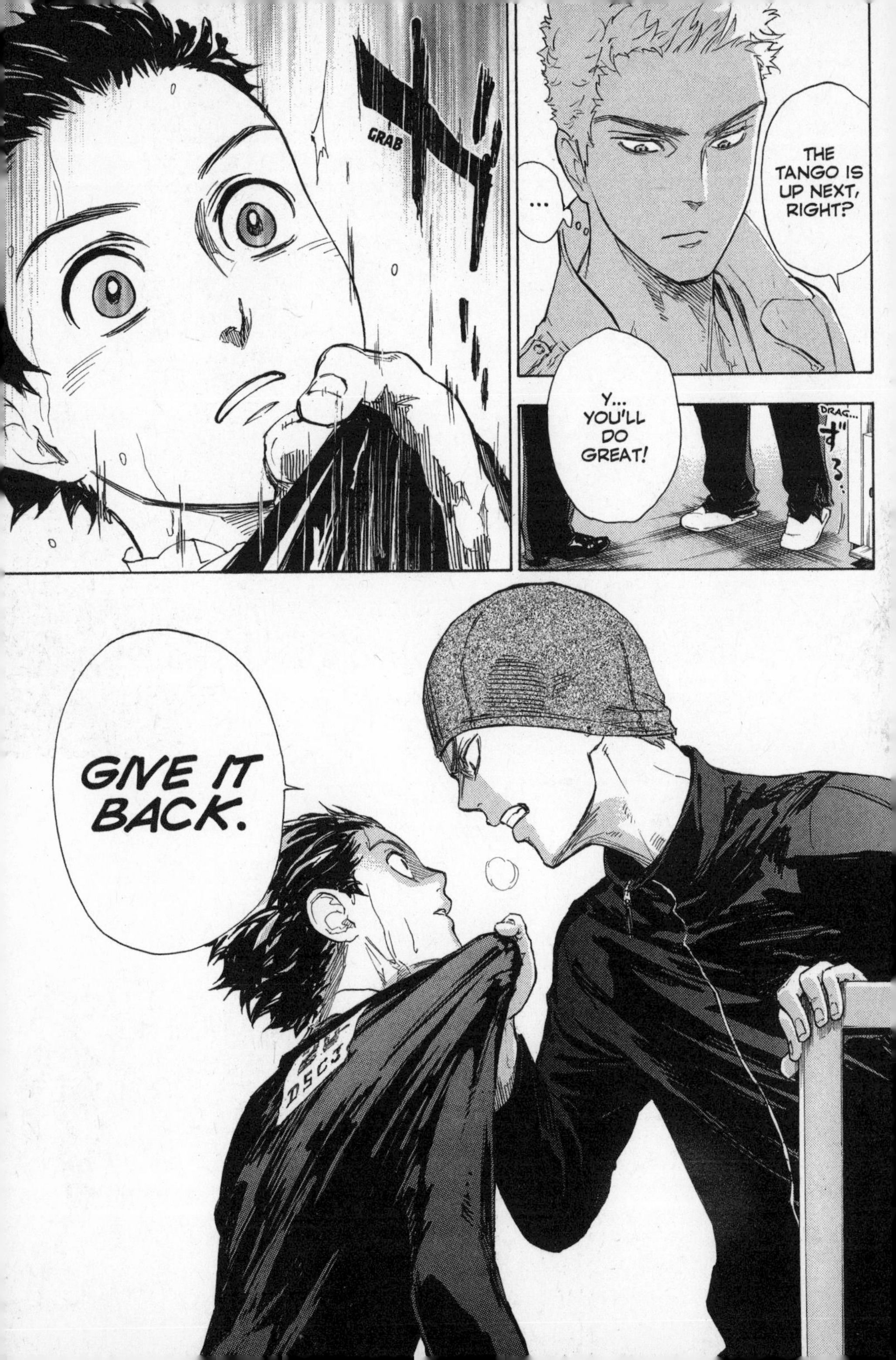
THE TANGO IS UP NEXT, RIGHT?
...
Y... YOU'LL DO GREAT!
DRAG...
GRAB
GIVE IT BACK.

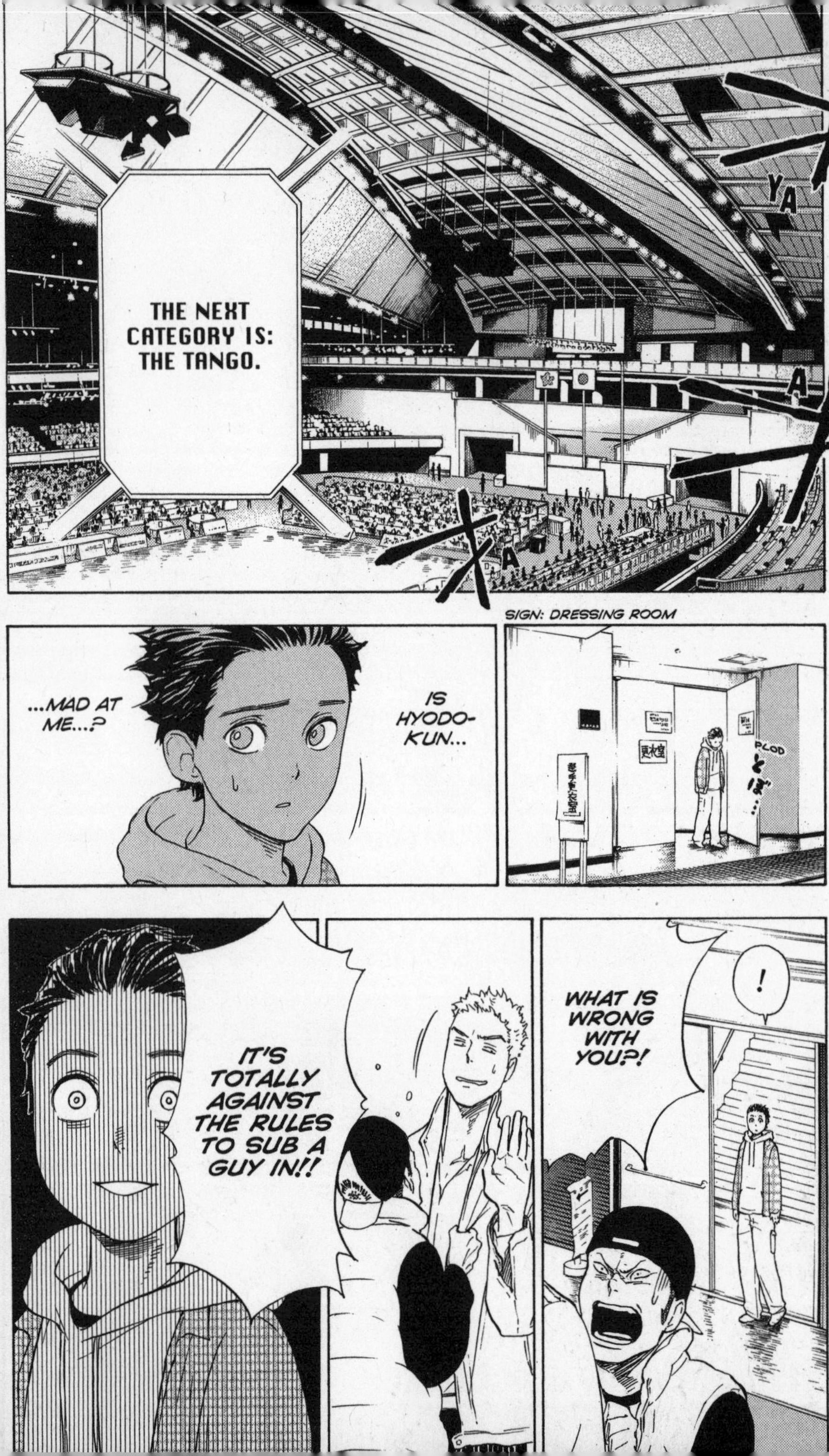
THE NEXT CATEGORY IS: THE TANGO.
YA
A
A
SIGN: DRESSING ROOM
PLOD
IS HYODO-KUN...
...MAD AT ME...?
!
WHAT IS WRONG WITH YOU?!
IT'S TOTALLY AGAINST THE RULES TO SUB A GUY IN!!

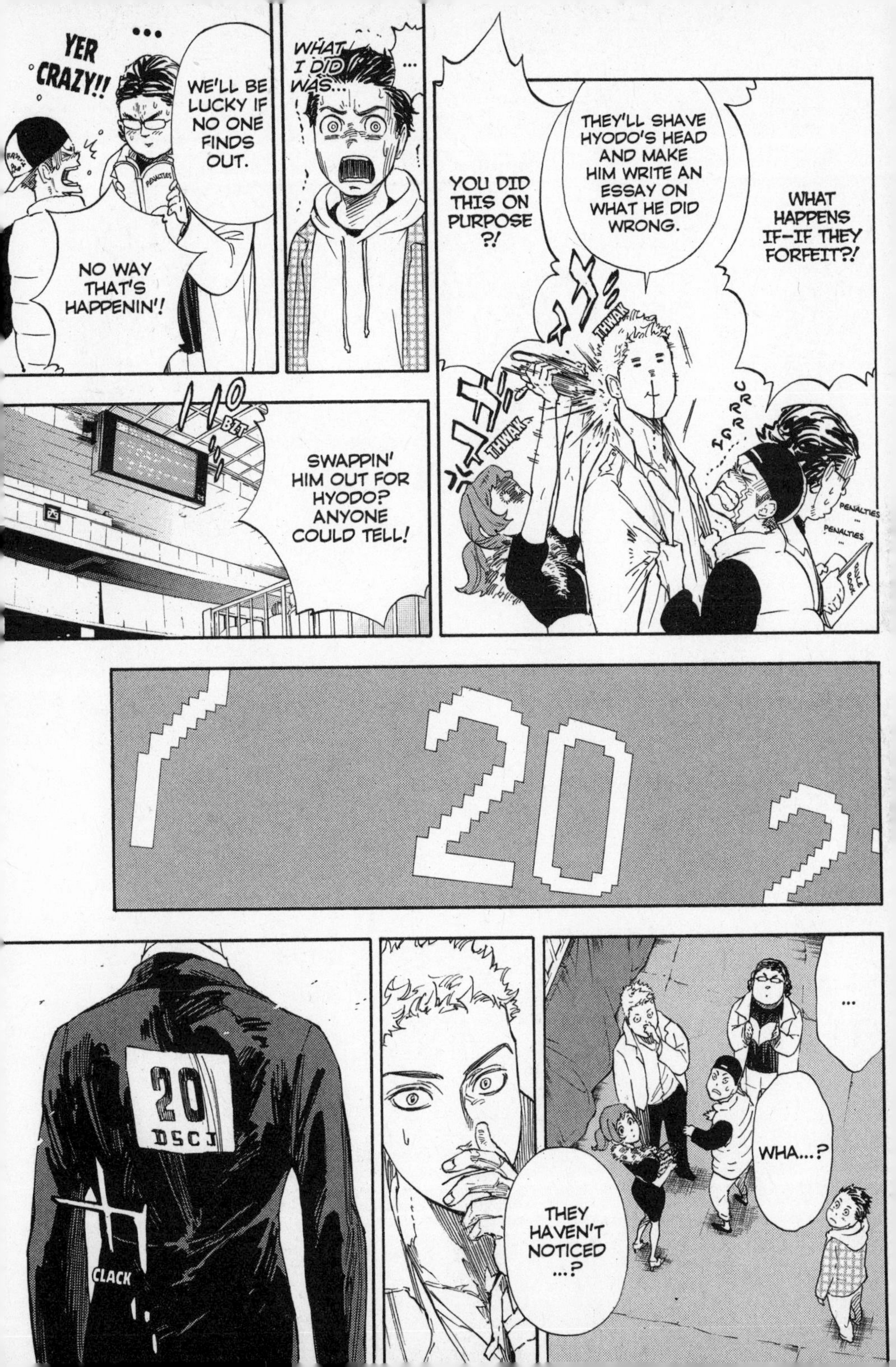
WHAT HAPPENS IF—IF THEY FORFEIT?!
THEY'LL SHAVE HYODO'S HEAD AND MAKE HIM WRITE AN ESSAY ON WHAT HE DID WRONG.
YOU DID THIS ON PURPOSE ?!
THWAK
THWAK
GRRR
PENALTIES ... PENALTIES ...
WHAT I DID WAS...
...
...
WE'LL BE LUCKY IF NO ONE FINDS OUT.
YER CRAZY!!
NO WAY THAT'S HAPPENIN'!
PENALTIES
BZT
SWAPPIN' HIM OUT FOR HYODO? ANYONE COULD TELL!
20
...
WHA...?
THEY HAVEN'T NOTICED ...?
20
DSCJ
CLACK

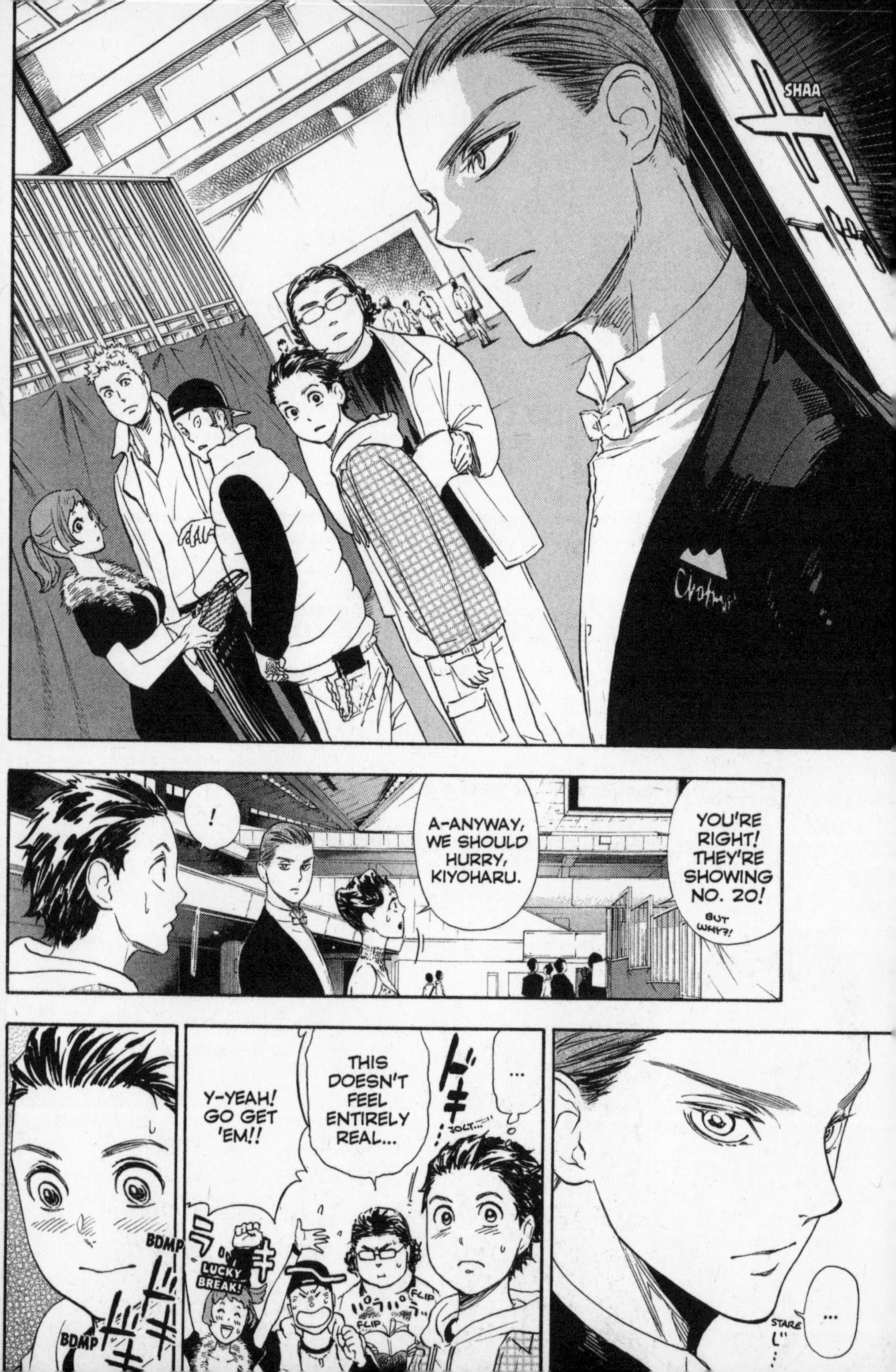
SHAA
YOU'RE RIGHT! THEY'RE SHOWING NO. 20!
BUT WHY?!
A-ANYWAY, WE SHOULD HURRY, KIYOHARU.
!
STARE
...
...
JOLT...
THIS DOESN'T FEEL ENTIRELY REAL...
Y-YEAH! GO GET 'EM!!
FLIP
FLIP
LUCKY BREAK!
BDMP
BDMP

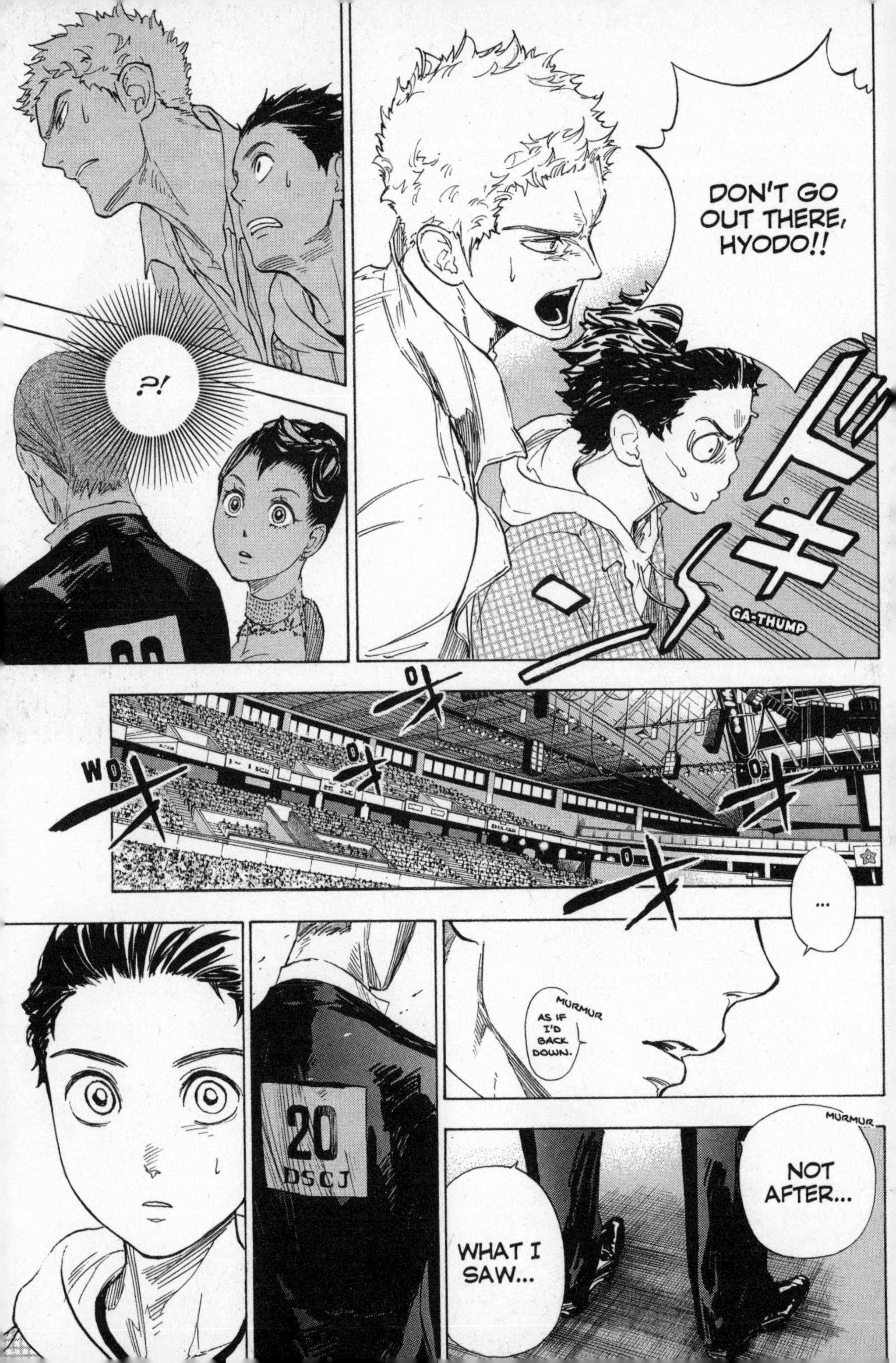
DON'T GO OUT THERE, HYODO!!
GA-THUMP
?!
WO
O
O
O
O
...
MURMUR
AS IF I'D BACK DOWN.
MURMUR
NOT AFTER...
WHAT I SAW...
20
DSCJ

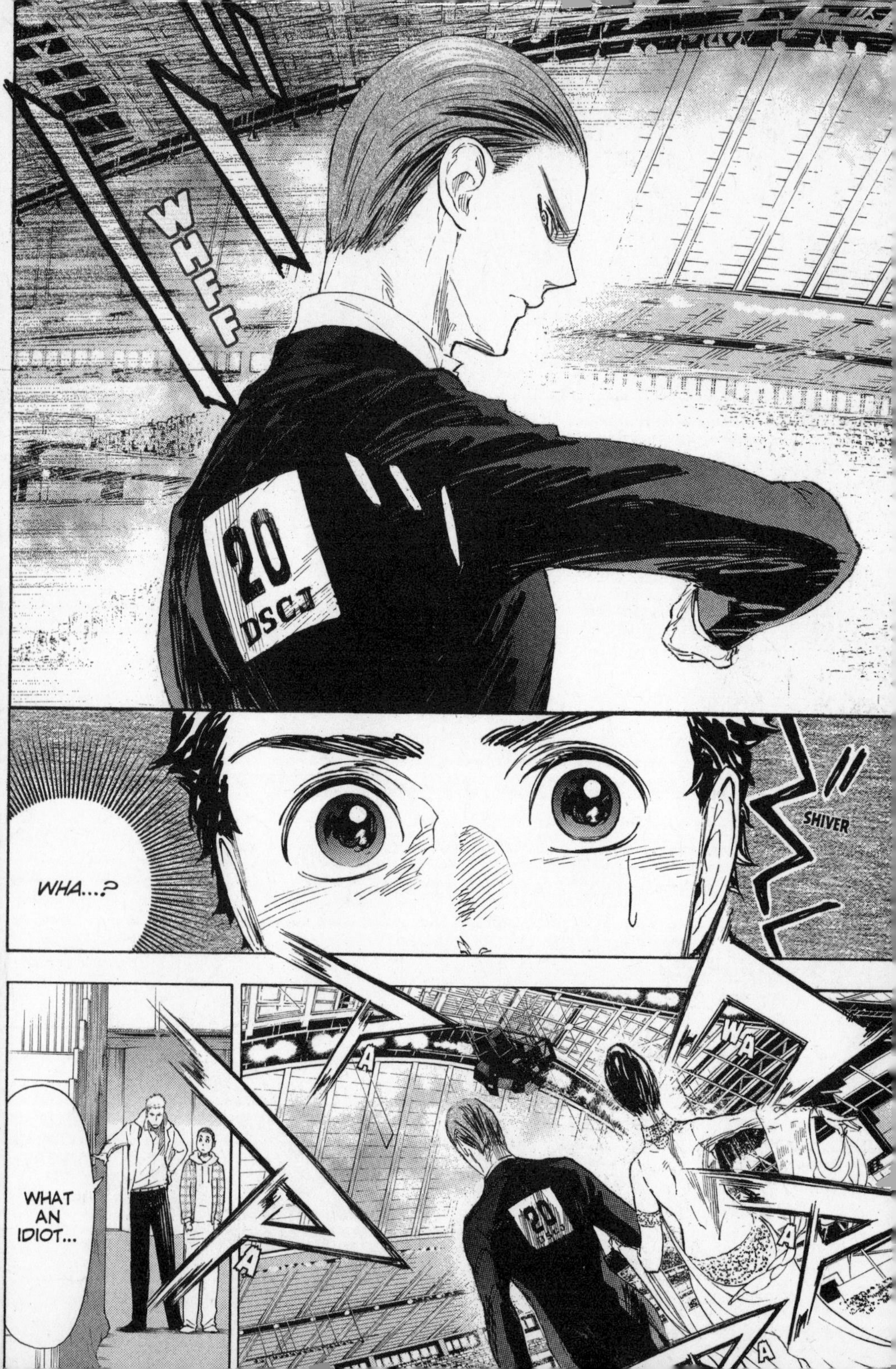
WHFF
20
DSCJ
SHIVER
WHA...?
WA
A
A
A
A
A
WHAT AN IDIOT...

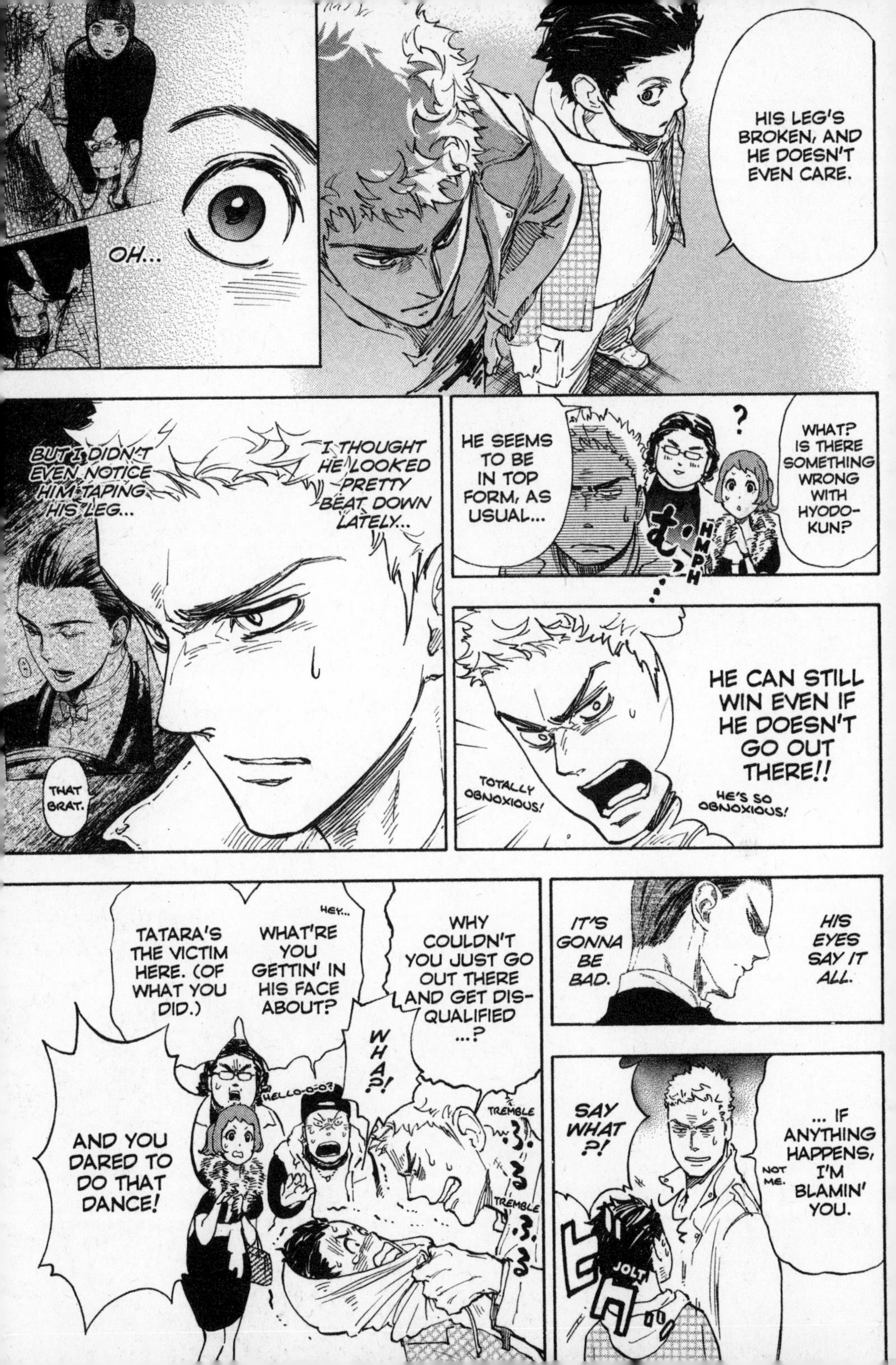
HIS LEG'S BROKEN, AND HE DOESN'T EVEN CARE.
OH...
WHAT? IS THERE SOMETHING WRONG WITH HYODO-KUN?
?
HE SEEMS TO BE IN TOP FORM, AS USUAL...
HMPH
HE CAN STILL WIN EVEN IF HE DOESN'T GO OUT THERE!!
HE'S SO OBNOXIOUS!
TOTALLY OBNOXIOUS!
I THOUGHT HE LOOKED PRETTY BEAT DOWN LATELY...
BUT I DIDN'T EVEN NOTICE HIM TAPING HIS LEG...
THAT BRAT.
HIS EYES SAY IT ALL.
IT'S GONNA BE BAD.
... IF ANYTHING HAPPENS, I'M BLAMIN' YOU.
NOT ME.
SAY WHAT?!
JOLT
WHY COULDN'T YOU JUST GO OUT THERE AND GET DIS-QUALIFIED ...?
HEY...
WHAT'RE YOU GETTIN' IN HIS FACE ABOUT?
TATARA'S THE VICTIM HERE. (OF WHAT YOU DID.)
WHA?!
HELLO-O-O?
TREMBLE
TREMBLE
AND YOU DARED TO DO THAT DANCE!

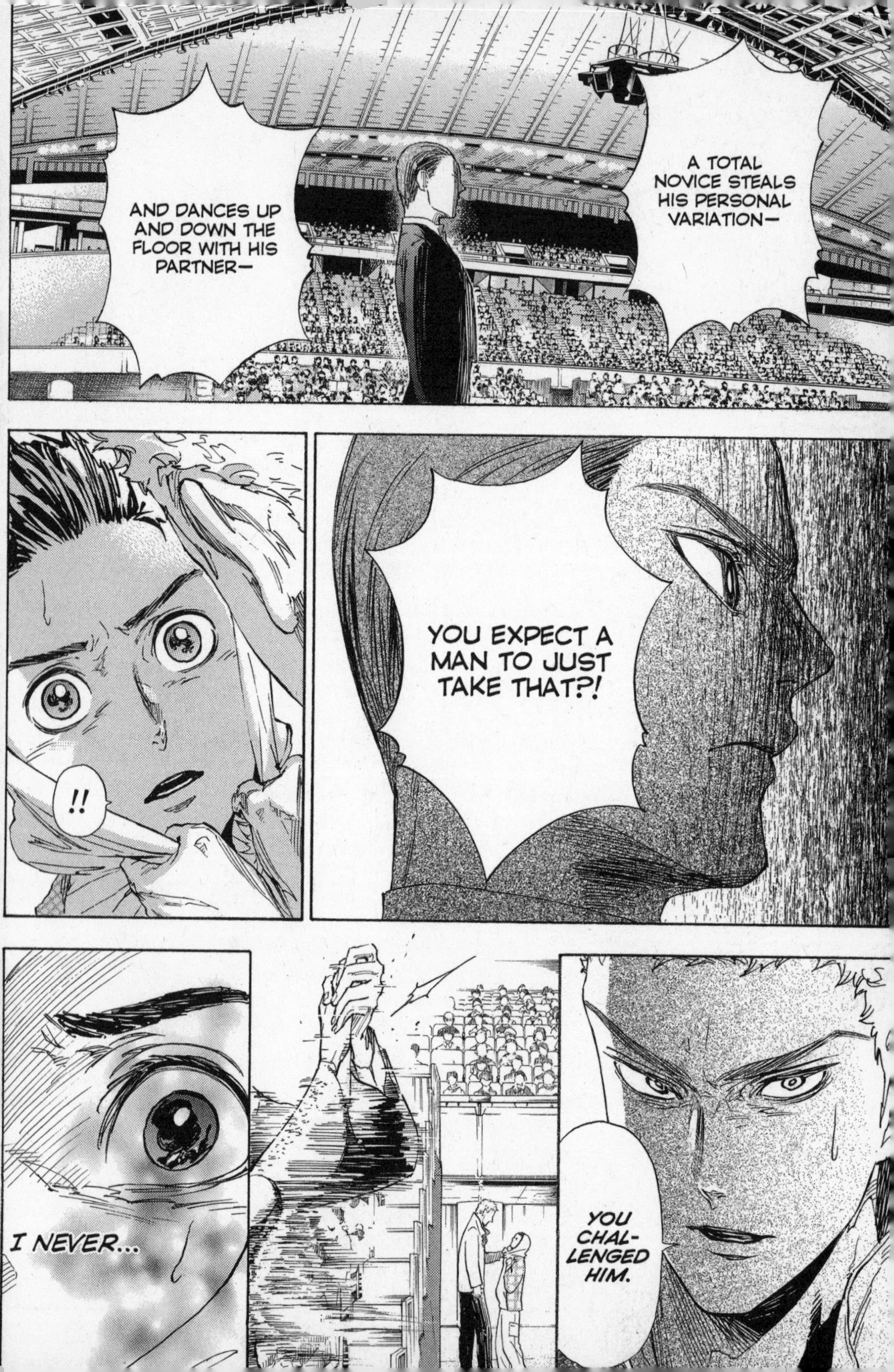
A TOTAL NOVICE STEALS HIS PERSONAL VARIATION—
AND DANCES UP AND DOWN THE FLOOR WITH HIS PARTNER—
YOU EXPECT A MAN TO JUST TAKE THAT?!
!!
YOU CHAL-LENGED HIM.
I NEVER...

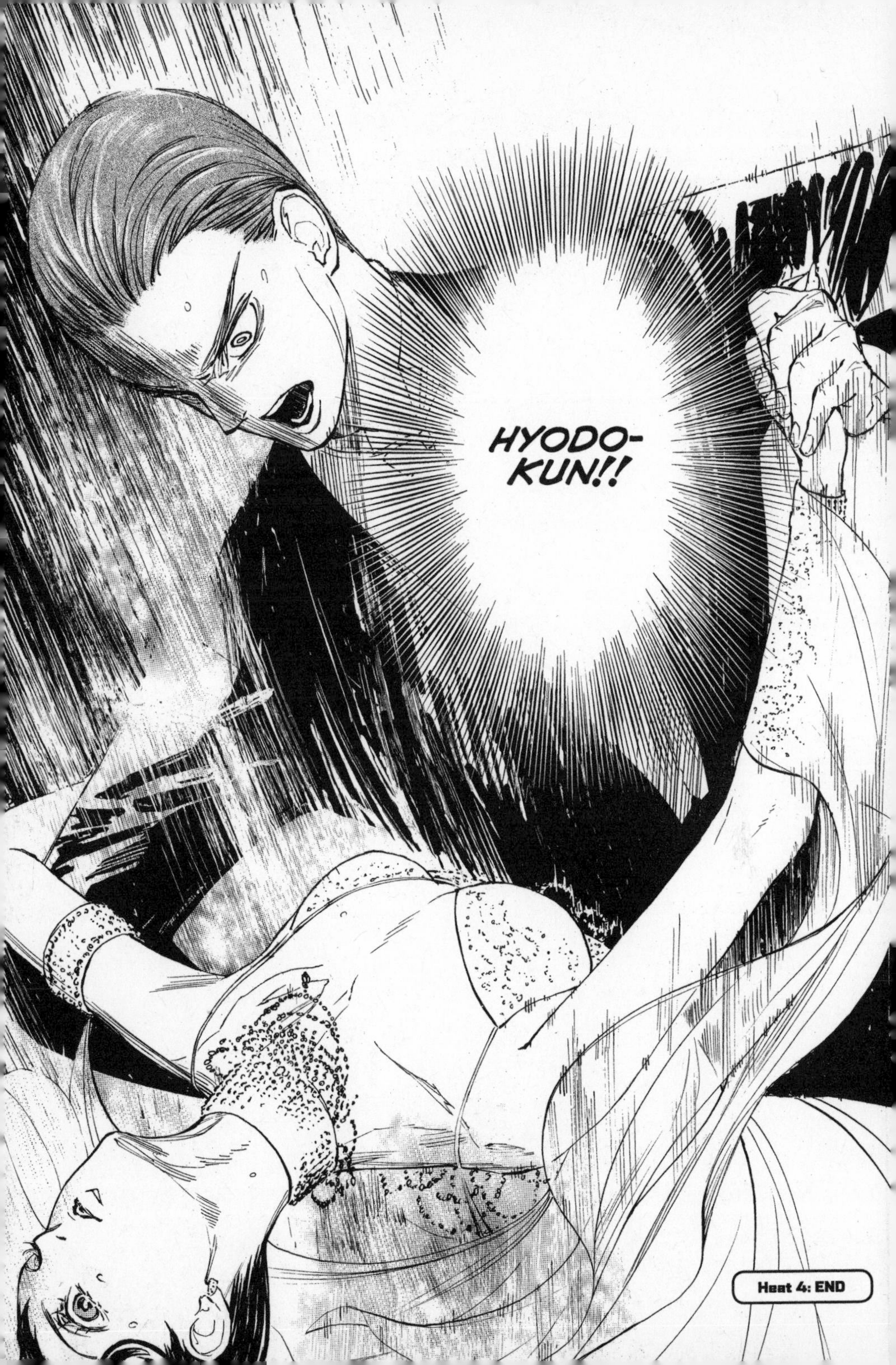
HYODO-KUN!!
Heat 4: END

WELCOME TO THE BALLROOM

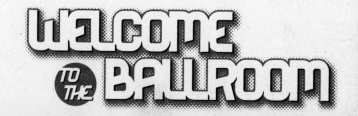

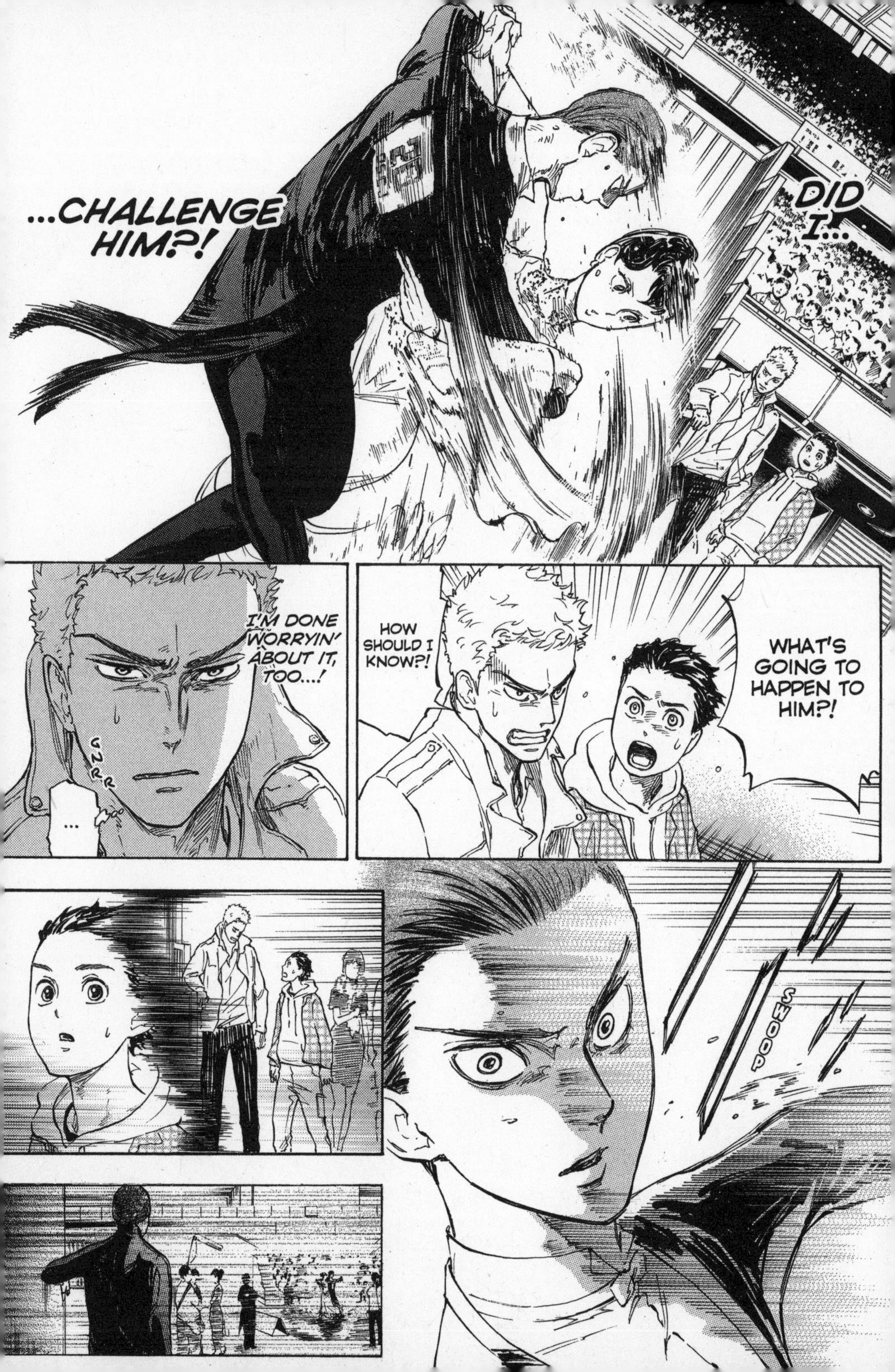
DID I...
...CHALLENGE HIM?!
WHAT'S GOING TO HAPPEN TO HIM?!
HOW SHOULD I KNOW?!
I'M DONE WORRYIN' ABOUT IT, TOO...!
...
SWOOP

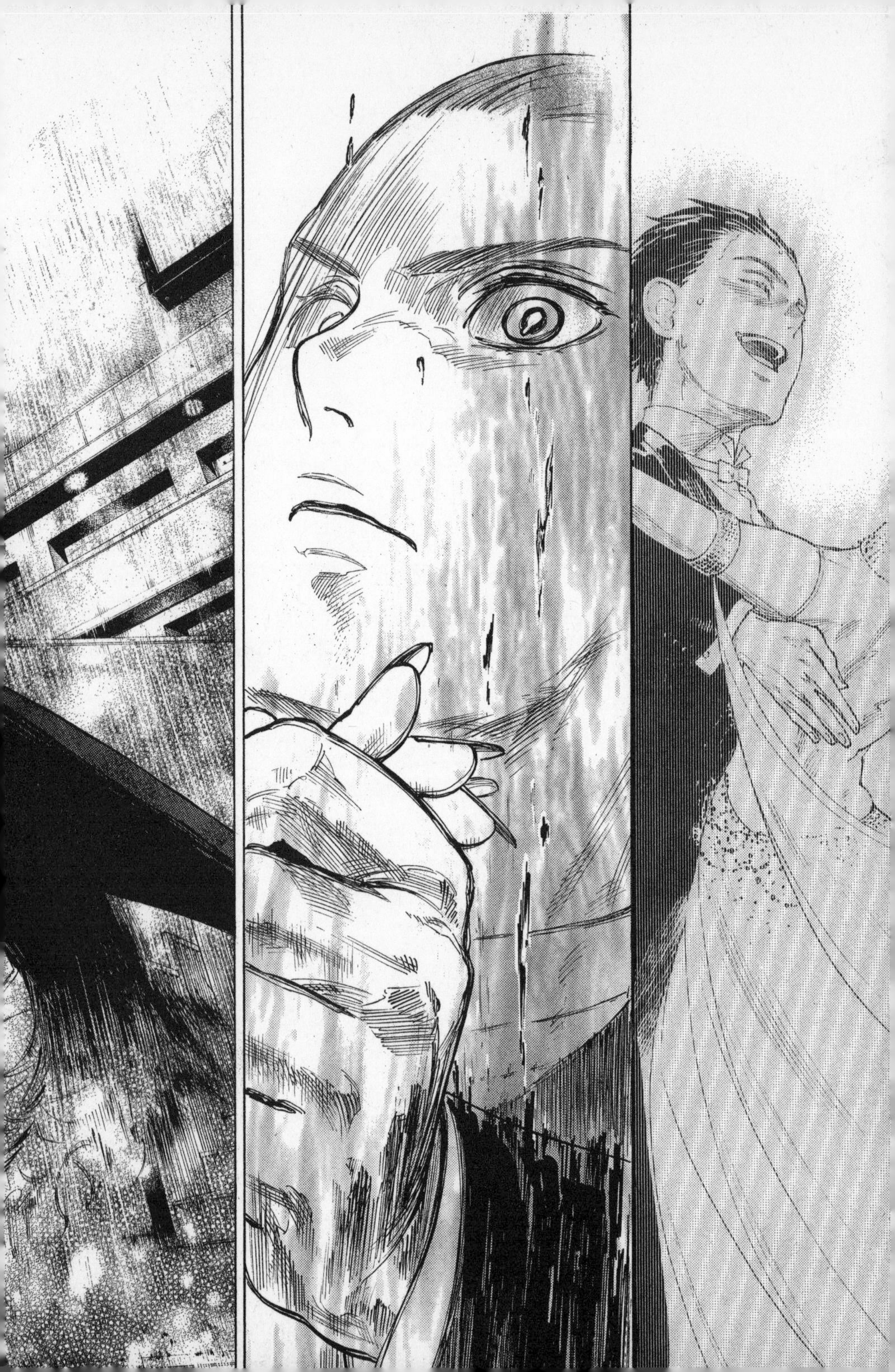

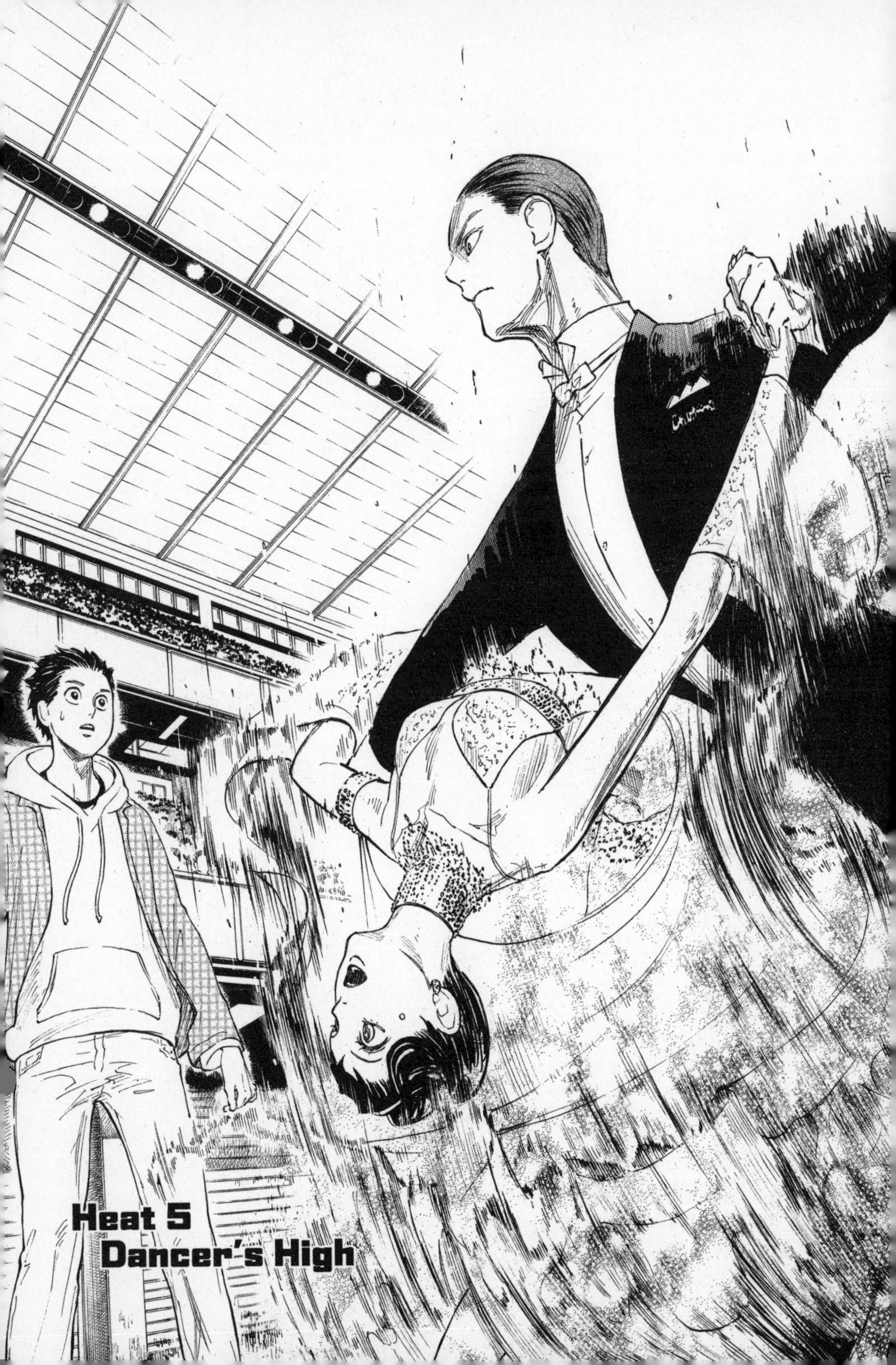
Heat 5
Dancer's High

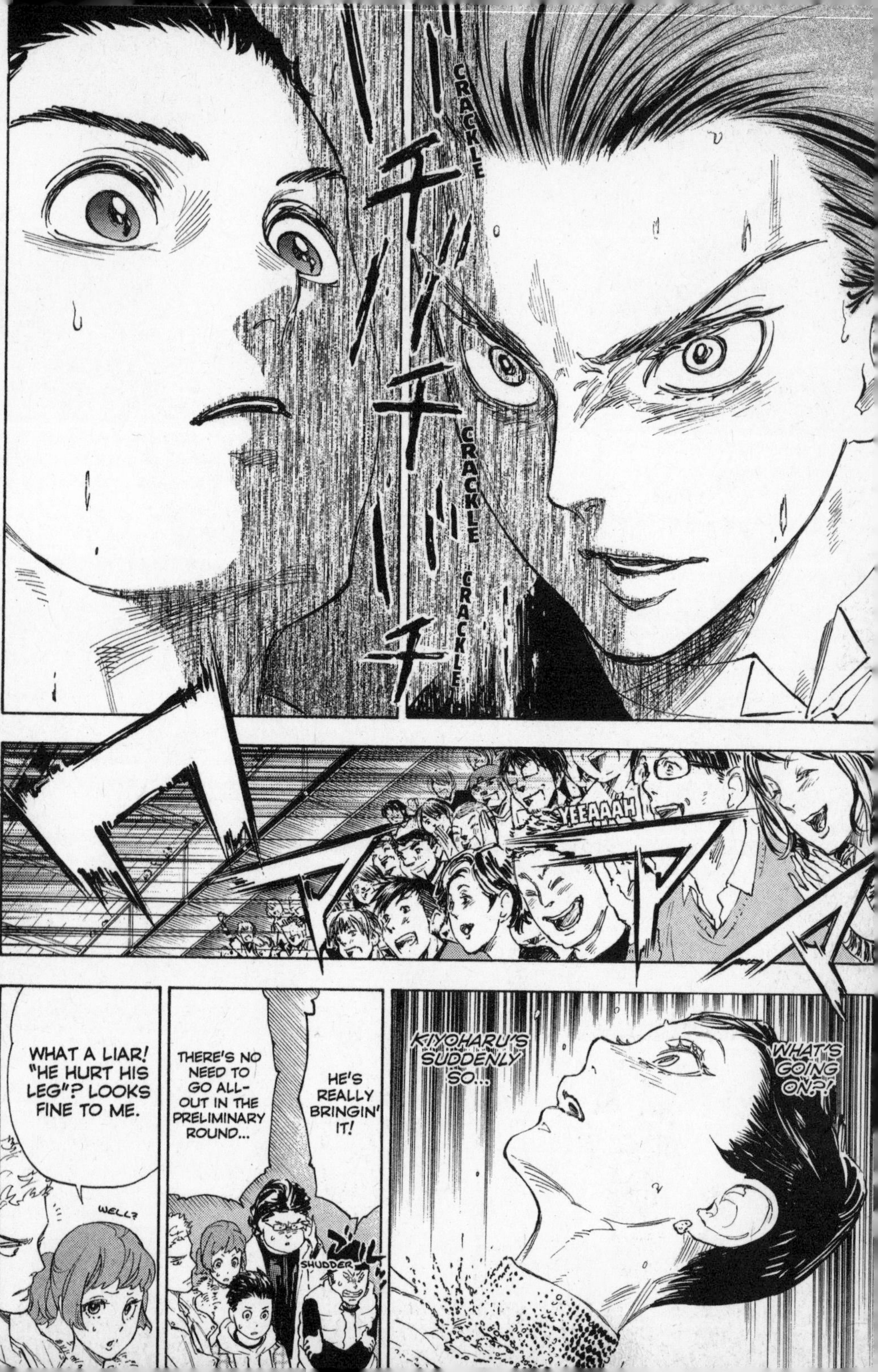
CRACKLE
CRACKLE
CRACKLE
CRACKLE
YEEAAAH
WHAT'S GOING ON?!
KIYOHARU'S SUDDENLY SO...
HE'S REALLY BRINGIN' IT!
THERE'S NO NEED TO GO ALL-OUT IN THE PRELIMINARY ROUND...
SHUDDER
WHAT A LIAR! "HE HURT HIS LEG"? LOOKS FINE TO ME.
WELL?

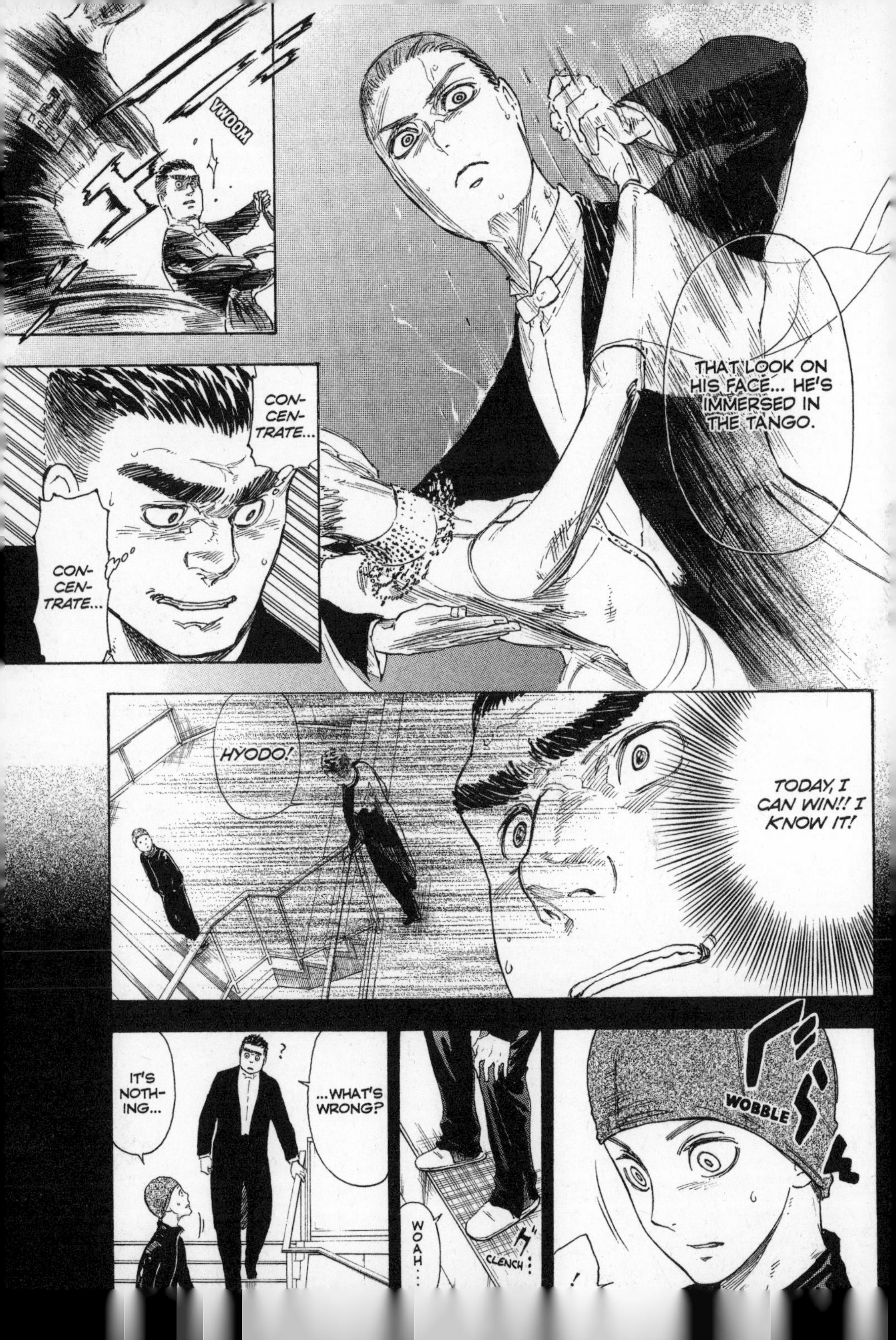
THAT LOOK ON HIS FACE... HE'S IMMERSED IN THE TANGO.
VWOOM
CON-CEN-TRATE...
CON-CEN-TRATE...
TODAY, I CAN WIN!! I KNOW IT!
HYODO!
WOBBLE
!
WOAH...
CLENCH
?
...WHAT'S WRONG?
IT'S NOTH-ING...

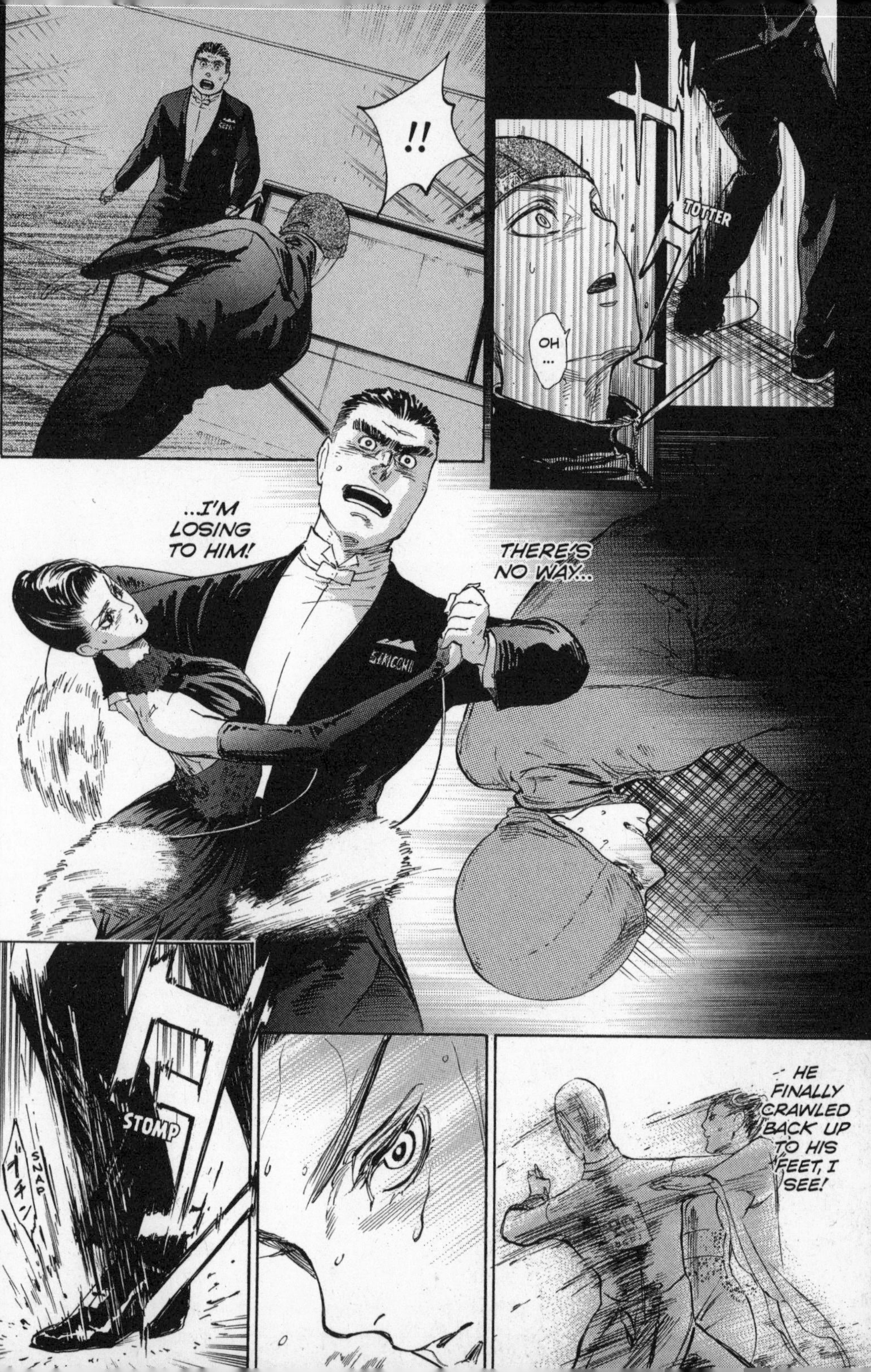
TOTTER
OH ...
!!
THERE'S NO WAY...
...I'M LOSING TO HIM!
HE FINALLY CRAWLED BACK UP TO HIS FEET, I SEE!
STOMP
SNAP

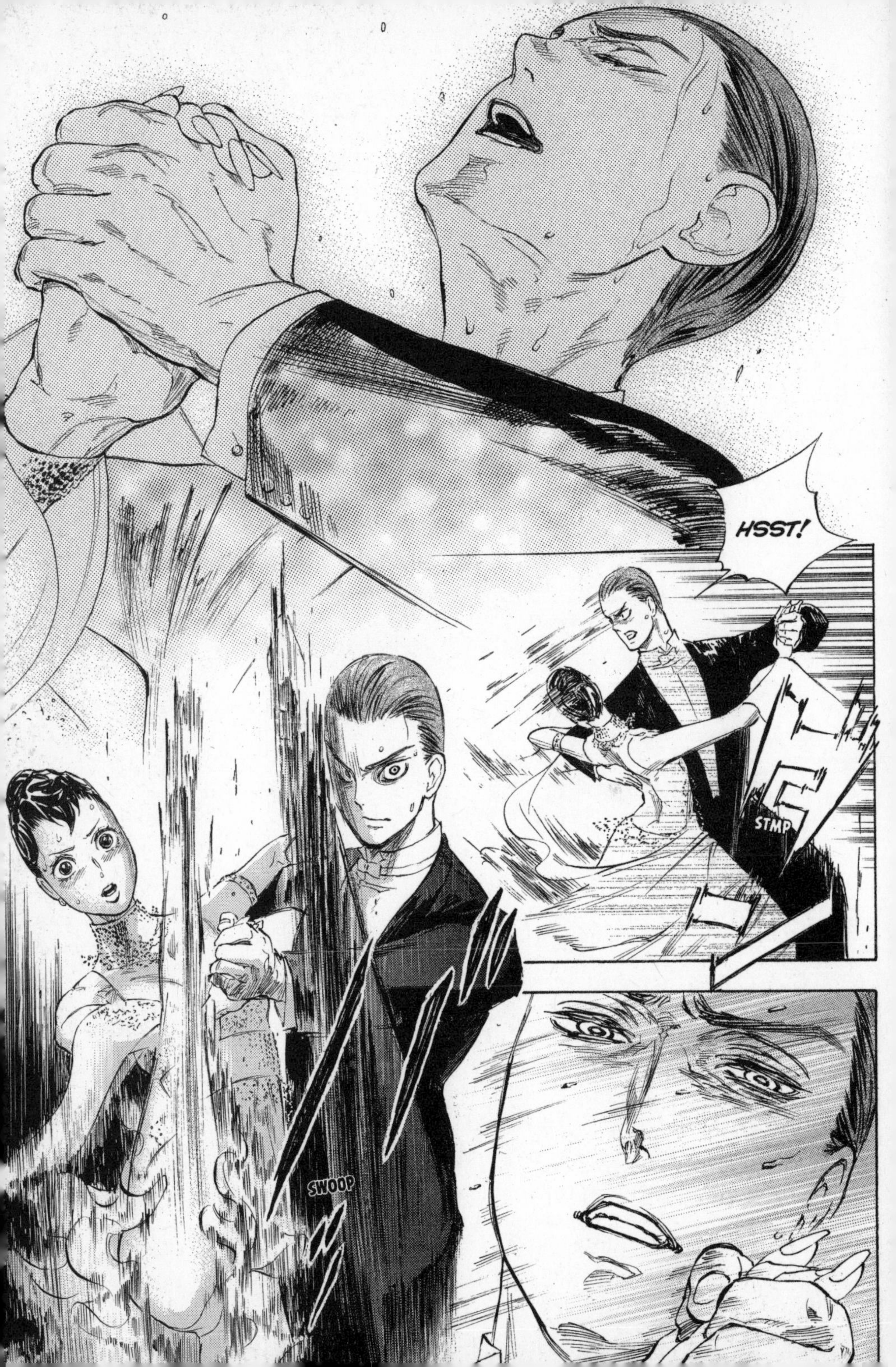
HSST!
STMP
SWOOP

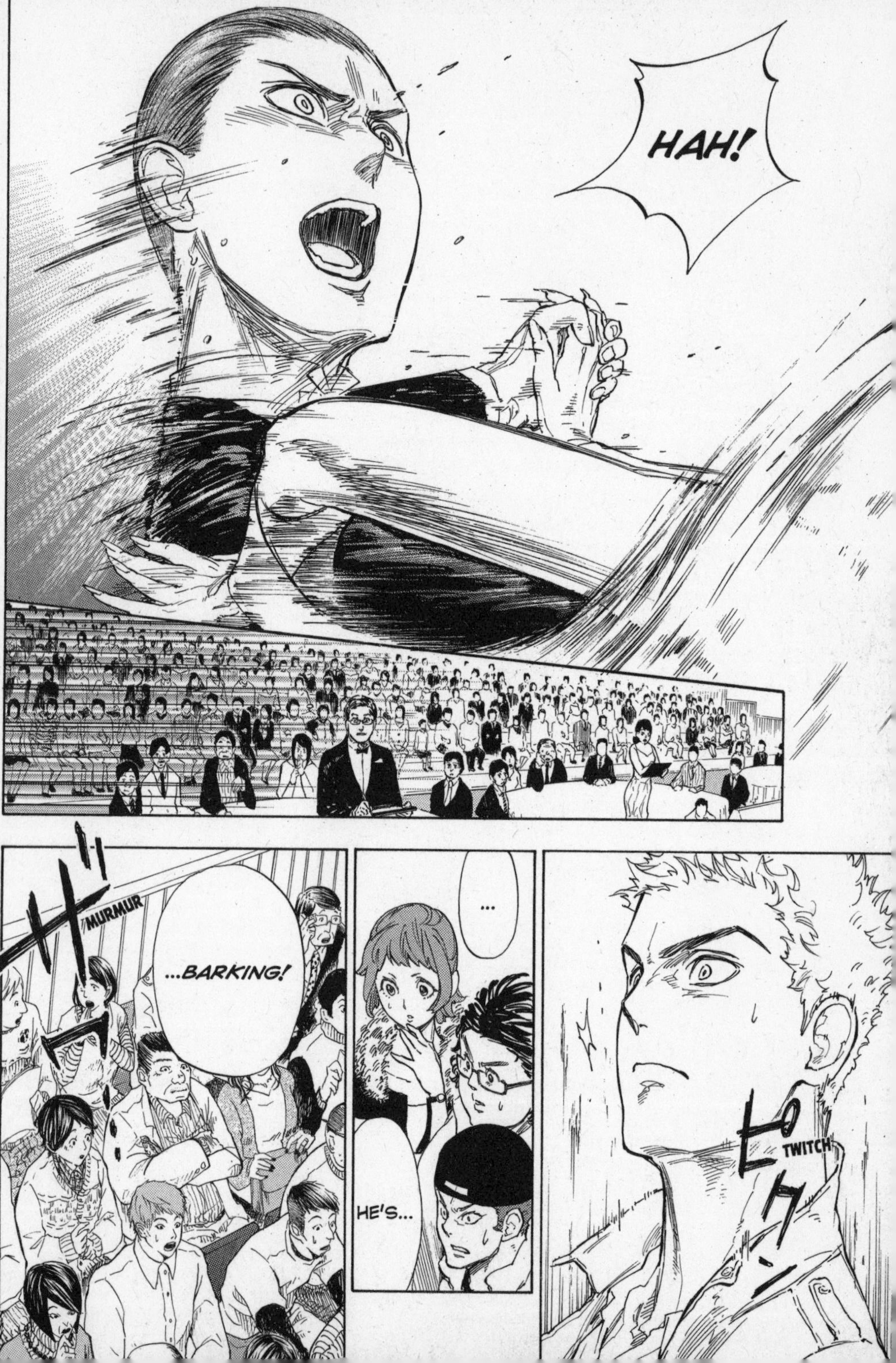
HAH!
TWITCH
...
HE'S...
MURMUR
...BARKING!

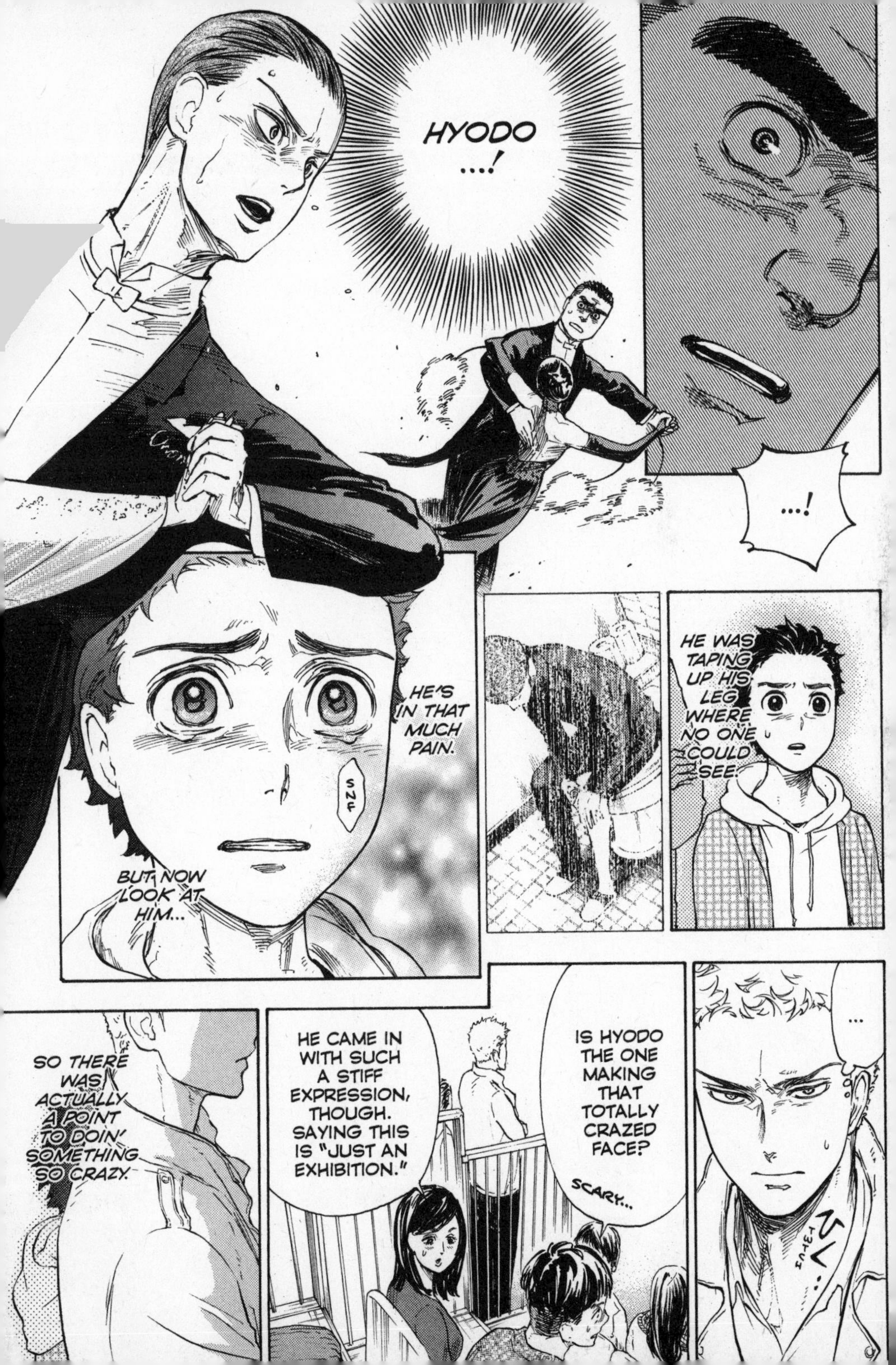
...!
HYODO ...!
HE WAS TAPING UP HIS LEG WHERE NO ONE COULD SEE.
HE'S IN THAT MUCH PAIN.
SNF
BUT NOW LOOK AT HIM...
...
IS HYODO THE ONE MAKING THAT TOTALLY CRAZED FACE?
HE CAME IN WITH SUCH A STIFF EXPRESSION, THOUGH. SAYING THIS IS "JUST AN EXHIBITION."
SCARY...
SO THERE WAS ACTUALLY A POINT TO DOIN' SOMETHING SO CRAZY.

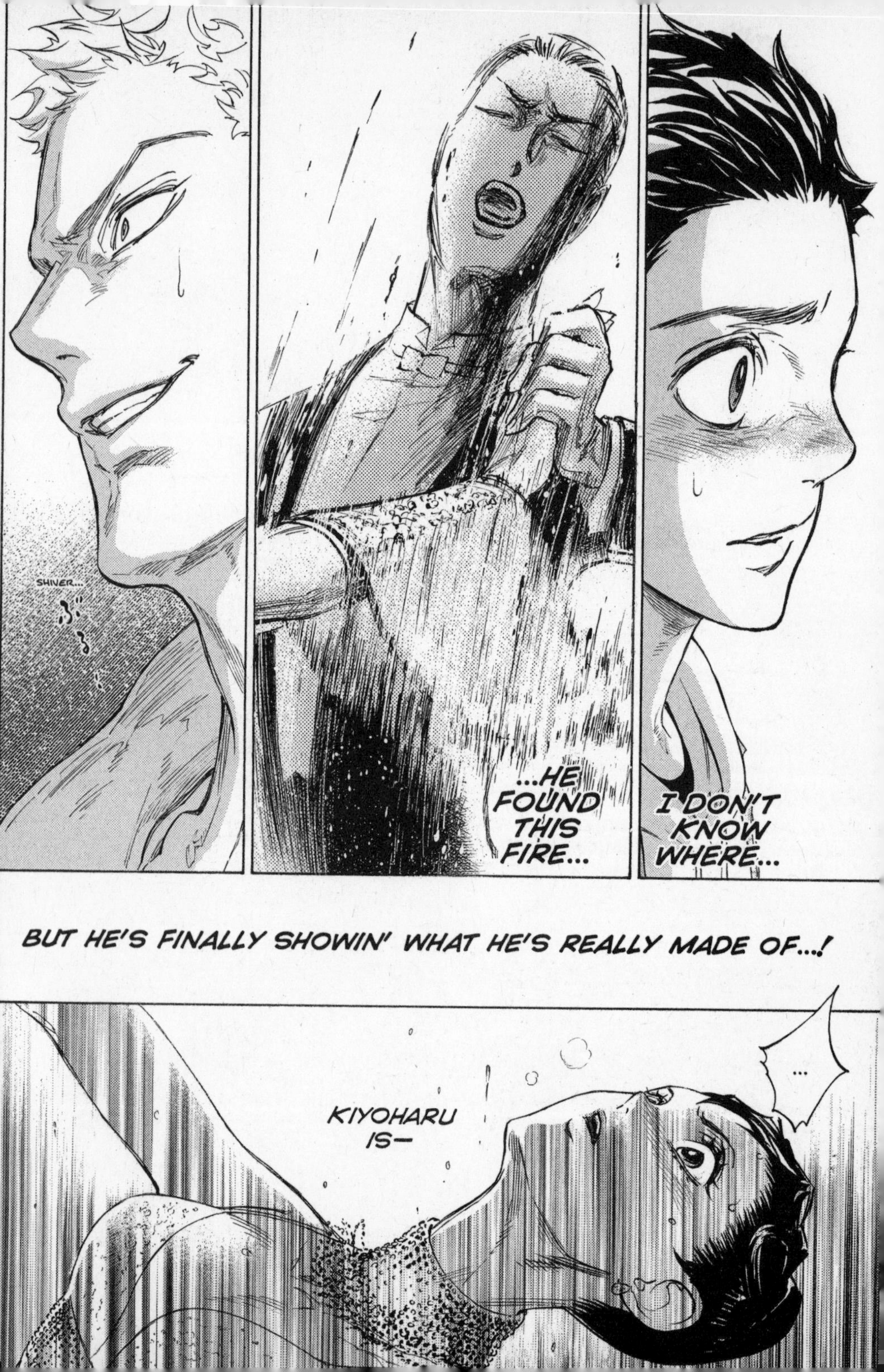
I DON'T KNOW WHERE...
...HE FOUND THIS FIRE...
SHIVER...
ぶる
BUT HE'S FINALLY SHOWIN' WHAT HE'S REALLY MADE OF...!
...
KIYOHARU IS—

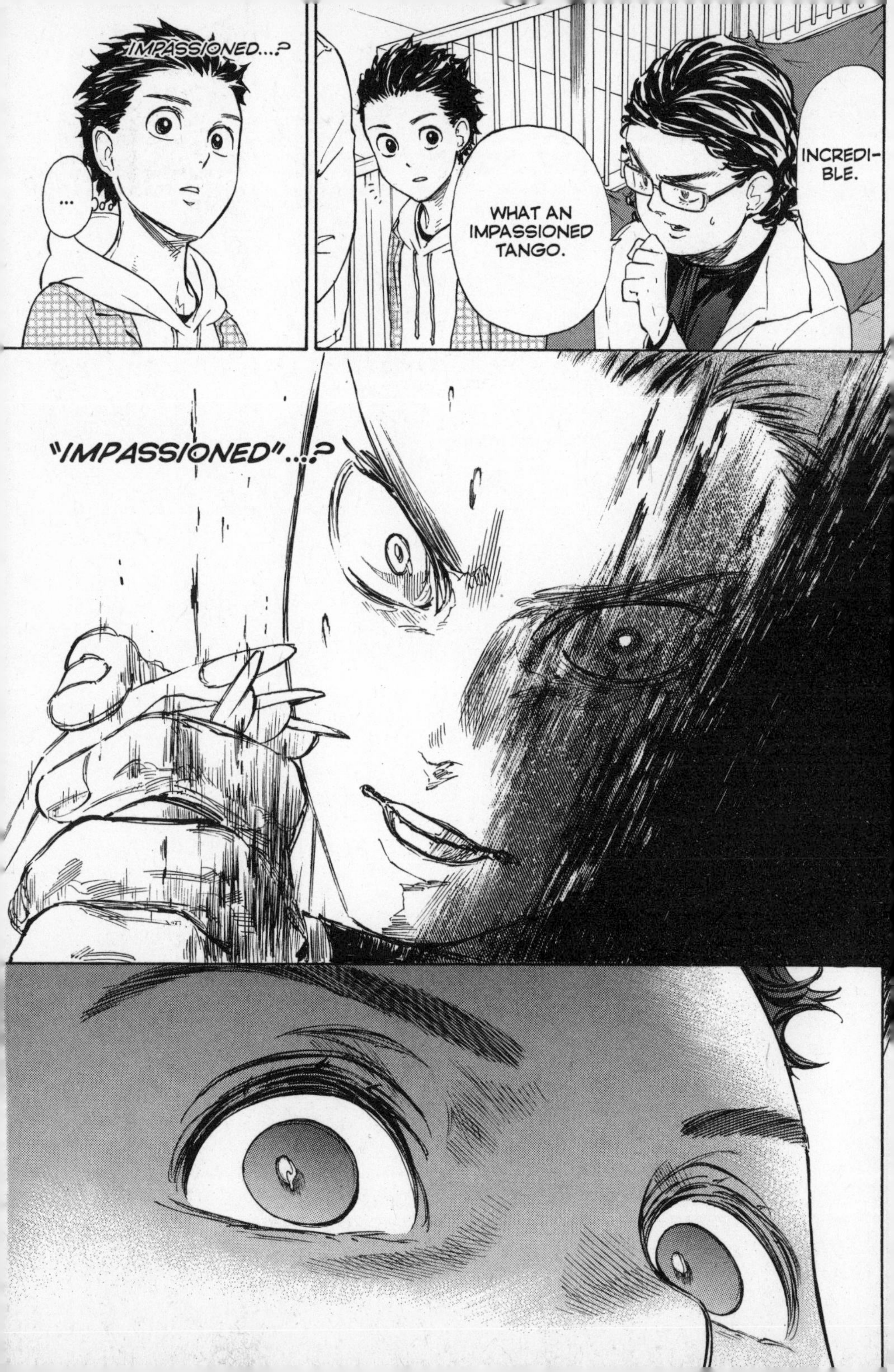
INCREDI-BLE.
WHAT AN IMPASSIONED TANGO.
IMPASSIONED...?
...
"IMPASSIONED"...?

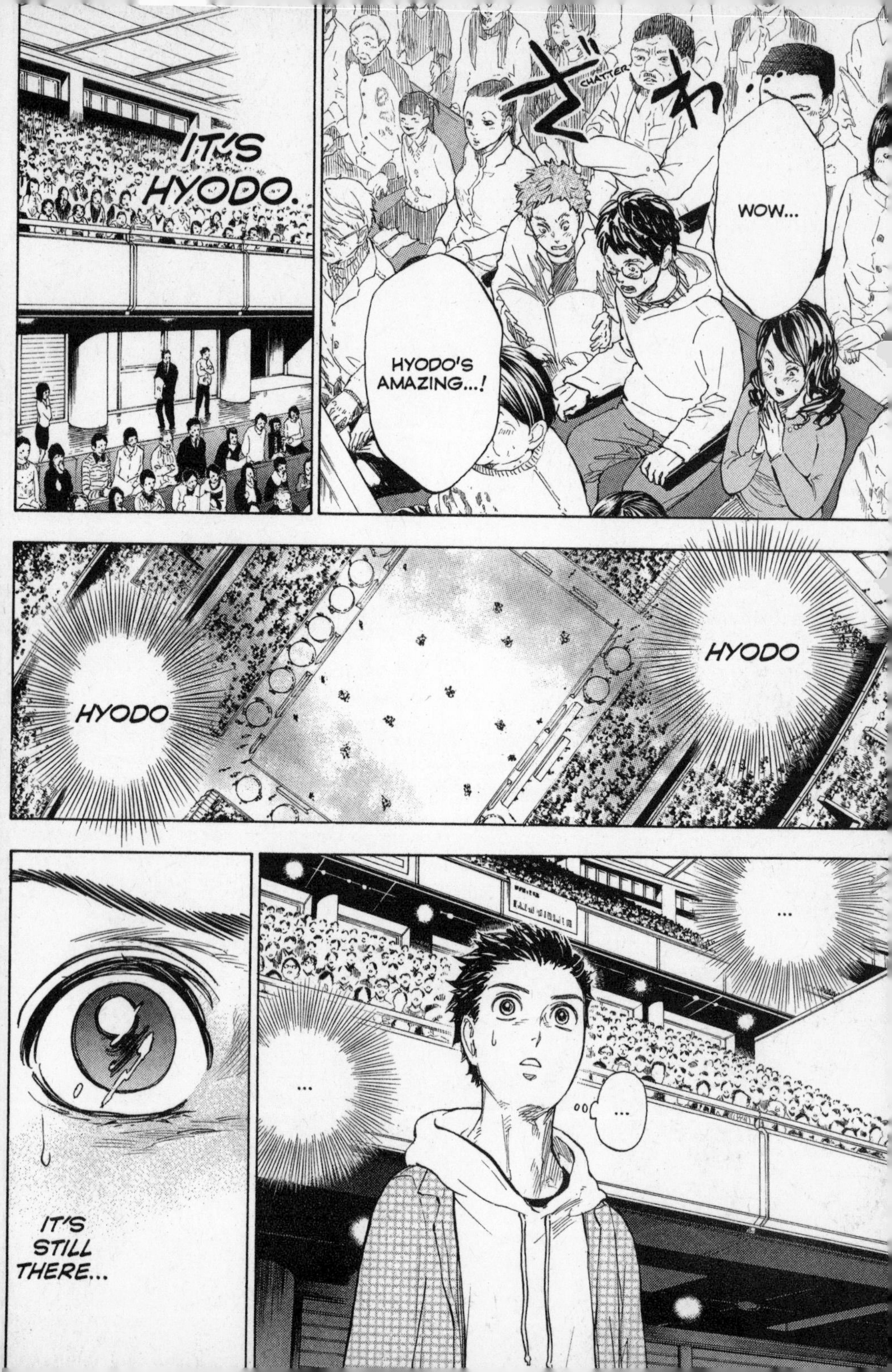

CHATTER
WOW...
HYODO'S AMAZING...!
IT'S HYODO.
HYODO
HYODO
...
...
...
IT'S STILL THERE...

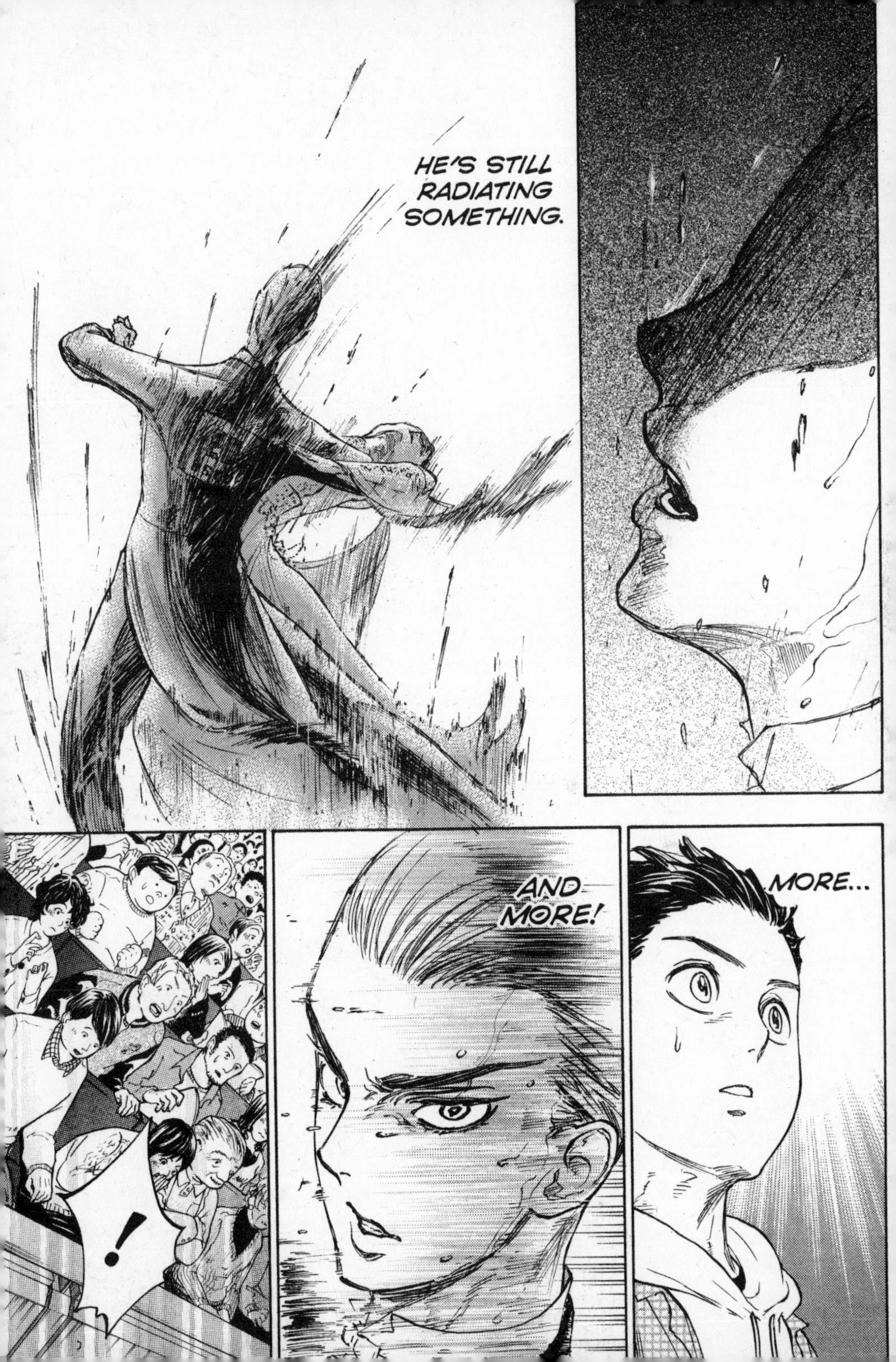
HE'S STILL RADIATING SOMETHING.
MORE...
AND MORE!
!

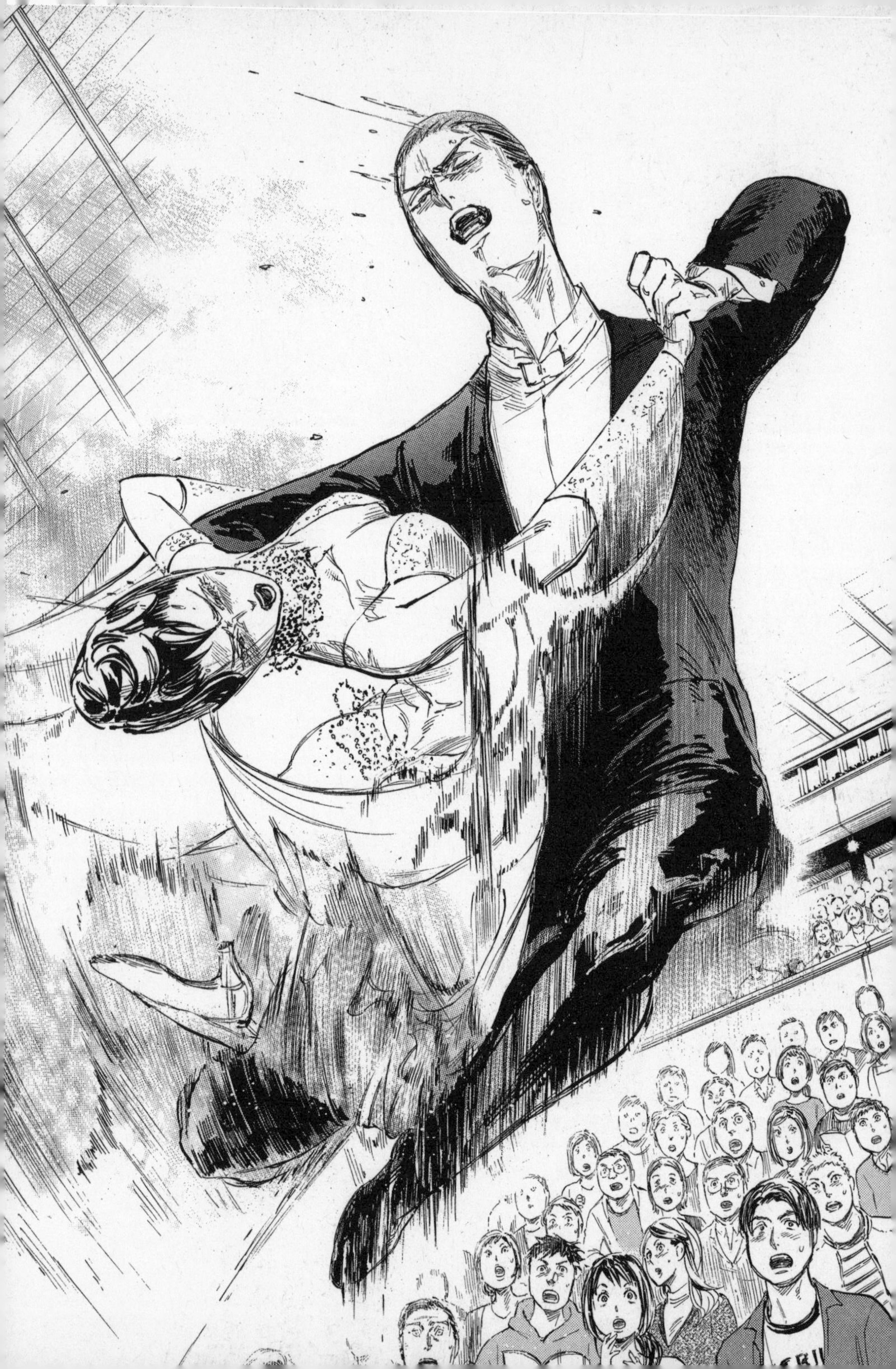

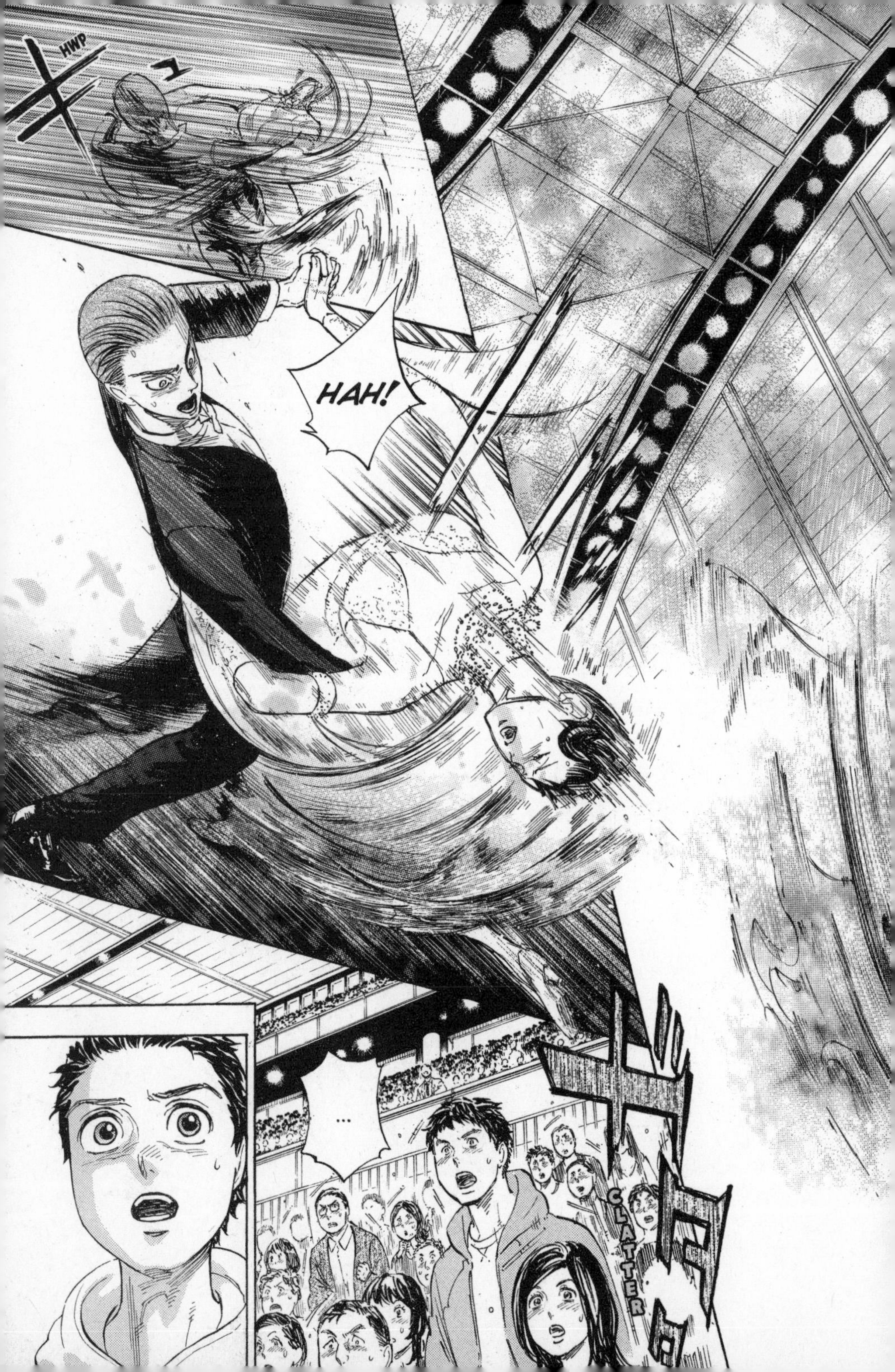
HWP
HAH!
...
CLATTER

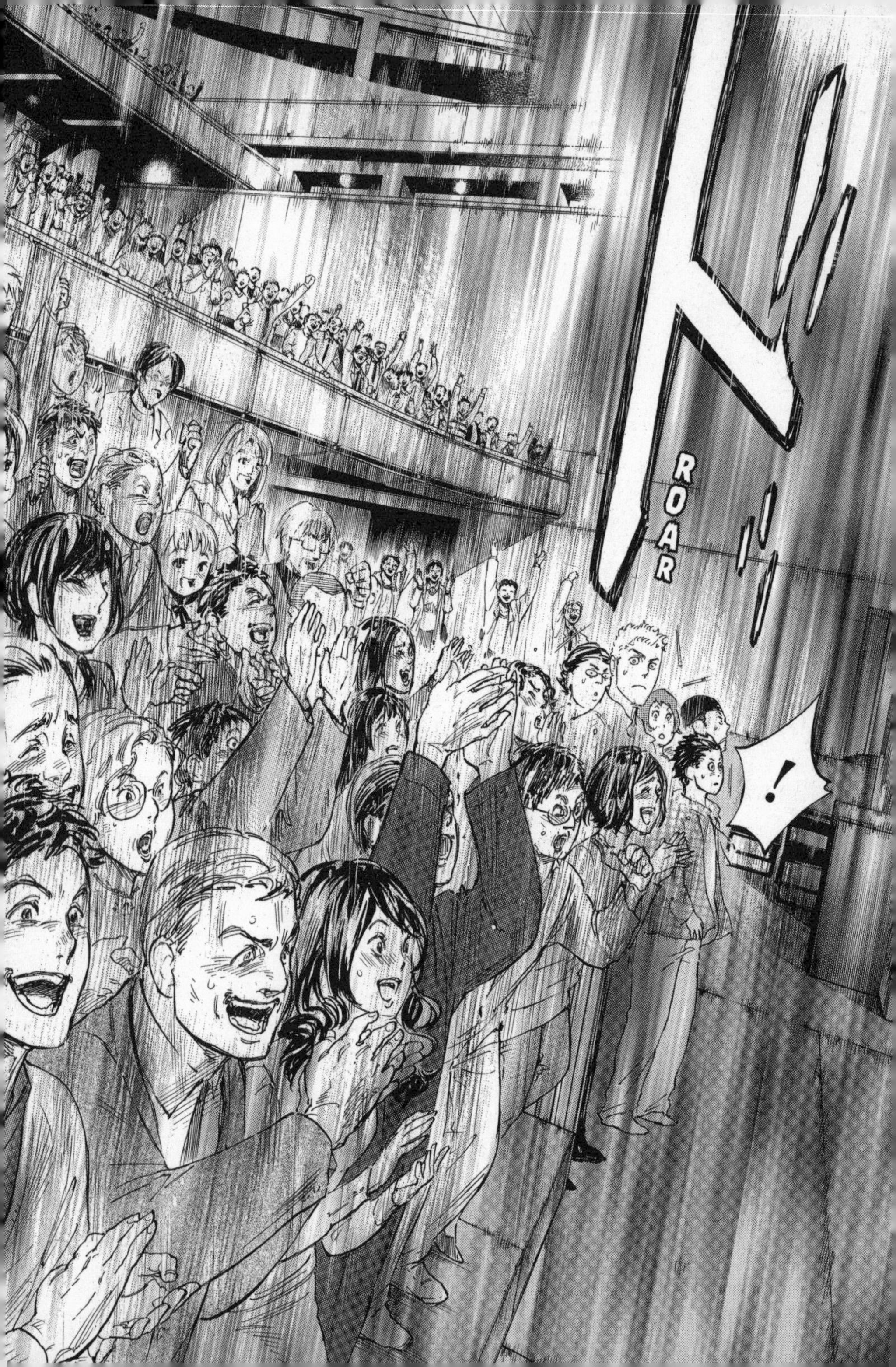

ROAR
!

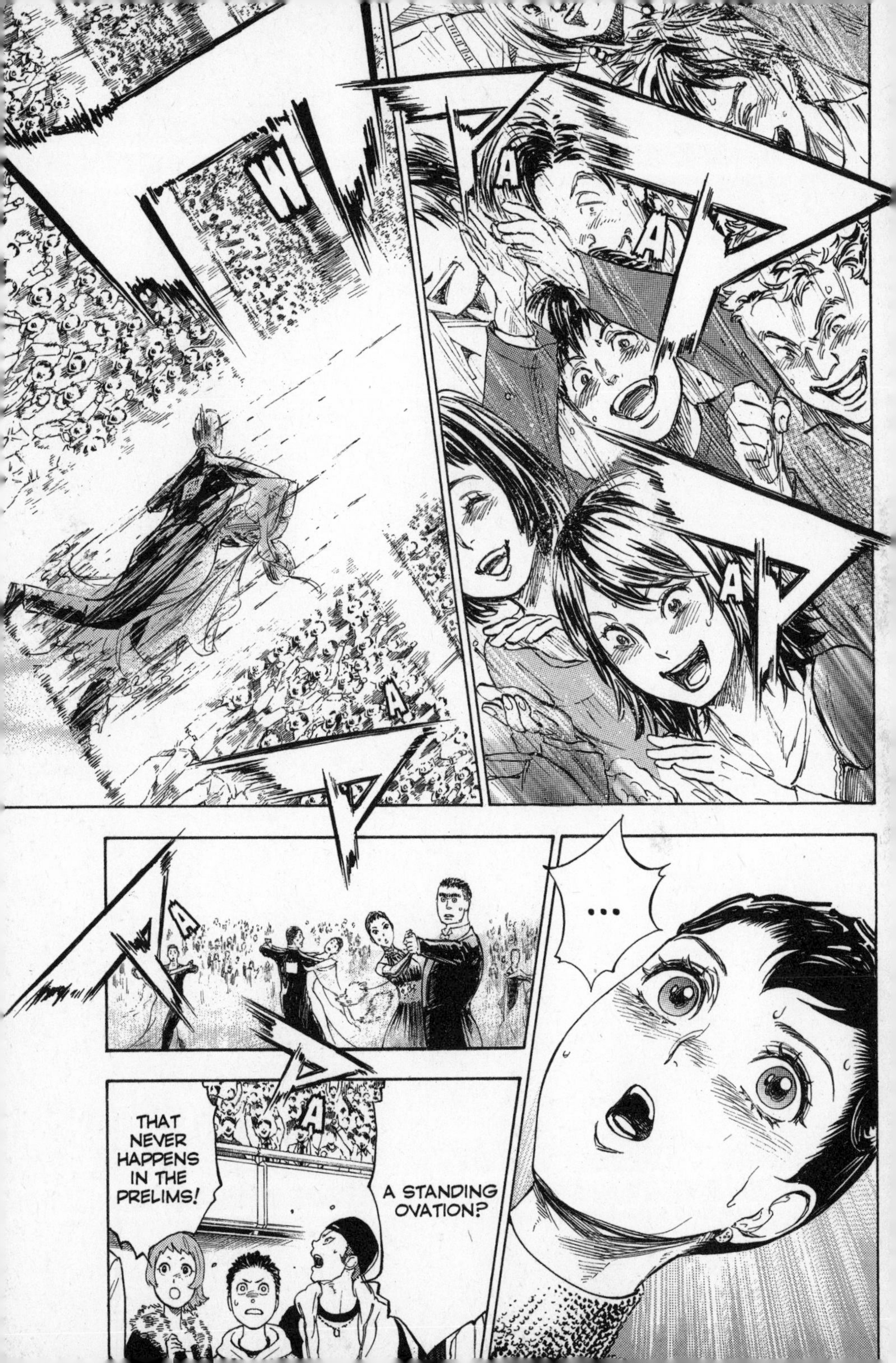

W
A
A
A
A
...
A
A STANDING OVATION?
THAT NEVER HAPPENS IN THE PRELIMS!

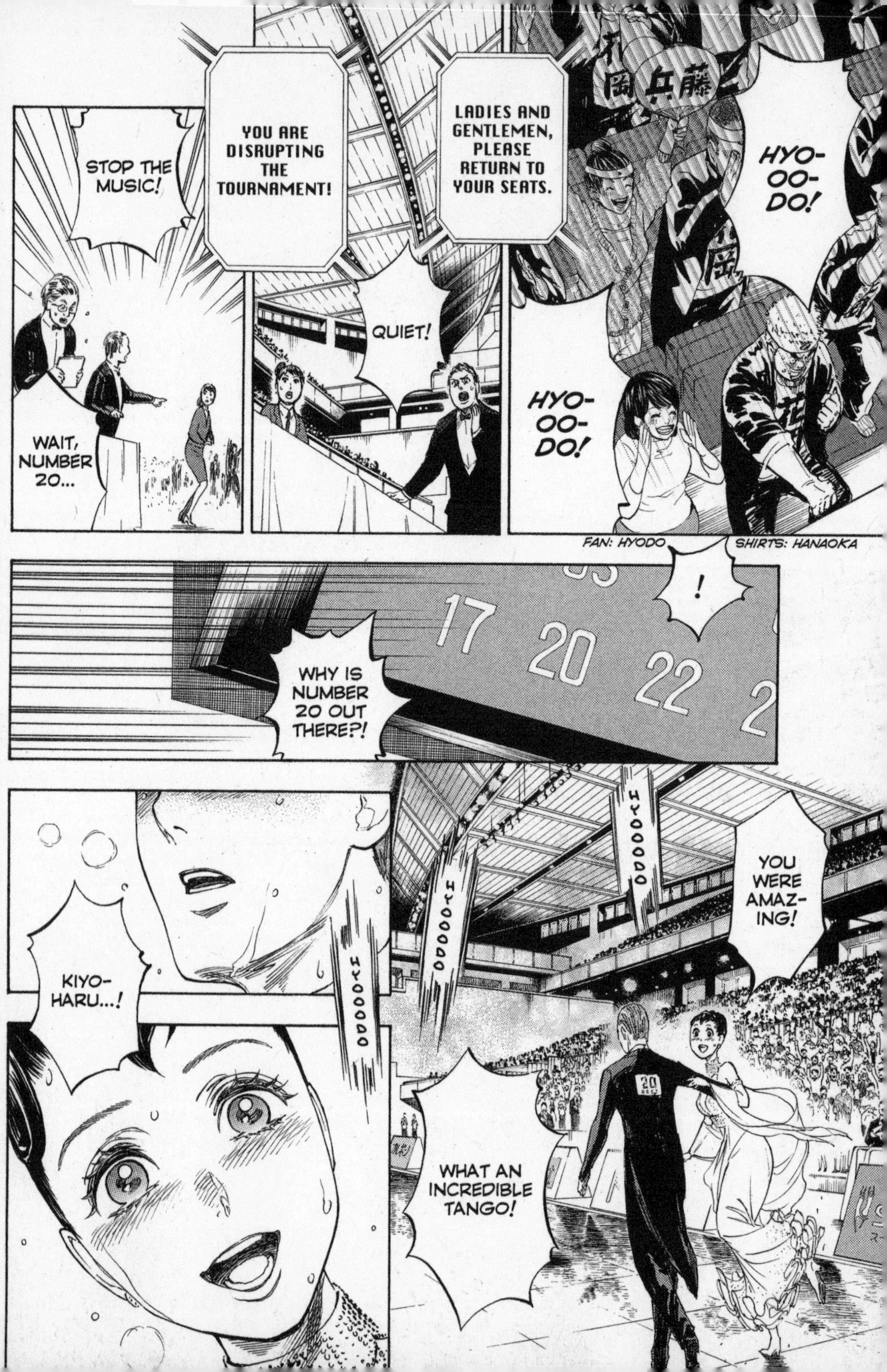
HYO-OO-DO!
HYO-OO-DO!
LADIES AND GENTLEMEN, PLEASE RETURN TO YOUR SEATS.
YOU ARE DISRUPTING THE TOURNAMENT!
QUIET!
STOP THE MUSIC!
WAIT, NUMBER 20...
FAN: HYODO
SHIRTS: HANAOKA
!
17 20 22
WHY IS NUMBER 20 OUT THERE?!
YOU WERE AMAZ-ING!
HYOOODO
HYOOODO
HYOOODO
WHAT AN INCREDIBLE TANGO!
KIYO-HARU...!

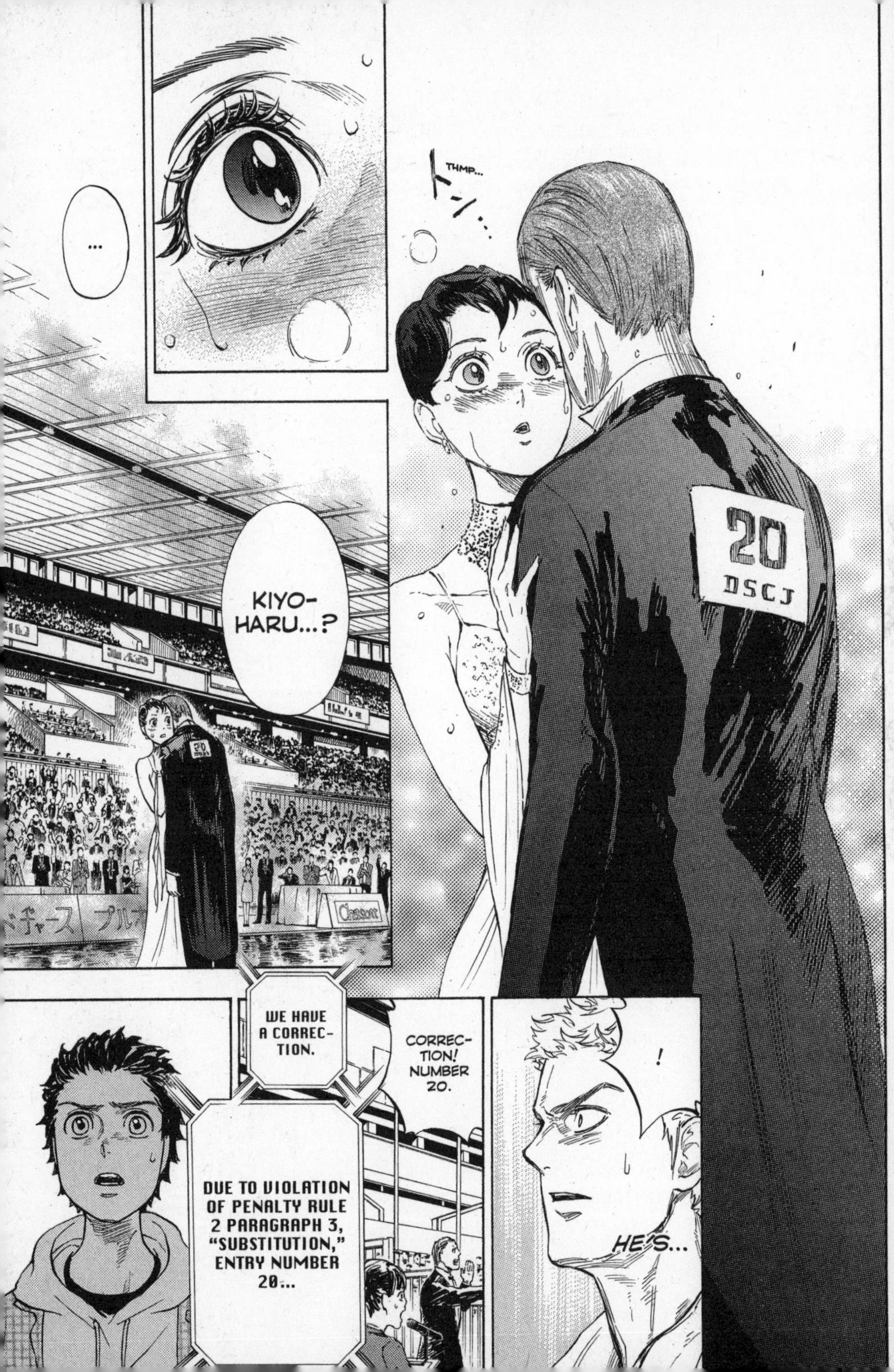
THMP...
...
KIYO-HARU...?
!
HE'S...
WE HAVE A CORRECTION.
CORRECTION! NUMBER 20.
DUE TO VIOLATION OF PENALTY RULE 2 PARAGRAPH 3, "SUBSTITUTION," ENTRY NUMBER 20...
20 DSCJ

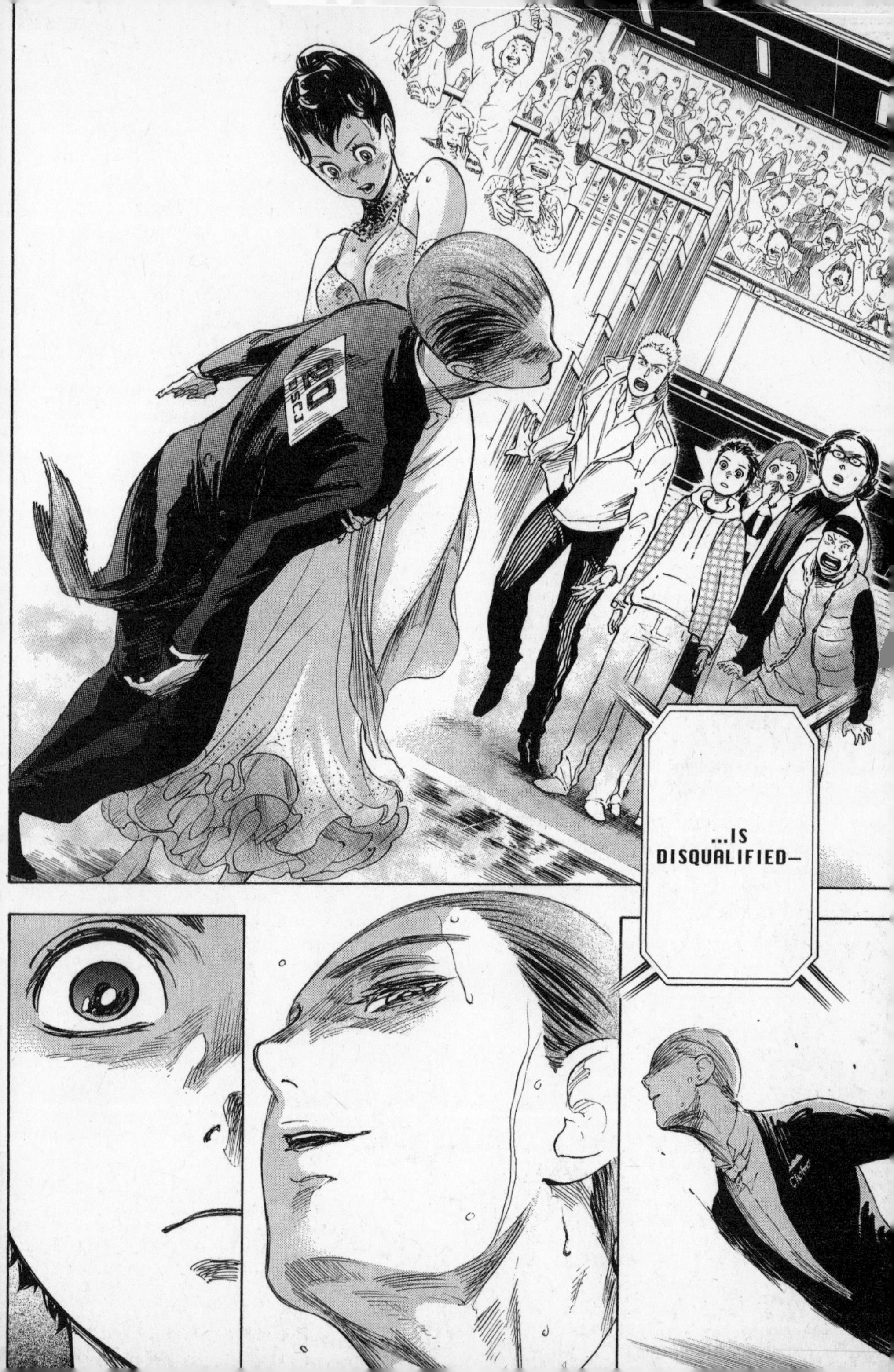

20
...IS
DISQUALIFIED—

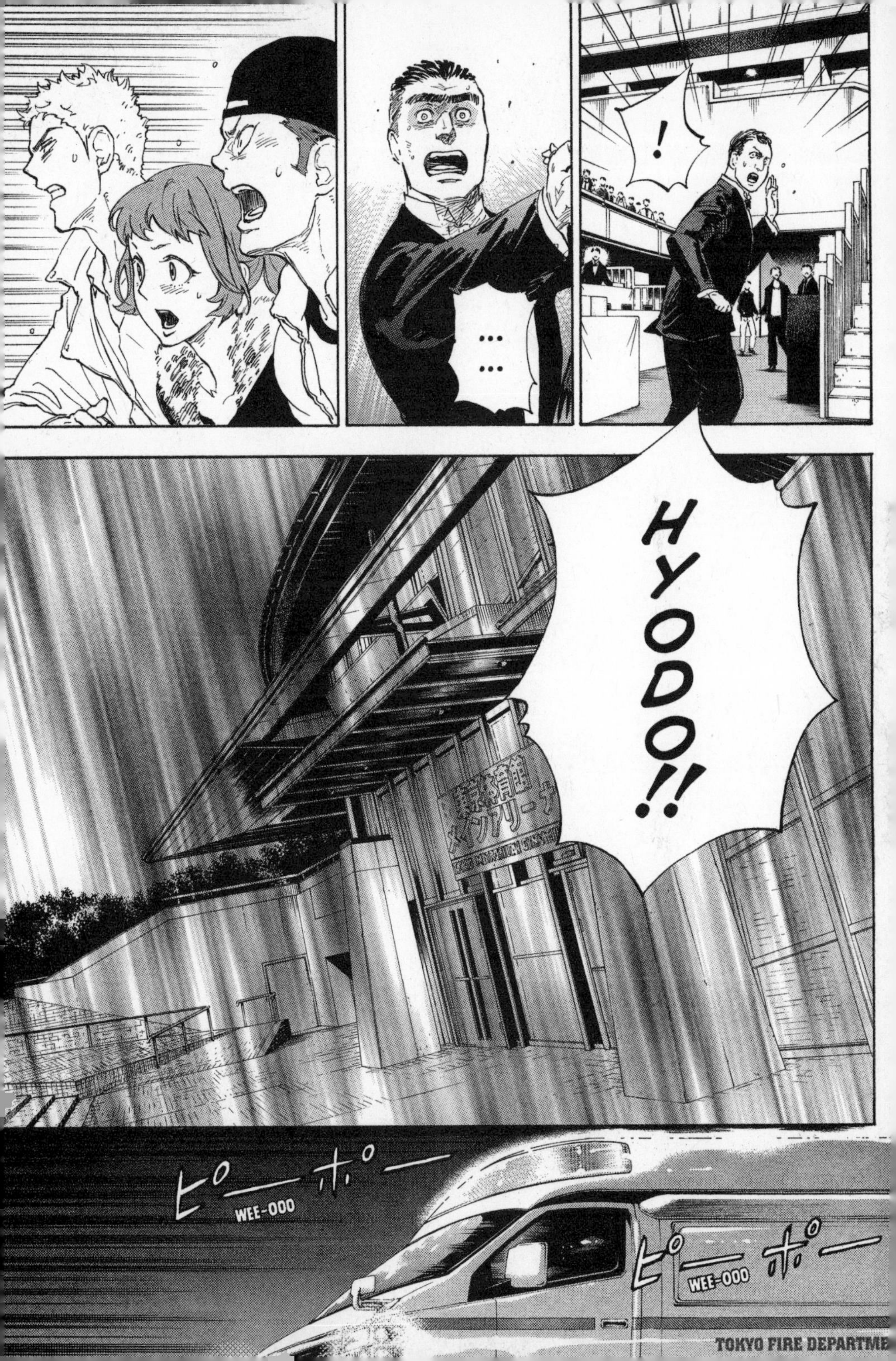
!
... ...
HYODO!!
ピー ポー
WEE-OOO
ピー ポー
WEE-OOO
TOKYO FIRE DEPARTM

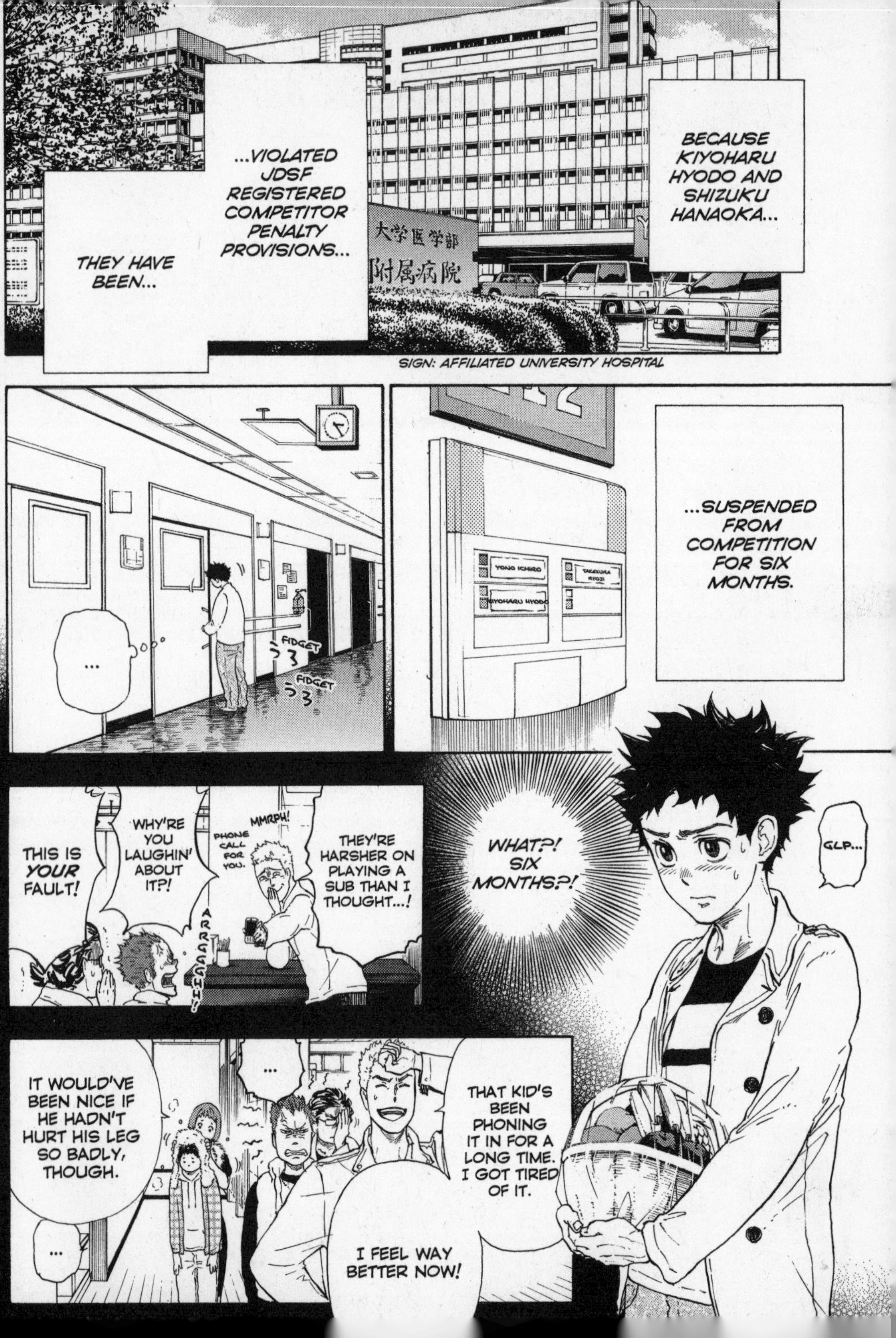
BECAUSE KIYOHARU HYODO AND SHIZUKU HANAOKA...
...VIOLATED JDSF REGISTERED COMPETITOR PENALTY PROVISIONS...
THEY HAVE BEEN...
大学医学部
附属病院
SIGN: AFFILIATED UNIVERSITY HOSPITAL
...SUSPENDED FROM COMPETITION FOR SIX MONTHS.
YONO ICHIRO
KIYOHARU HYODO
FIDGET
FIDGET
...
GLP...
WHAT?! SIX MONTHS?!
THEY'RE HARSHER ON PLAYING A SUB THAN I THOUGHT...!
MMRPH!
PHONE CALL FOR YOU.
WHY'RE YOU LAUGHIN' ABOUT IT?!
THIS IS *YOUR* FAULT!
ARRGGHH!
THAT KID'S BEEN PHONING IT IN FOR A LONG TIME. I GOT TIRED OF IT.
...
IT WOULD'VE BEEN NICE IF HE HADN'T HURT HIS LEG SO BADLY, THOUGH.
I FEEL WAY BETTER NOW!
...

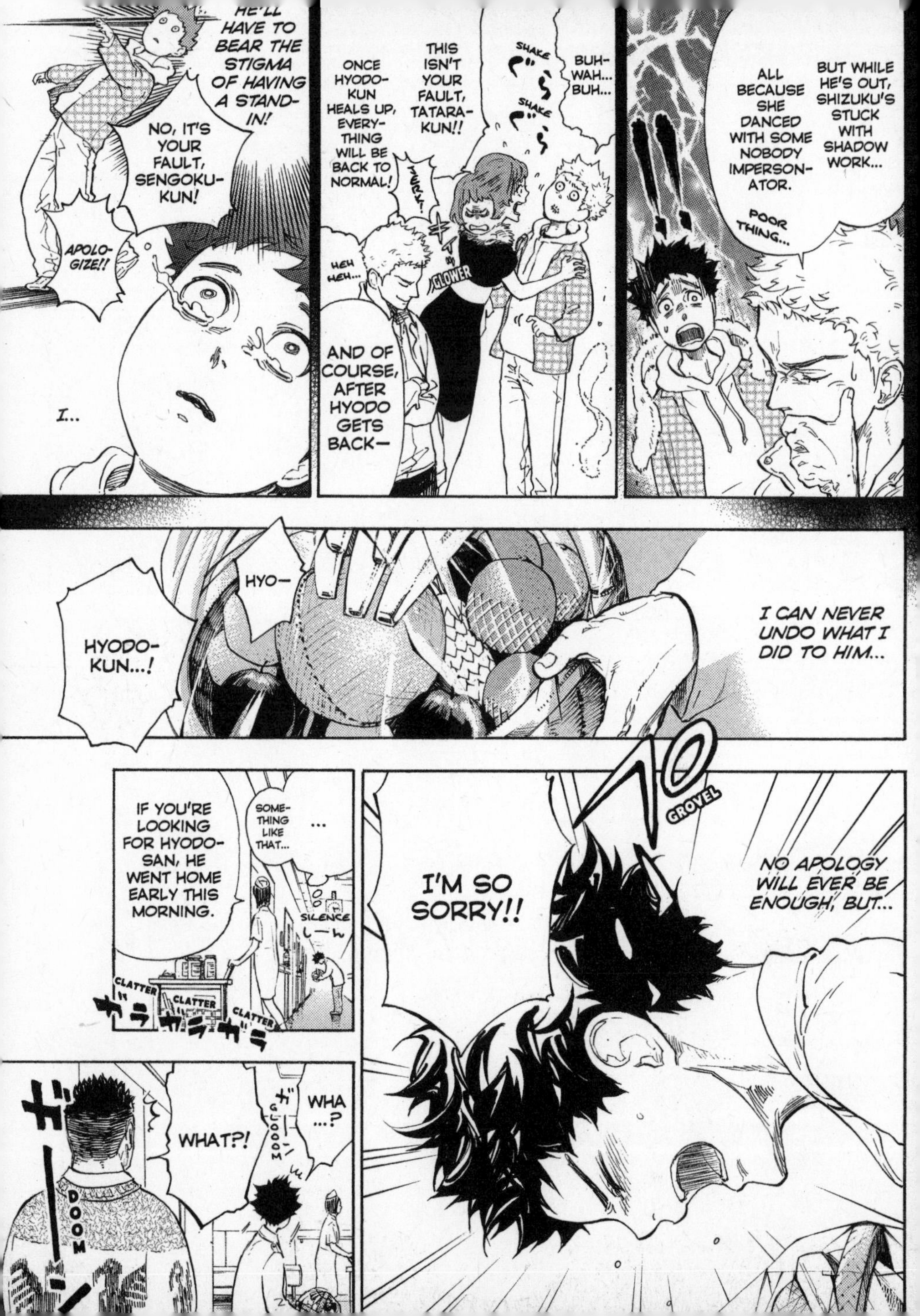
BUT WHILE HE'S OUT, SHIZUKU'S STUCK WITH SHADOW WORK...
ALL BECAUSE SHE DANCED WITH SOME NOBODY IMPERSONATOR.
POOR THING...
BUH-WAH... BUH...
SHAKE
SHAKE
THIS ISN'T YOUR FAULT, TATARA-KUN!!
ONCE HYODO-KUN HEALS UP, EVERYTHING WILL BE BACK TO NORMAL!
HURK
GLOWER
HEH HEH...
AND OF COURSE, AFTER HYODO GETS BACK—
HE'LL HAVE TO BEAR THE STIGMA OF HAVING A STAND-IN!
NO, IT'S YOUR FAULT, SENGOKU-KUN!
APOLOGIZE!!
I...
I CAN NEVER UNDO WHAT I DID TO HIM...
HYO—
HYODO-KUN...!
GROVEL
NO APOLOGY WILL EVER BE ENOUGH, BUT...
I'M SO SORRY!!
SOMETHING LIKE THAT...
...
IF YOU'RE LOOKING FOR HYODO-SAN, HE WENT HOME EARLY THIS MORNING.
SILENCE
CLATTER
CLATTER
CLATTER
WHA...?
GLOOOM
WHAT?!
DOOM

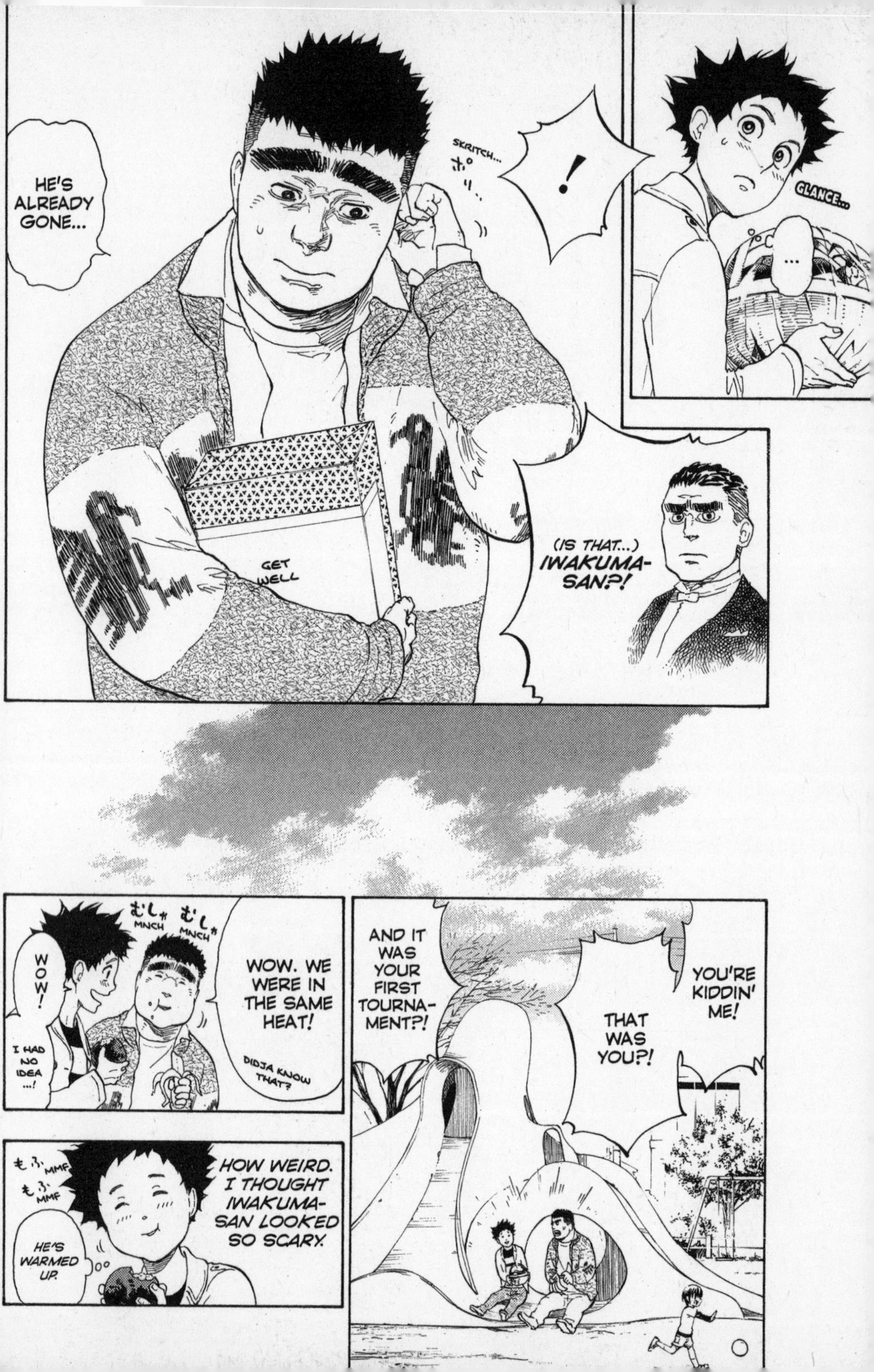
GLANCE...
...
!
(IS THAT...) IWAKUMA-SAN?!
HE'S ALREADY GONE...
SKRITCH... ポリ..
GET WELL
YOU'RE KIDDIN' ME!
THAT WAS YOU?!
AND IT WAS YOUR FIRST TOURNAMENT?!
WOW. WE WERE IN THE SAME HEAT!
DIDJA KNOW THAT?
むしゃ MNCH むしゃ MNCH
WOW!
I HAD NO IDEA...!
HOW WEIRD. I THOUGHT IWAKUMA-SAN LOOKED SO SCARY.
もふ MMF もふ MMF
HE'S WARMED UP.

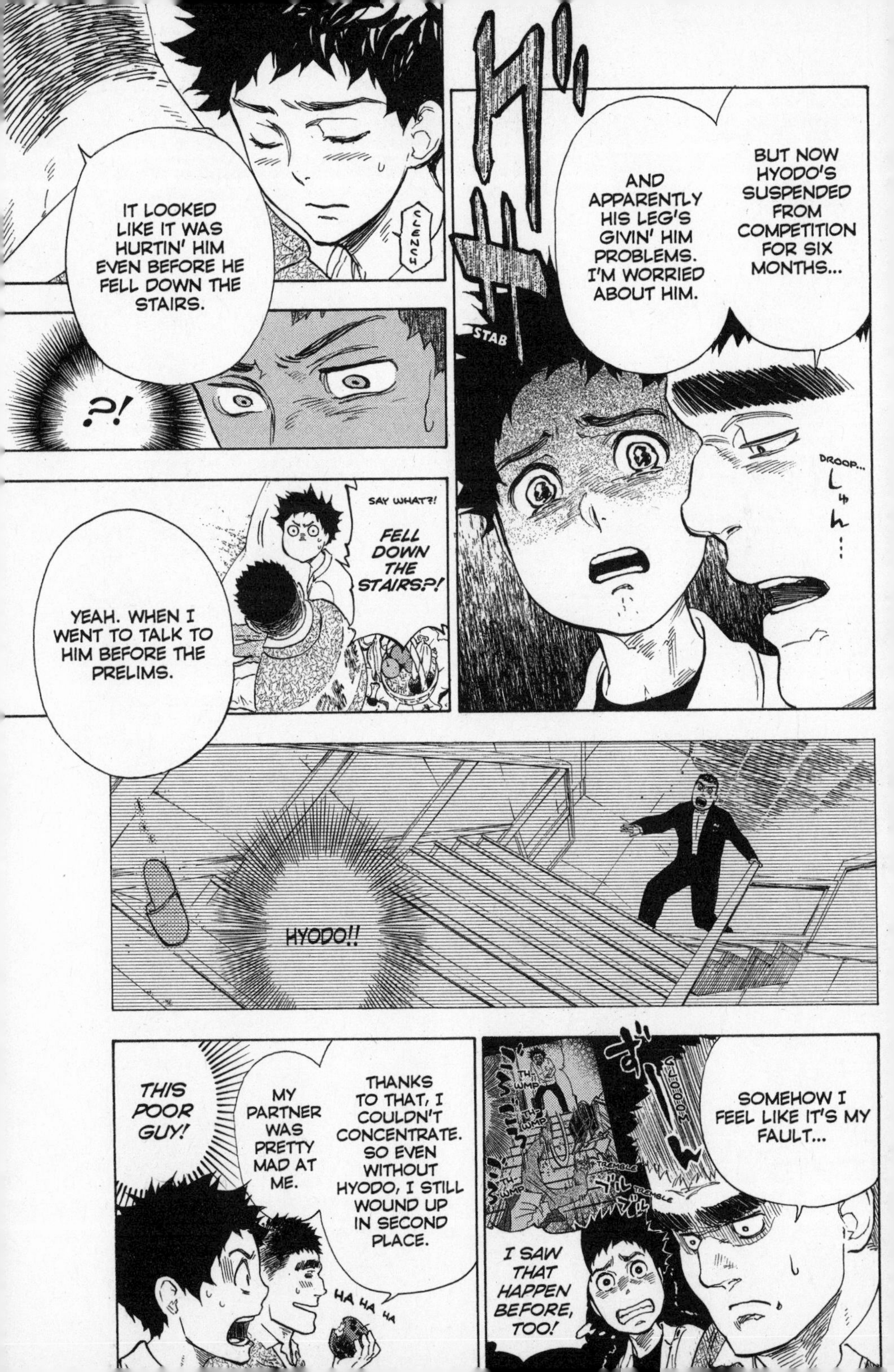
BUT NOW HYODO'S SUSPENDED FROM COMPETITION FOR SIX MONTHS...
AND APPARENTLY HIS LEG'S GIVIN' HIM PROBLEMS. I'M WORRIED ABOUT HIM.
STAB
DROOP...
CLENCH
IT LOOKED LIKE IT WAS HURTIN' HIM EVEN BEFORE HE FELL DOWN THE STAIRS.
?!
SAY WHAT?!
FELL DOWN THE STAIRS?!
YEAH. WHEN I WENT TO TALK TO HIM BEFORE THE PRELIMS.
HYODO!!
SOMEHOW I FEEL LIKE IT'S MY FAULT...
TH-WMP
TH-WMP
TH-WMP
TREMBLE
TREMBLE
I SAW THAT HAPPEN BEFORE, TOO!
THANKS TO THAT, I COULDN'T CONCENTRATE. SO EVEN WITHOUT HYODO, I STILL WOUND UP IN SECOND PLACE.
MY PARTNER WAS PRETTY MAD AT ME.
HA HA HA
THIS POOR GUY!

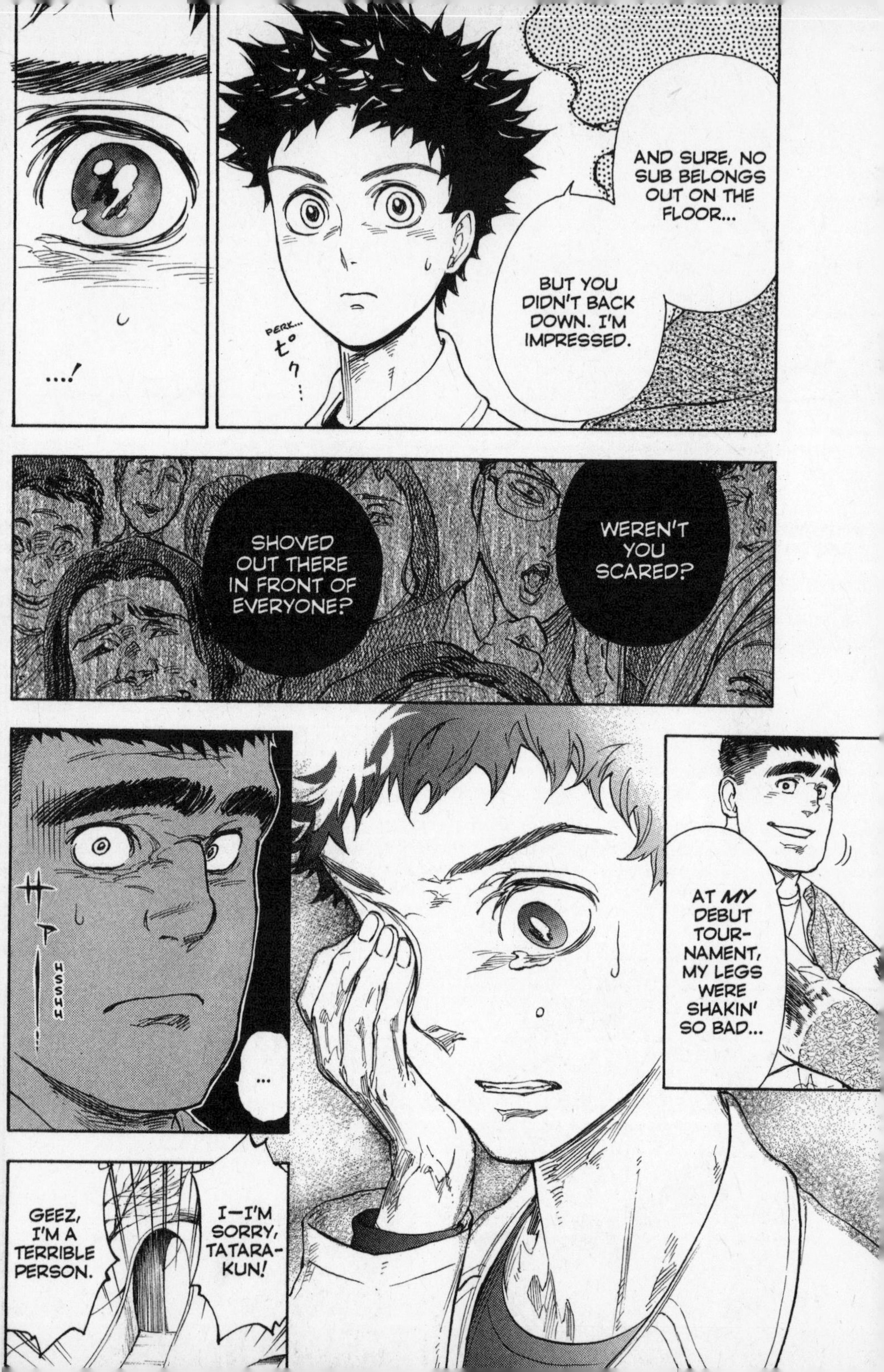
AND SURE, NO SUB BELONGS OUT ON THE FLOOR...
BUT YOU DIDN'T BACK DOWN. I'M IMPRESSED.
PERK...
...!
WEREN'T YOU SCARED?
SHOVED OUT THERE IN FRONT OF EVERYONE?
AT *MY* DEBUT TOUR-NAMENT, MY LEGS WERE SHAKIN' SO BAD...
HSSHH
...
I—I'M SORRY, TATARA-KUN!
GEEZ, I'M A TERRIBLE PERSON.

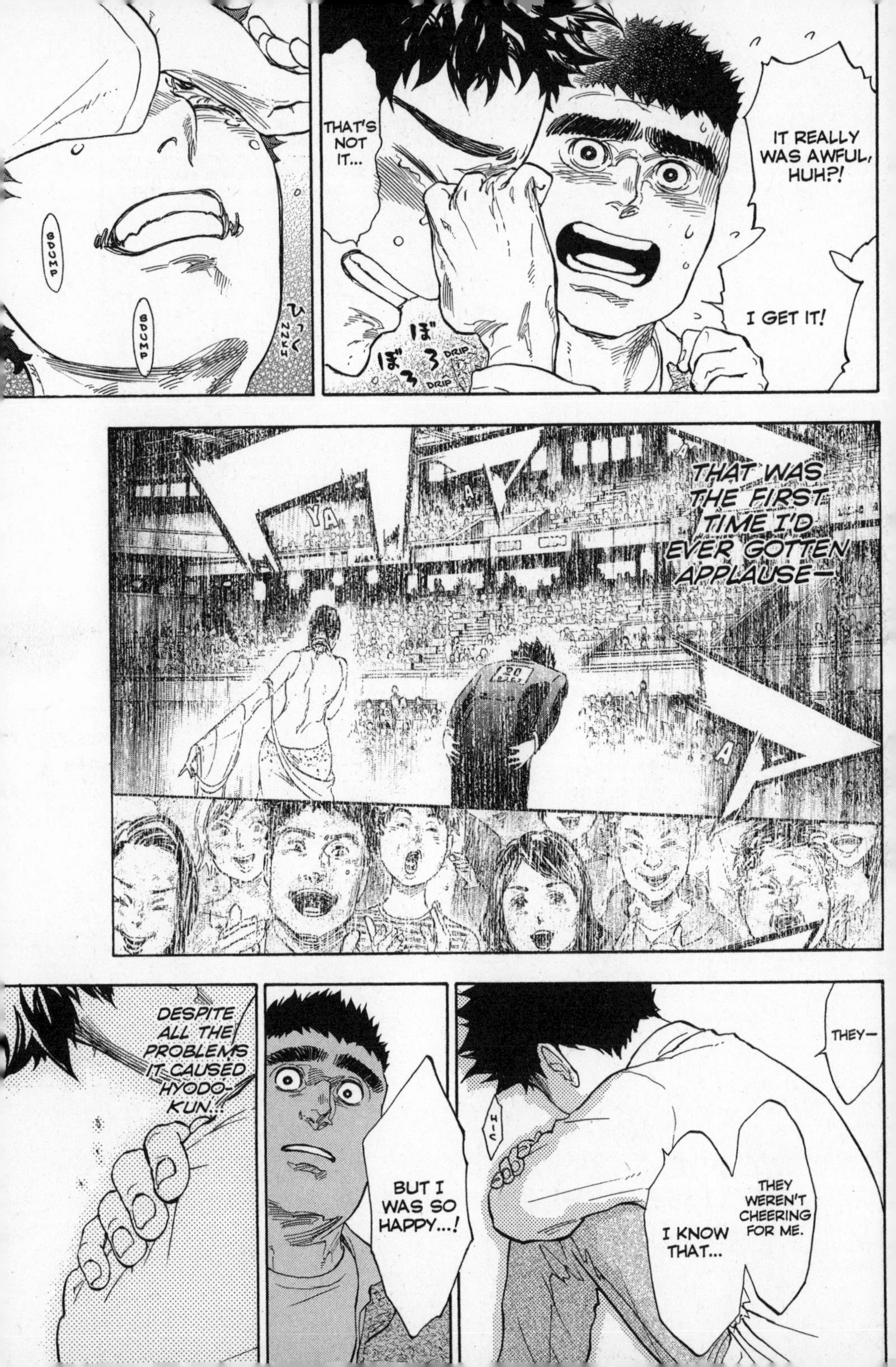
IT REALLY WAS AWFUL, HUH?!
I GET IT!
THAT'S NOT IT...
ぼろぼろ DRIP DRIP
ひっく NNKH
BDUMP
BDUMP
THAT WAS THE FIRST TIME I'D EVER GOTTEN APPLAUSE—
THEY—
THEY WEREN'T CHEERING FOR ME.
I KNOW THAT...
HIC
BUT I WAS SO HAPPY...!
DESPITE ALL THE PROBLEMS IT CAUSED HYODO-KUN...

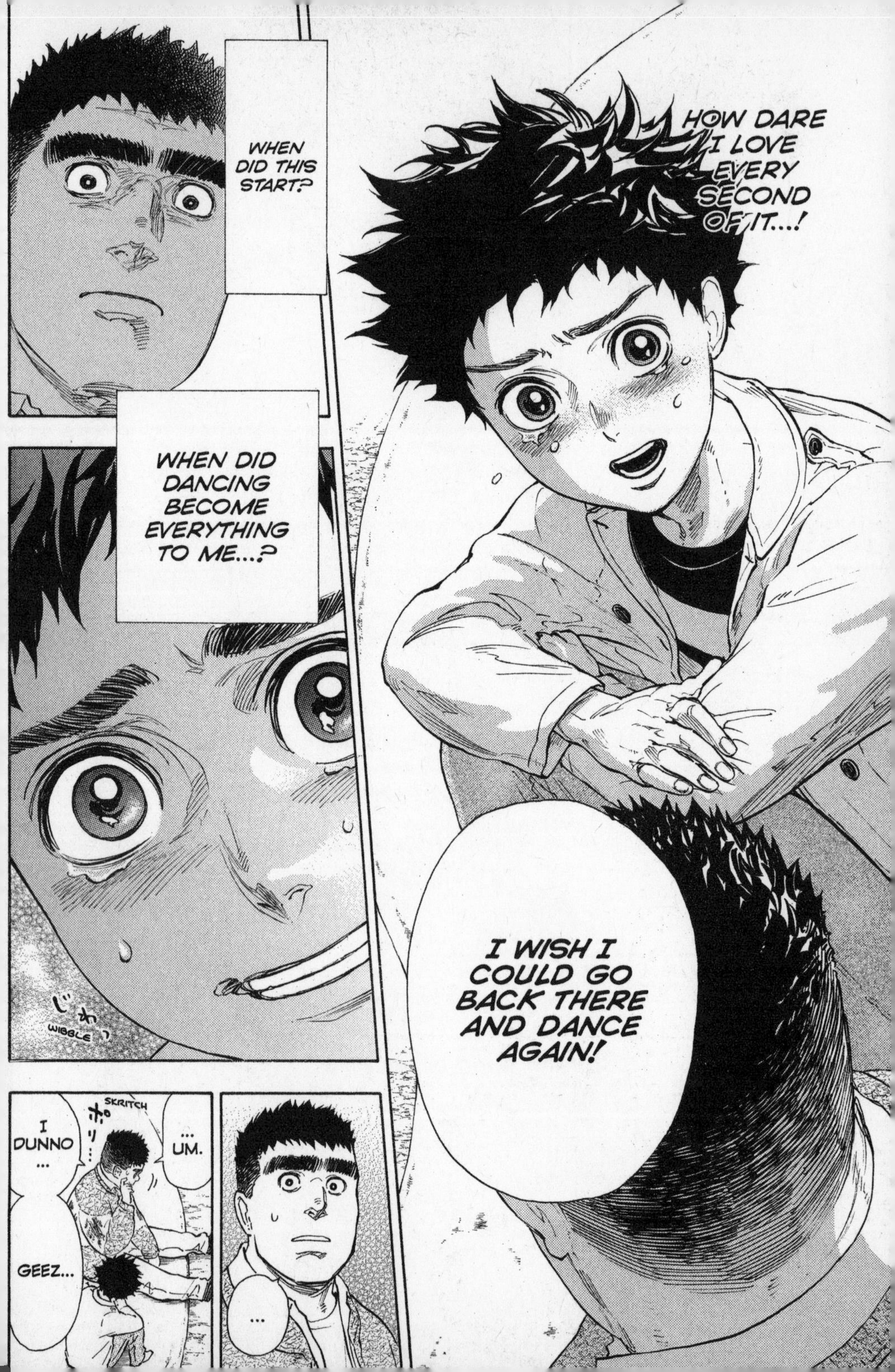
HOW DARE I LOVE EVERY SECOND OF IT...!
I WISH I COULD GO BACK THERE AND DANCE AGAIN!
WHEN DID THIS START?
WHEN DID DANCING BECOME EVERYTHING TO ME...?
じわ
WIBBLE
...
... UM.
ポリ...
SKRITCH
I DUNNO ...
GEEZ...

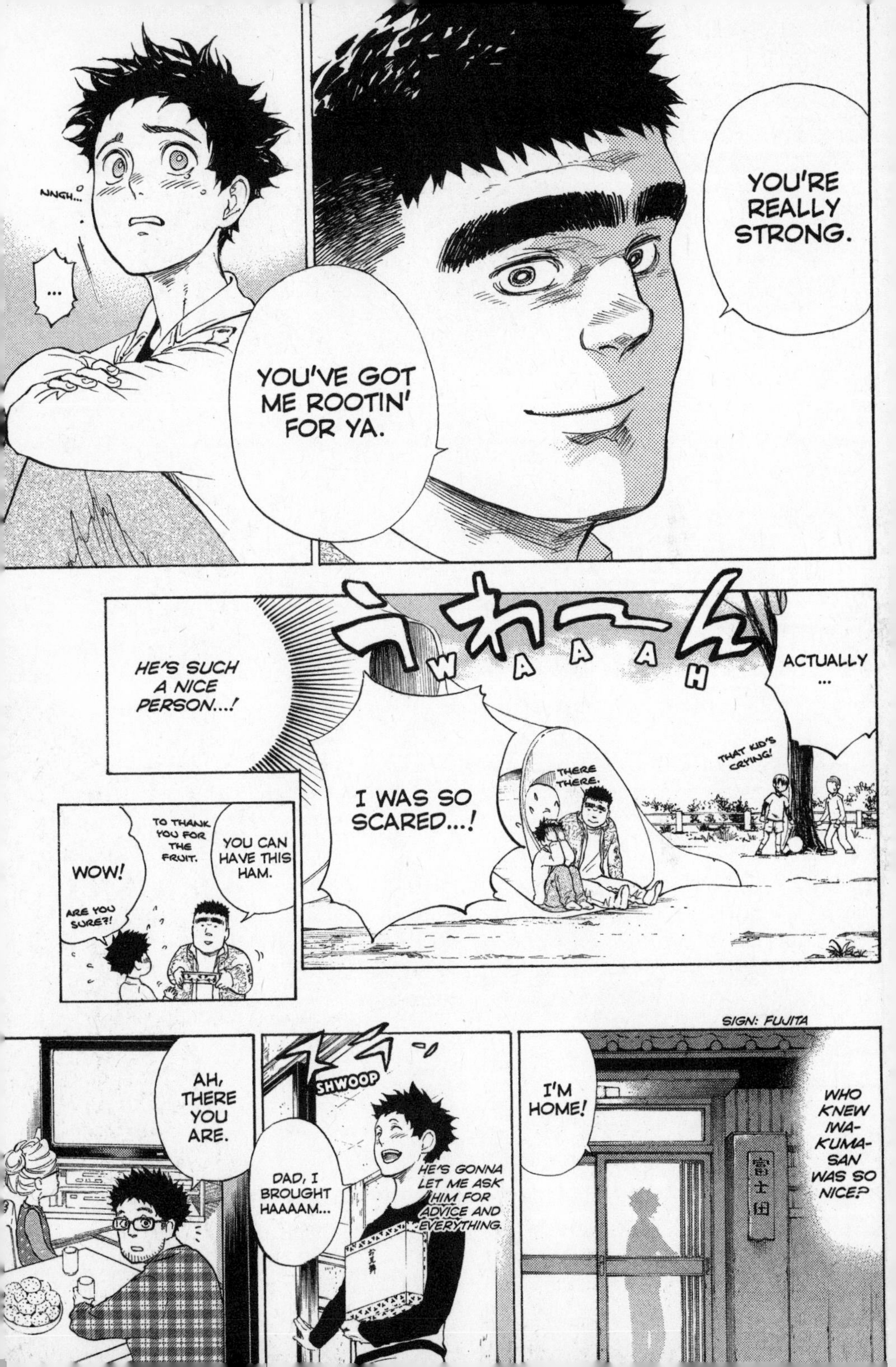
YOU'RE REALLY STRONG.
YOU'VE GOT ME ROOTIN' FOR YA.
NNGH...
...
ACTUALLY ...
THAT KID'S CRYING!
THERE THERE.
うわ～ん
WAAAAH
I WAS SO SCARED...!
HE'S SUCH A NICE PERSON...!
TO THANK YOU FOR THE FRUIT.
YOU CAN HAVE THIS HAM.
WOW!
ARE YOU SURE?!
SIGN: FUJITA
WHO KNEW IWA-KUMA-SAN WAS SO NICE?
富士田
I'M HOME!
SHWOOP
HE'S GONNA LET ME ASK HIM FOR ADVICE AND EVERYTHING.
DAD, I BROUGHT HAAAAM...
AH, THERE YOU ARE.

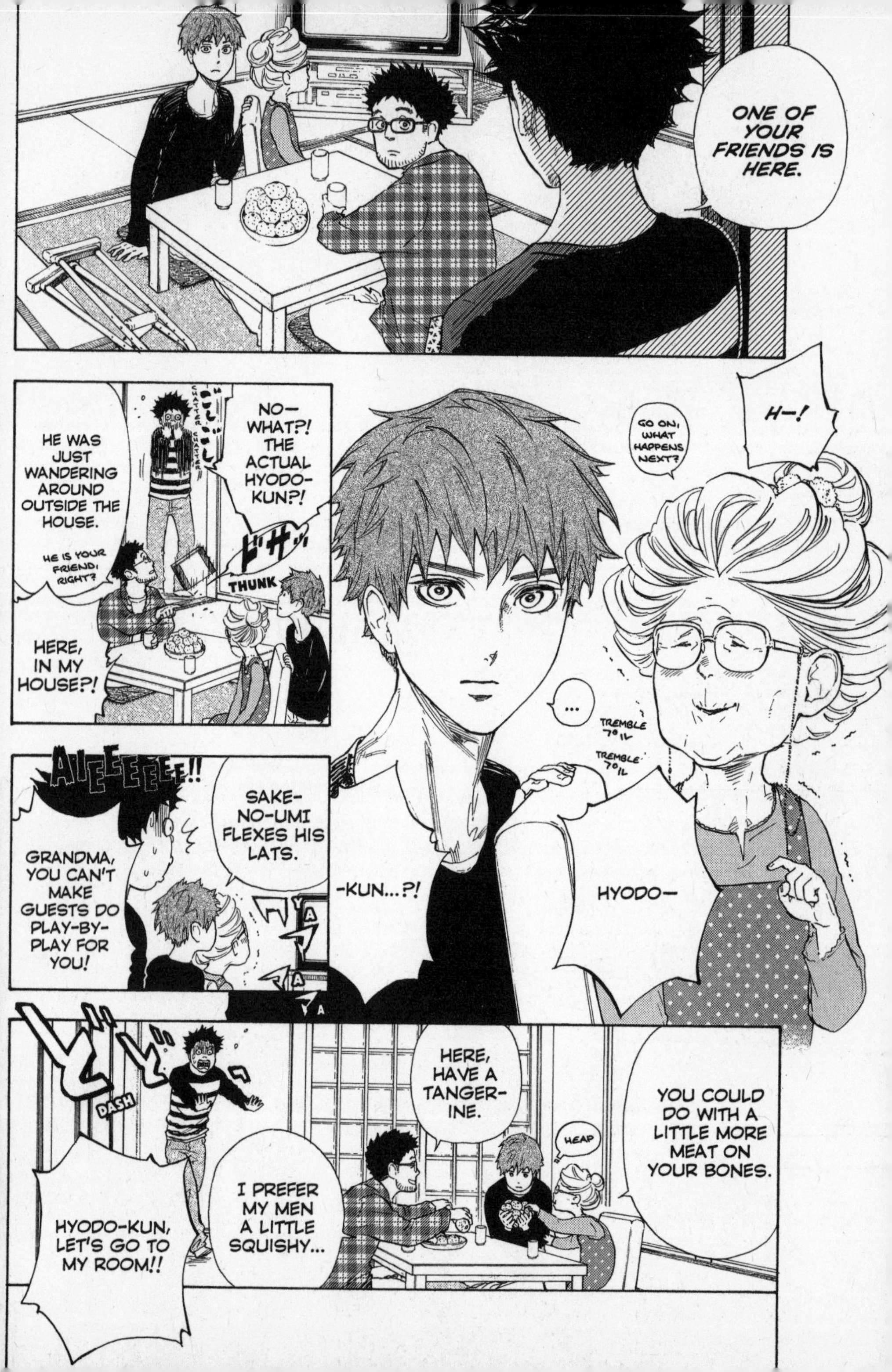
ONE OF YOUR FRIENDS IS HERE.
H—!
GO ON, WHAT HAPPENS NEXT?
TREMBLE
TREMBLE
...
HYODO—
-KUN...?!
NO— WHAT?! THE ACTUAL HYODO-KUN?!
CHATTER CHATTER
HE WAS JUST WANDERING AROUND OUTSIDE THE HOUSE.
THUNK
HE IS YOUR FRIEND, RIGHT?
HERE, IN MY HOUSE?!
SAKE-NO-UMI FLEXES HIS LATS.
AIEEEEEEE!!
GRANDMA, YOU CAN'T MAKE GUESTS DO PLAY-BY-PLAY FOR YOU!
YOU COULD DO WITH A LITTLE MORE MEAT ON YOUR BONES.
HERE, HAVE A TANGERINE.
HEAP
I PREFER MY MEN A LITTLE SQUISHY...
DASH
HYODO-KUN, LET'S GO TO MY ROOM!!

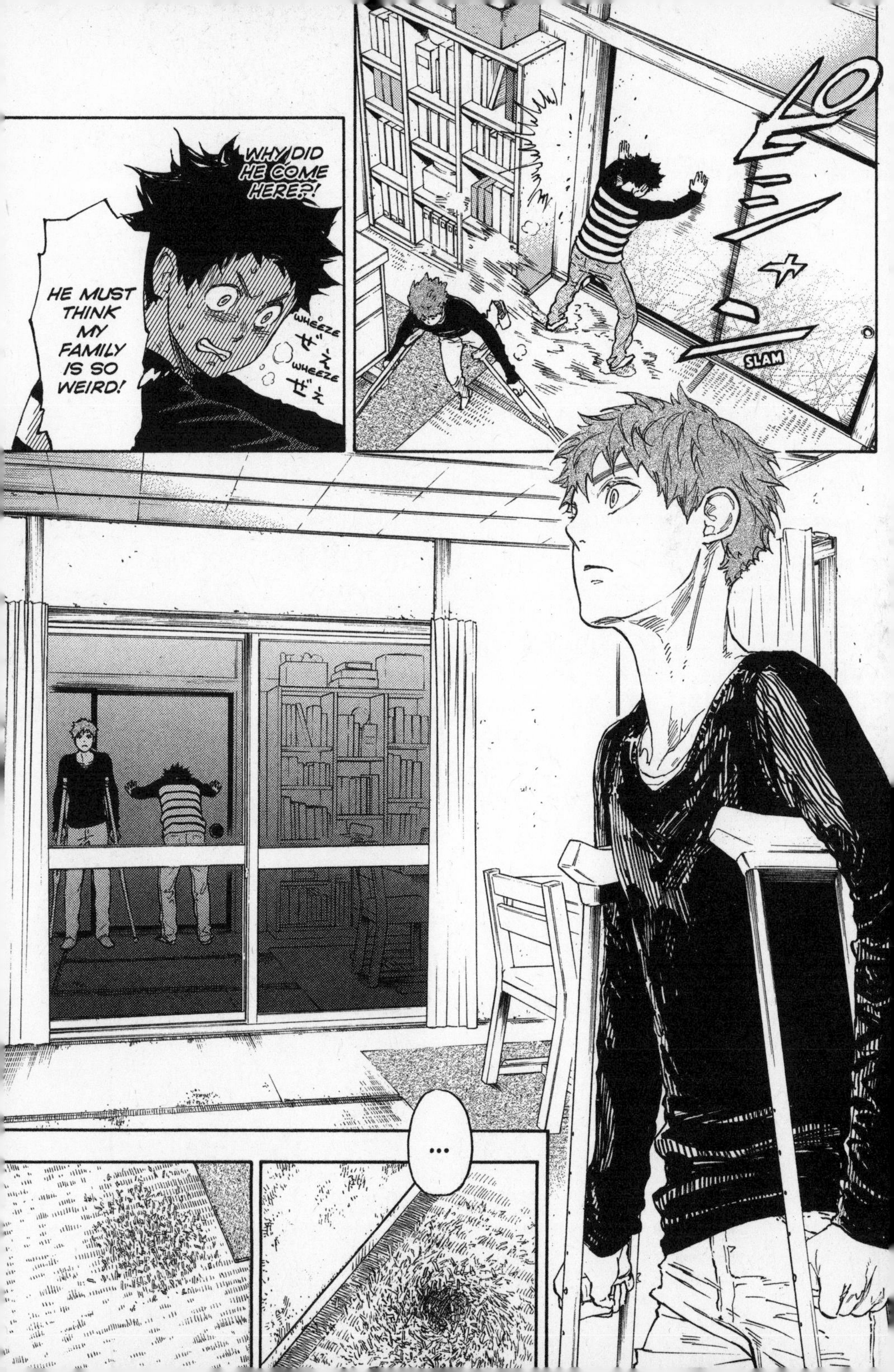
SLAM
WHY DID HE COME HERE?!
HE MUST THINK MY FAMILY IS SO WEIRD!
WHEEZE ぜぇ
WHEEZE ぜぇ
...

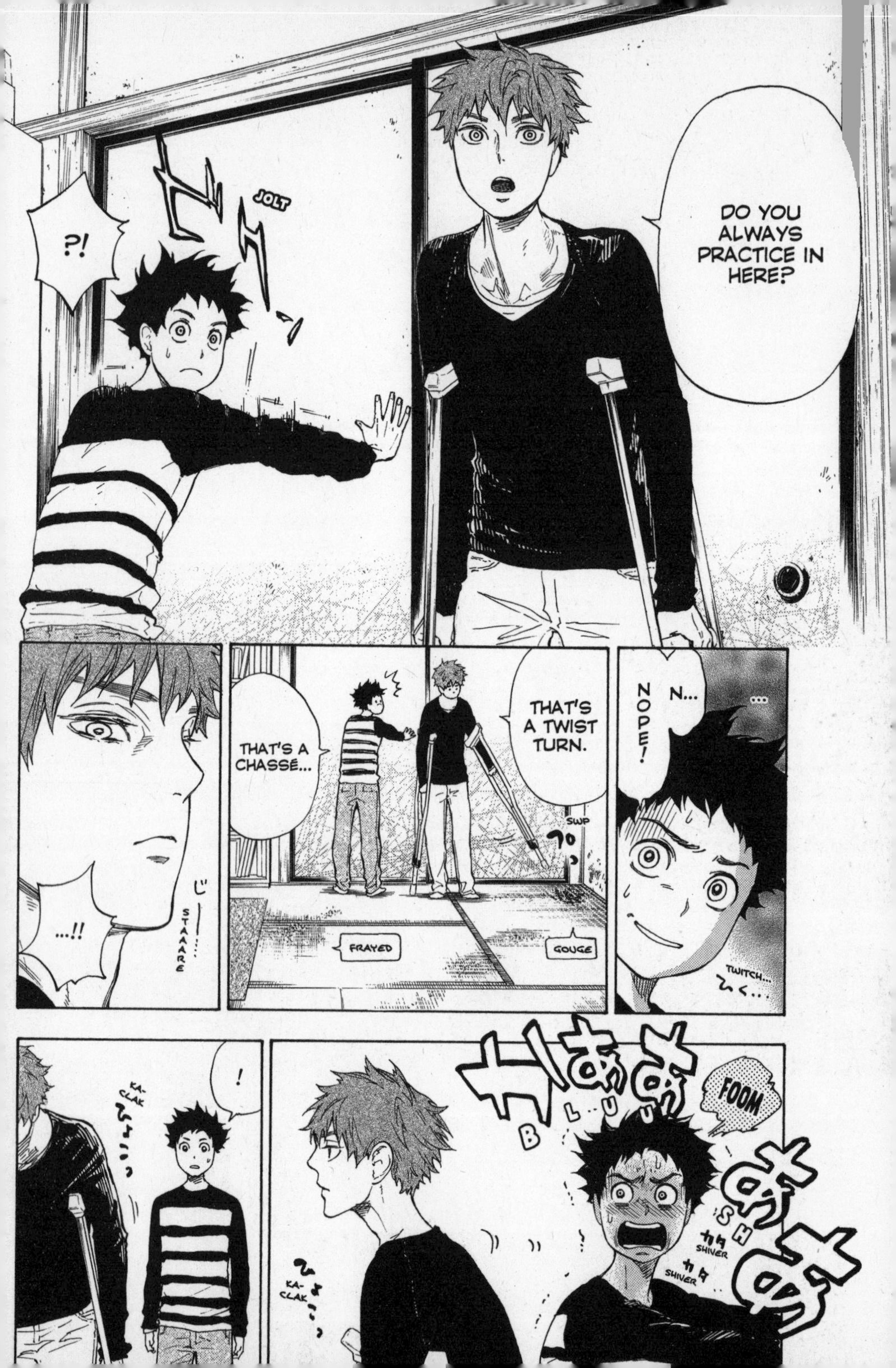

DO YOU ALWAYS PRACTICE IN HERE?
JOLT
?!
...
N... NOPE!
TWITCH...
ひく...
THAT'S A TWIST TURN.
SWP
THAT'S A CHASSÉ...
GOUGE
FRAYED
STAAARE
じー...
...!!
FOOM
BLUUSH
カタ
SHIVER
カタ
SHIVER
!
KA-CLAK
KA-CLAK

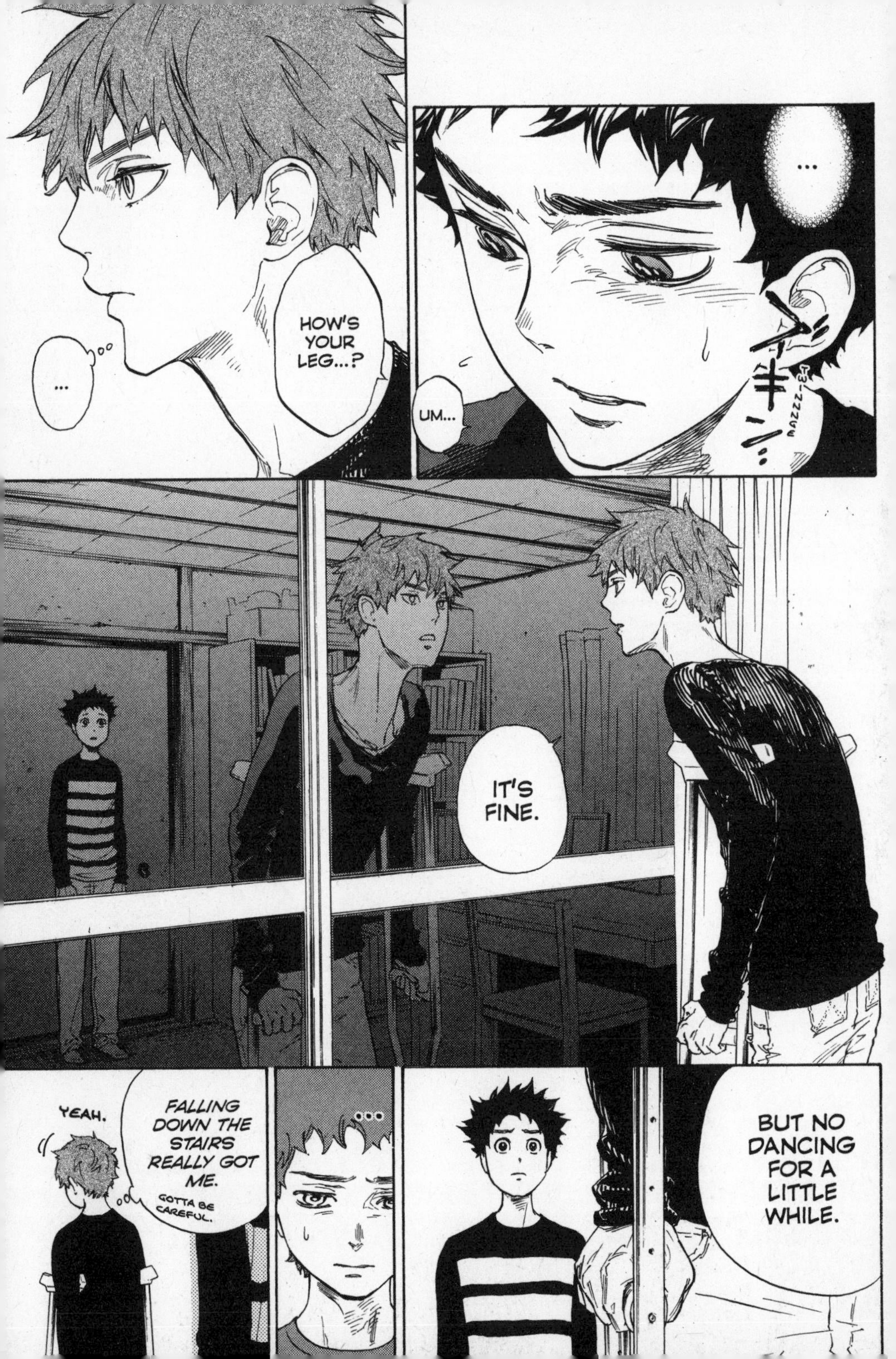

...
UM...
TWINNNGE
HOW'S YOUR LEG...?
...
IT'S FINE.
BUT NO DANCING FOR A LITTLE WHILE.
...
FALLING DOWN THE STAIRS REALLY GOT ME.
GOTTA BE CAREFUL.
YEAH.

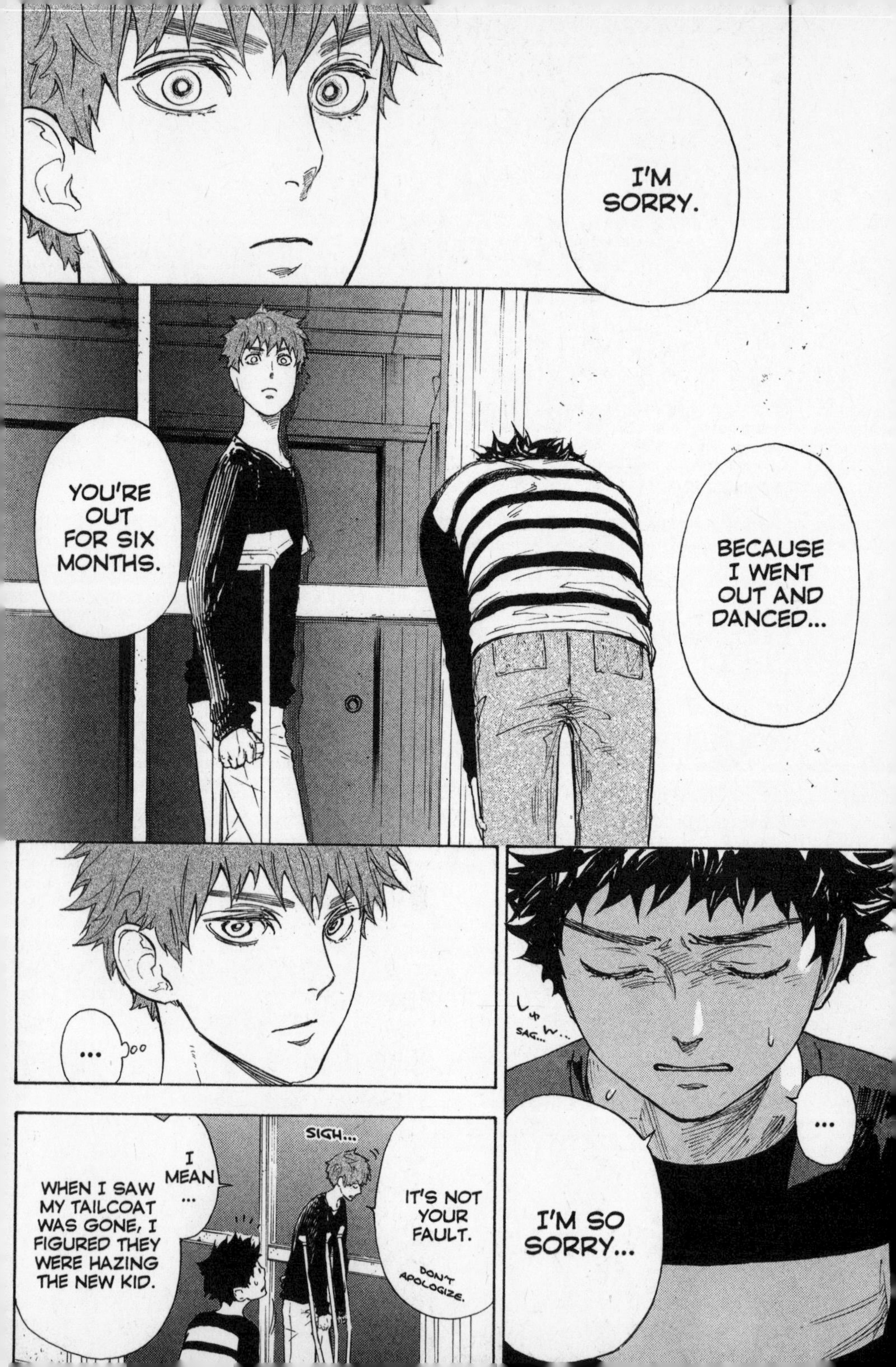
I'M SORRY.
BECAUSE I WENT OUT AND DANCED...
YOU'RE OUT FOR SIX MONTHS.
SAG...
...
I'M SO SORRY...
...
SIGH...
IT'S NOT YOUR FAULT.
DON'T APOLOGIZE.
I MEAN ...
WHEN I SAW MY TAILCOAT WAS GONE, I FIGURED THEY WERE HAZING THE NEW KID.

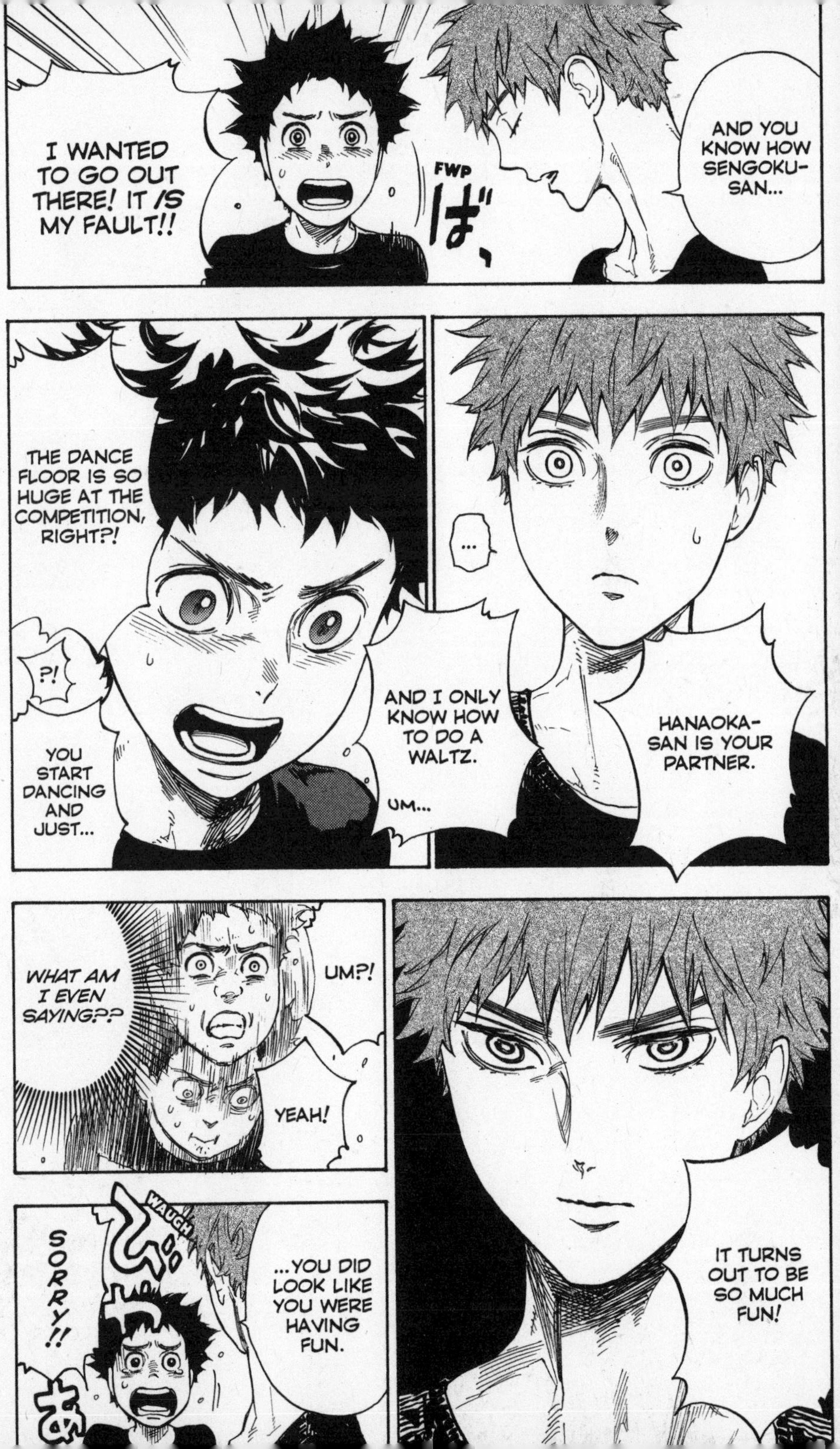
AND YOU KNOW HOW SENGOKU-SAN...
FWP
ば、
I WANTED TO GO OUT THERE! IT IS MY FAULT!!
HANAOKA-SAN IS YOUR PARTNER.
...
THE DANCE FLOOR IS SO HUGE AT THE COMPETITION, RIGHT?!
AND I ONLY KNOW HOW TO DO A WALTZ.
?!
YOU START DANCING AND JUST...
UM...
IT TURNS OUT TO BE SO MUCH FUN!
UM?!
WHAT AM I EVEN SAYING??
YEAH!
...YOU DID LOOK LIKE YOU WERE HAVING FUN.
WAUGH
ひっ
SORRY!!
あ

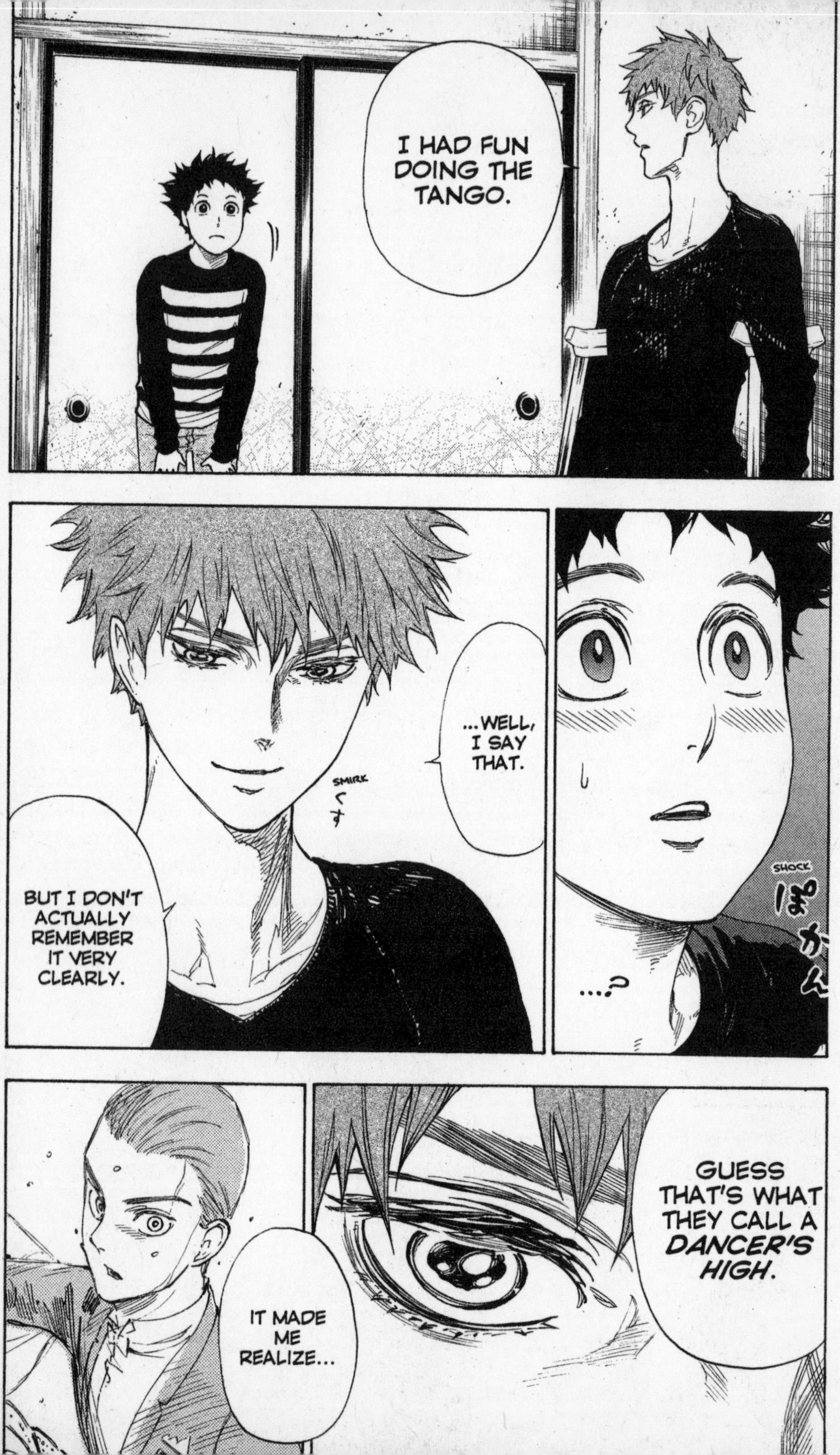
I HAD FUN DOING THE TANGO.
SHOCK
ぽかん
...?
...WELL, I SAY THAT.
SMIRK
くす
BUT I DON'T ACTUALLY REMEMBER IT VERY CLEARLY.
GUESS THAT'S WHAT THEY CALL A *DANCER'S HIGH*.
IT MADE ME REALIZE...

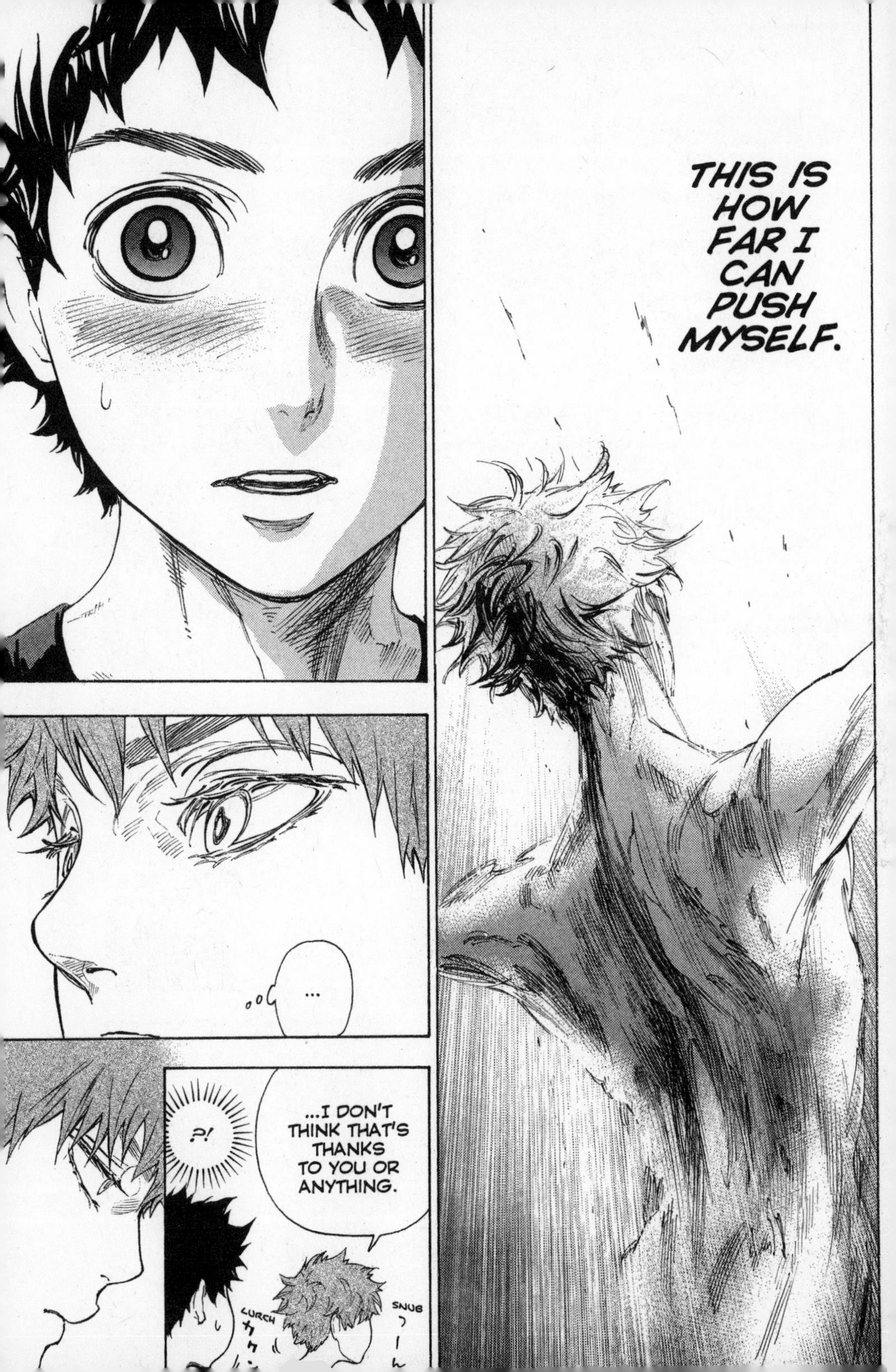
THIS IS HOW FAR I CAN PUSH MYSELF.
...
...I DON'T THINK THAT'S THANKS TO YOU OR ANYTHING.
?!
SNUB
LURCH

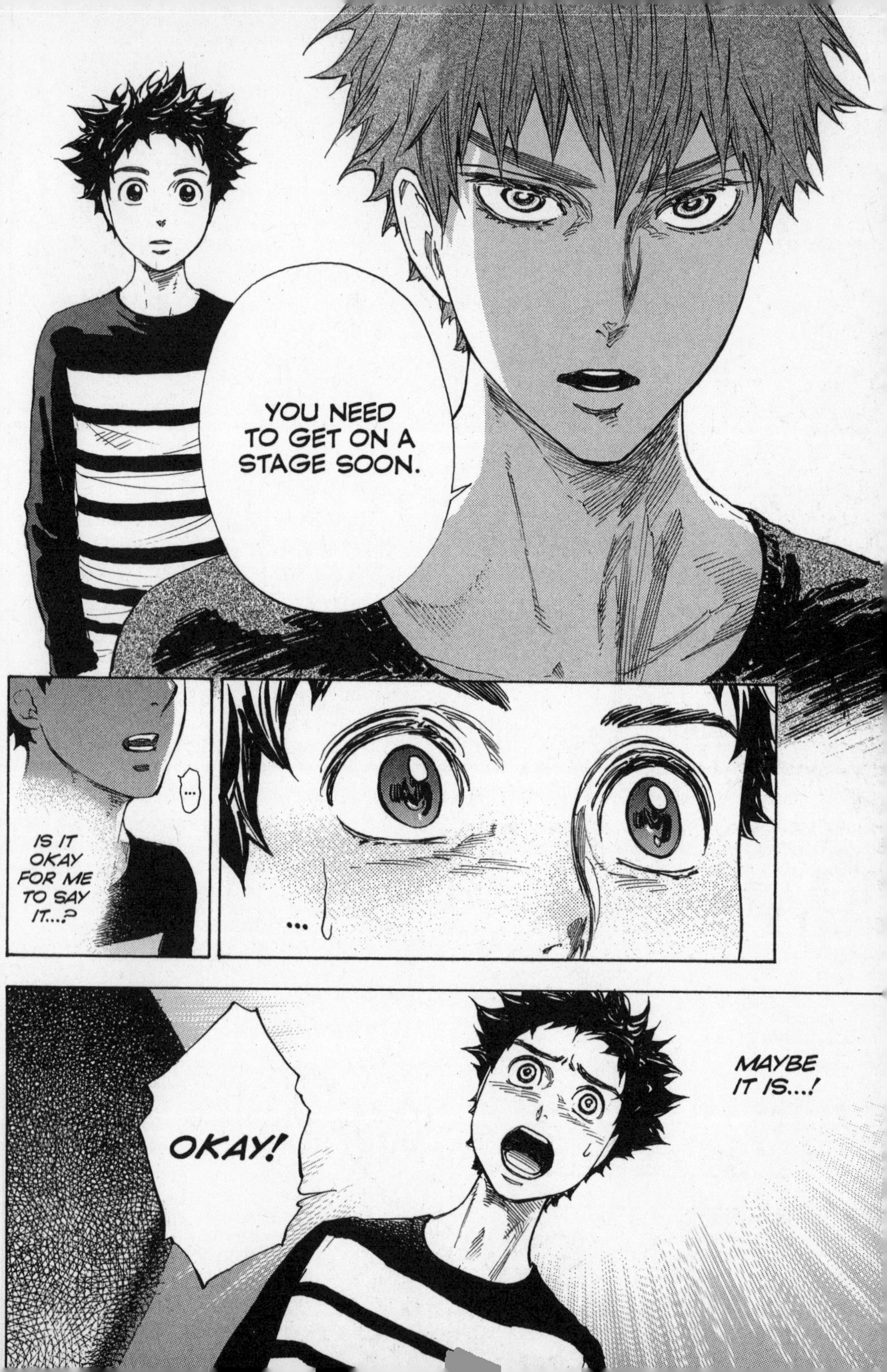
YOU NEED TO GET ON A STAGE SOON.
...
...
IS IT OKAY FOR ME TO SAY IT...?
MAYBE IT IS...!
OKAY!

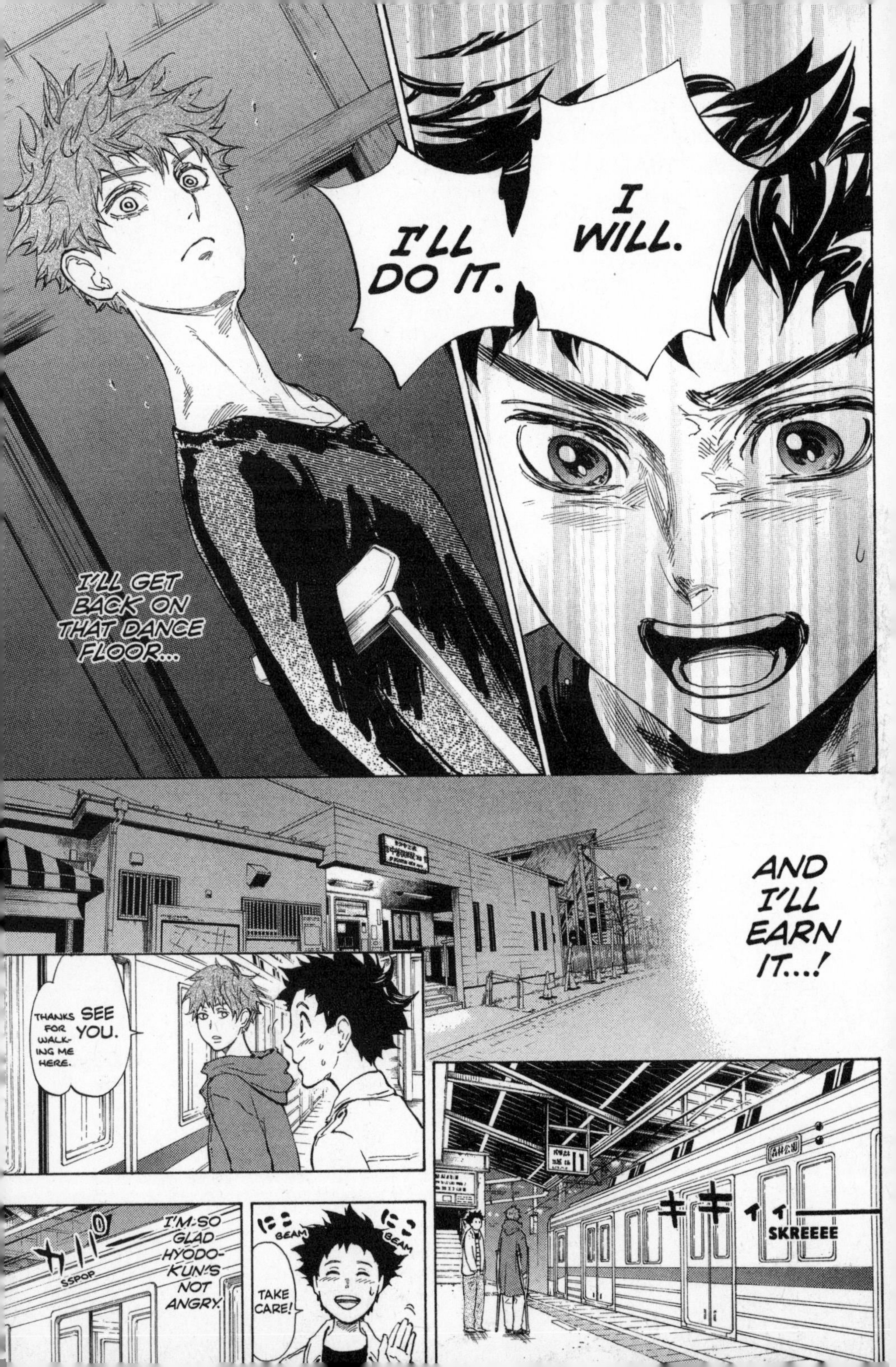
I WILL.
I'LL DO IT.
I'LL GET BACK ON THAT DANCE FLOOR...
AND I'LL EARN IT...!
SEE YOU.
THANKS FOR WALKING ME HERE.
キキィィ
SKREEEE
にこ
BEAM
にこ
BEAM
TAKE CARE!
I'M SO GLAD HYODO-KUN'S NOT ANGRY.
カパ
SSPOP

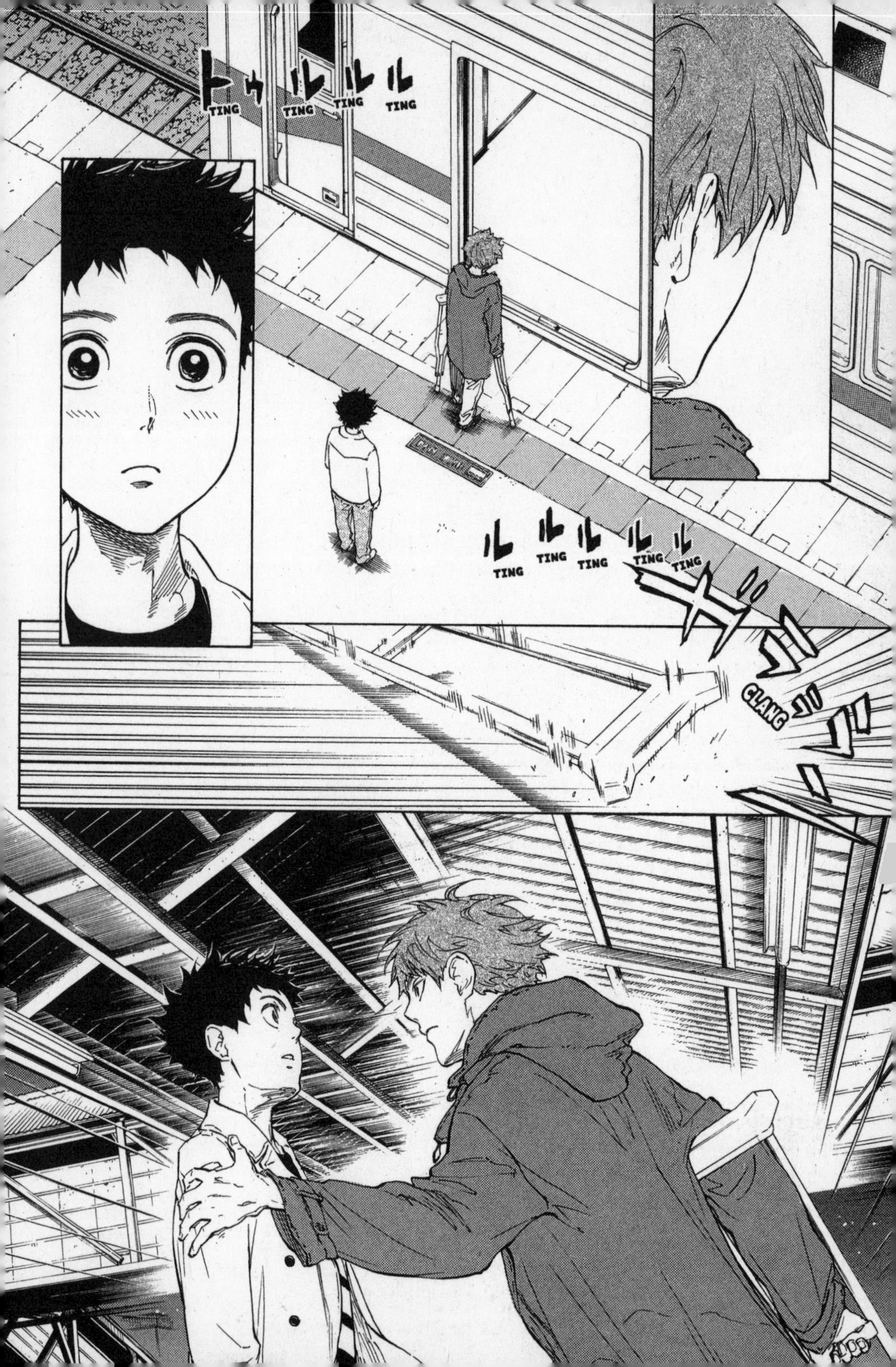

トゥルルル
TING TING TING TING
ルルルルル
TING TING TING TING TING
CLANG

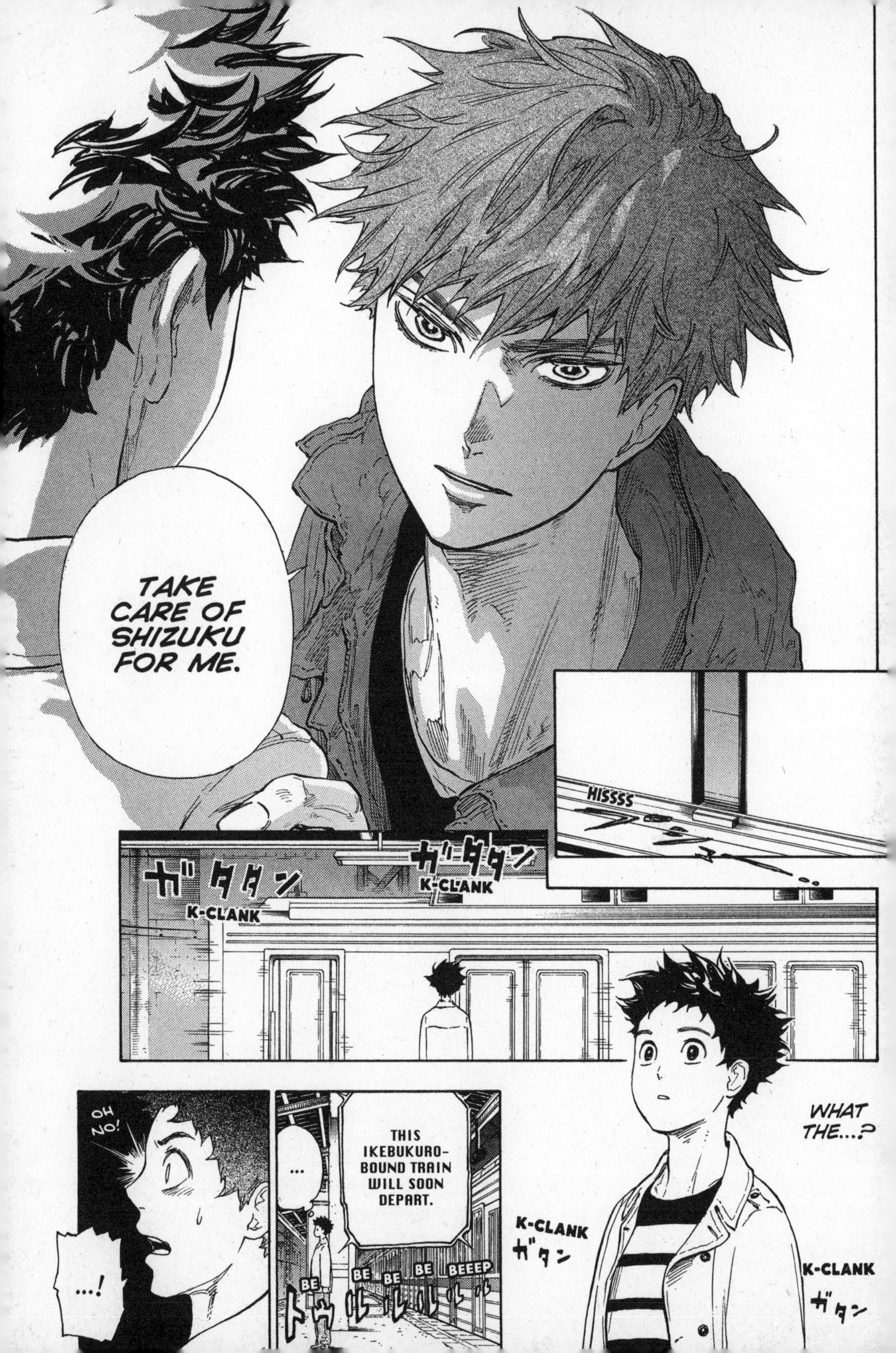
TAKE CARE OF SHIZUKU FOR ME.
HISSSS
ガタタン
K-CLANK
ガタタン
K-CLANK
WHAT THE...?
K-CLANK
ガタン
K-CLANK
ガタン
THIS IKEBUKURO-BOUND TRAIN WILL SOON DEPART.
...
BE BE BE BE BEEEP
OH NO!
...!

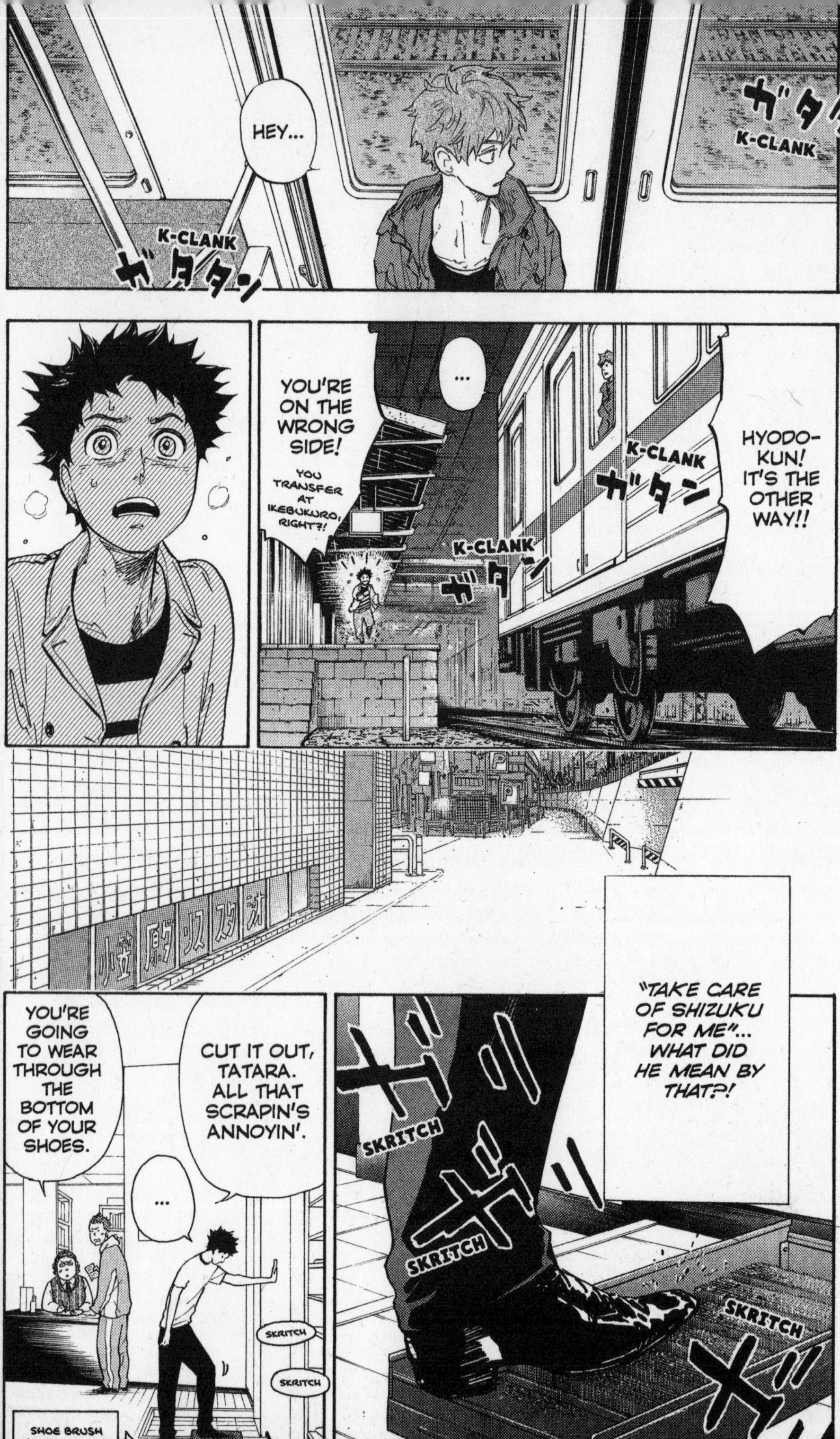
ガタタン
K-CLANK
HEY...
K-CLANK
ガタタン
HYODO-KUN! IT'S THE OTHER WAY!!
K-CLANK
ガタン
...
YOU'RE ON THE WRONG SIDE!
YOU TRANSFER AT IKEBUKURO, RIGHT?!
K-CLANK
"TAKE CARE OF SHIZUKU FOR ME"... WHAT DID HE MEAN BY THAT?!
SKRITCH
SKRITCH
SKRITCH
CUT IT OUT, TATARA. ALL THAT SCRAPIN'S ANNOYIN'.
YOU'RE GOING TO WEAR THROUGH THE BOTTOM OF YOUR SHOES.
...
SKRITCH
SKRITCH
SHOE BRUSH (ALSO CALLED "GARIGARI-KUN")

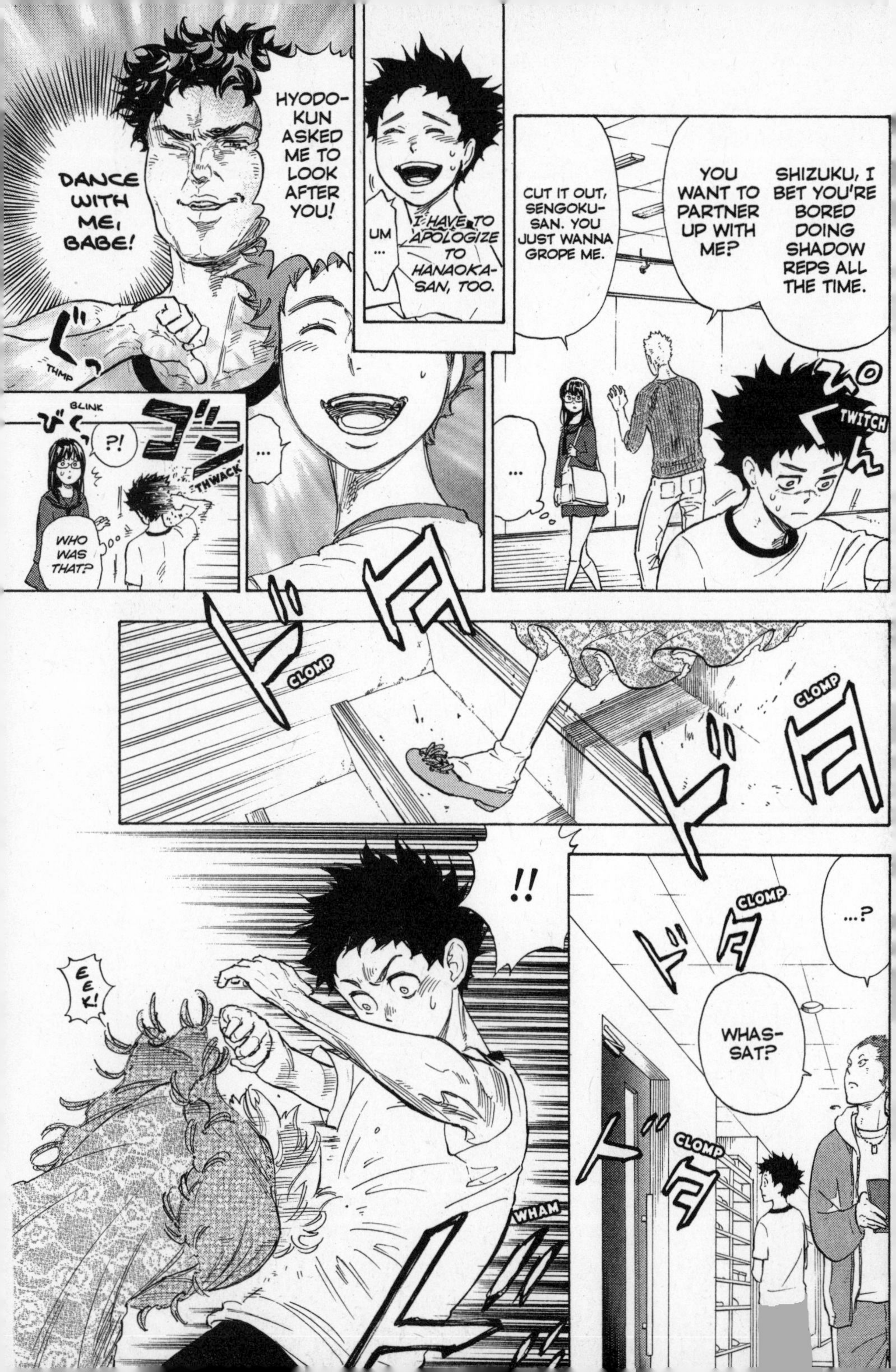
SHIZUKU, I BET YOU'RE BORED DOING SHADOW REPS ALL THE TIME.
YOU WANT TO PARTNER UP WITH ME?
CUT IT OUT, SENGOKU-SAN. YOU JUST WANNA GROPE ME.
...
TWITCH
UM ...
I HAVE TO APOLOGIZE TO HANAOKA-SAN, TOO.
...
HYODO-KUN ASKED ME TO LOOK AFTER YOU!
DANCE WITH ME, BABE!
THMP
THWACK
BLINK
?!
WHO WAS THAT?
CLOMP
CLOMP
...?
CLOMP
WHAS-SAT?
CLOMP
!!
EEK!
WHAM

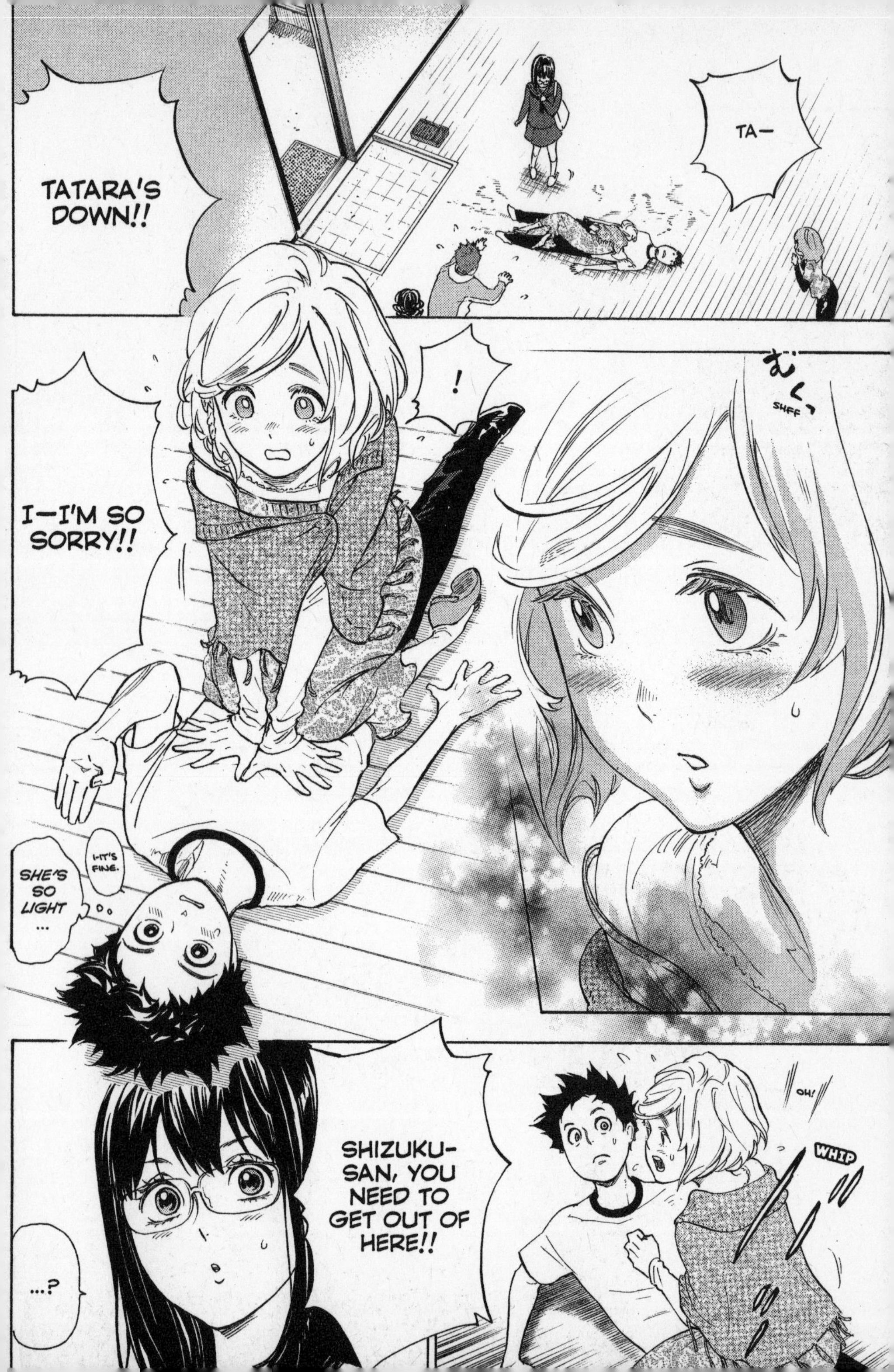
TA—
TATARA'S DOWN!!
むく
SHFF
!
I—I'M SO SORRY!!
I-IT'S FINE.
SHE'S SO LIGHT ...
OH!
WHIP
SHIZUKU-SAN, YOU NEED TO GET OUT OF HERE!!
...?

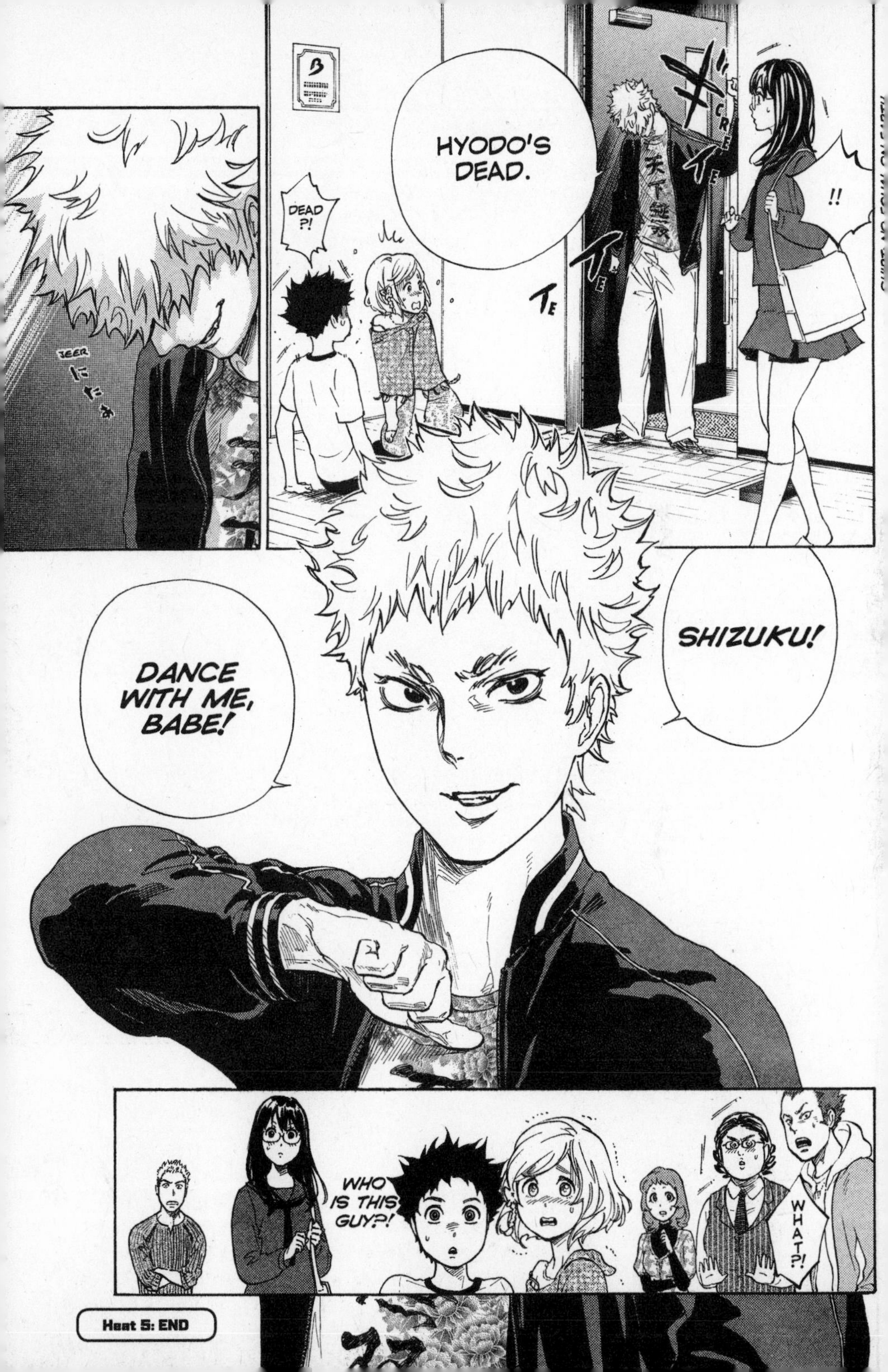
CREEE
!!
HYODO'S DEAD.
DEAD?!
TE
JEER
SHIZUKU!
DANCE WITH ME, BABE!
WHAT?!
WHO IS THIS GUY?!

Heat 5: END

WELCOME TO THE BALLROOM

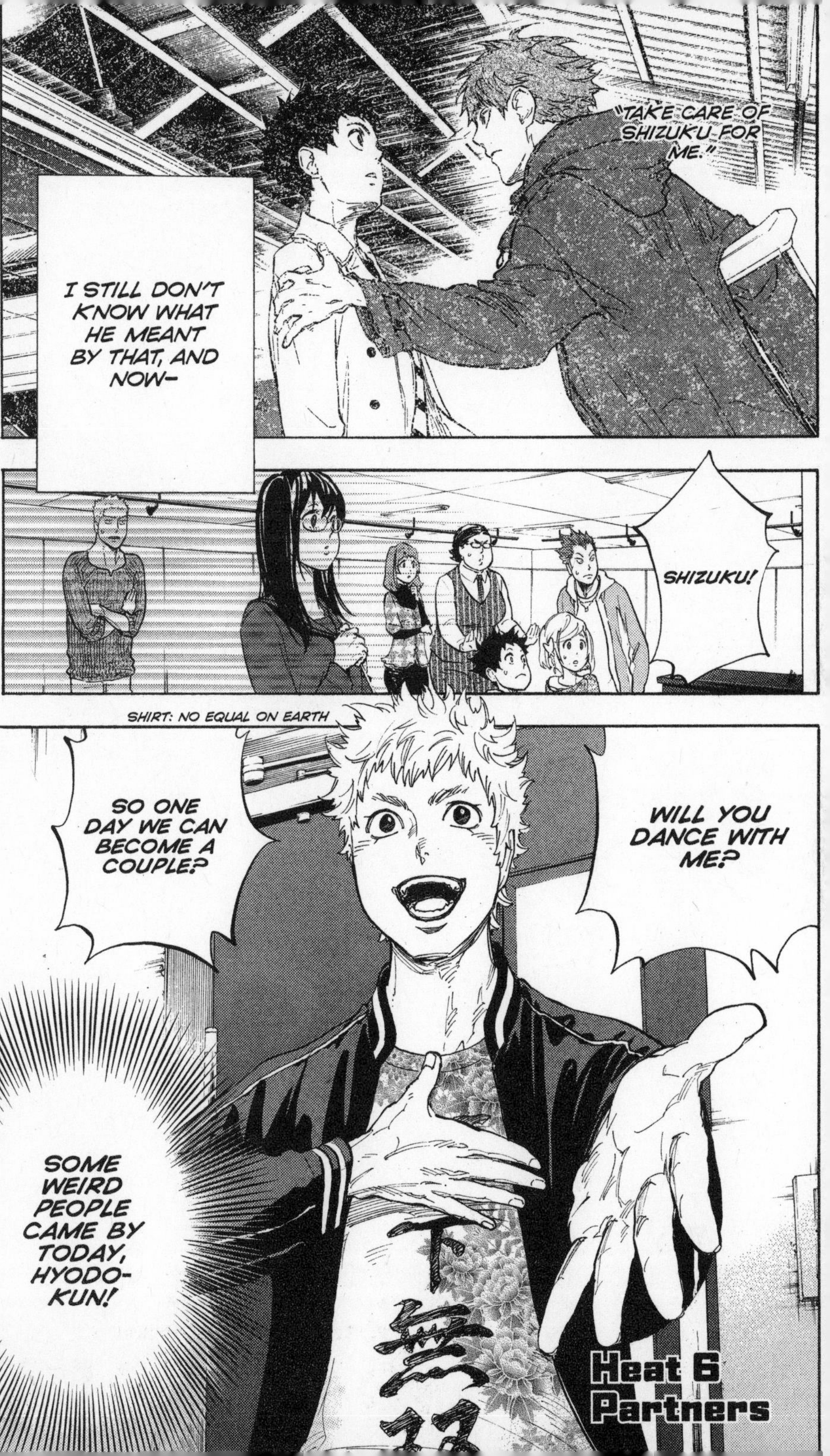
"TAKE CARE OF SHIZUKU FOR ME."
I STILL DON'T KNOW WHAT HE MEANT BY THAT, AND NOW-
SHIZUKU!
SHIRT: NO EQUAL ON EARTH
WILL YOU DANCE WITH ME?
SO ONE DAY WE CAN BECOME A COUPLE?
SOME WEIRD PEOPLE CAME BY TODAY, HYODO-KUN!

Heat 6 Partners

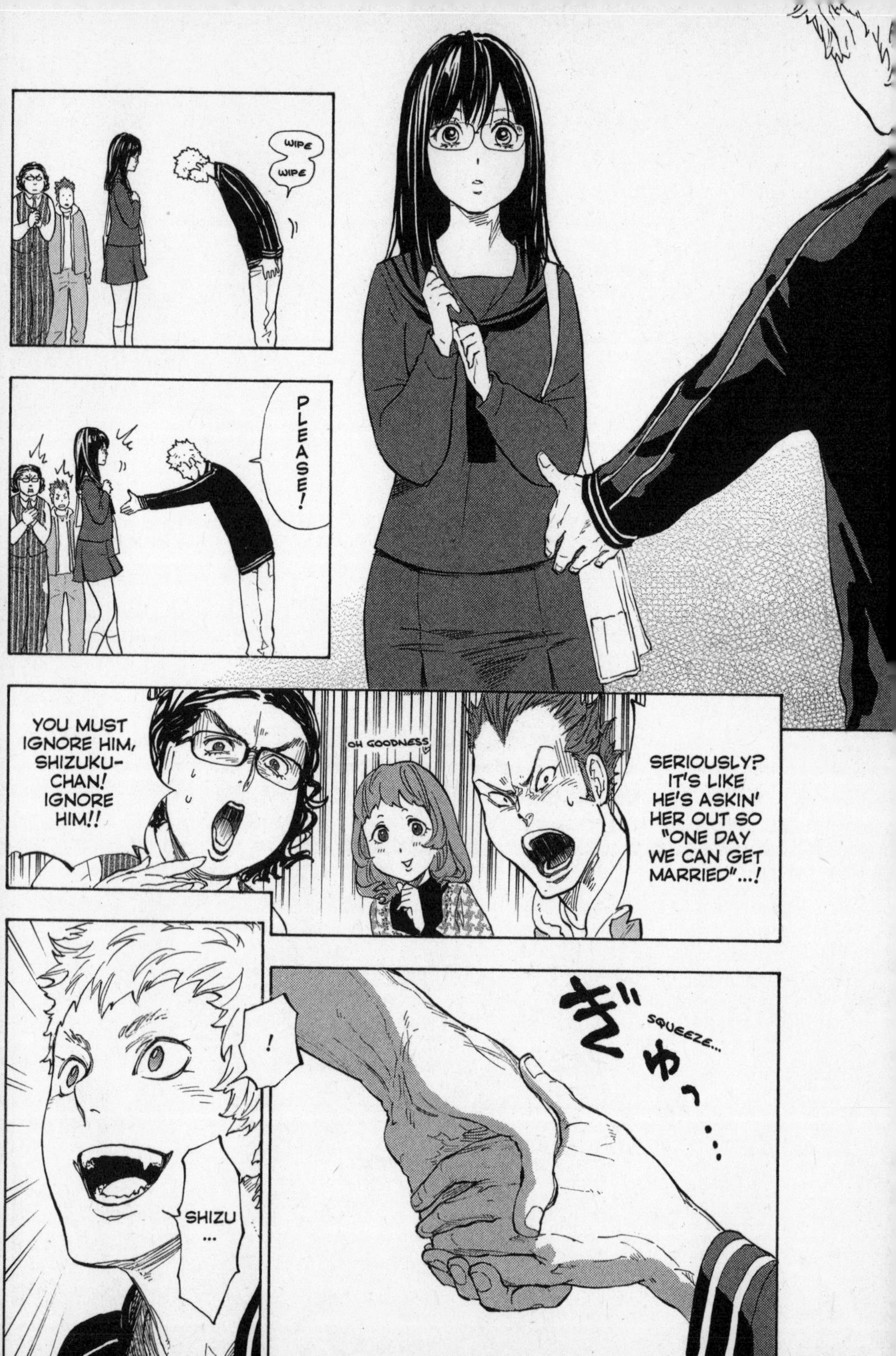
WIPE
WIPE
PLEASE!
SERIOUSLY? IT'S LIKE HE'S ASKIN' HER OUT SO "ONE DAY WE CAN GET MARRIED"...!
OH GOODNESS
YOU MUST IGNORE HIM, SHIZUKU-CHAN! IGNORE HIM!!
ぎゅ、、、
SQUEEZE...
!
SHIZU
...

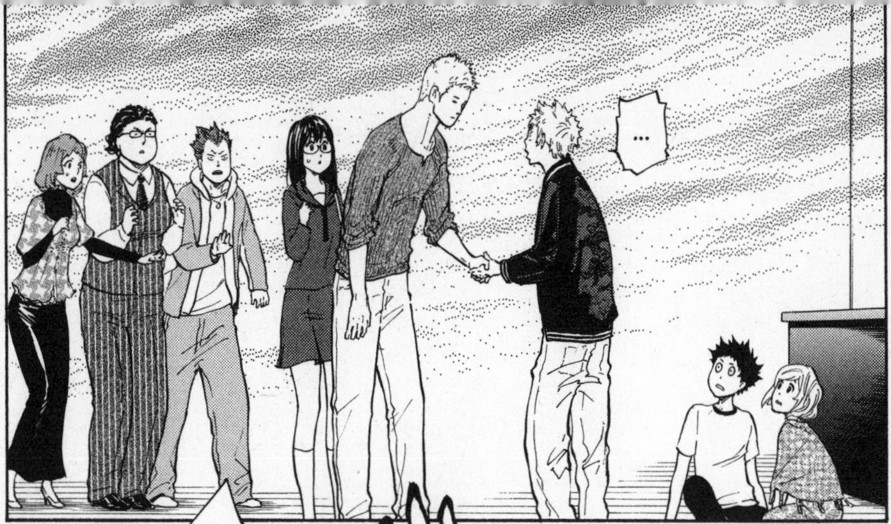
...

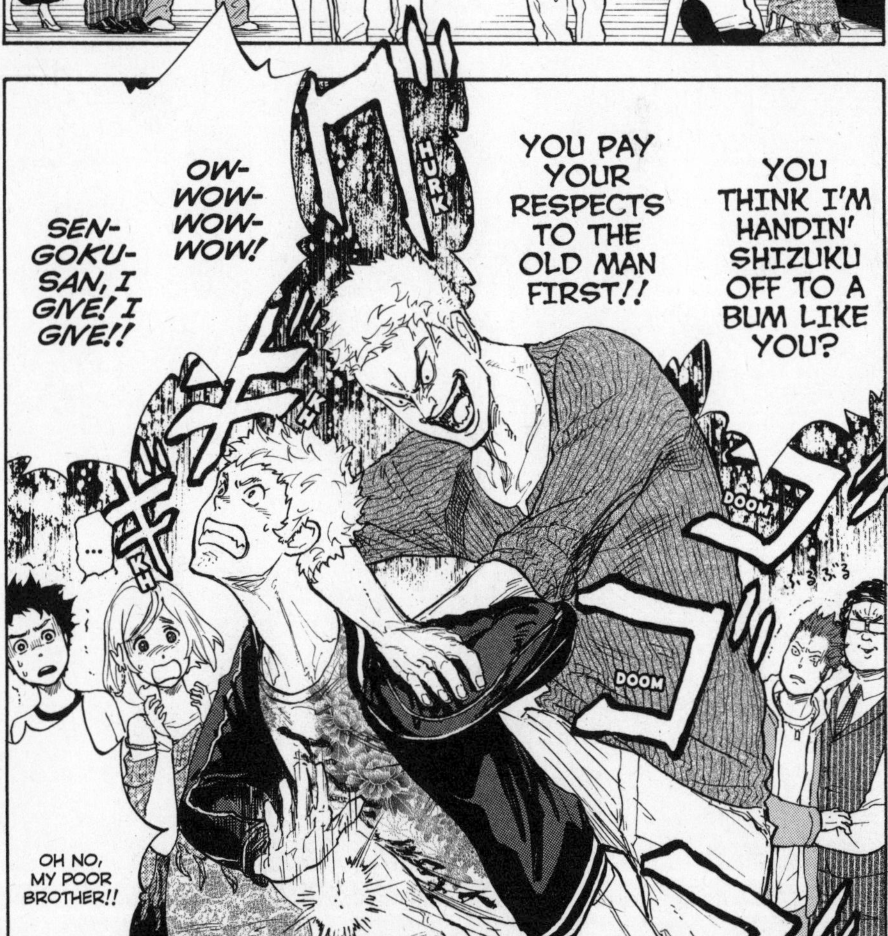
YOU THINK I'M HANDIN' SHIZUKU OFF TO A BUM LIKE YOU?
YOU PAY YOUR RESPECTS TO THE OLD MAN FIRST!!
HURK
OW-WOW-WOW-WOW!
SEN-GOKU-SAN, I GIVE! I GIVE!!
KH
KH
DOOM
...
DOOM
DOOM
OH NO, MY POOR BROTHER!!
WHAP
WHAP

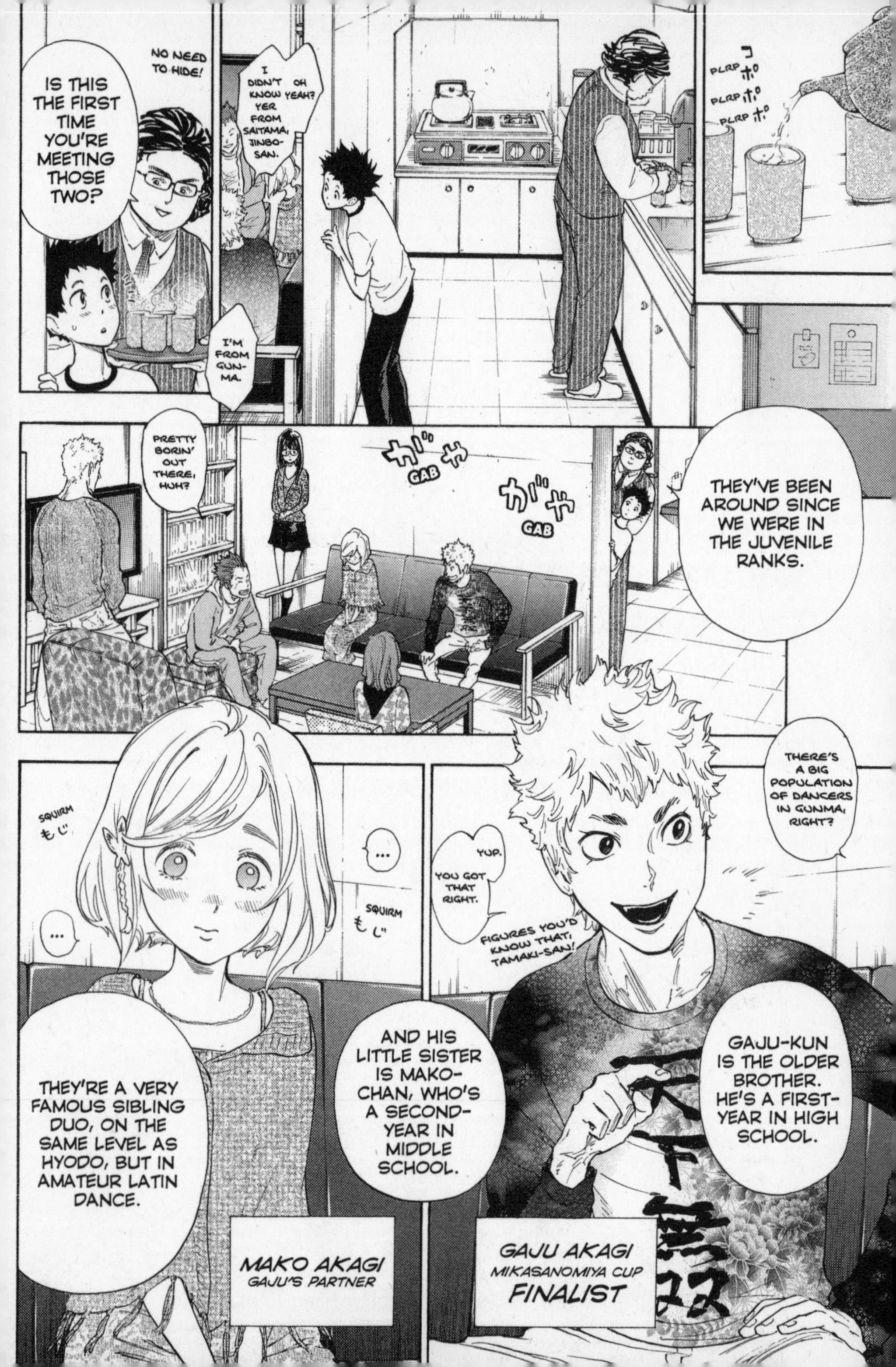
PLRP コポ
PLRP ポ
PLRP ポ
OH YEAH?
I DIDN'T KNOW YER FROM SAITAMA, JINBO-SAN.
I'M FROM GUNMA.
NO NEED TO HIDE!
IS THIS THE FIRST TIME YOU'RE MEETING THOSE TWO?
THEY'VE BEEN AROUND SINCE WE WERE IN THE JUVENILE RANKS.
がや GAB
がや GAB
PRETTY BORIN' OUT THERE, HUH?
THERE'S A BIG POPULATION OF DANCERS IN GUNMA, RIGHT?
YUP.
YOU GOT THAT RIGHT.
FIGURES YOU'D KNOW THAT, TAMAKI-SAN!
GAJU-KUN IS THE OLDER BROTHER. HE'S A FIRST-YEAR IN HIGH SCHOOL.
GAJU AKAGI MIKASANOMIYA CUP FINALIST
SQUIRM もじ
...
SQUIRM もじ
...
AND HIS LITTLE SISTER IS MAKO-CHAN, WHO'S A SECOND-YEAR IN MIDDLE SCHOOL.
THEY'RE A VERY FAMOUS SIBLING DUO, ON THE SAME LEVEL AS HYODO, BUT IN AMATEUR LATIN DANCE.
MAKO AKAGI GAJU'S PARTNER

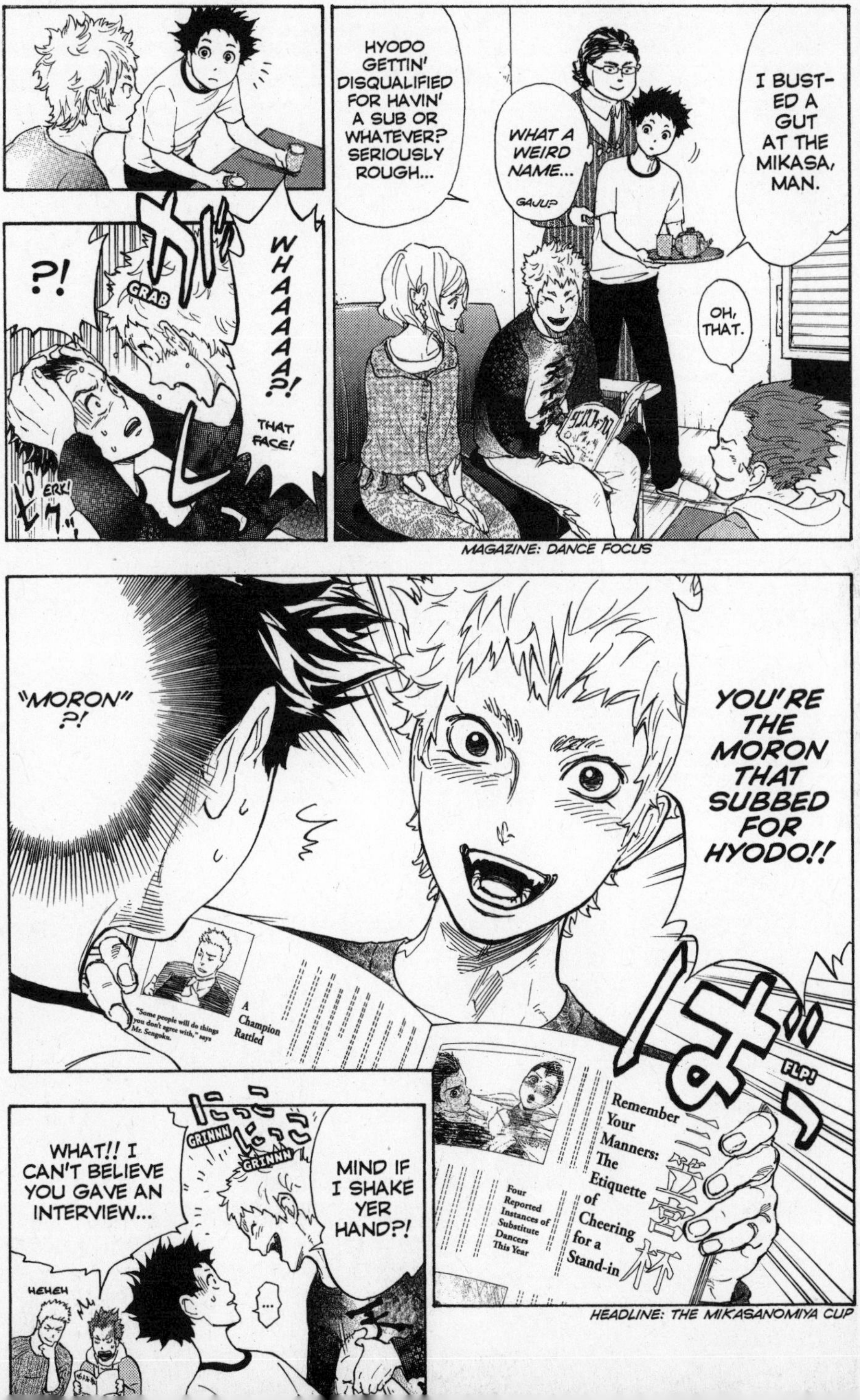
I BUST-ED A GUT AT THE MIKASA, MAN.
HYODO GETTIN' DISQUALIFIED FOR HAVIN' A SUB OR WHATEVER? SERIOUSLY ROUGH...
WHAT A WEIRD NAME...
GAJU?
OH, THAT.
MAGAZINE: DANCE FOCUS
WHAAAAAA?!
GRAB
?!
THAT FACE!
ERK!
YOU'RE THE MORON THAT SUBBED FOR HYODO!!
"MORON" ?!
A Champion Rattled
"Some people will do things you don't agree with," says Mr. Sengoku.
FLP!
Remember Your Manners: The Etiquette of Cheering for a Stand-in
三笠宮杯
Four Reported Instances of Substitute Dancers This Year
HEADLINE: THE MIKASANOMIYA CUP
MIND IF I SHAKE YER HAND?!
GRINNN
GRINNN
WHAT!! I CAN'T BELIEVE YOU GAVE AN INTERVIEW...
...
HEHEH

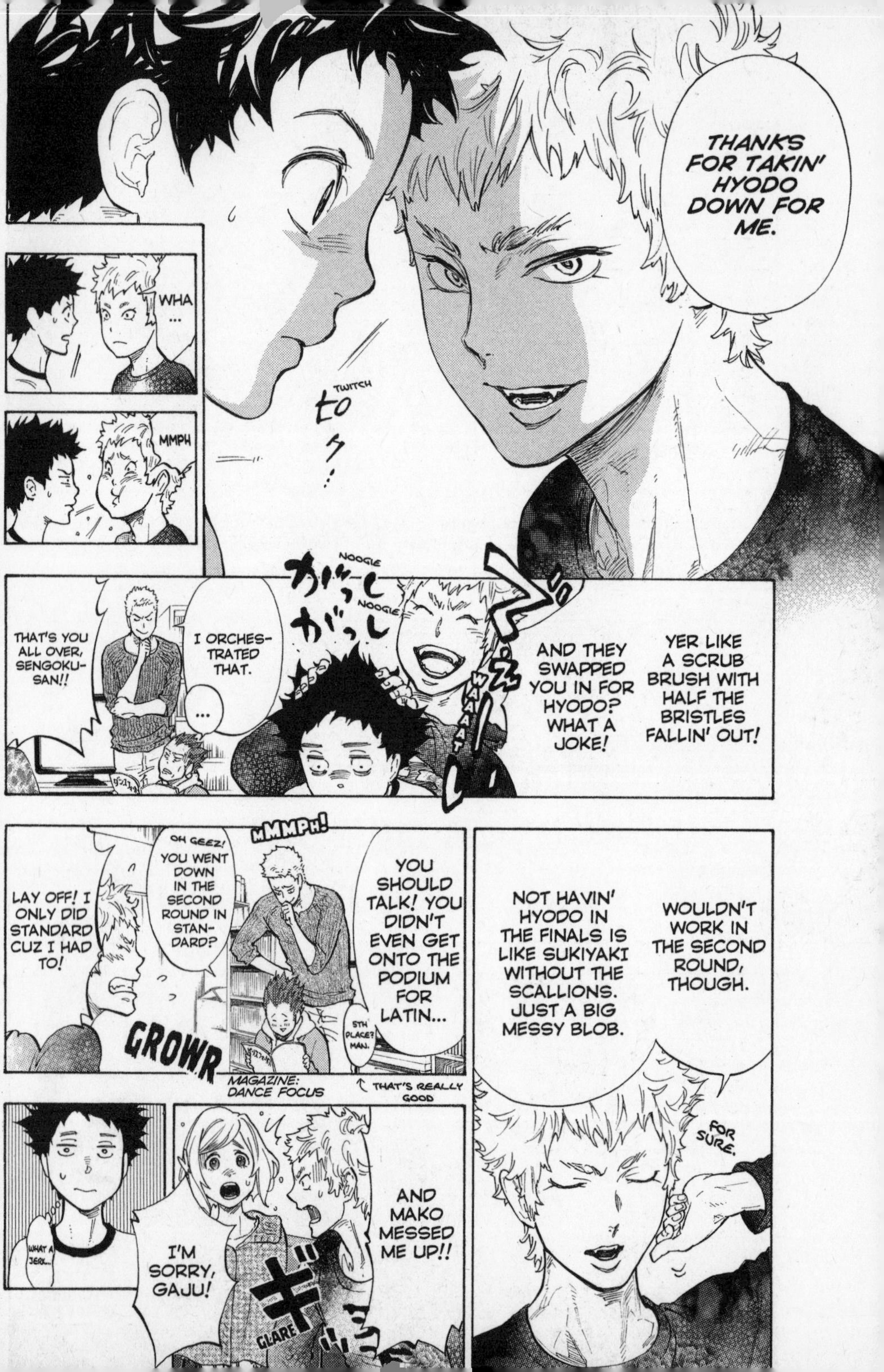
THANKS FOR TAKIN' HYODO DOWN FOR ME.
TWITCH
WHA ...
MMPH
YER LIKE A SCRUB BRUSH WITH HALF THE BRISTLES FALLIN' OUT!
AND THEY SWAPPED YOU IN FOR HYODO? WHAT A JOKE!
WAAAAT
NOOGIE
NOOGIE
I ORCHESTRATED THAT.
...
THAT'S YOU ALL OVER, SENGOKU-SAN!!
WOULDN'T WORK IN THE SECOND ROUND, THOUGH.
NOT HAVIN' HYODO IN THE FINALS IS LIKE SUKIYAKI WITHOUT THE SCALLIONS. JUST A BIG MESSY BLOB.
FOR SURE.
YOU SHOULD TALK! YOU DIDN'T EVEN GET ONTO THE PODIUM FOR LATIN...
MMMPH!
OH GEEZ! YOU WENT DOWN IN THE SECOND ROUND IN STAN-DARD?
LAY OFF! I ONLY DID STANDARD CUZ I HAD TO!
GROWR
5TH PLACE? MAN.
MAGAZINE: DANCE FOCUS
↑ THAT'S REALLY GOOD
AND MAKO MESSED ME UP!!
GLARE
I'M SORRY, GAJU!
WHAT A JERK...

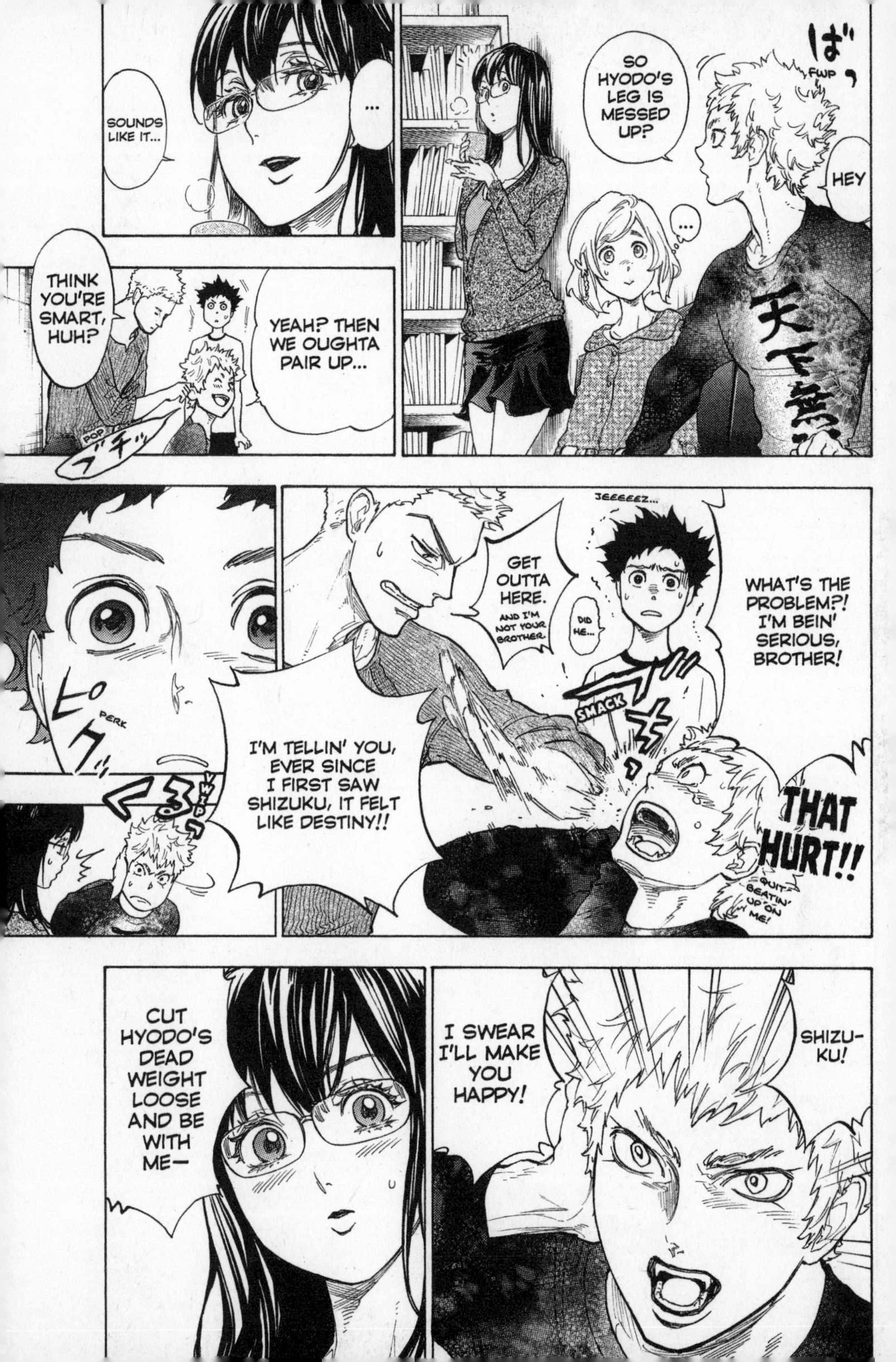

ばっ
FWP
HEY
SO HYODO'S LEG IS MESSED UP?
...
...
SOUNDS LIKE IT...
YEAH? THEN WE OUGHTA PAIR UP...
THINK YOU'RE SMART, HUH?
ブチッ
POP
WHAT'S THE PROBLEM?! I'M BEIN' SERIOUS, BROTHER!
JEEEEEZ...
DID HE...
GET OUTTA HERE.
AND I'M NOT YOUR BROTHER.
SMACK
THAT HURT!!
QUIT BEATIN' UP ON ME!
ピクッ
PERK
I'M TELLIN' YOU, EVER SINCE I FIRST SAW SHIZUKU, IT FELT LIKE DESTINY!!
くるっ
VWIP
SHIZU-KU!
I SWEAR I'LL MAKE YOU HAPPY!
CUT HYODO'S DEAD WEIGHT LOOSE AND BE WITH ME—

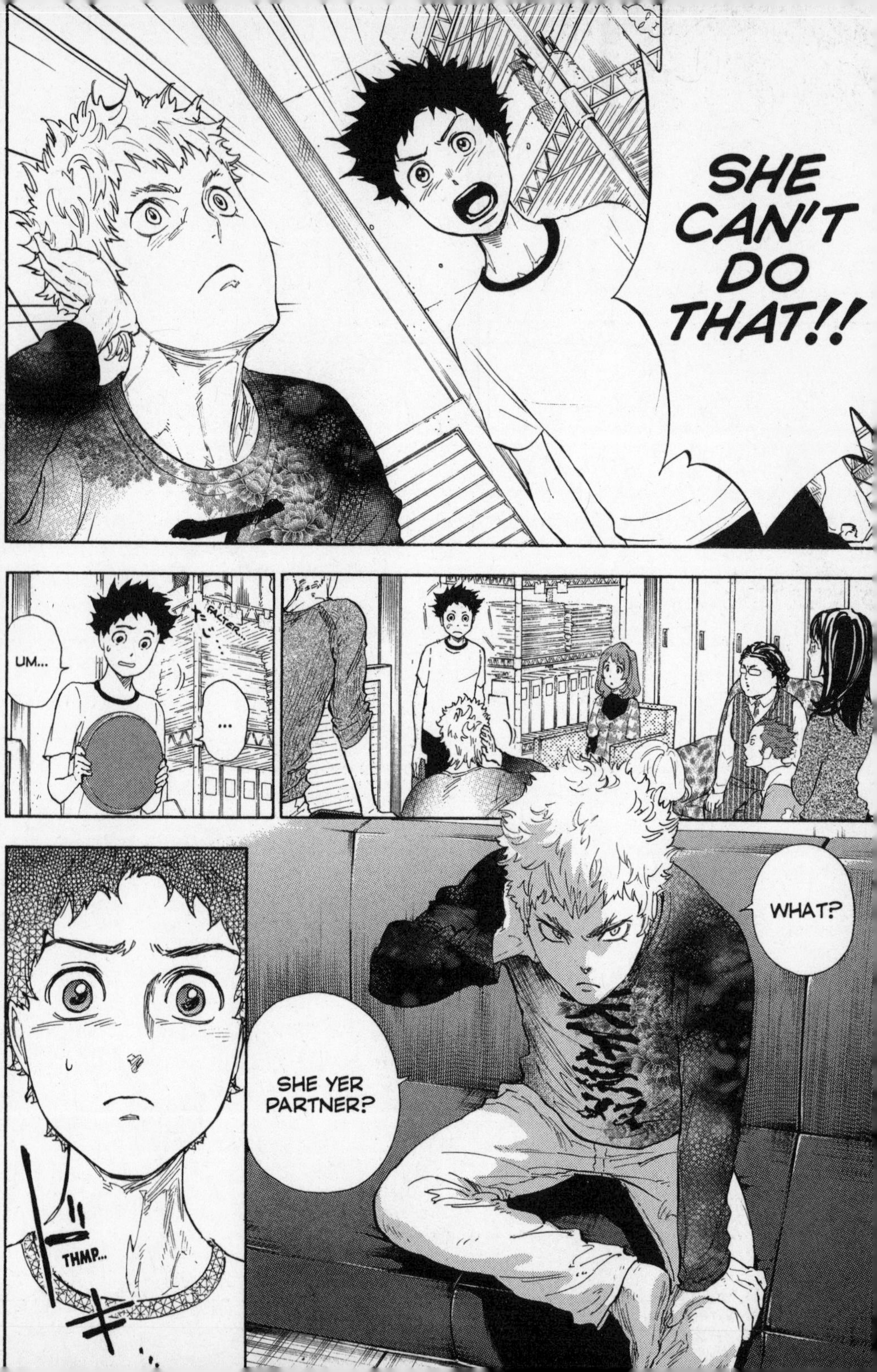
SHE CAN'T DO THAT!!
FALTER...
UM...
...
WHAT?
SHE YER PARTNER?
THMP...
...

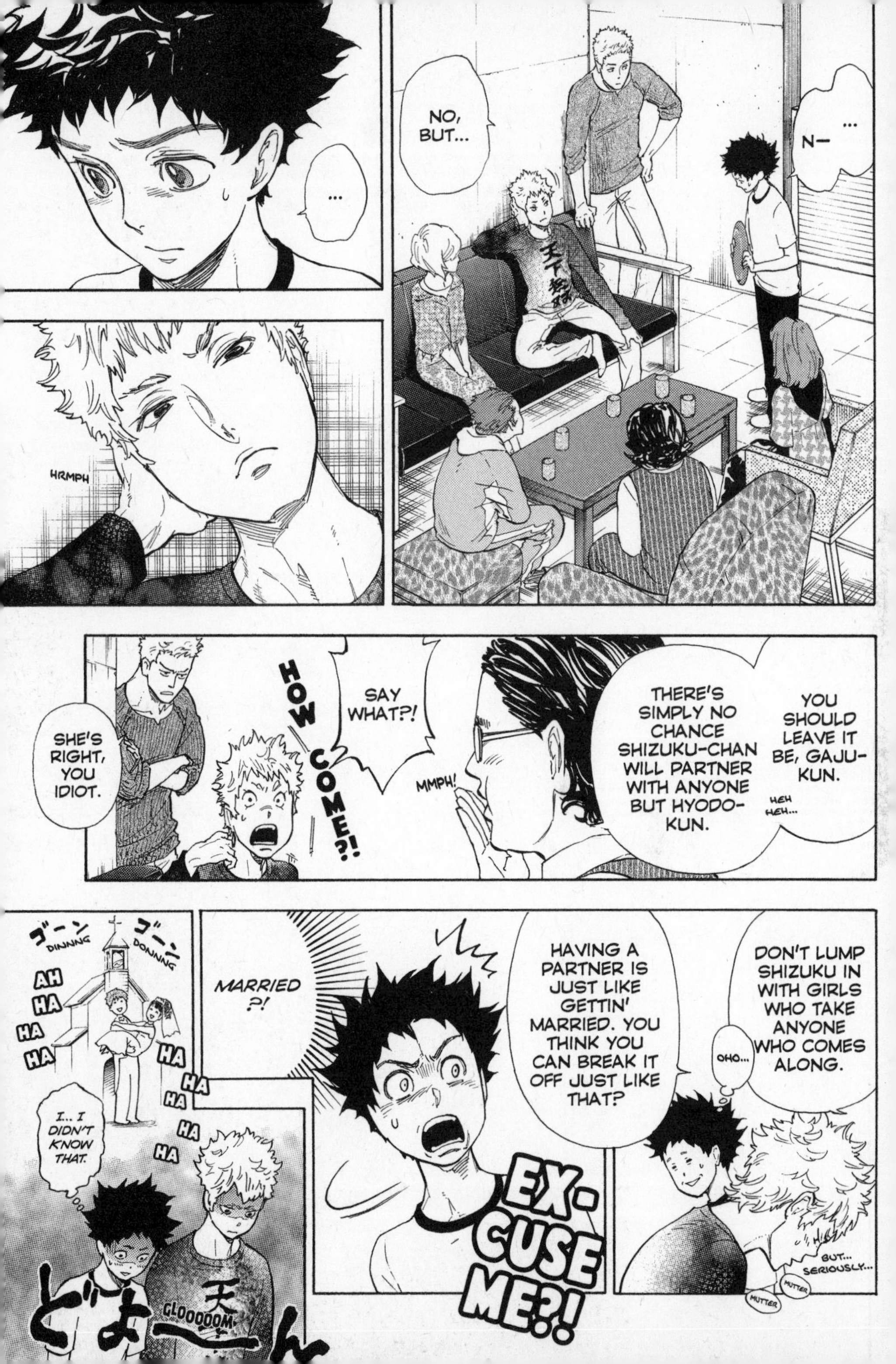
... N—
NO, BUT...
...
HRMPH
YOU SHOULD LEAVE IT BE, GAJU-KUN.
HEH HEH...
THERE'S SIMPLY NO CHANCE SHIZUKU-CHAN WILL PARTNER WITH ANYONE BUT HYODO-KUN.
MMPH!
SAY WHAT?!
HOW COME?!
SHE'S RIGHT, YOU IDIOT.
DON'T LUMP SHIZUKU IN WITH GIRLS WHO TAKE ANYONE WHO COMES ALONG.
OHO...
BUT... SERIOUSLY...
MUTTER MUTTER
HAVING A PARTNER IS JUST LIKE GETTIN' MARRIED. YOU THINK YOU CAN BREAK IT OFF JUST LIKE THAT?
MARRIED ?!
EX-CUSE ME?!
ゴーン DINNNG
ゴーン DONNNG
AH HA HA HA
HA HA HA HA HA
I... I DIDN'T KNOW THAT.
どよ～ん GLOOOOOM

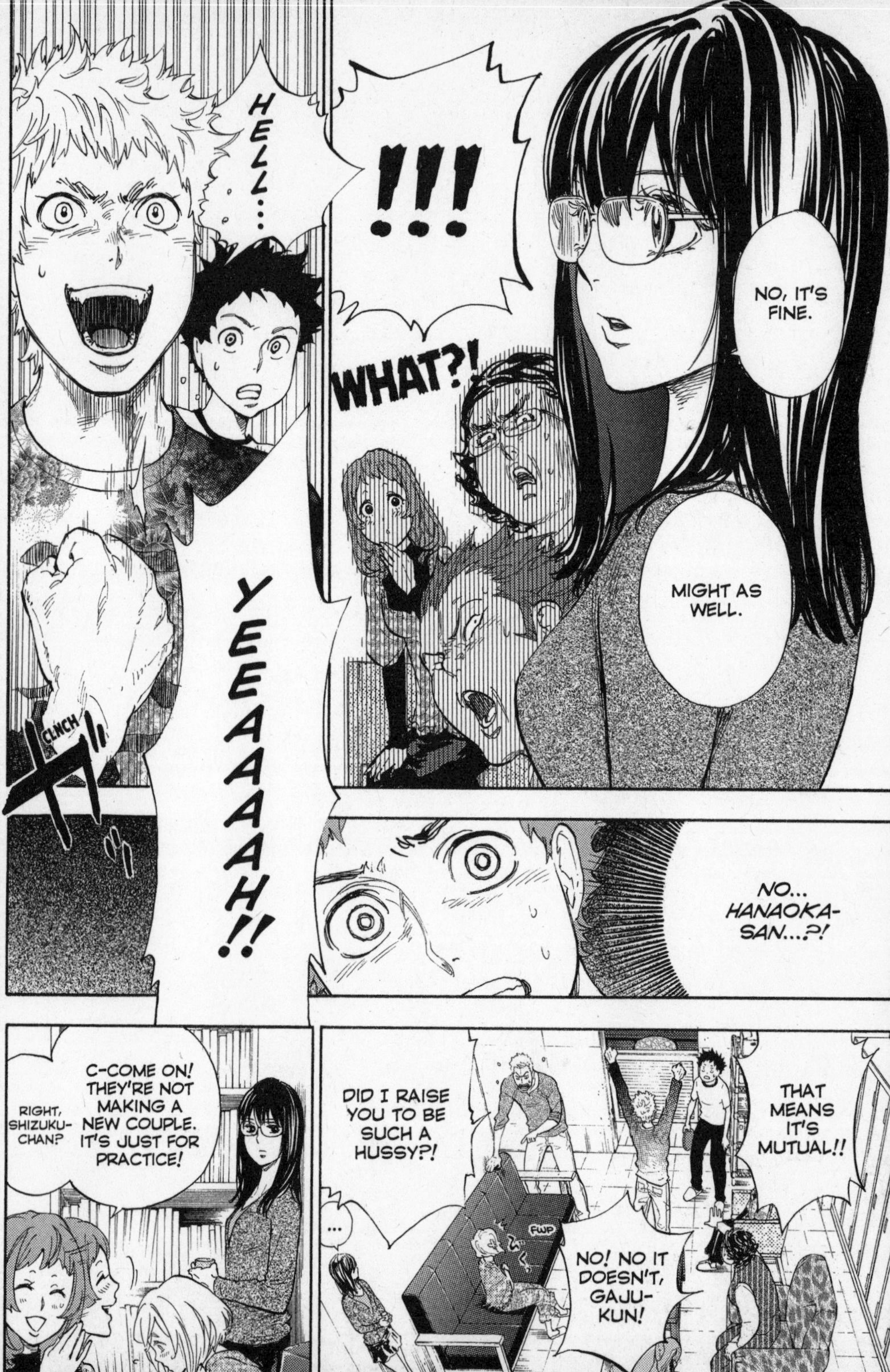
NO, IT'S FINE.
!!!
WHAT?!
MIGHT AS WELL.
NO... HANAOKA-SAN...?!
HELL...
YEEAAAAAAH!!
CLNCH
THAT MEANS IT'S MUTUAL!!
DID I RAISE YOU TO BE SUCH A HUSSY?!
FWP
NO! NO IT DOESN'T, GAJU-KUN!
...
C-COME ON! THEY'RE NOT MAKING A NEW COUPLE. IT'S JUST FOR PRACTICE!
RIGHT, SHIZUKU-CHAN?

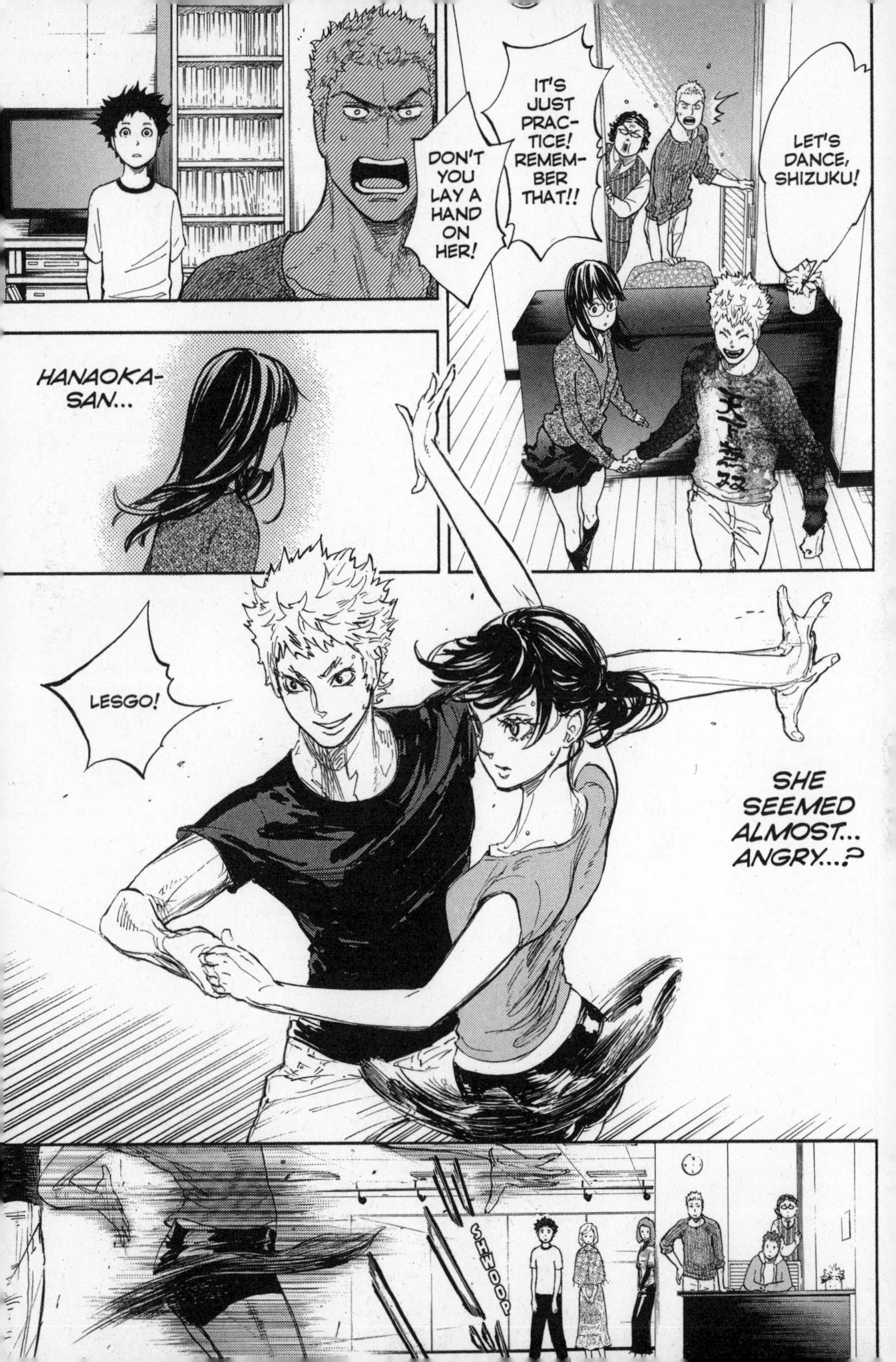
LET'S DANCE, SHIZUKU!
IT'S JUST PRACTICE! REMEMBER THAT!!
DON'T YOU LAY A HAND ON HER!
HANAOKA-SAN...
SHE SEEMED ALMOST... ANGRY...?
LESGO!
SHWOOP

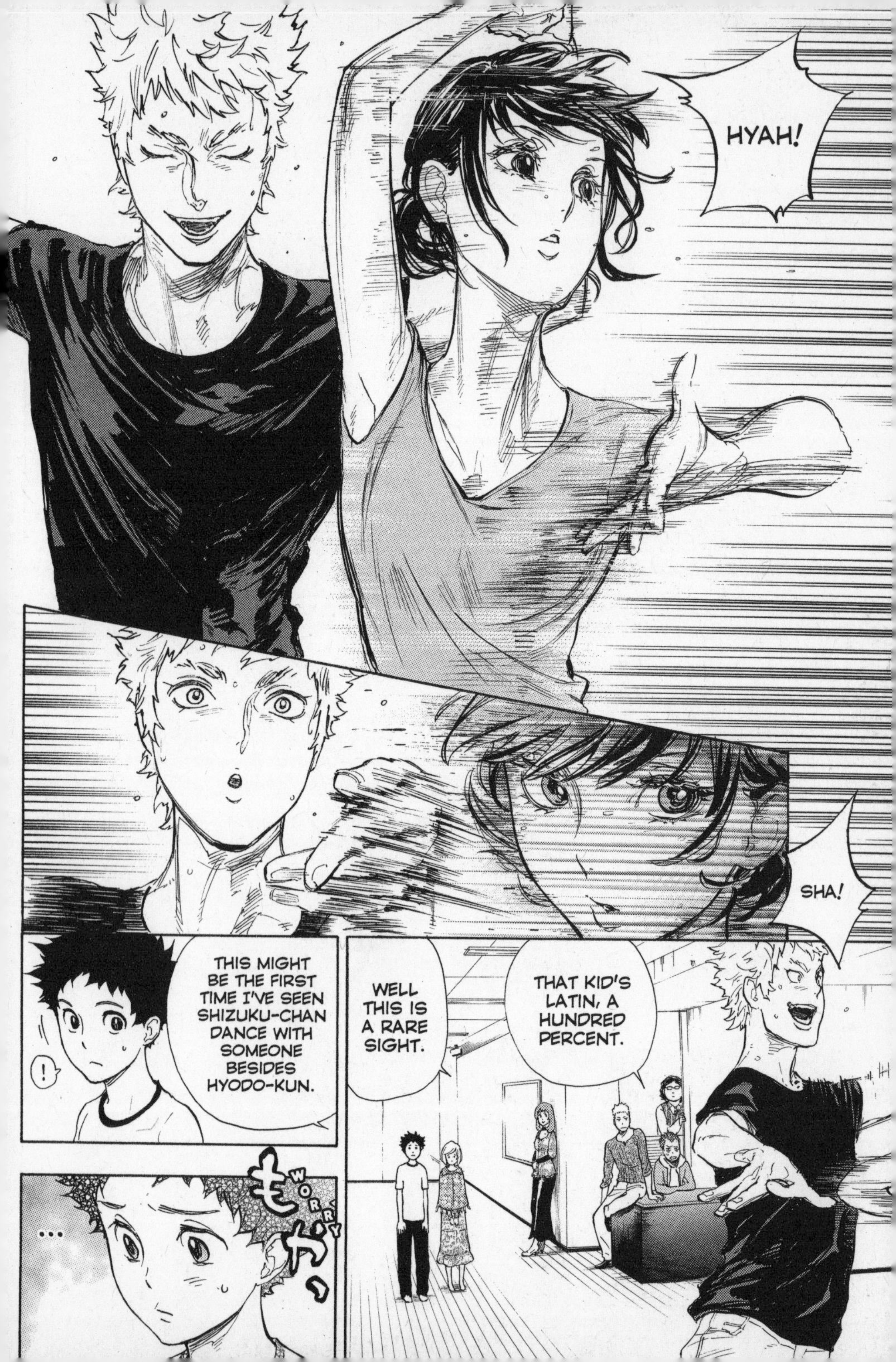

HYAH!
SHA!
THAT KID'S LATIN, A HUNDRED PERCENT.
WELL THIS IS A RARE SIGHT.
THIS MIGHT BE THE FIRST TIME I'VE SEEN SHIZUKU-CHAN DANCE WITH SOMEONE BESIDES HYODO-KUN.
!
もやっ
WORRY
...

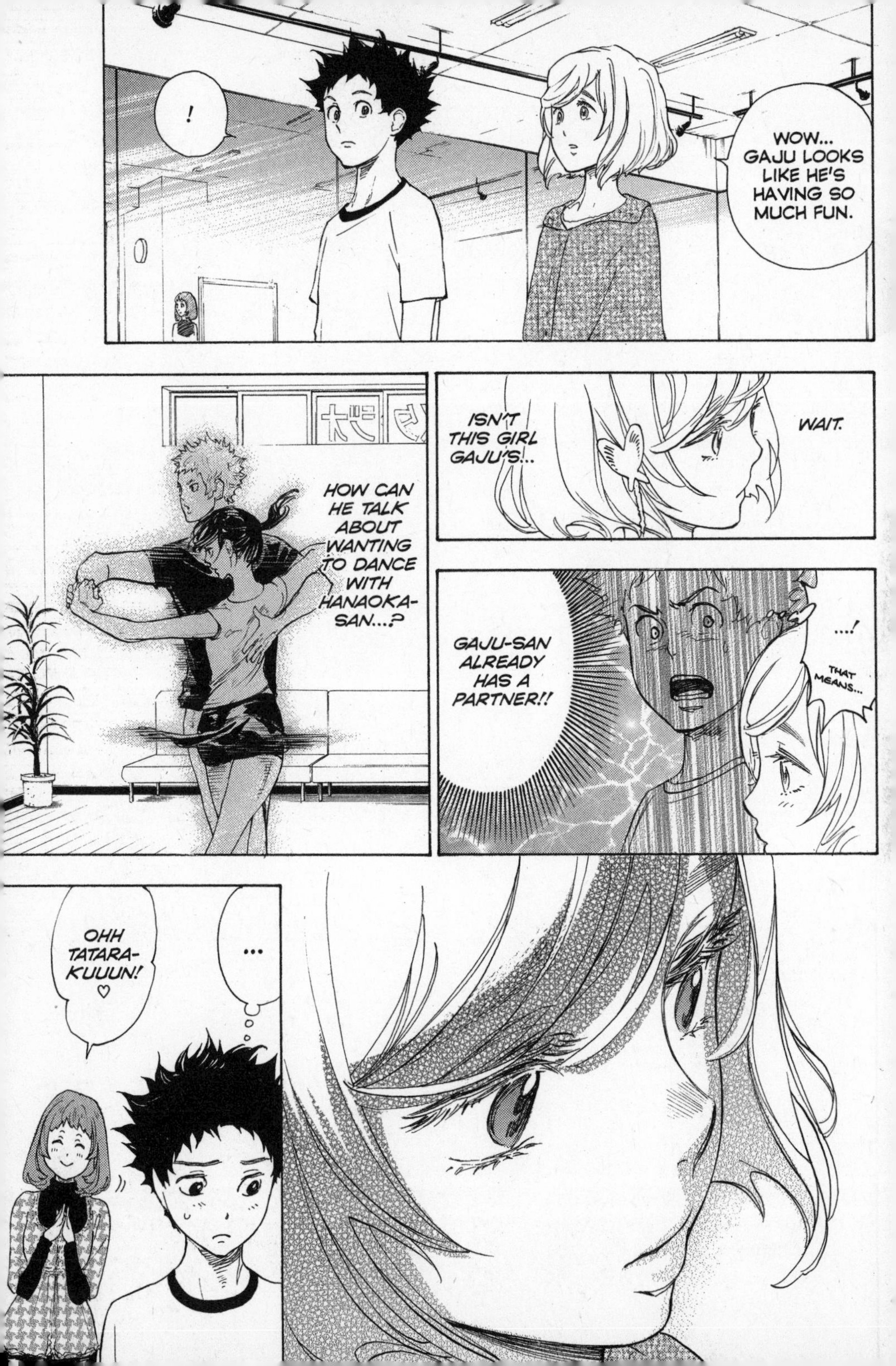
WOW... GAJU LOOKS LIKE HE'S HAVING SO MUCH FUN.
!
WAIT.
ISN'T THIS GIRL GAJU'S...
...!
THAT MEANS...
GAJU-SAN ALREADY HAS A PARTNER!!
HOW CAN HE TALK ABOUT WANTING TO DANCE WITH HANAOKA-SAN...?
...
OHH TATARA-KUUUN! ♡

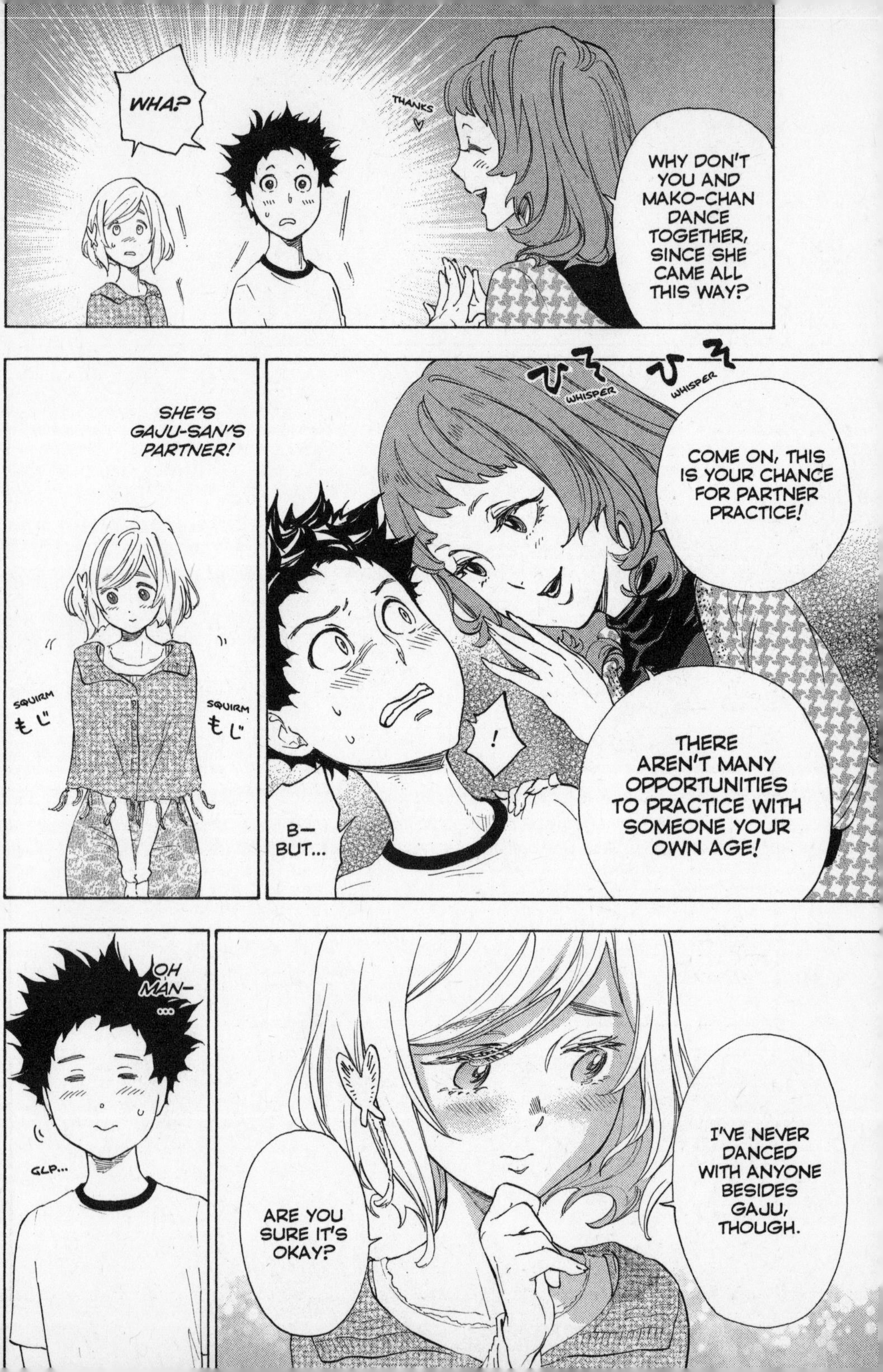
WHY DON'T YOU AND MAKO-CHAN DANCE TOGETHER, SINCE SHE CAME ALL THIS WAY?
THANKS
WHA?
ひそ WHISPER
ひそ WHISPER
COME ON, THIS IS YOUR CHANCE FOR PARTNER PRACTICE!
THERE AREN'T MANY OPPORTUNITIES TO PRACTICE WITH SOMEONE YOUR OWN AGE!
!
B— BUT...
SHE'S GAJU-SAN'S PARTNER!
SQUIRM もじ
SQUIRM もじ
I'VE NEVER DANCED WITH ANYONE BESIDES GAJU, THOUGH.
ARE YOU SURE IT'S OKAY?
OH MAN—...
GLP...

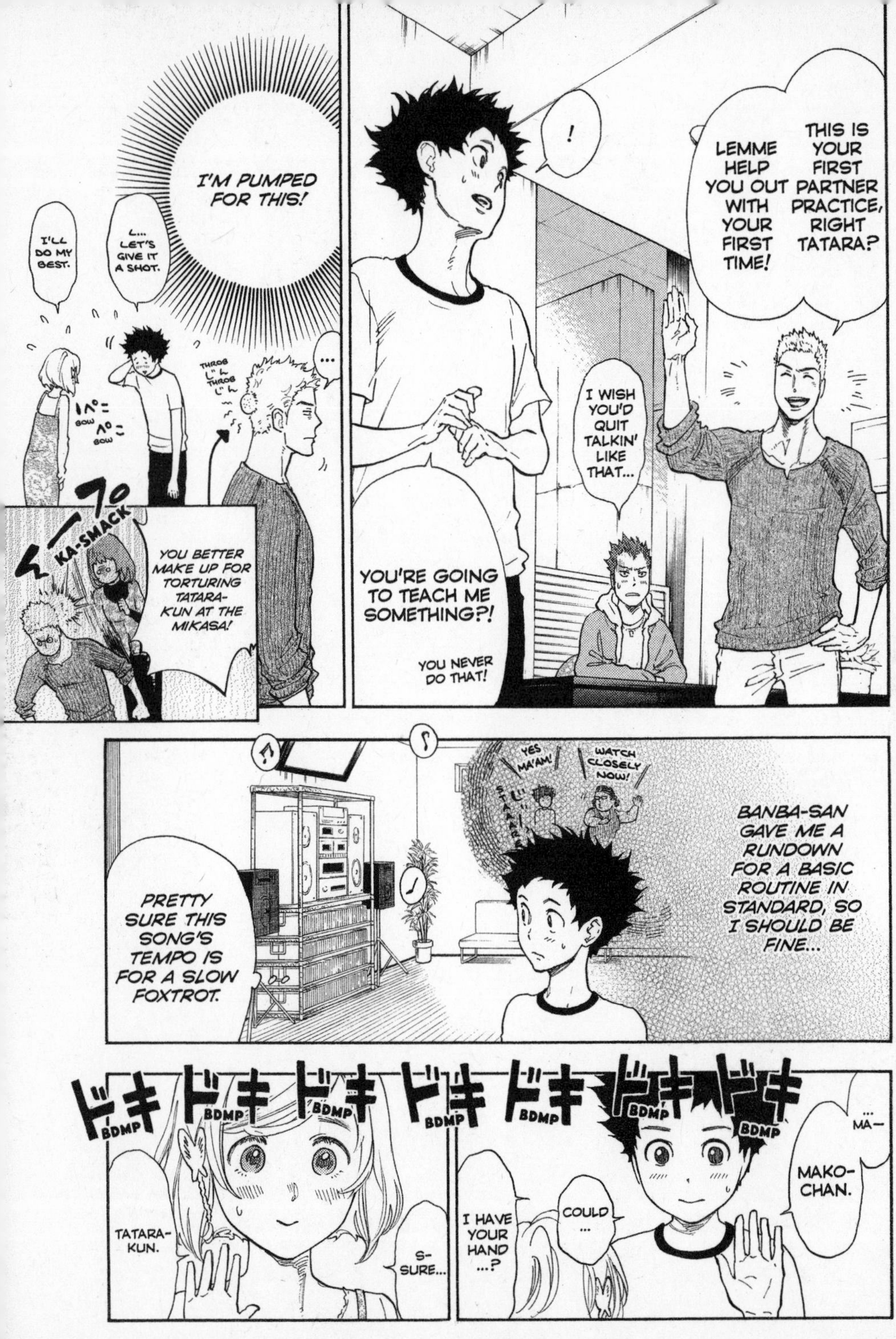
THIS IS YOUR FIRST PARTNER PRACTICE, RIGHT TATARA?
LEMME HELP YOU OUT WITH YOUR FIRST TIME!
I WISH YOU'D QUIT TALKIN' LIKE THAT...
!
YOU'RE GOING TO TEACH ME SOMETHING?!
YOU NEVER DO THAT!
I'M PUMPED FOR THIS!
L... LET'S GIVE IT A SHOT.
I'LL DO MY BEST.
...
THROB THROB
BOW BOW
KA-SMACK
YOU BETTER MAKE UP FOR TORTURING TATARA-KUN AT THE MIKASA!
BANBA-SAN GAVE ME A RUNDOWN FOR A BASIC ROUTINE IN STANDARD, SO I SHOULD BE FINE...
WATCH CLOSELY NOW!
YES MA'AM!
STAAARE
PRETTY SURE THIS SONG'S TEMPO IS FOR A SLOW FOXTROT.
ドキ ドキ ドキ ドキ ドキ ドキ ドキ
BDMP BDMP BDMP BDMP BDMP BDMP BDMP
... MA—
MAKO-CHAN.
COULD ...
I HAVE YOUR HAND ...?
S-SURE...
TATARA-KUN.

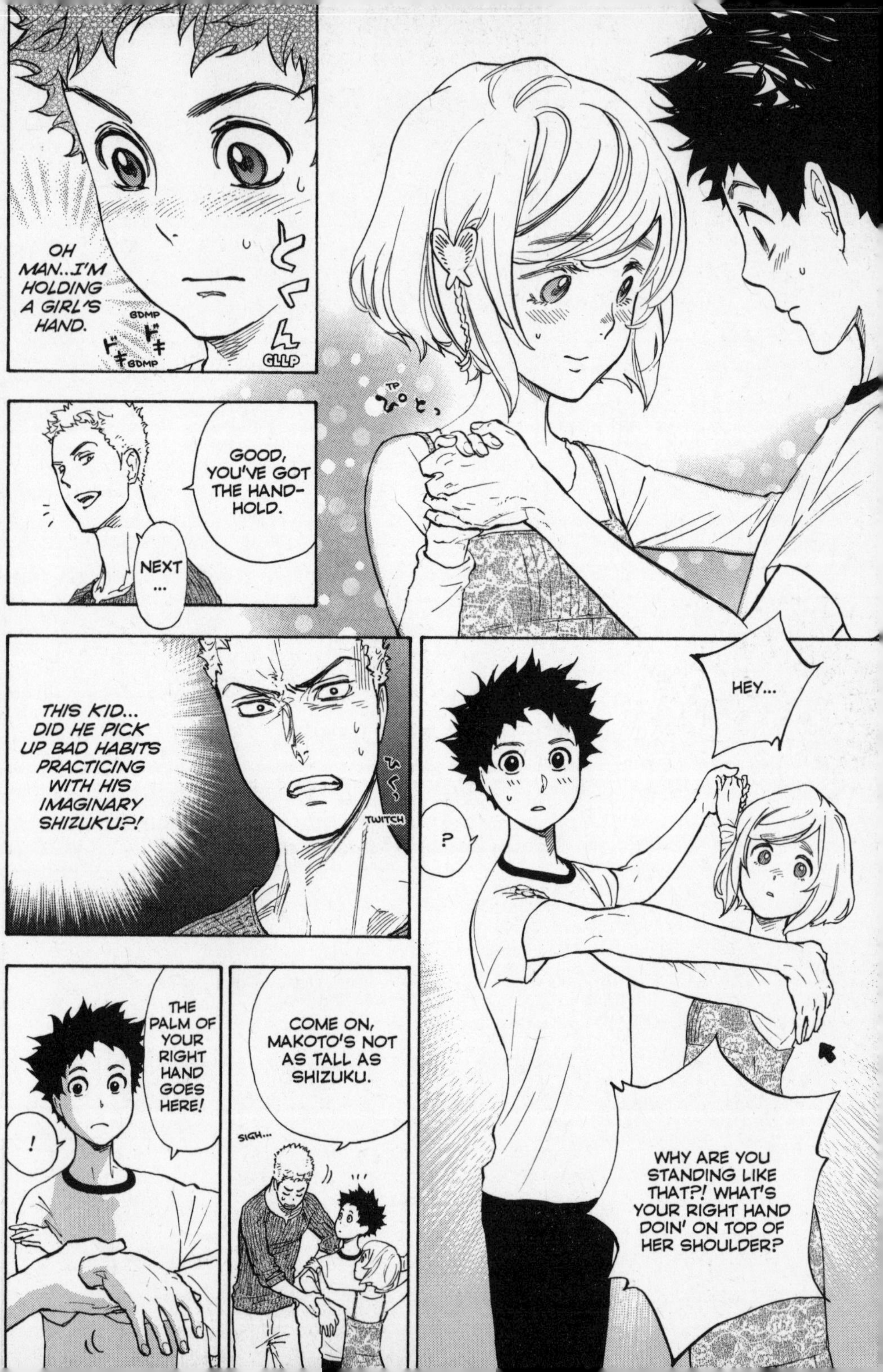
TP
OH MAN...I'M HOLDING A GIRL'S HAND.
BDMP
BDMP
GLLP
GOOD, YOU'VE GOT THE HAND-HOLD.
NEXT...
HEY...
?
WHY ARE YOU STANDING LIKE THAT?! WHAT'S YOUR RIGHT HAND DOIN' ON TOP OF HER SHOULDER?
THIS KID... DID HE PICK UP BAD HABITS PRACTICING WITH HIS IMAGINARY SHIZUKU?!
TWITCH
COME ON, MAKOTO'S NOT AS TALL AS SHIZUKU.
SIGH...
THE PALM OF YOUR RIGHT HAND GOES HERE!
!

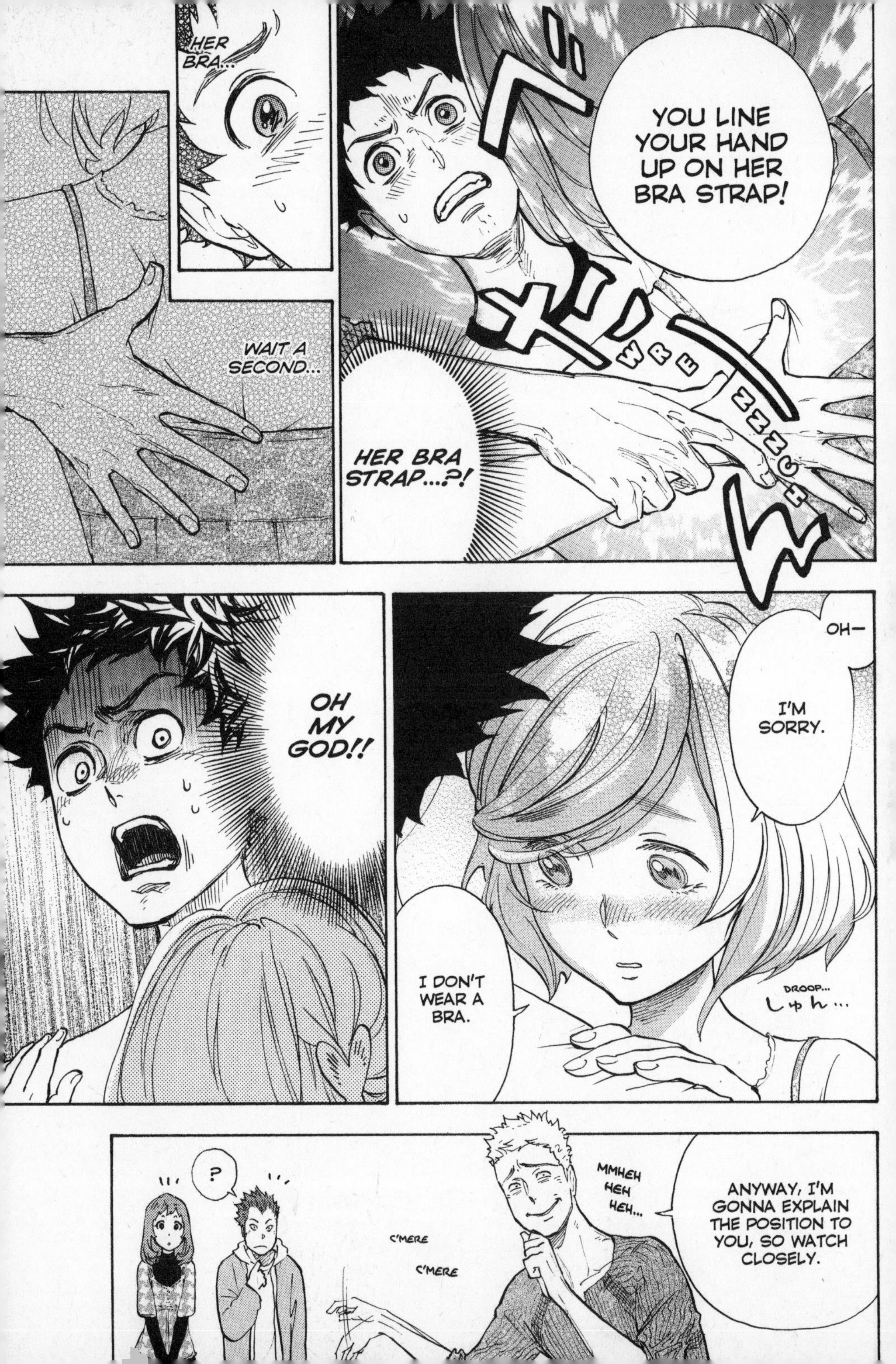
YOU LINE YOUR HAND UP ON HER BRA STRAP!
WRENNNGH
HER BRA STRAP...?!
HER BRA...
WAIT A SECOND...
OH—
I'M SORRY.
I DON'T WEAR A BRA.
DROOP...
しゅん...
OH MY GOD!!
ANYWAY, I'M GONNA EXPLAIN THE POSITION TO YOU, SO WATCH CLOSELY.
MMHEH HEH HEH...
C'MERE
C'MERE
?

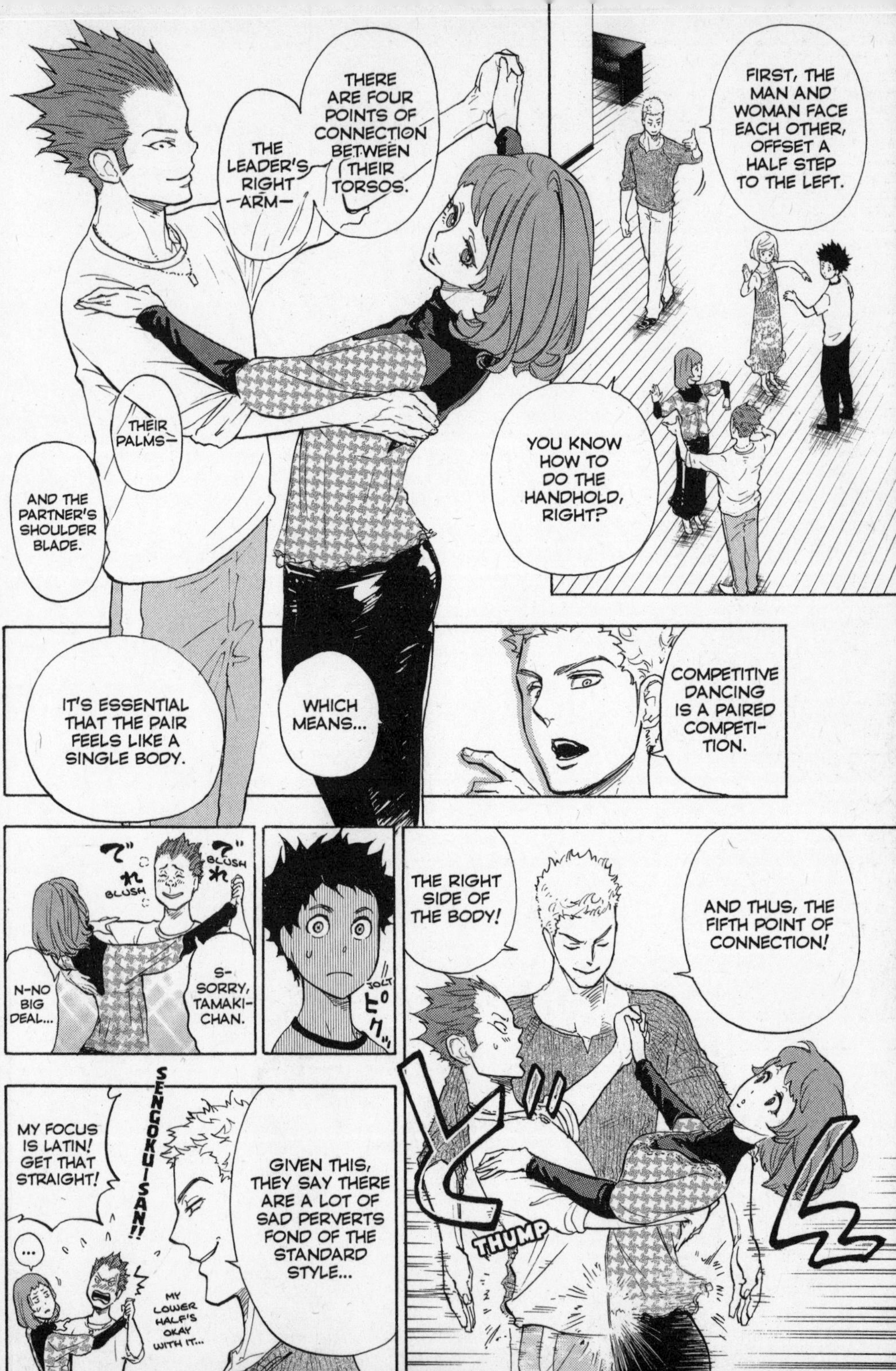
FIRST, THE MAN AND WOMAN FACE EACH OTHER, OFFSET A HALF STEP TO THE LEFT.
YOU KNOW HOW TO DO THE HANDHOLD, RIGHT?
THERE ARE FOUR POINTS OF CONNECTION BETWEEN THEIR TORSOS.
THE LEADER'S RIGHT ARM—
THEIR PALMS—
AND THE PARTNER'S SHOULDER BLADE.
COMPETITIVE DANCING IS A PAIRED COMPETITION.
WHICH MEANS...
IT'S ESSENTIAL THAT THE PAIR FEELS LIKE A SINGLE BODY.
AND THUS, THE FIFTH POINT OF CONNECTION!
THE RIGHT SIDE OF THE BODY!
THUMP
JOLT
BLUSH
BLUSH
S-SORRY, TAMAKI-CHAN.
N-NO BIG DEAL...
GIVEN THIS, THEY SAY THERE ARE A LOT OF SAD PERVERTS FOND OF THE STANDARD STYLE...
SENGOKU-SAN!!
MY FOCUS IS LATIN! GET THAT STRAIGHT!
...
MY LOWER HALF'S OKAY WITH IT...

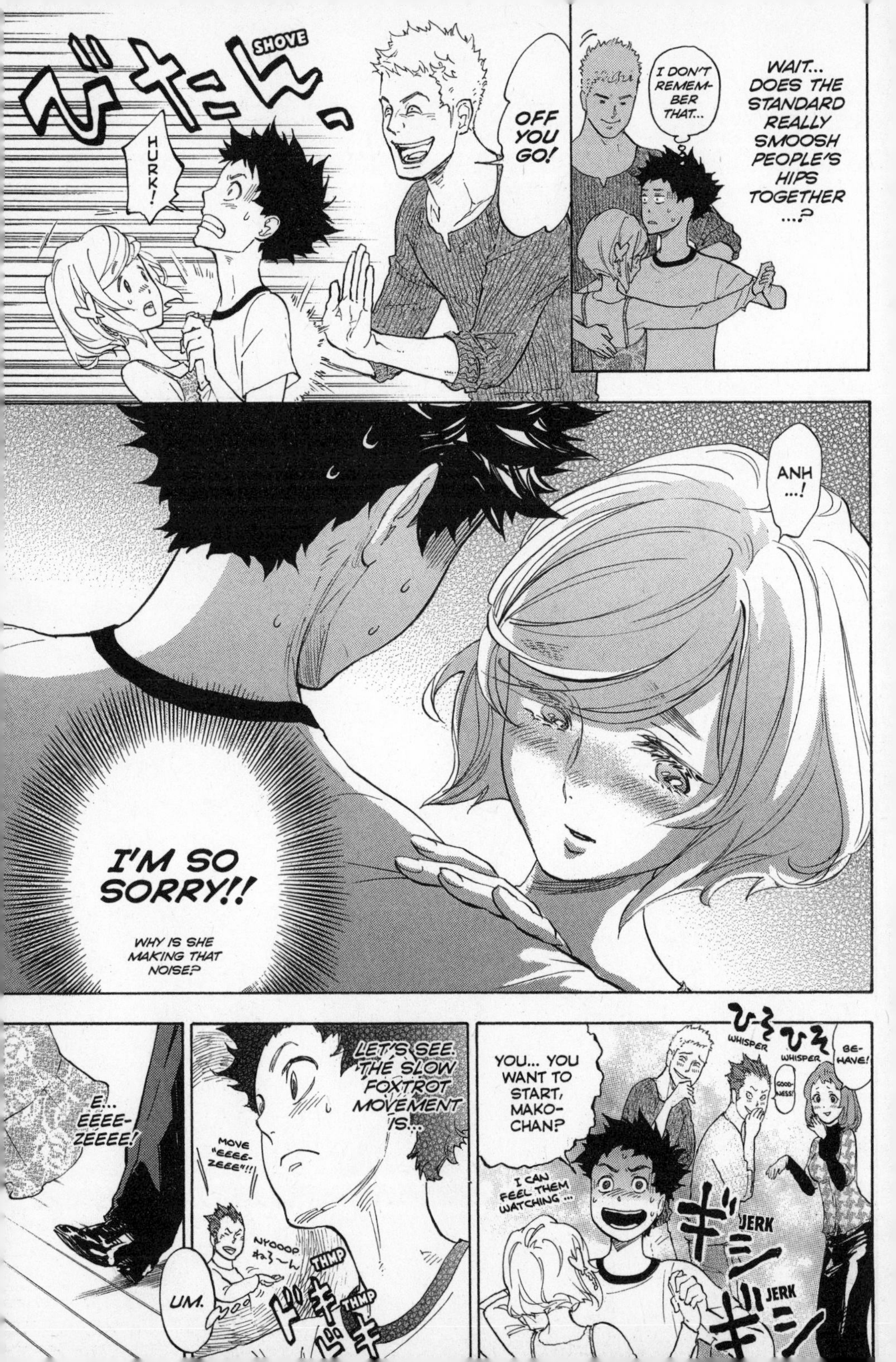
WAIT... DOES THE STANDARD REALLY SMOOSH PEOPLE'S HIPS TOGETHER...?
I DON'T REMEM-BER THAT...
OFF YOU GO!
SHOVE
HURK!
ANH...!
I'M SO SORRY!!
WHY IS SHE MAKING THAT NOISE?
BE-HAVE!
WHISPER
GOOD-NESS!
WHISPER
YOU... YOU WANT TO START, MAKO-CHAN?
I CAN FEEL THEM WATCHING...
JERK
JERK
LET'S SEE. THE SLOW FOXTROT MOVEMENT IS...
MOVE "EEEE-ZEEE"!!!
NYOOOP
THMP
THMP
UM.
E... EEEE-ZEEEE!

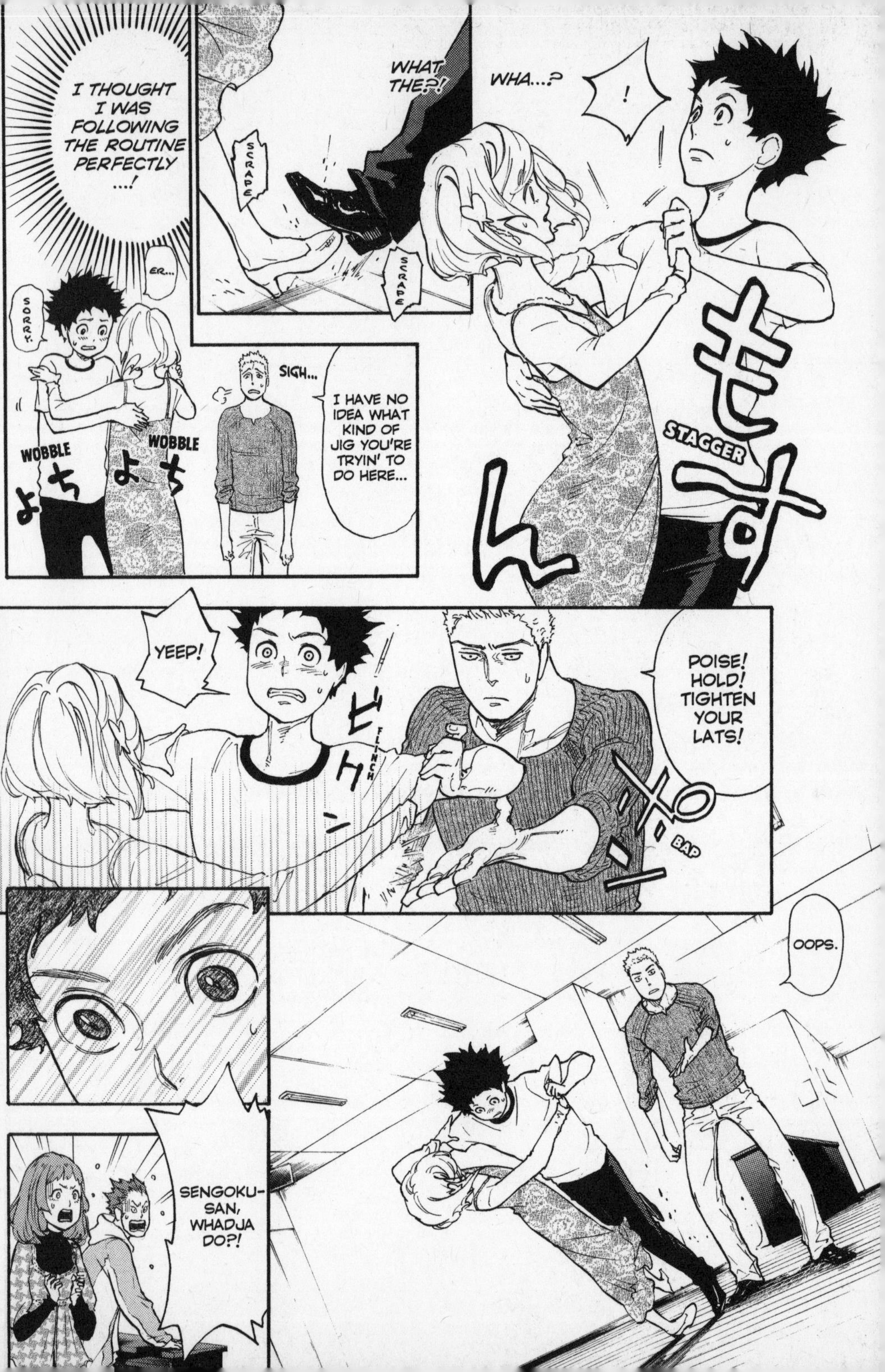
WHA...?
!
STAGGER
WHAT THE?!
SCRAPE
SCRAPE
I THOUGHT I WAS FOLLOWING THE ROUTINE PERFECTLY ...!
ER...
SORRY.
WOBBLE
WOBBLE
よち よち
SIGH...
I HAVE NO IDEA WHAT KIND OF JIG YOU'RE TRYIN' TO DO HERE...
POISE! HOLD! TIGHTEN YOUR LATS!
BAP
FLINCH
YEEP!
OOPS.
SENGOKU-SAN, WHADJA DO?!

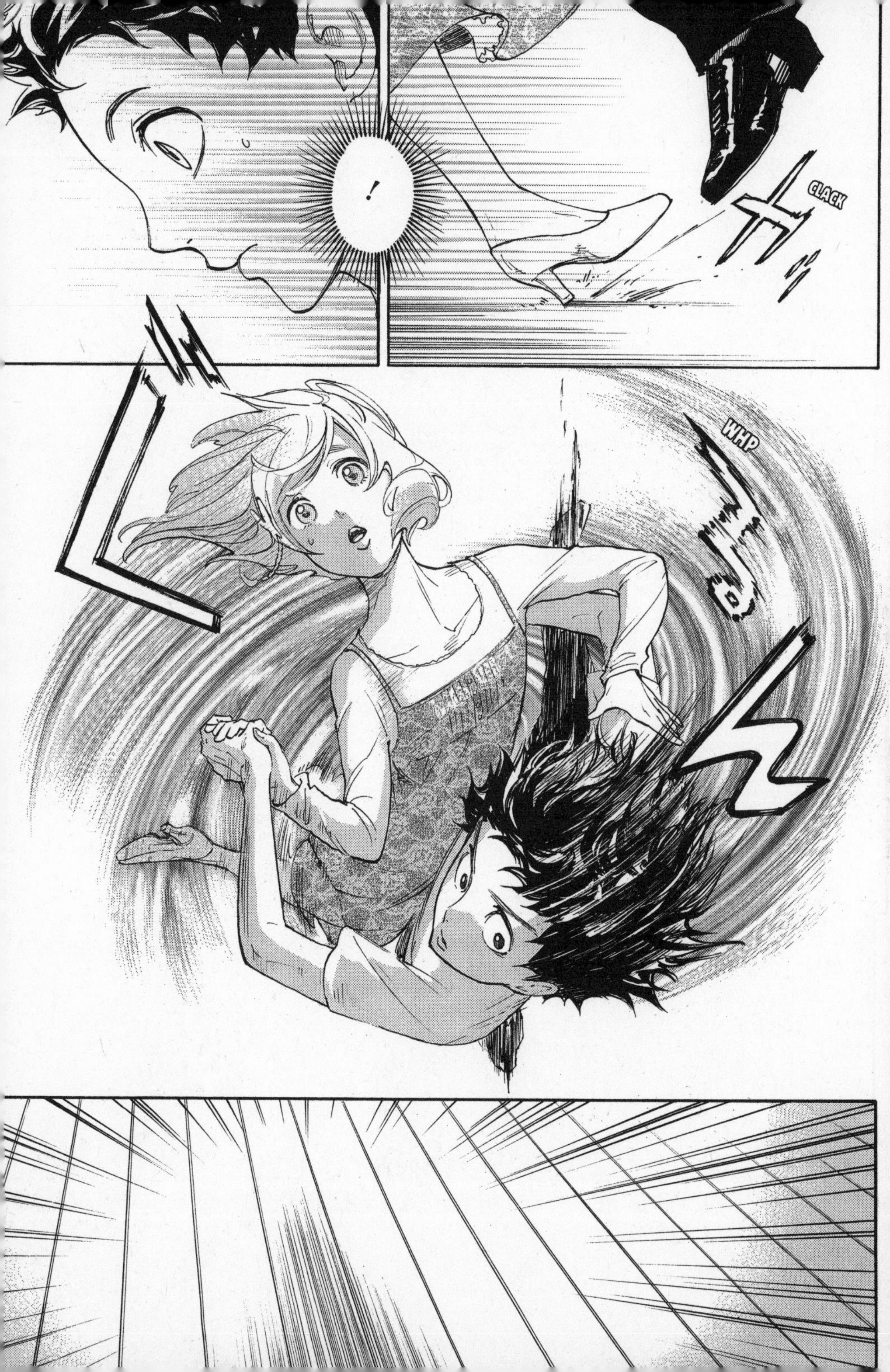
CLACK
!
WHP

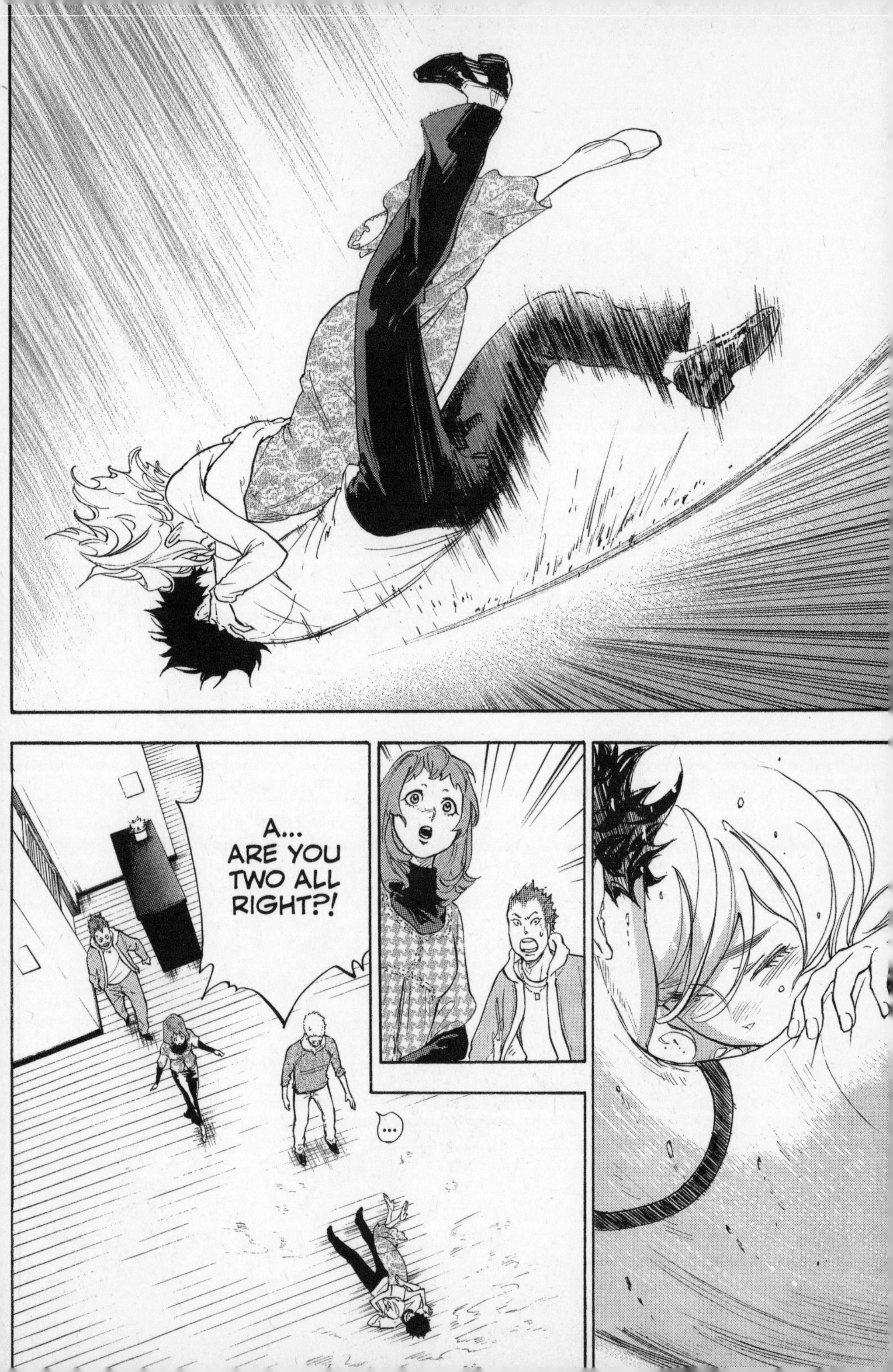
A... ARE YOU TWO ALL RIGHT?!
...

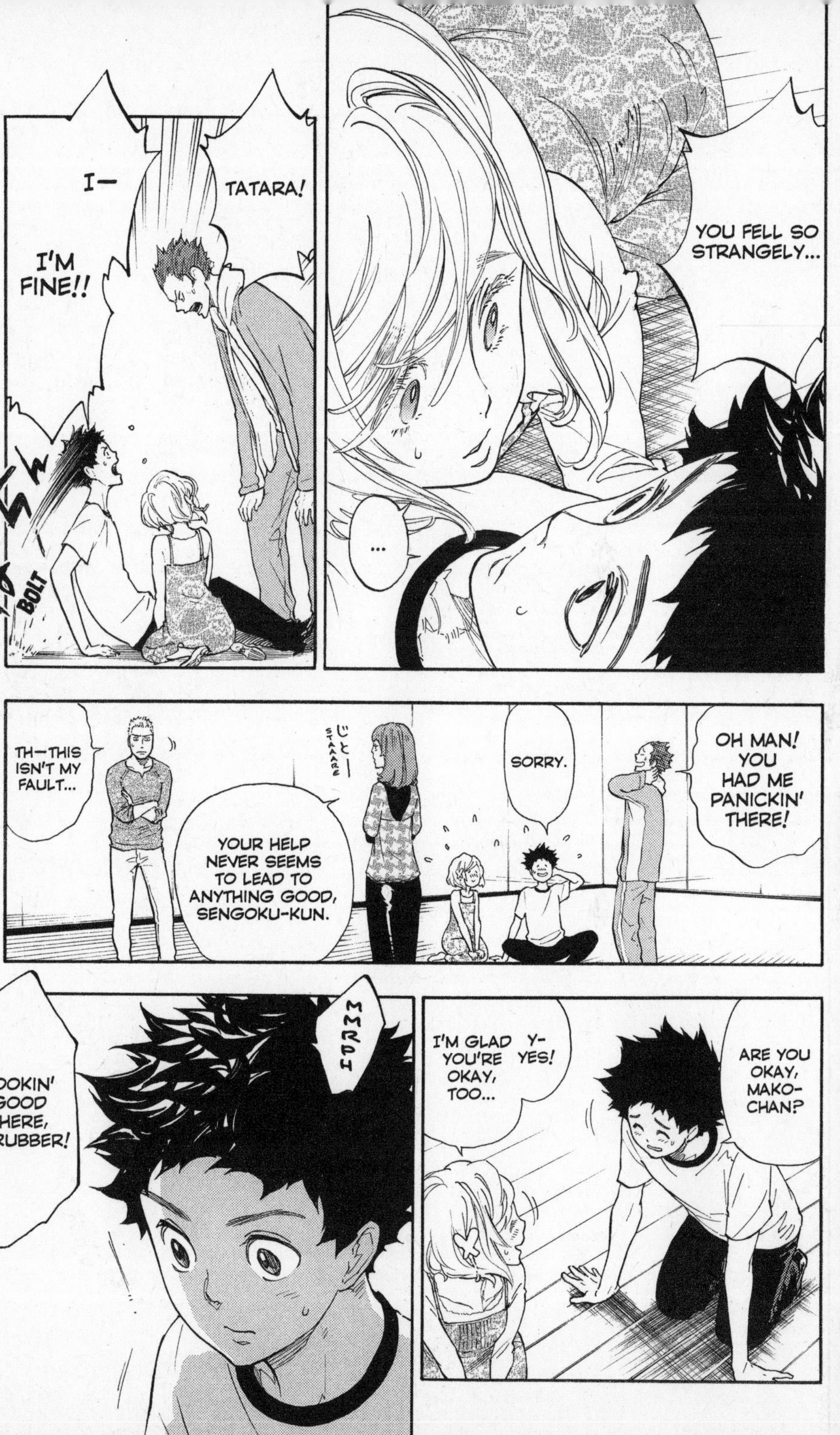
YOU FELL SO STRANGELY...
...
TATARA!
I—
I'M FINE!!
BOLT
OH MAN! YOU HAD ME PANICKIN' THERE!
SORRY.
STAARE
YOUR HELP NEVER SEEMS TO LEAD TO ANYTHING GOOD, SENGOKU-KUN.
TH—THIS ISN'T MY FAULT...
ARE YOU OKAY, MAKO-CHAN?
Y-YES!
I'M GLAD YOU'RE OKAY, TOO...
MMRPH
LOOKIN' GOOD THERE, SCRUBBER!

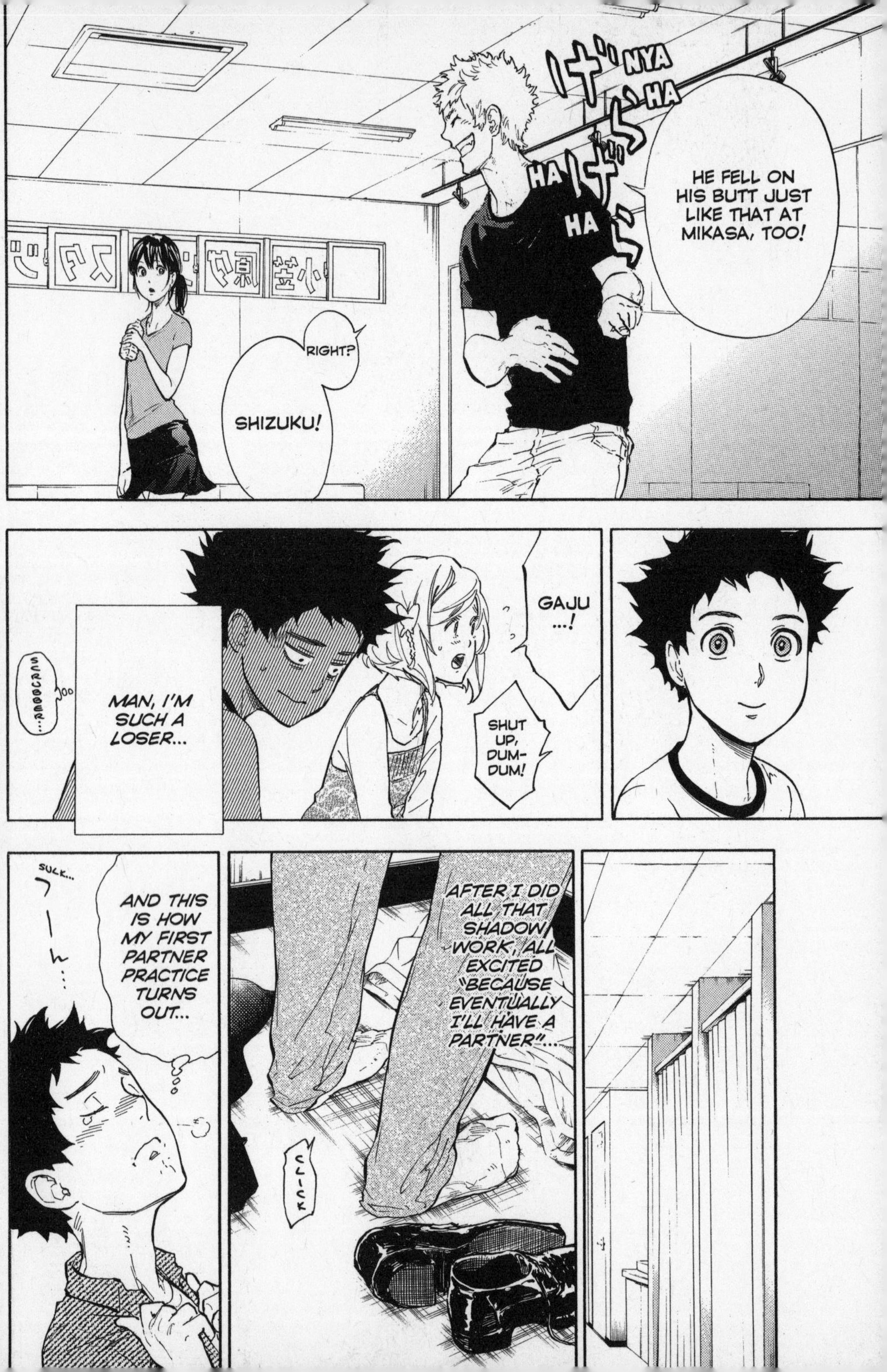
HE FELL ON HIS BUTT JUST LIKE THAT AT MIKASA, TOO!
NYA HA HA HA
RIGHT?
SHIZUKU!
GAJU ...!
SHUT UP, DUM-DUM!
MAN, I'M SUCH A LOSER...
SCRUBBER...
AFTER I DID ALL THAT SHADOW WORK, ALL EXCITED "BECAUSE EVENTUALLY I'LL HAVE A PARTNER"...
CLICK
AND THIS IS HOW MY FIRST PARTNER PRACTICE TURNS OUT...
SULK...

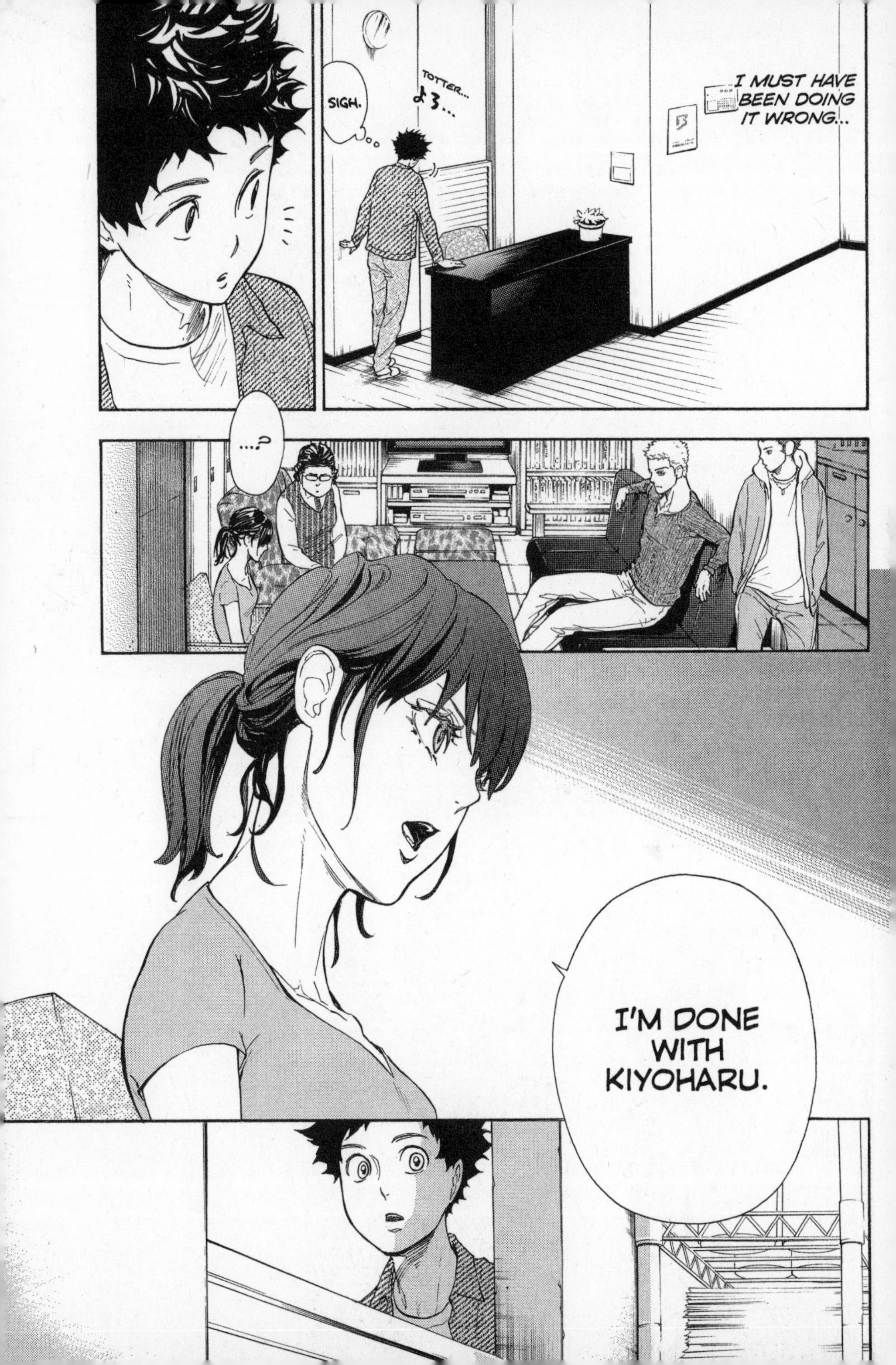
I MUST HAVE BEEN DOING IT WRONG...
TOTTER... よろ...
SIGH.
...?
I'M DONE WITH KIYOHARU.

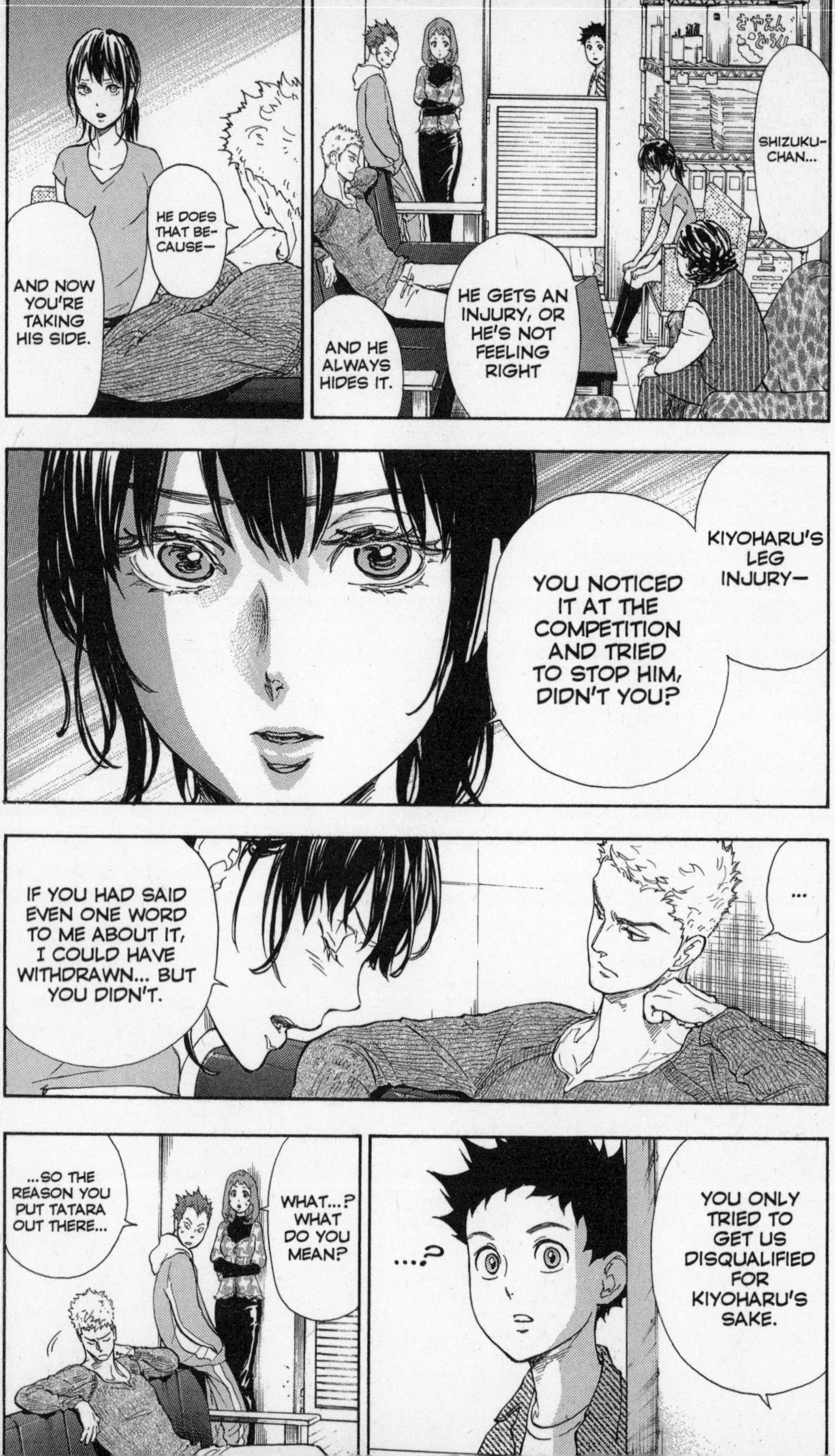
SHIZUKU-CHAN...
HE GETS AN INJURY, OR HE'S NOT FEELING RIGHT
AND HE ALWAYS HIDES IT.
HE DOES THAT BE-CAUSE—
AND NOW YOU'RE TAKING HIS SIDE.
KIYOHARU'S LEG INJURY—
YOU NOTICED IT AT THE COMPETITION AND TRIED TO STOP HIM, DIDN'T YOU?
...
IF YOU HAD SAID EVEN ONE WORD TO ME ABOUT IT, I COULD HAVE WITHDRAWN... BUT YOU DIDN'T.
YOU ONLY TRIED TO GET US DISQUALIFIED FOR KIYOHARU'S SAKE.
...?
WHAT...? WHAT DO YOU MEAN?
...SO THE REASON YOU PUT TATARA OUT THERE...

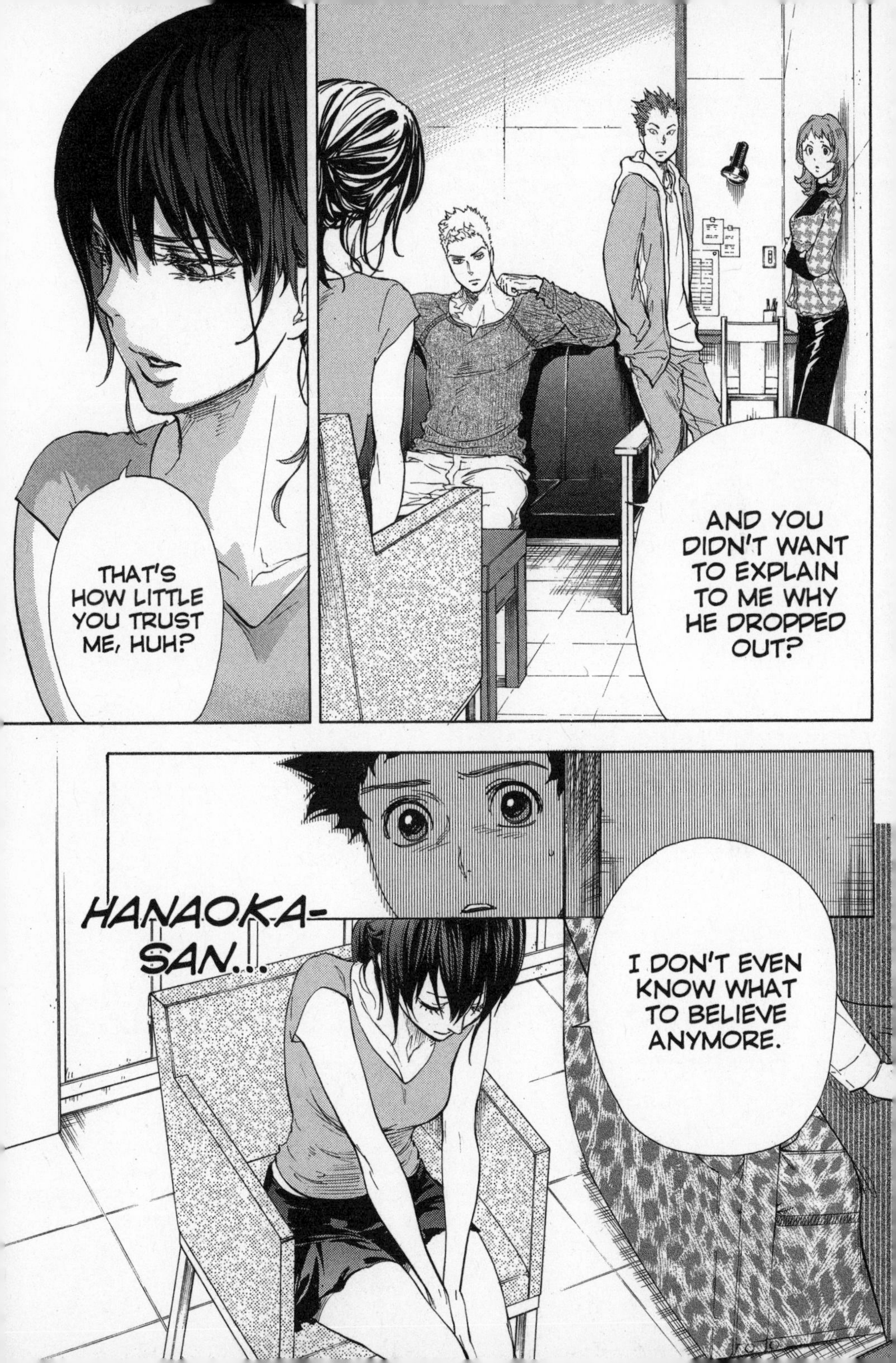
AND YOU DIDN'T WANT TO EXPLAIN TO ME WHY HE DROPPED OUT?
THAT'S HOW LITTLE YOU TRUST ME, HUH?
I DON'T EVEN KNOW WHAT TO BELIEVE ANYMORE.
HANAOKA-SAN...

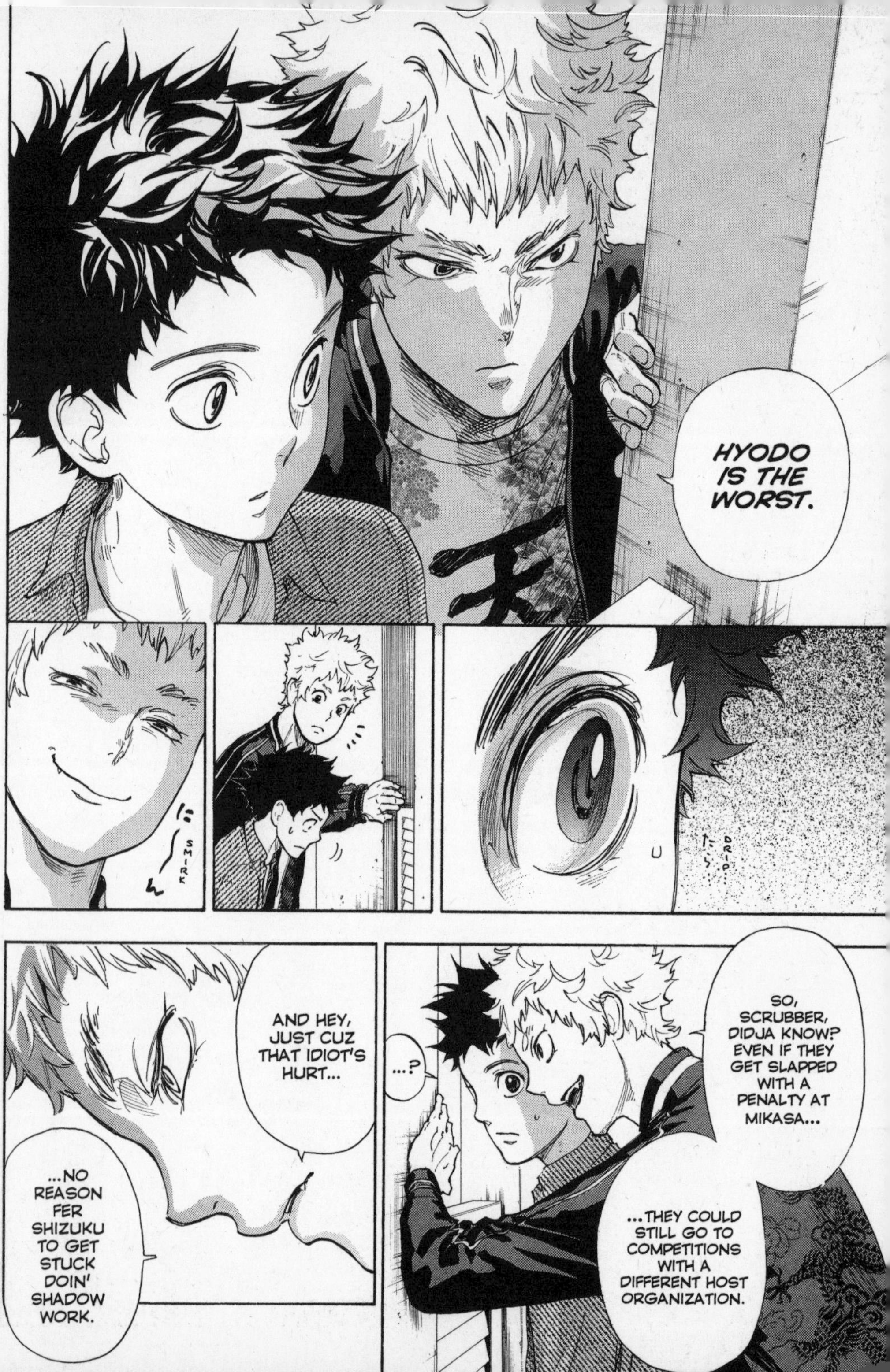
HYODO IS THE WORST.
DRIP...
SMIRK
SO, SCRUBBER, DIDJA KNOW? EVEN IF THEY GET SLAPPED WITH A PENALTY AT MIKASA...
...?
...THEY COULD STILL GO TO COMPETITIONS WITH A DIFFERENT HOST ORGANIZATION.
AND HEY, JUST CUZ THAT IDIOT'S HURT...
...NO REASON FER SHIZUKU TO GET STUCK DOIN' SHADOW WORK.

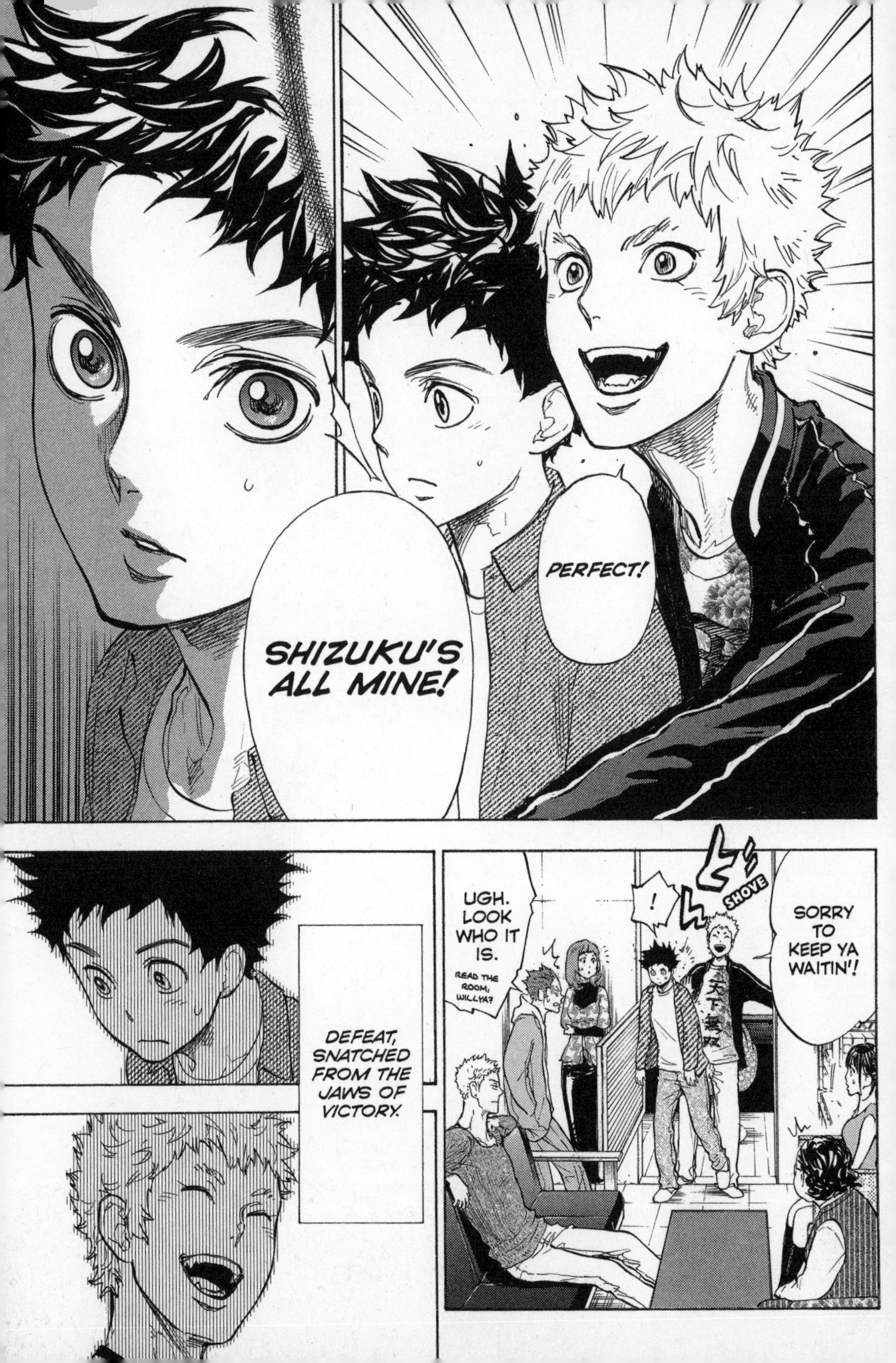
PERFECT!
SHIZUKU'S ALL MINE!
SHOVE
SORRY TO KEEP YA WAITIN'!
!
UGH. LOOK WHO IT IS.
READ THE ROOM, WILLYA?
DEFEAT, SNATCHED FROM THE JAWS OF VICTORY.

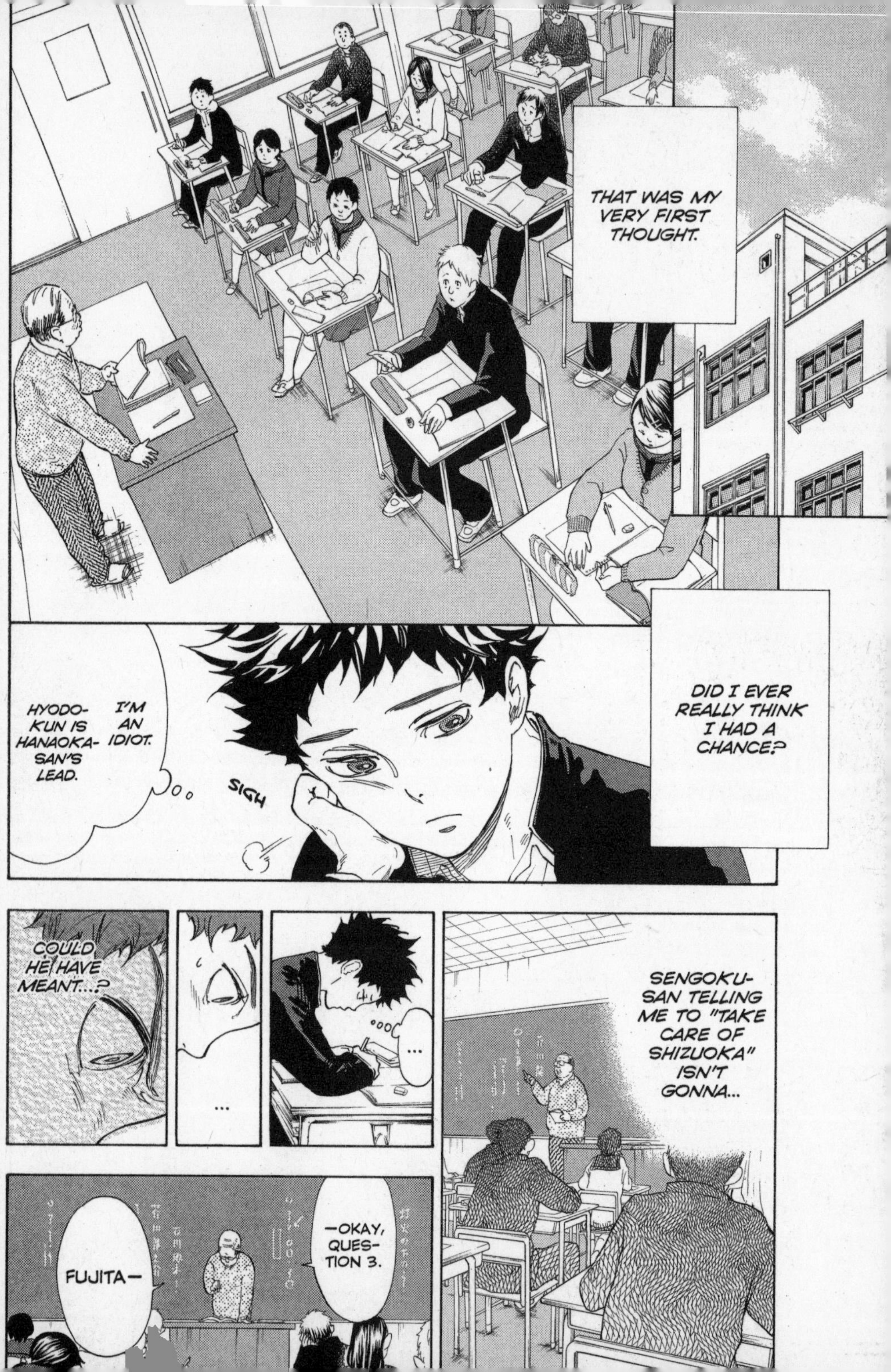
THAT WAS MY VERY FIRST THOUGHT.
DID I EVER REALLY THINK I HAD A CHANCE?
I'M AN IDIOT.
HYODO-KUN IS HANAOKA-SAN'S LEAD.
SIGH
SENGOKU-SAN TELLING ME TO "TAKE CARE OF SHIZUOKA" ISN'T GONNA...
...
...
COULD HE HAVE MEANT...?
—OKAY, QUESTION 3.
FUJITA—

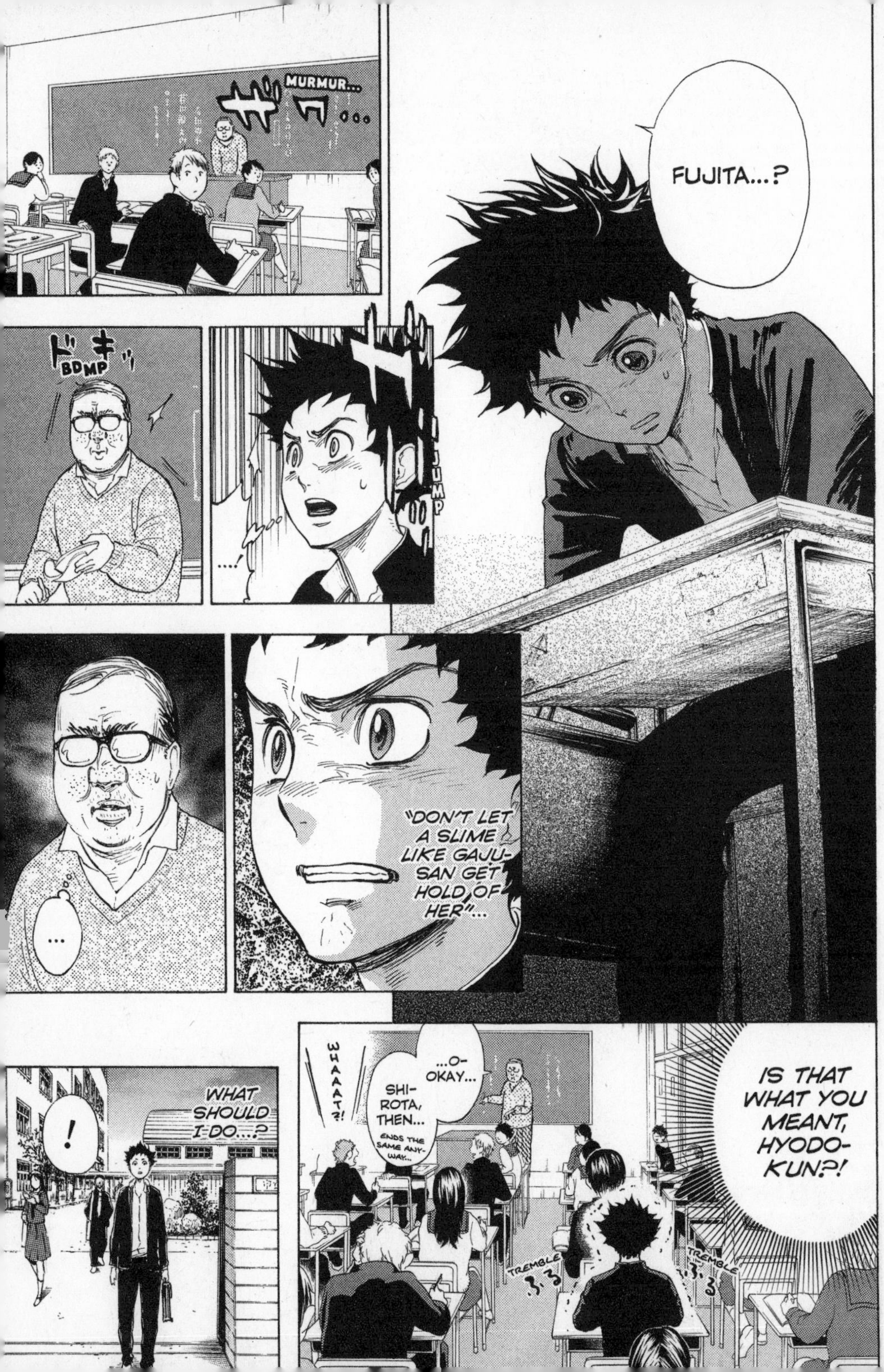
FUJITA...?
MURMUR...
ザワ…
JUMP
...!
BDMP
ドキッ
"DON'T LET A SLIME LIKE GAJU-SAN GET HOLD OF HER"...
...
IS THAT WHAT YOU MEANT, HYODO-KUN?!
...O-OKAY...
SHI-ROTA, THEN...
ENDS THE SAME ANY-WAY...
WHAAAAT?!
TREMBLE
TREMBLE
WHAT SHOULD I DO...?
!

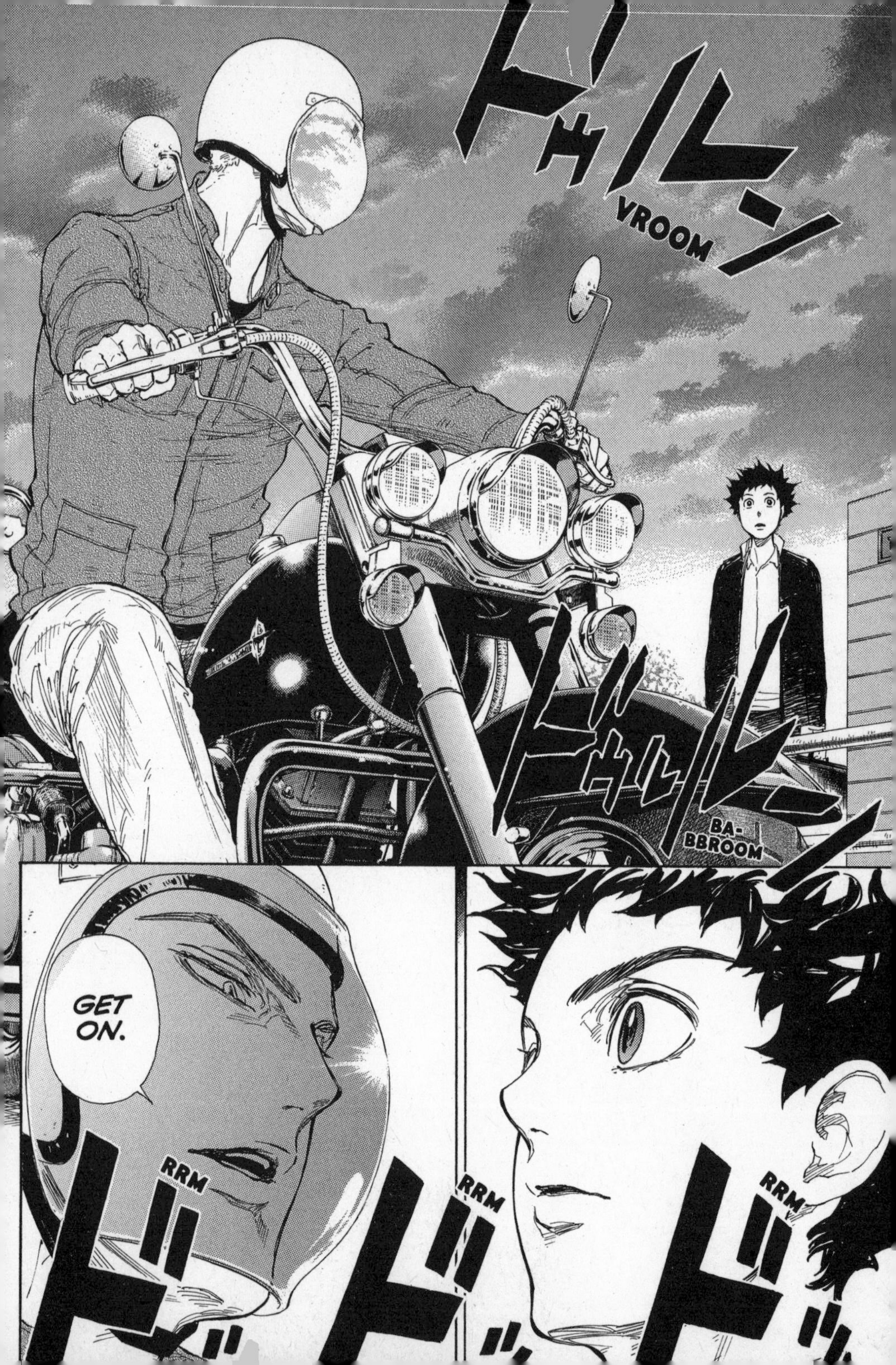

VROOM
BA-BBROOM
RRM
RRM
GET ON.
RRM

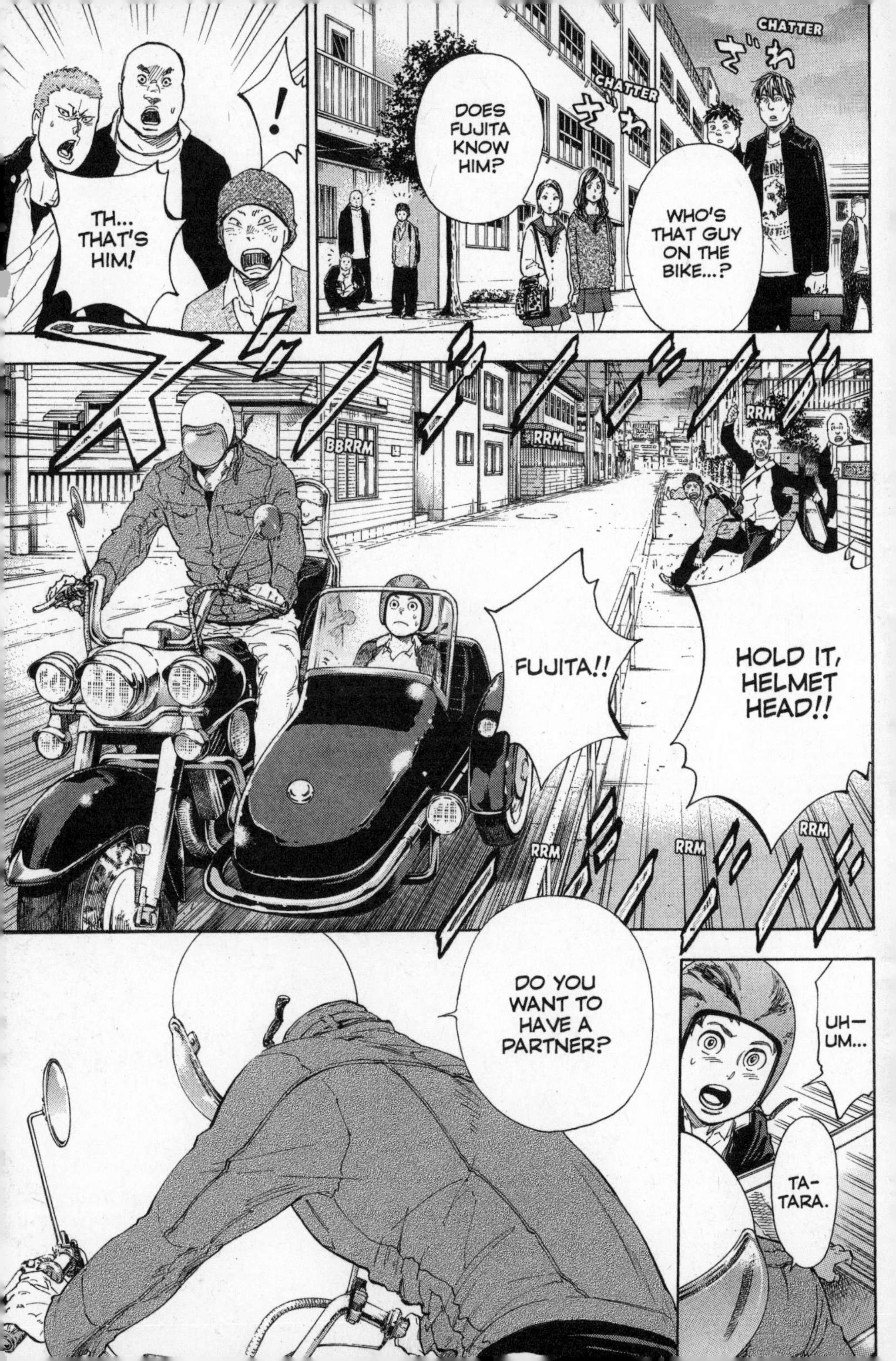
CHATTER
ざわ
CHATTER
ざわ
WHO'S THAT GUY ON THE BIKE...?
DOES FUJITA KNOW HIM?
!
TH... THAT'S HIM!
RRM
RRM
BBRRRM
HOLD IT, HELMET HEAD!!
FUJITA!!
RRM
RRM
RRM
UH— UM...
TA-TARA.
DO YOU WANT TO HAVE A PARTNER?

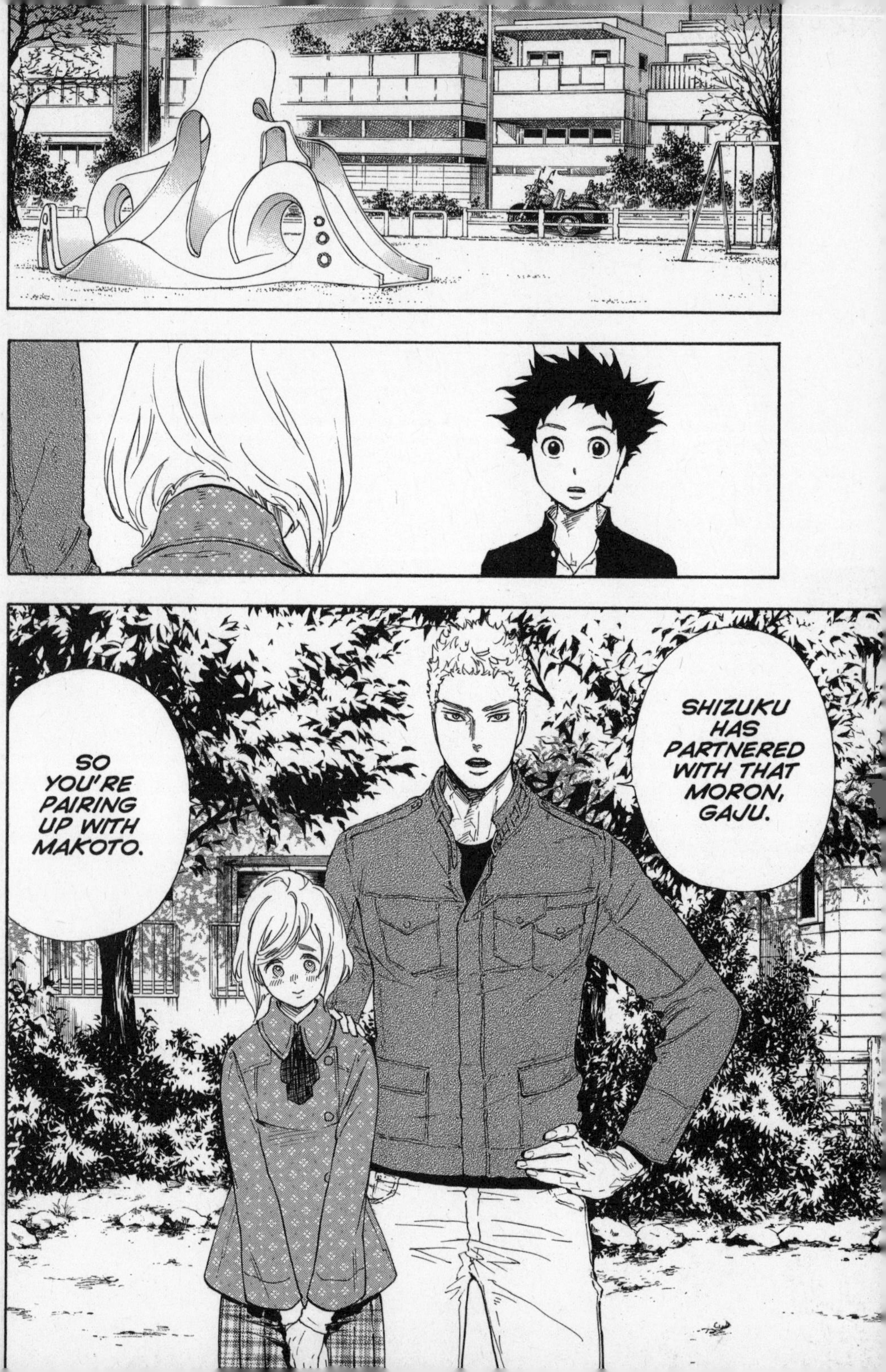
SHIZUKU HAS PARTNERED WITH THAT MORON, GAJU.
SO YOU'RE PAIRING UP WITH MAKOTO.

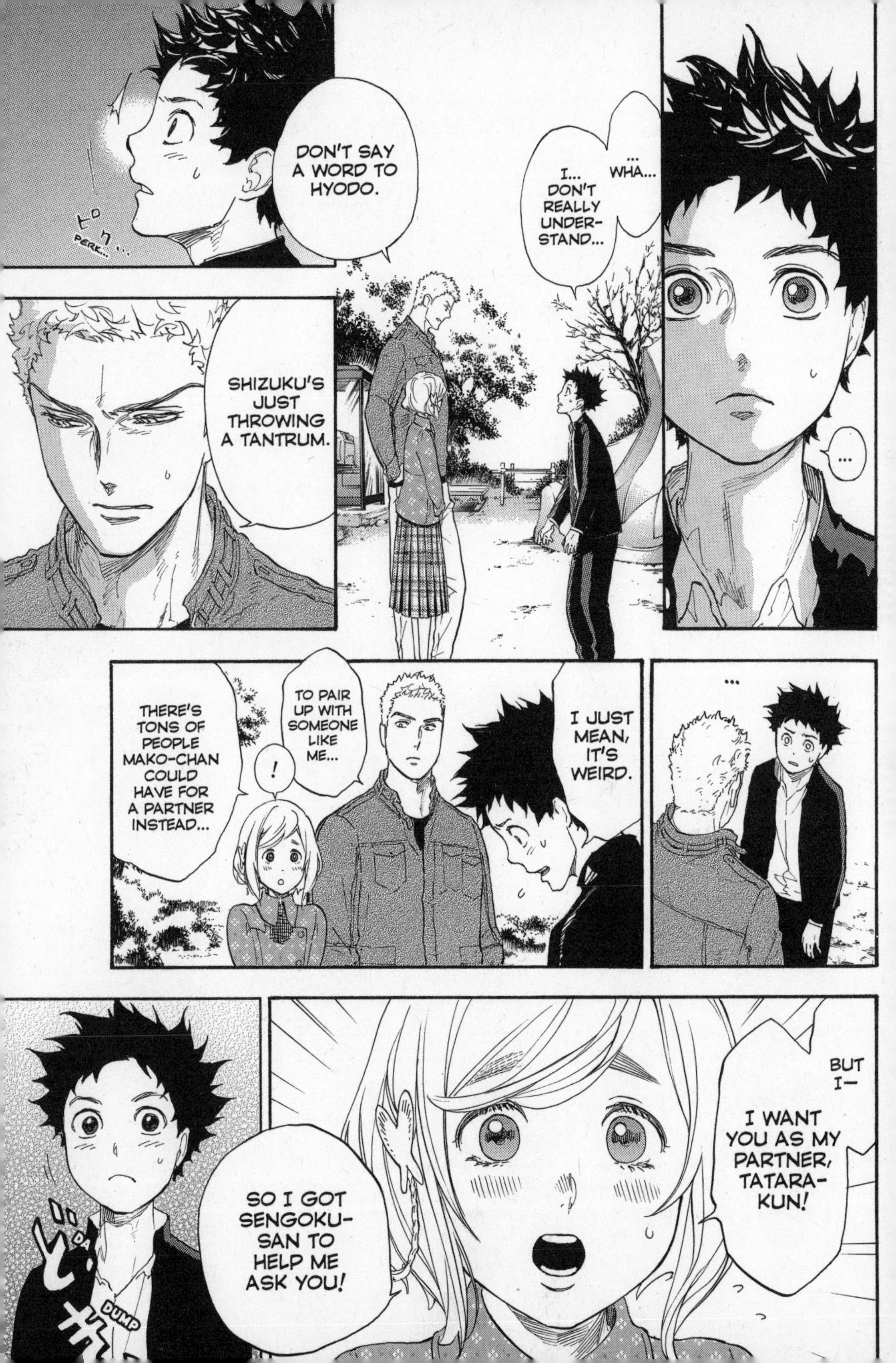

... WHA...
I... DON'T REALLY UNDERSTAND...
DON'T SAY A WORD TO HYODO.
PERK...
SHIZUKU'S JUST THROWING A TANTRUM.
...
...
I JUST MEAN, IT'S WEIRD.
TO PAIR UP WITH SOMEONE LIKE ME...
!
THERE'S TONS OF PEOPLE MAKO-CHAN COULD HAVE FOR A PARTNER INSTEAD...
BUT I—
I WANT YOU AS MY PARTNER, TATARA-KUN!
SO I GOT SENGOKU-SAN TO HELP ME ASK YOU!
DA
DUMP

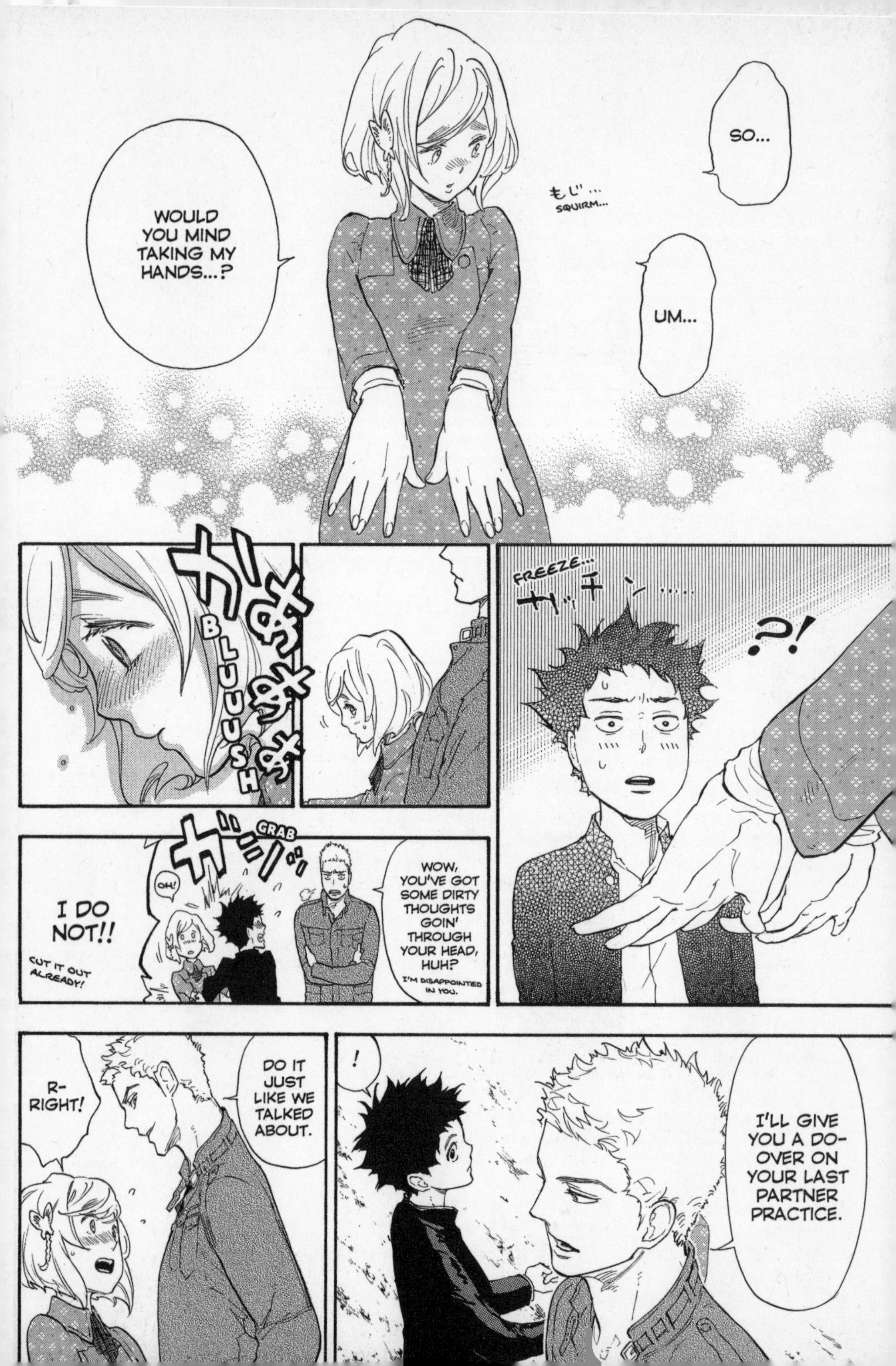
SO...
もじ… SQUIRM...
UM...
WOULD YOU MIND TAKING MY HANDS...?
FREEZE...
ガッチーン.....
?!
かあああ
BLUUUSH
GRAB
ガバッ
WOW, YOU'VE GOT SOME DIRTY THOUGHTS GOIN' THROUGH YOUR HEAD, HUH?
I'M DISAPPOINTED IN YOU.
OH!
I DO NOT!!
CUT IT OUT ALREADY!
!
I'LL GIVE YOU A DO-OVER ON YOUR LAST PARTNER PRACTICE.
DO IT JUST LIKE WE TALKED ABOUT.
R-RIGHT!

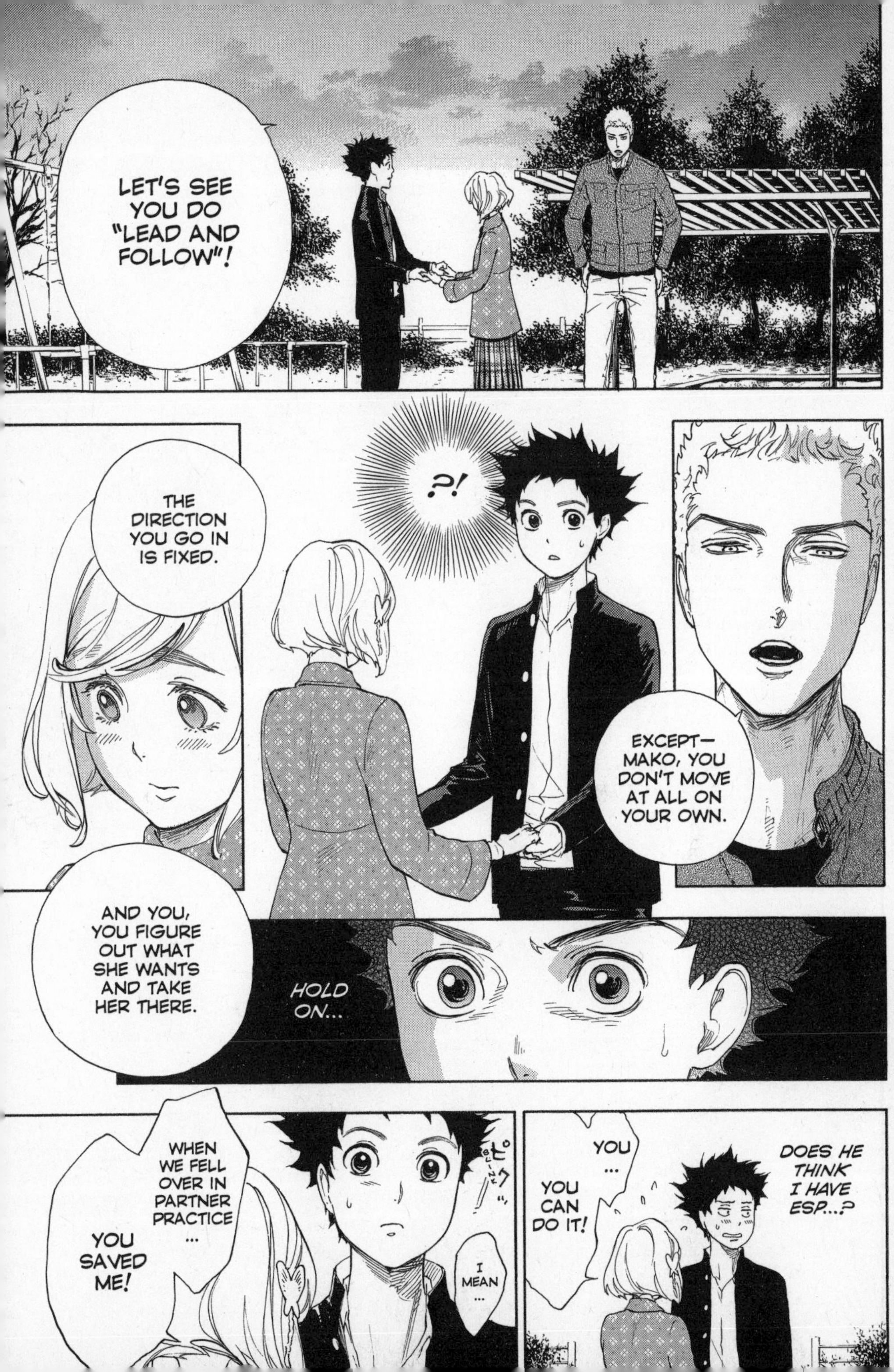
LET'S SEE YOU DO "LEAD AND FOLLOW"!
EXCEPT— MAKO, YOU DON'T MOVE AT ALL ON YOUR OWN.
?!
THE DIRECTION YOU GO IN IS FIXED.
HOLD ON...
AND YOU, YOU FIGURE OUT WHAT SHE WANTS AND TAKE HER THERE.
DOES HE THINK I HAVE ESP...?
YOU ...
YOU CAN DO IT!
BLINK
WHEN WE FELL OVER IN PARTNER PRACTICE ...
I MEAN ...
YOU SAVED ME!

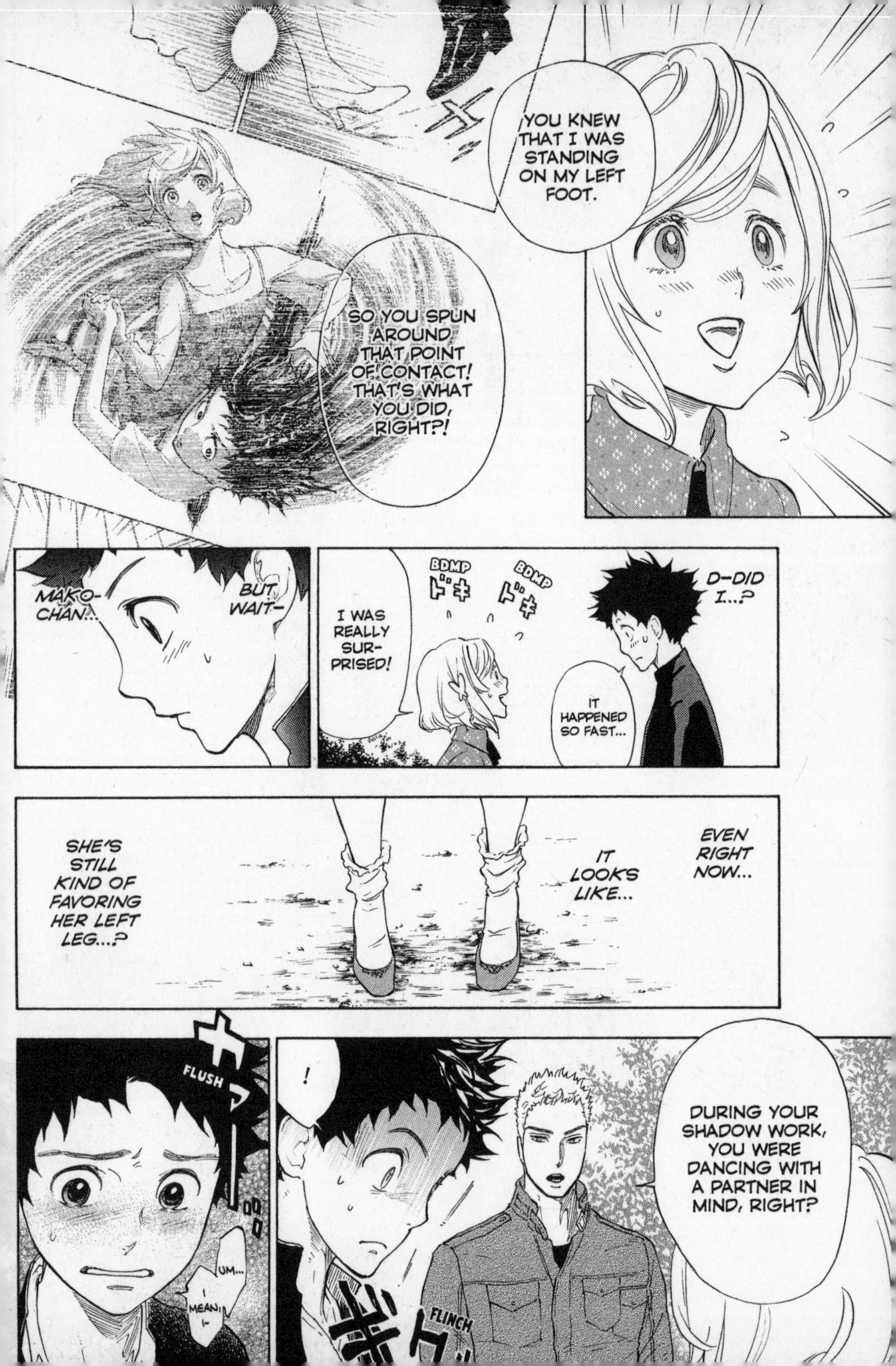
YOU KNEW THAT I WAS STANDING ON MY LEFT FOOT.
SO YOU SPUN AROUND THAT POINT OF CONTACT! THAT'S WHAT YOU DID, RIGHT?!
D-DID I...?
BDMP
BDMP
I WAS REALLY SUR-PRISED!
IT HAPPENED SO FAST...
BUT WAIT-
MAKO-CHAN...
EVEN RIGHT NOW...
IT LOOKS LIKE...
SHE'S STILL KIND OF FAVORING HER LEFT LEG...?
DURING YOUR SHADOW WORK, YOU WERE DANCING WITH A PARTNER IN MIND, RIGHT?
!
FLINCH
FLUSH
UM...
I MEAN I-

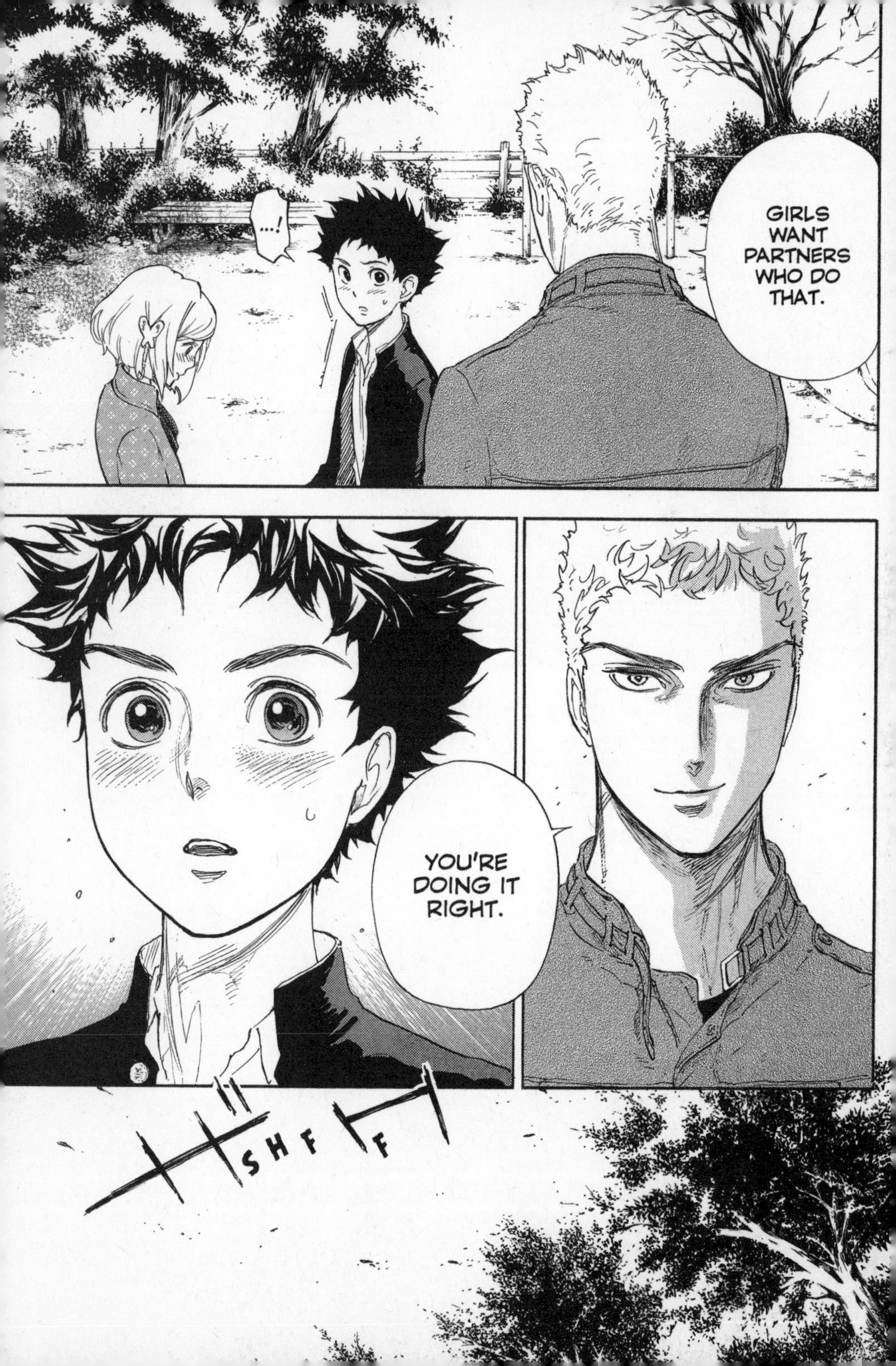
GIRLS WANT PARTNERS WHO DO THAT.
...!
YOU'RE DOING IT RIGHT.
SHFF

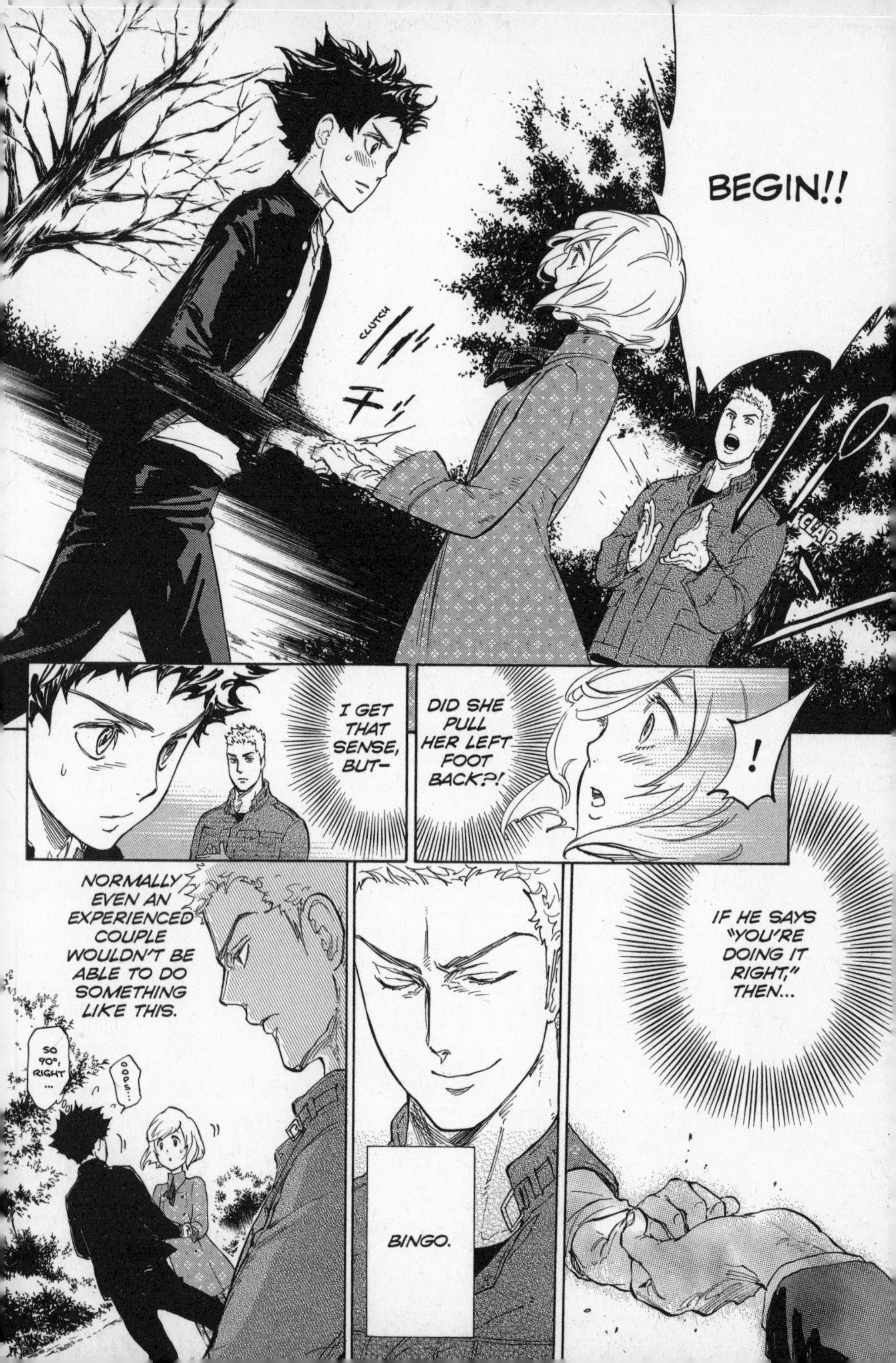
BEGIN!!
CLAP
CLUTCH
DID SHE PULL HER LEFT FOOT BACK?!
!
I GET THAT SENSE, BUT-
IF HE SAYS "YOU'RE DOING IT RIGHT," THEN...
BINGO.
NORMALLY EVEN AN EXPERIENCED COUPLE WOULDN'T BE ABLE TO DO SOMETHING LIKE THIS.
SO 90°, RIGHT...
OOPS...

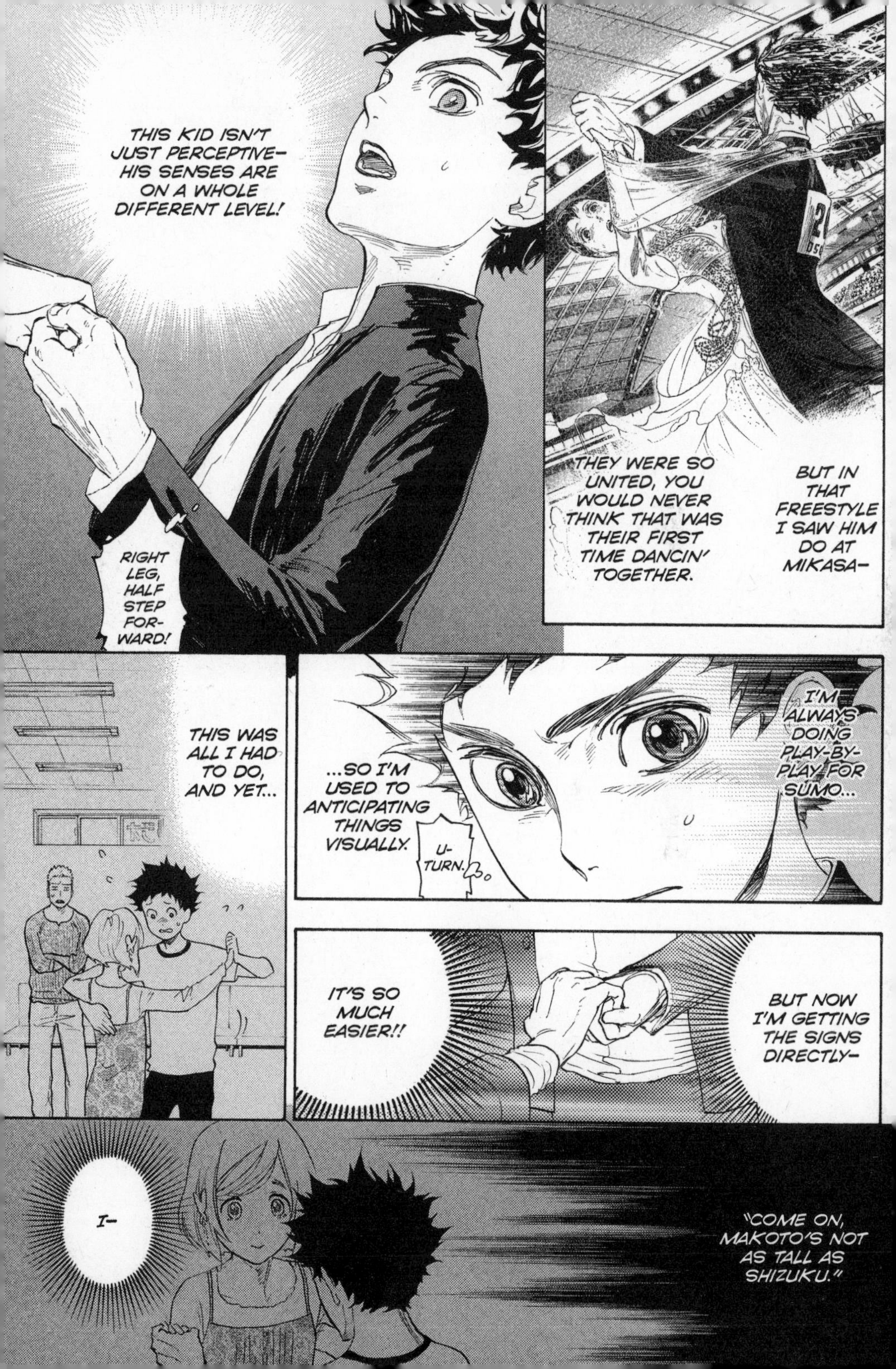

BUT IN THAT FREESTYLE I SAW HIM DO AT MIKASA–
THEY WERE SO UNITED, YOU WOULD NEVER THINK THAT WAS THEIR FIRST TIME DANCIN' TOGETHER.
THIS KID ISN'T JUST PERCEPTIVE– HIS SENSES ARE ON A WHOLE DIFFERENT LEVEL!
RIGHT LEG, HALF STEP FOR-WARD!
I'M ALWAYS DOING PLAY-BY-PLAY FOR SUMO...
...SO I'M USED TO ANTICIPATING THINGS VISUALLY.
U-TURN.
BUT NOW I'M GETTING THE SIGNS DIRECTLY–
IT'S SO MUCH EASIER!!
THIS WAS ALL I HAD TO DO, AND YET...
"COME ON, MAKOTO'S NOT AS TALL AS SHIZUKU."
I–

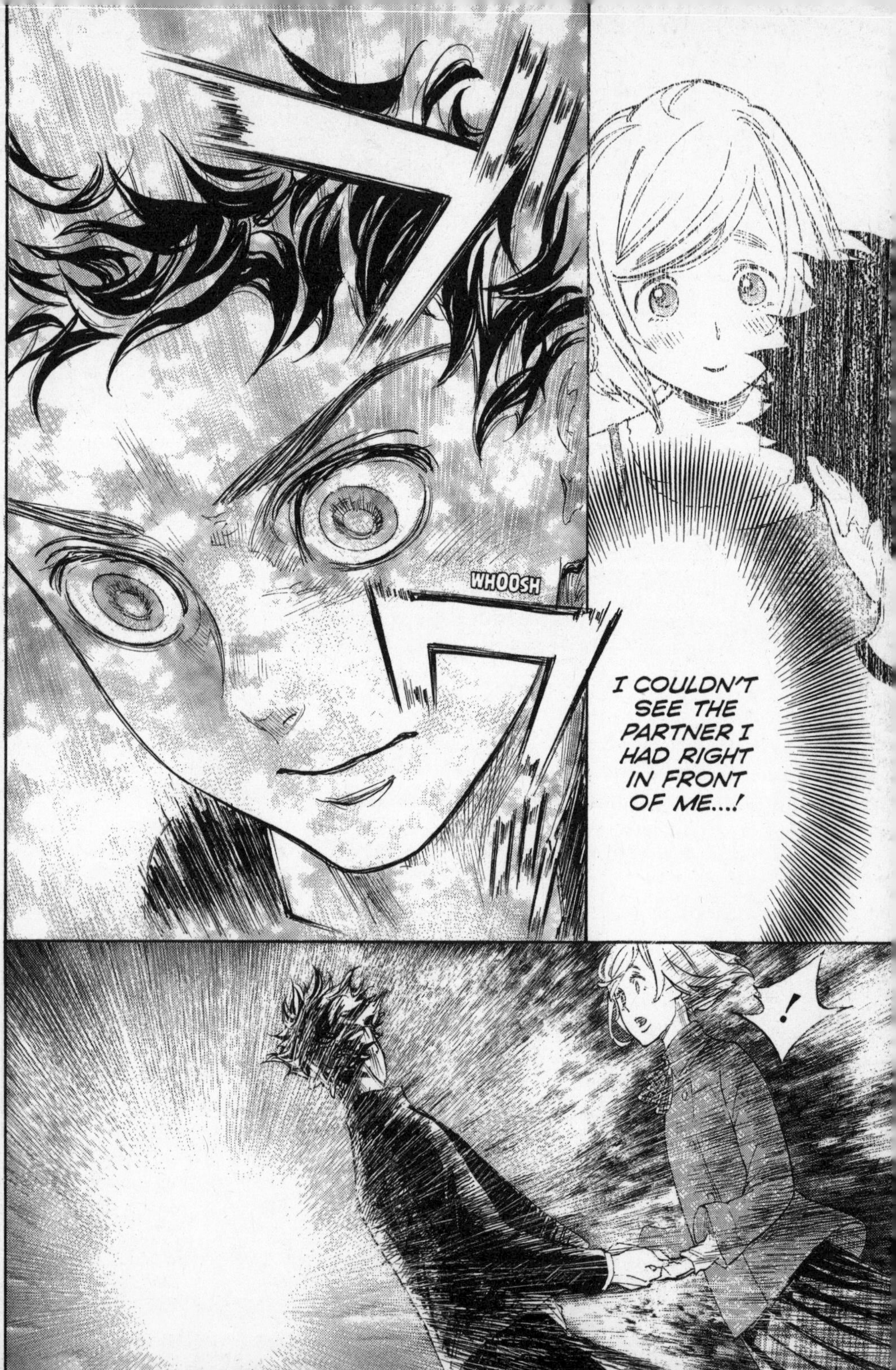
I COULDN'T SEE THE PARTNER I HAD RIGHT IN FRONT OF ME...!
WHOOSH
!

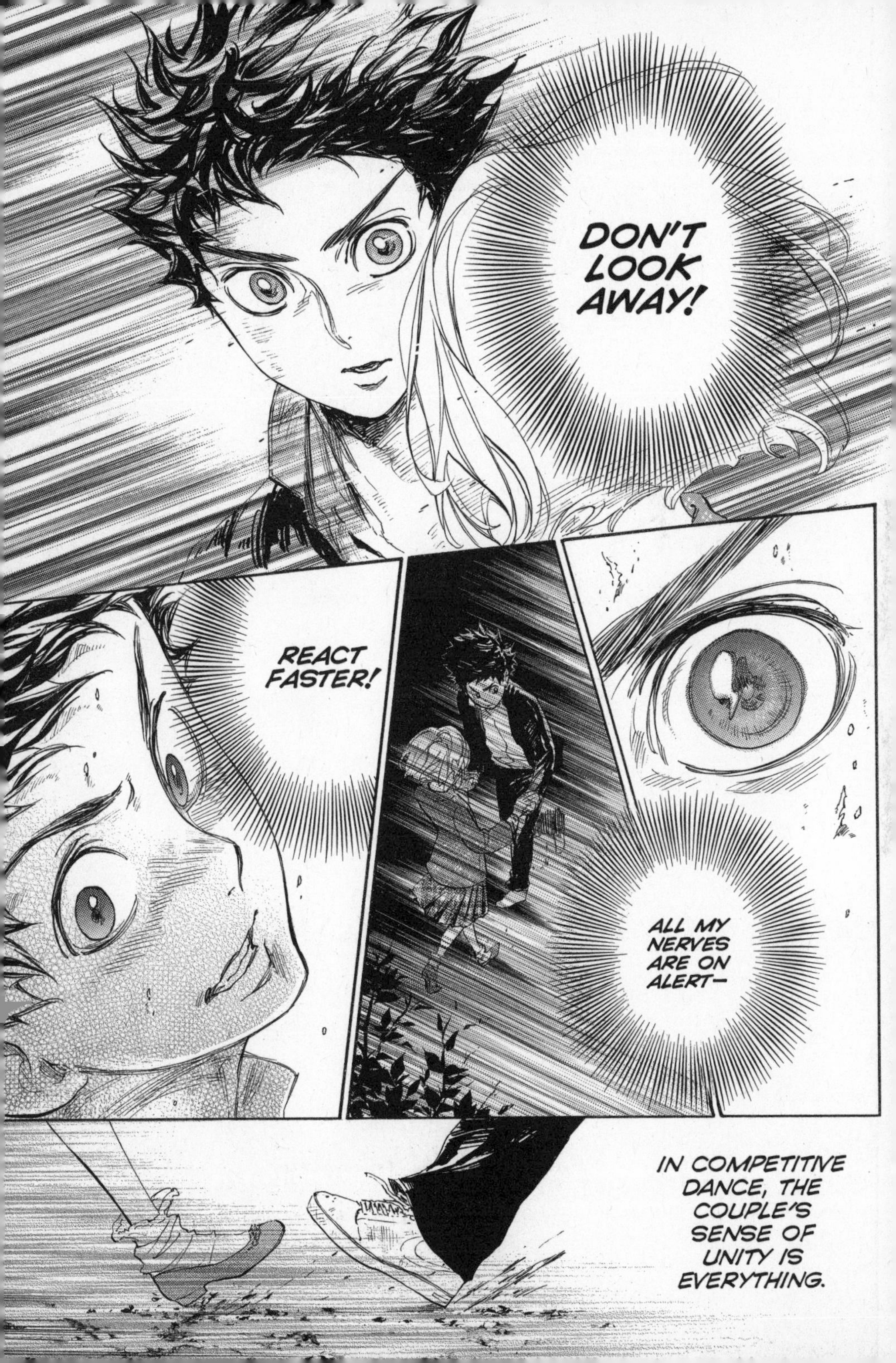
DON'T LOOK AWAY!
ALL MY NERVES ARE ON ALERT—
REACT FASTER!
IN COMPETITIVE DANCE, THE COUPLE'S SENSE OF UNITY IS EVERYTHING.

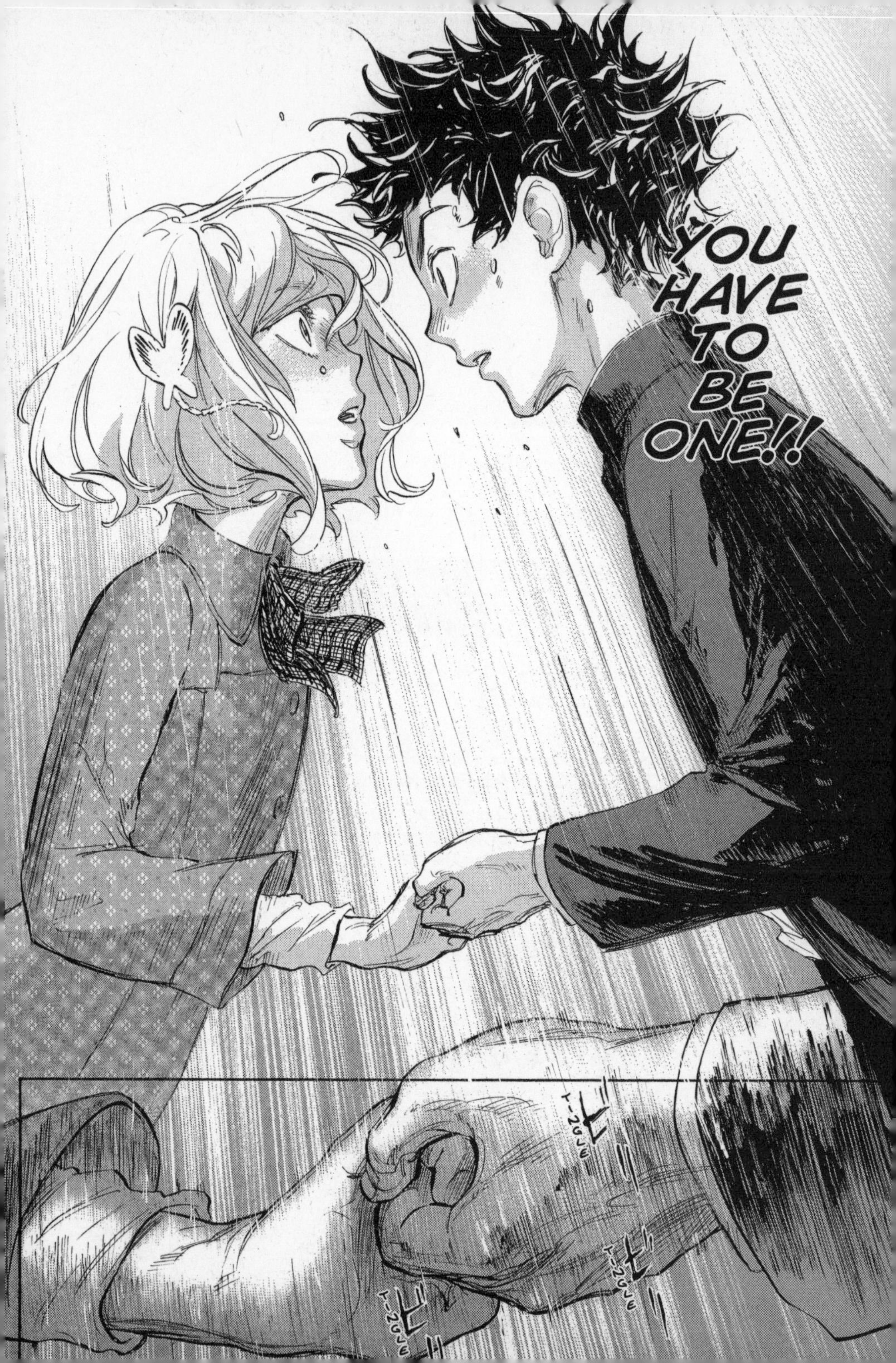
YOU HAVE TO BE ONE!!
TINGLE
TINGLE
TINGLE

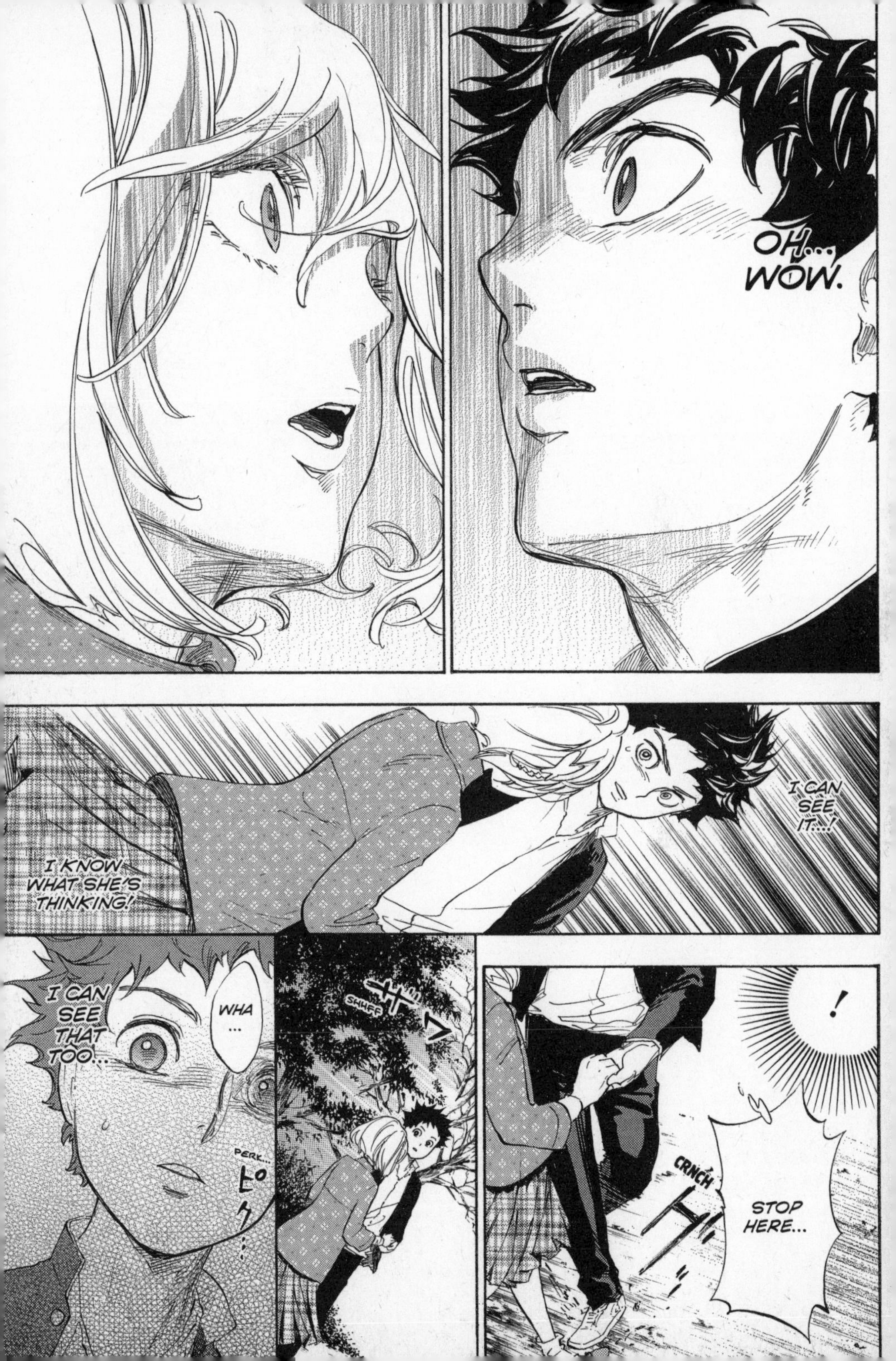
OH... WOW.
I CAN SEE IT...!
I KNOW WHAT SHE'S THINKING!
!
STOP HERE...
CRNCH
SHHFF
I CAN SEE THAT TOO...
WHA ...
PERK...

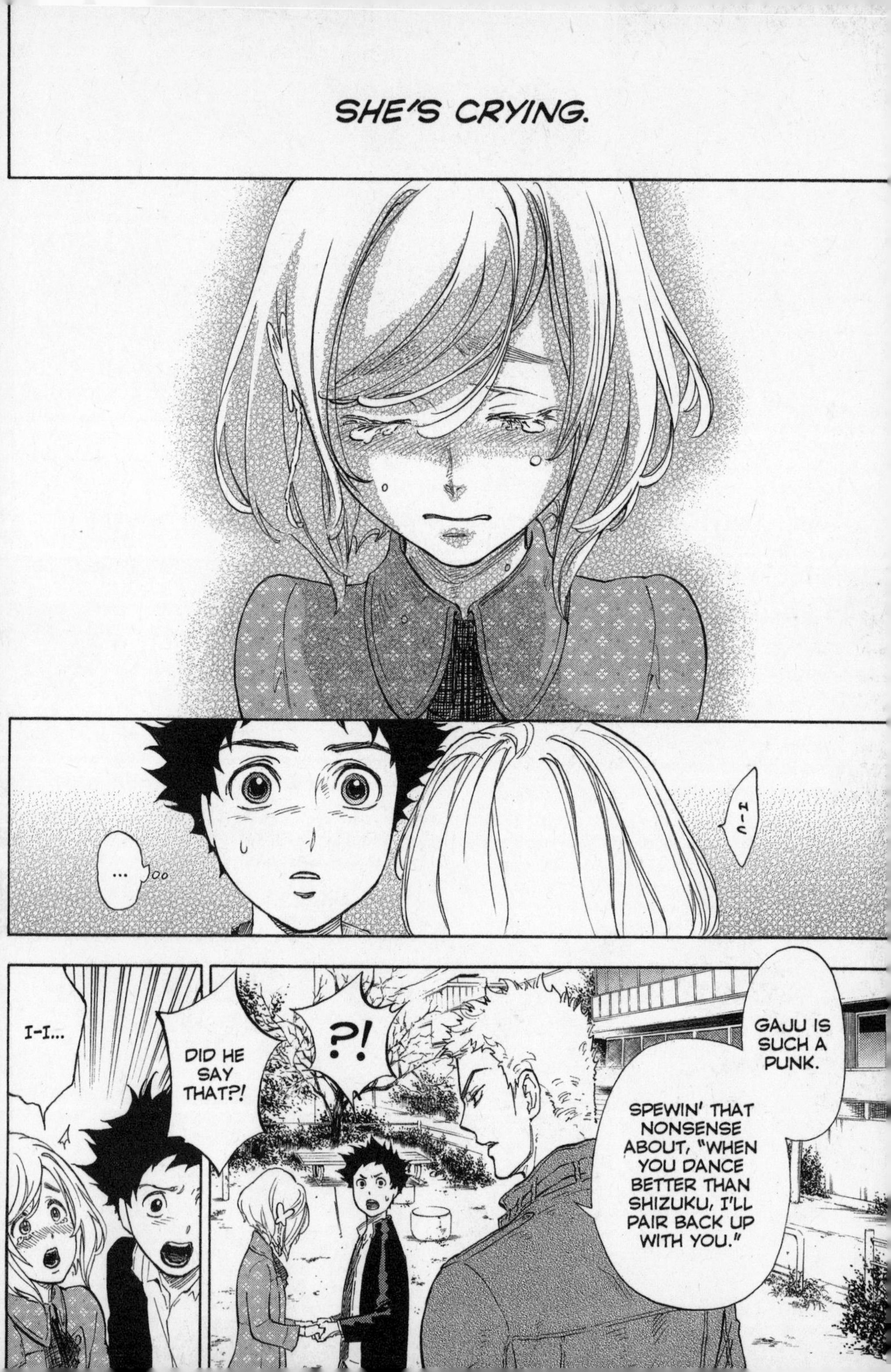
SHE'S CRYING.
...
GAJU IS SUCH A PUNK.
SPEWIN' THAT NONSENSE ABOUT, "WHEN YOU DANCE BETTER THAN SHIZUKU, I'LL PAIR BACK UP WITH YOU."
?!
DID HE SAY THAT?!
I-I...

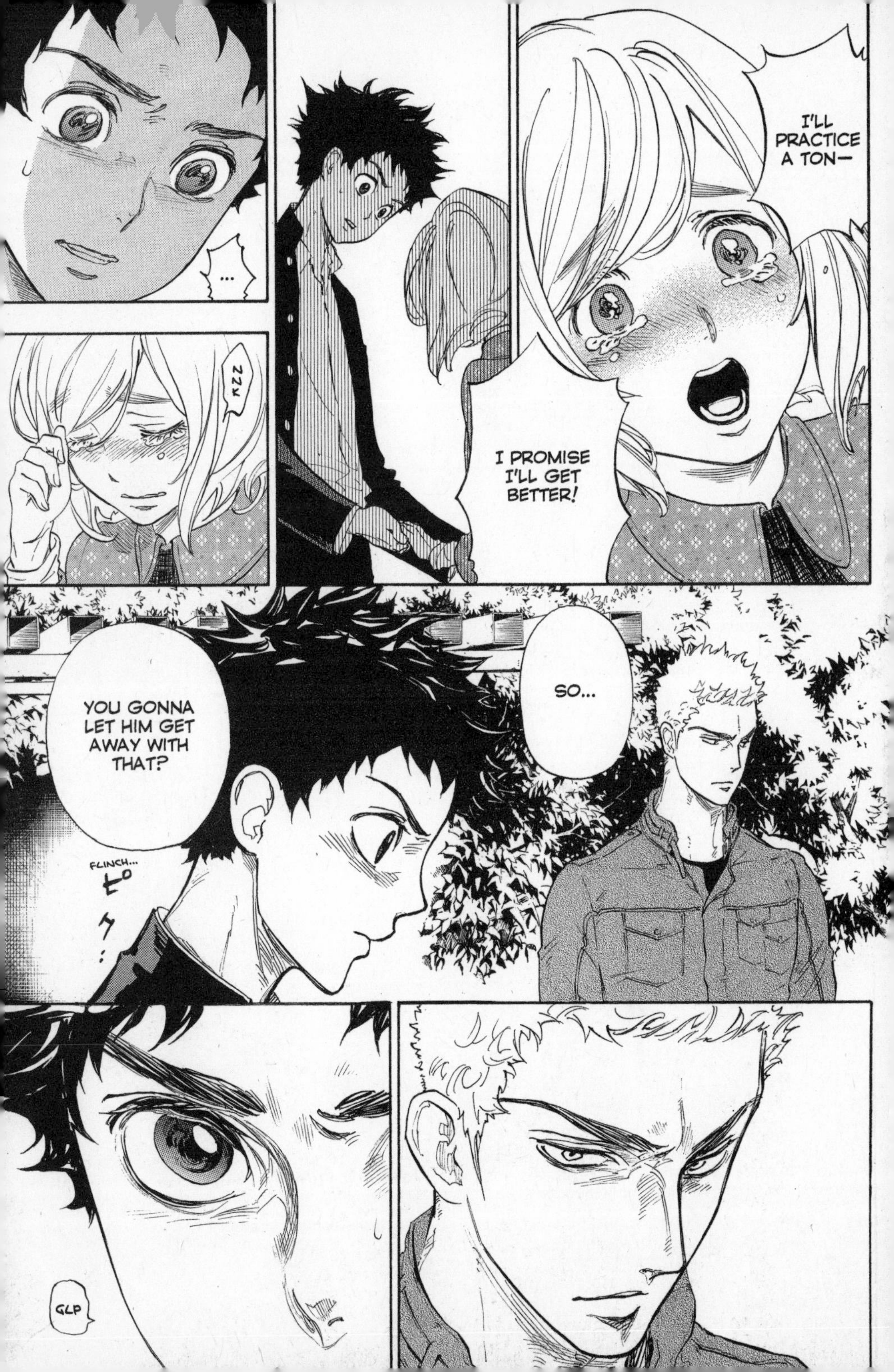
I'LL PRACTICE A TON—
I PROMISE I'LL GET BETTER!
...
ZNK
SO...
YOU GONNA LET HIM GET AWAY WITH THAT?
FLINCH...
GLP

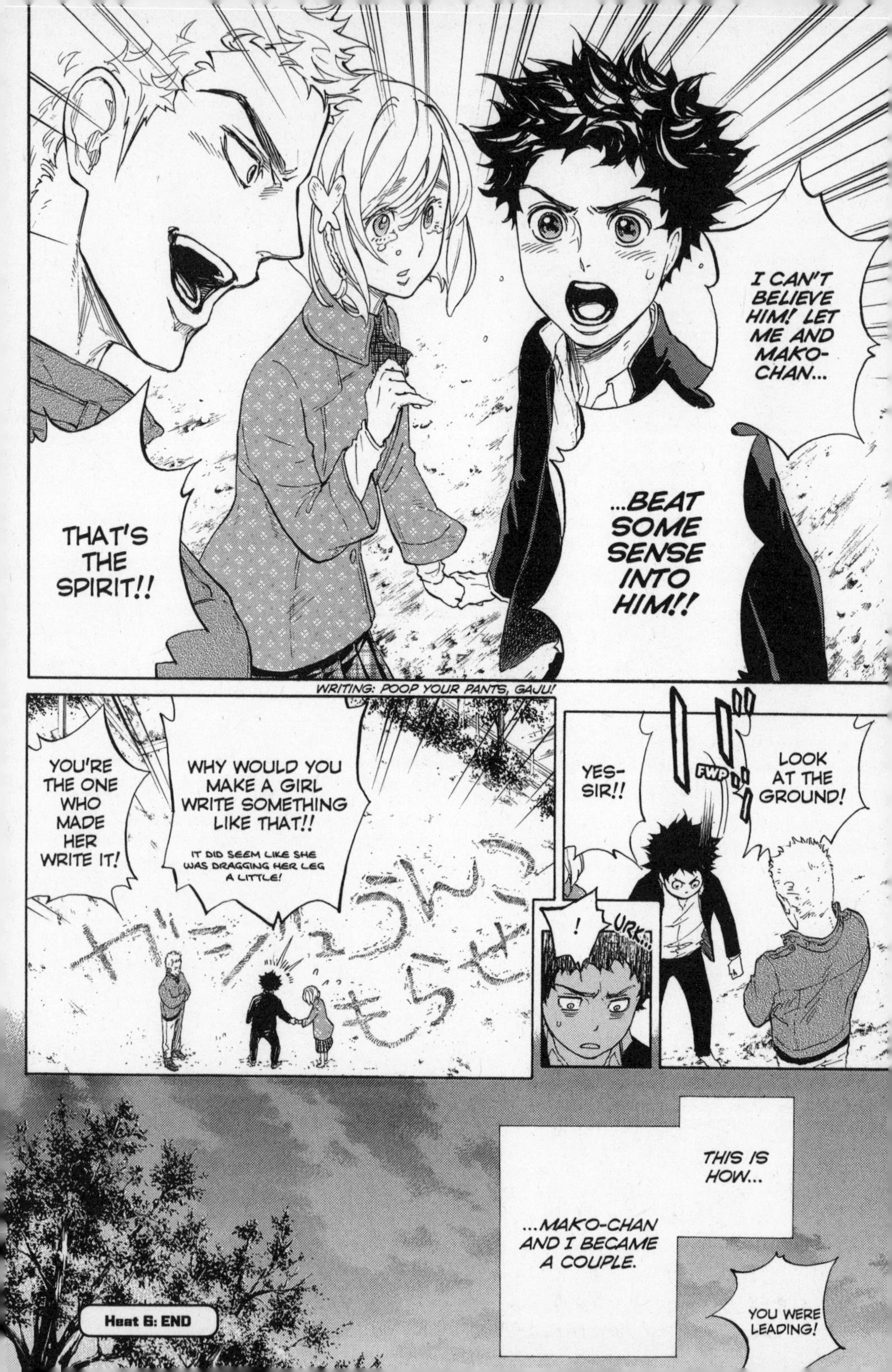
I CAN'T BELIEVE HIM! LET ME AND MAKO-CHAN...
...BEAT SOME SENSE INTO HIM!!
THAT'S THE SPIRIT!!
LOOK AT THE GROUND!
FWP
YES-SIR!!
!
URK!!
WRITING: POOP YOUR PANTS, GAJU!
WHY WOULD YOU MAKE A GIRL WRITE SOMETHING LIKE THAT!!
IT DID SEEM LIKE SHE WAS DRAGGING HER LEG A LITTLE!
YOU'RE THE ONE WHO MADE HER WRITE IT!
THIS IS HOW...
...MAKO-CHAN AND I BECAME A COUPLE.
YOU WERE LEADING!
Heat 6: END

WELCOME TO THE BALLROOM

Special Thanks!

Quickstep choreography asssistance

Mr. Masayuki Ishihara

Ms. Saori Ito

Background Assistance

Fuji Gakuin
(Dance rehearsal facility)

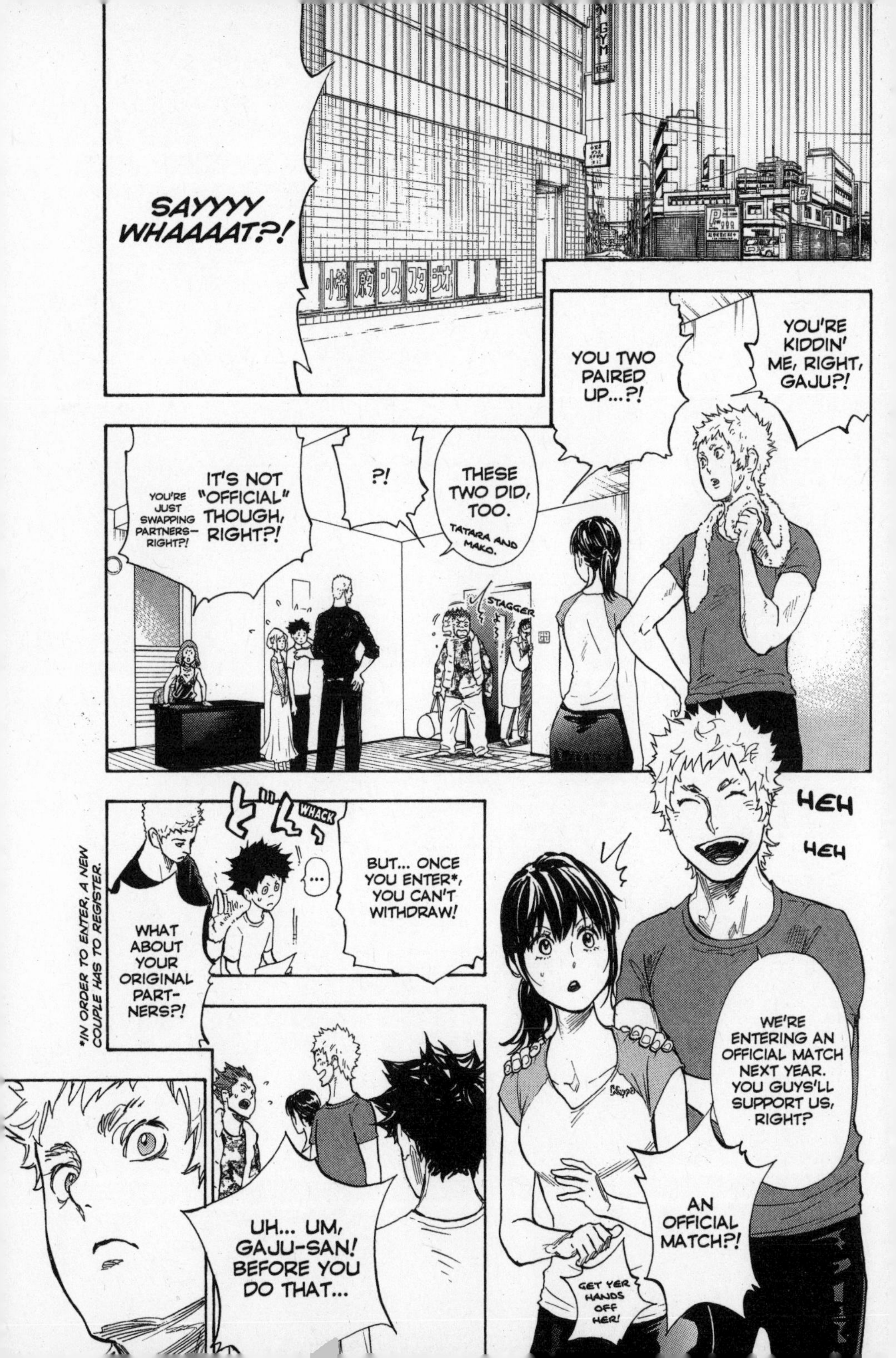
SAYYYY WHAAAAT?!
YOU'RE KIDDIN' ME, RIGHT, GAJU?!
YOU TWO PAIRED UP...?!
THESE TWO DID, TOO.
TATARA AND MAKO.
STAGGER
?!
IT'S NOT "OFFICIAL" THOUGH, RIGHT?!
YOU'RE JUST SWAPPING PARTNERS-RIGHT?!
HEH
HEH
WE'RE ENTERING AN OFFICIAL MATCH NEXT YEAR. YOU GUYS'LL SUPPORT US, RIGHT?
AN OFFICIAL MATCH?!
GET YER HANDS OFF HER!
WHACK
BUT... ONCE YOU ENTER*, YOU CAN'T WITHDRAW!
...
WHAT ABOUT YOUR ORIGINAL PARTNERS?!
UH... UM, GAJU-SAN! BEFORE YOU DO THAT...

*IN ORDER TO ENTER, A NEW COUPLE HAS TO REGISTER.

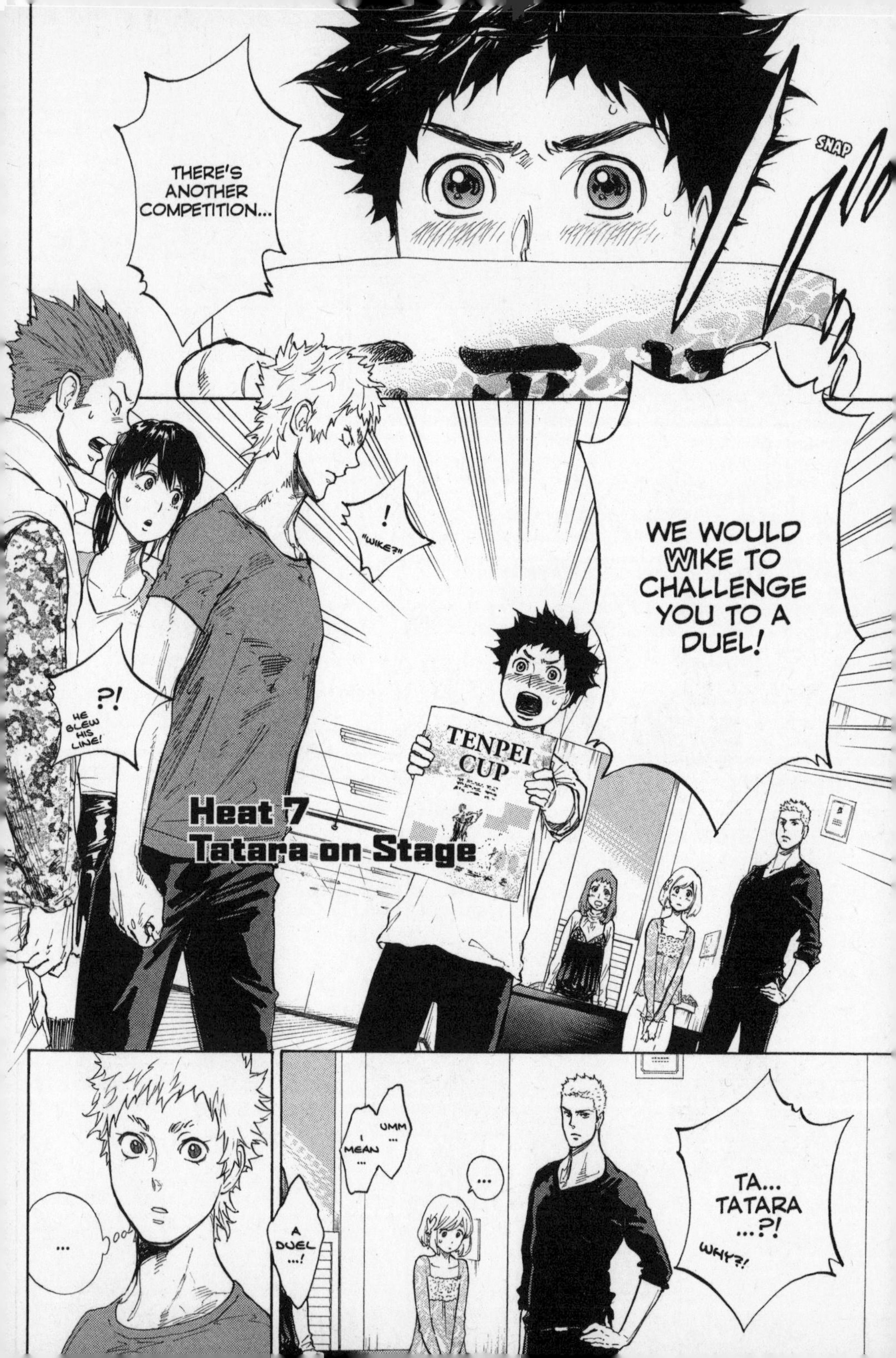
SNAP
THERE'S ANOTHER COMPETITION...
WE WOULD WIKE TO CHALLENGE YOU TO A DUEL!
!
"WIKE?"
TENPEI CUP
?!
HE BLEW HIS LINE!
Heat 7
Tatara on Stage
TA... TATARA ...?!
WHY?!
UMM ...
I MEAN ...
...
A DUEL ...!
...

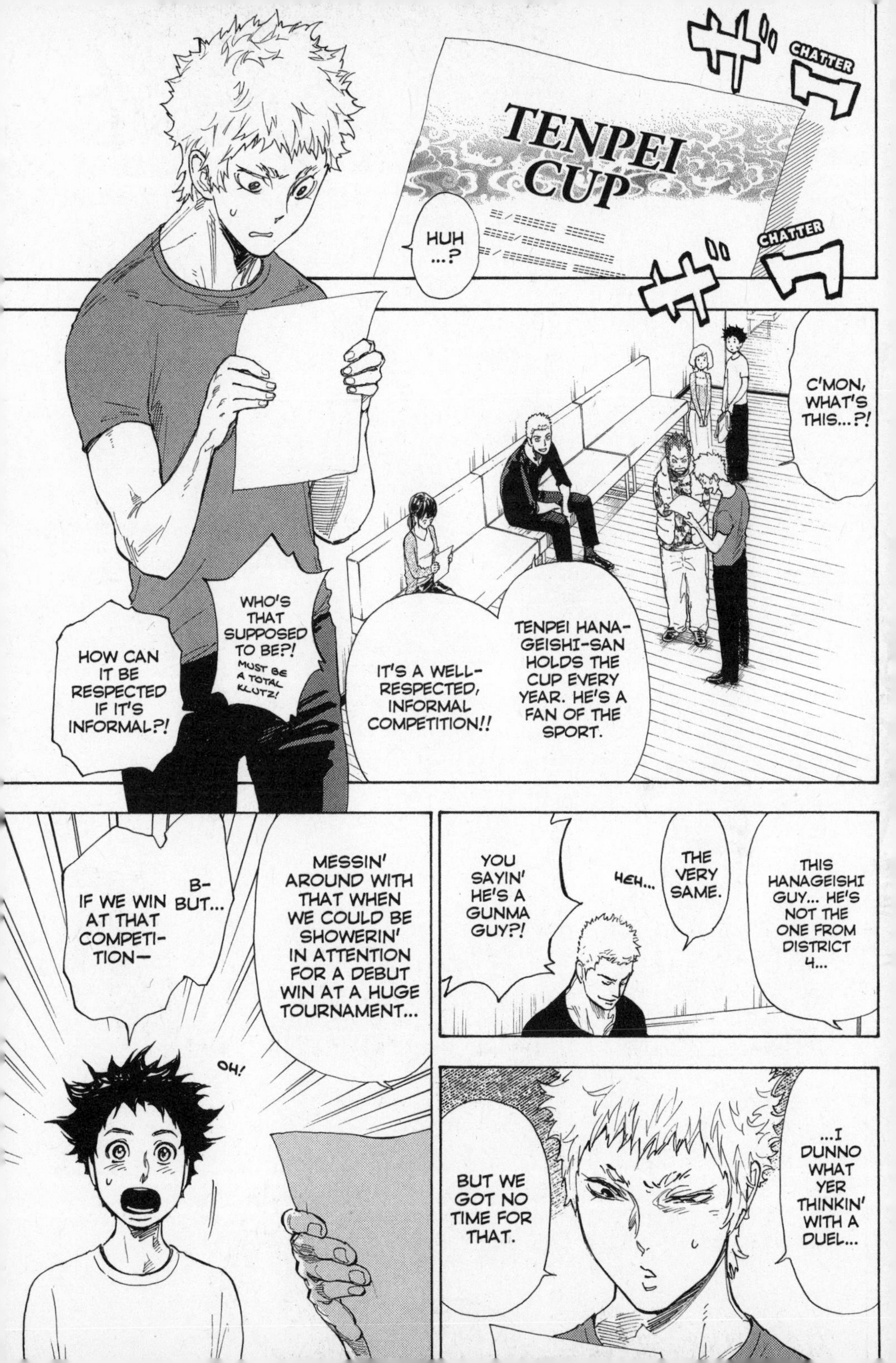
CHATTER
CHATTER
TENPEI CUP
HUH ...?
C'MON, WHAT'S THIS...?!
TENPEI HANAGEISHI-SAN HOLDS THE CUP EVERY YEAR. HE'S A FAN OF THE SPORT.
IT'S A WELL-RESPECTED, INFORMAL COMPETITION!!
WHO'S THAT SUPPOSED TO BE?! MUST BE A TOTAL KLUTZ!
HOW CAN IT BE RESPECTED IF IT'S INFORMAL?!
THIS HANAGEISHI GUY... HE'S NOT THE ONE FROM DISTRICT 4...
THE VERY SAME.
HEH...
YOU SAYIN' HE'S A GUNMA GUY?!
...I DUNNO WHAT YER THINKIN' WITH A DUEL...
BUT WE GOT NO TIME FOR THAT.
MESSIN' AROUND WITH THAT WHEN WE COULD BE SHOWERIN' IN ATTENTION FOR A DEBUT WIN AT A HUGE TOURNAMENT...
B-BUT...
IF WE WIN AT THAT COMPETITION—
OH!

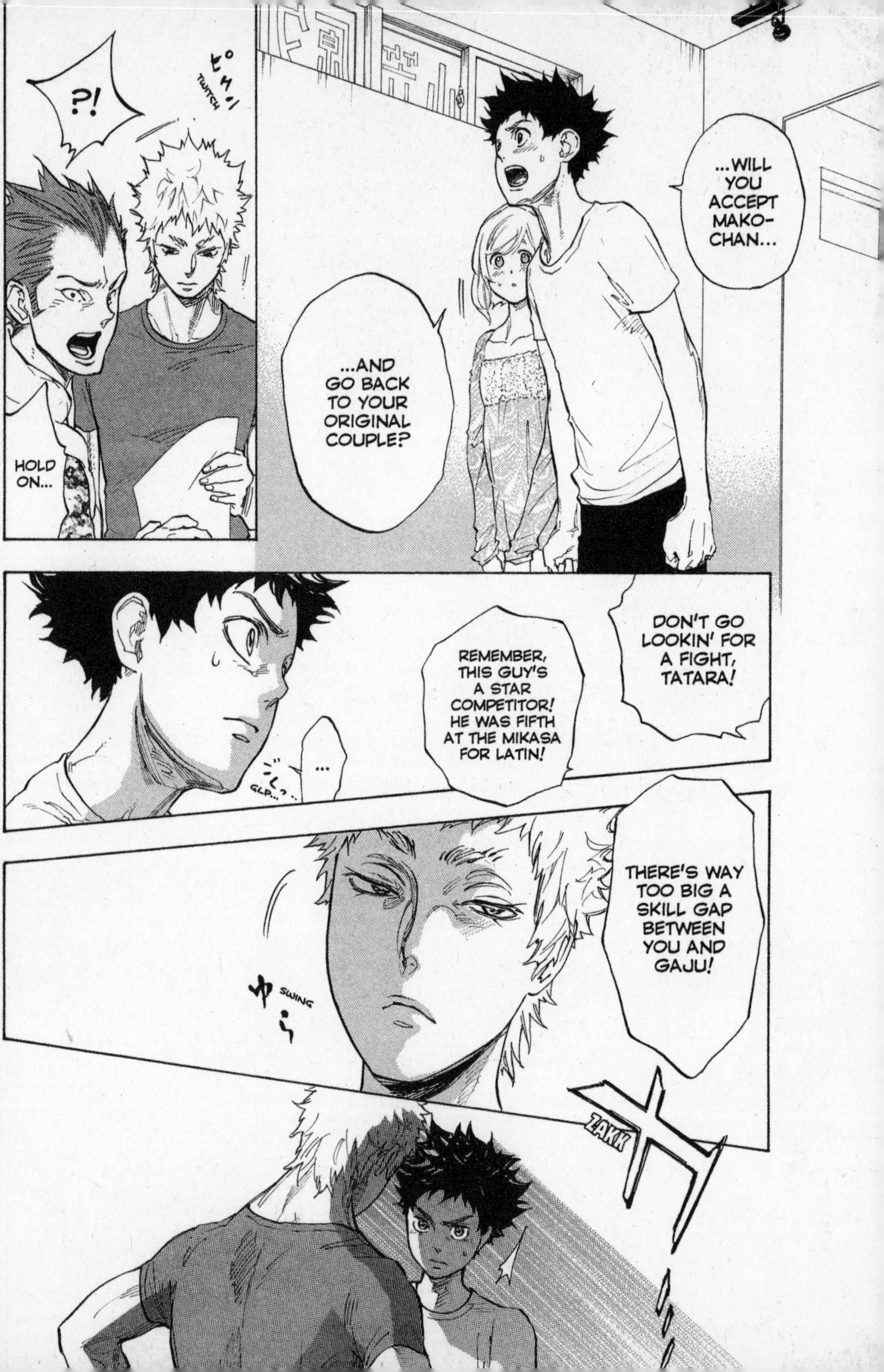
...WILL YOU ACCEPT MAKO-CHAN...
...AND GO BACK TO YOUR ORIGINAL COUPLE?
TWITCH
?!
HOLD ON...
DON'T GO LOOKIN' FOR A FIGHT, TATARA!
REMEMBER, THIS GUY'S A STAR COMPETITOR! HE WAS FIFTH AT THE MIKASA FOR LATIN!
...
GLP...
THERE'S WAY TOO BIG A SKILL GAP BETWEEN YOU AND GAJU!
SWING
ZAKK

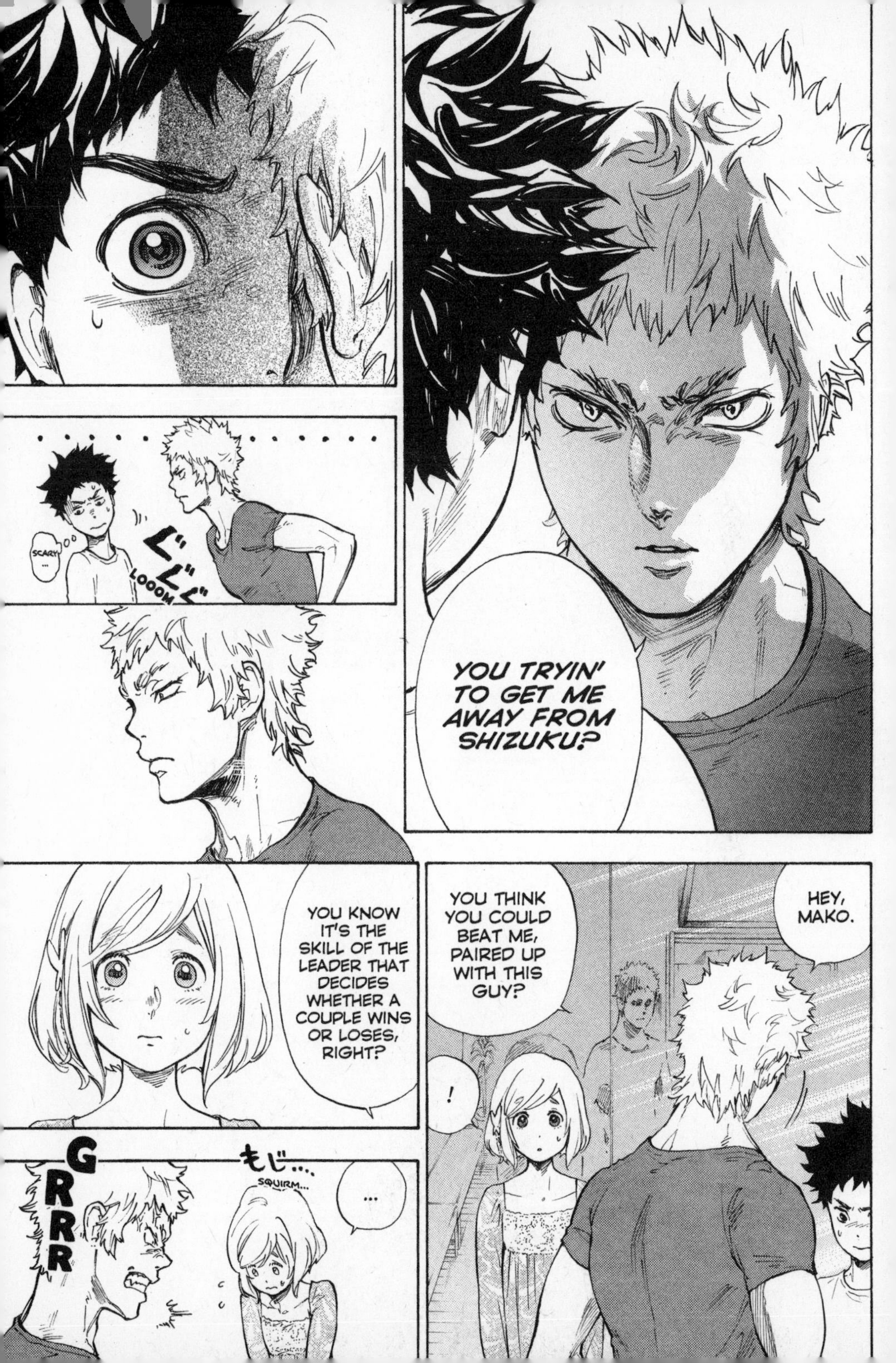
YOU TRYIN' TO GET ME AWAY FROM SHIZUKU?
. . . .
ぐ ぐ ぐ
LOOOM
SCARY...
HEY, MAKO.
YOU THINK YOU COULD BEAT ME, PAIRED UP WITH THIS GUY?
!
YOU KNOW IT'S THE SKILL OF THE LEADER THAT DECIDES WHETHER A COUPLE WINS OR LOSES, RIGHT?
...
もじ....
SQUIRM...
GRRR

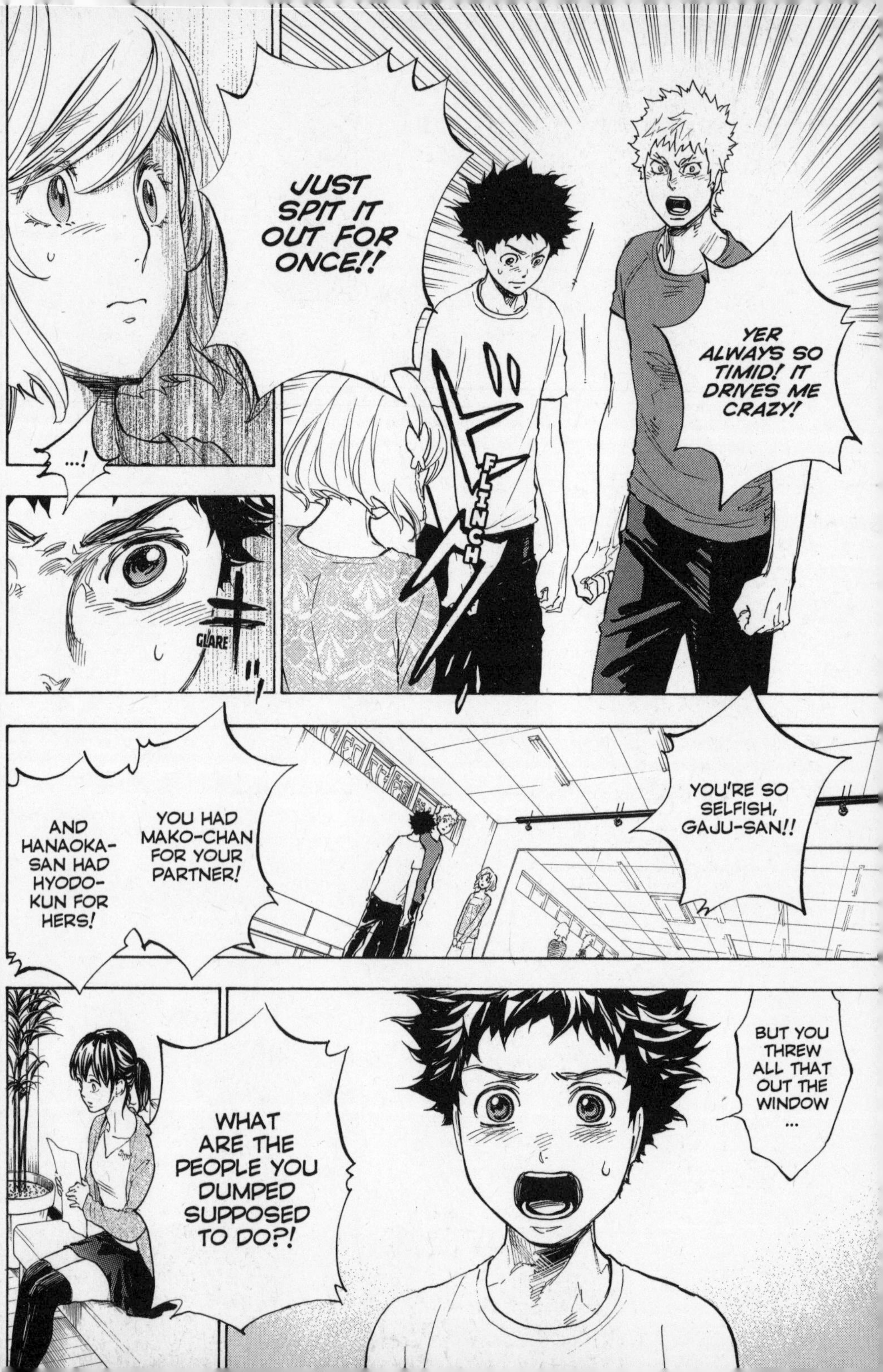
JUST SPIT IT OUT FOR ONCE!!
YER ALWAYS SO TIMID! IT DRIVES ME CRAZY!
FLINCH
...!
GLARE
YOU'RE SO SELFISH, GAJU-SAN!!
YOU HAD MAKO-CHAN FOR YOUR PARTNER!
AND HANAOKA-SAN HAD HYODO-KUN FOR HERS!
BUT YOU THREW ALL THAT OUT THE WINDOW ...
WHAT ARE THE PEOPLE YOU DUMPED SUPPOSED TO DO?!

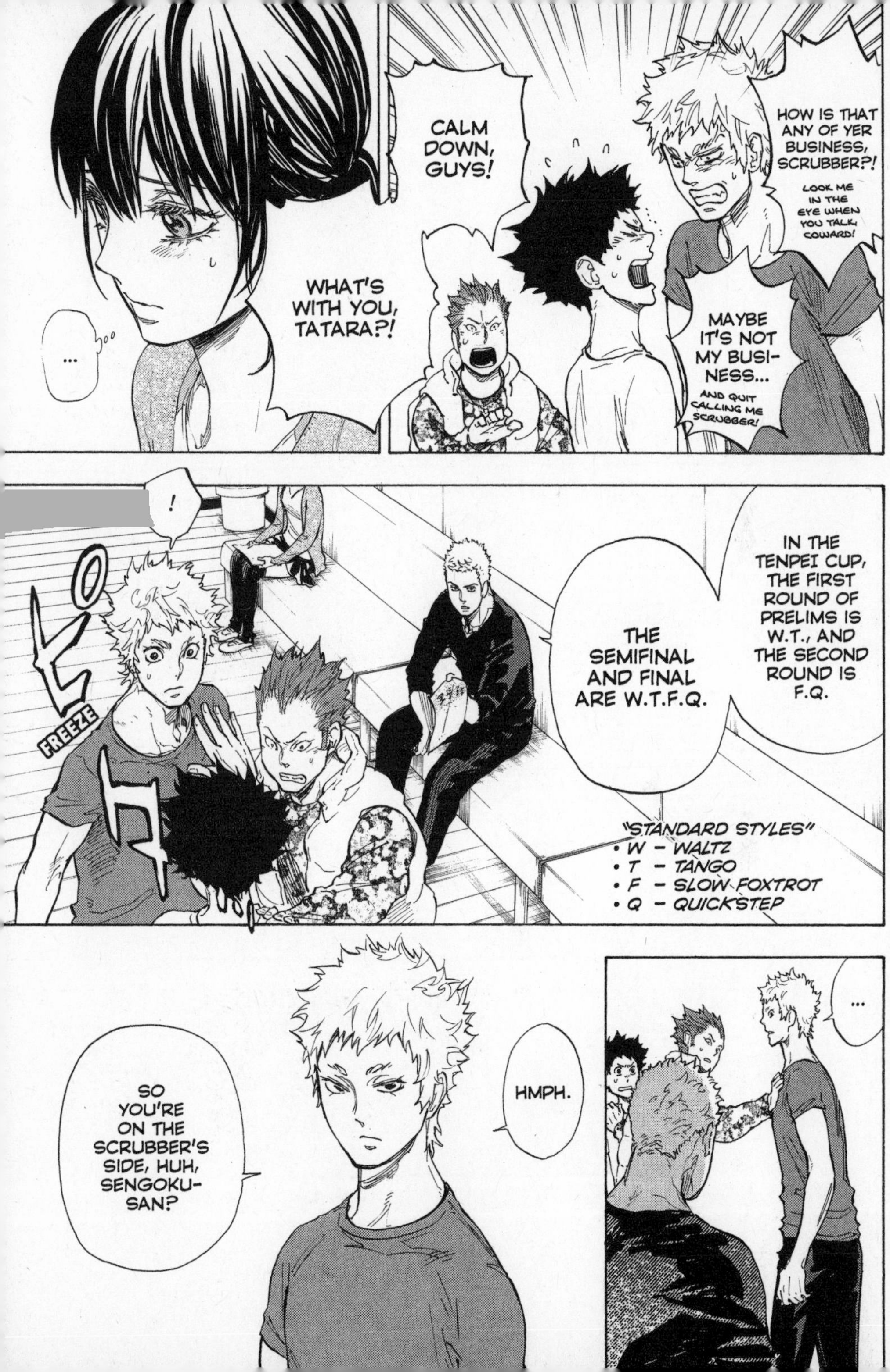
HOW IS THAT ANY OF YER BUSINESS, SCRUBBER?!
LOOK ME IN THE EYE WHEN YOU TALK, COWARD!
MAYBE IT'S NOT MY BUSINESS...
AND QUIT CALLING ME SCRUBBER!
CALM DOWN, GUYS!
WHAT'S WITH YOU, TATARA?!
...
IN THE TENPEI CUP, THE FIRST ROUND OF PRELIMS IS W.T., AND THE SECOND ROUND IS F.Q.
THE SEMIFINAL AND FINAL ARE W.T.F.Q.
"STANDARD STYLES"
• W - WALTZ
• T - TANGO
• F - SLOW FOXTROT
• Q - QUICKSTEP
!
FREEZE
...
HMPH.
SO YOU'RE ON THE SCRUBBER'S SIDE, HUH, SENGOKU-SAN?

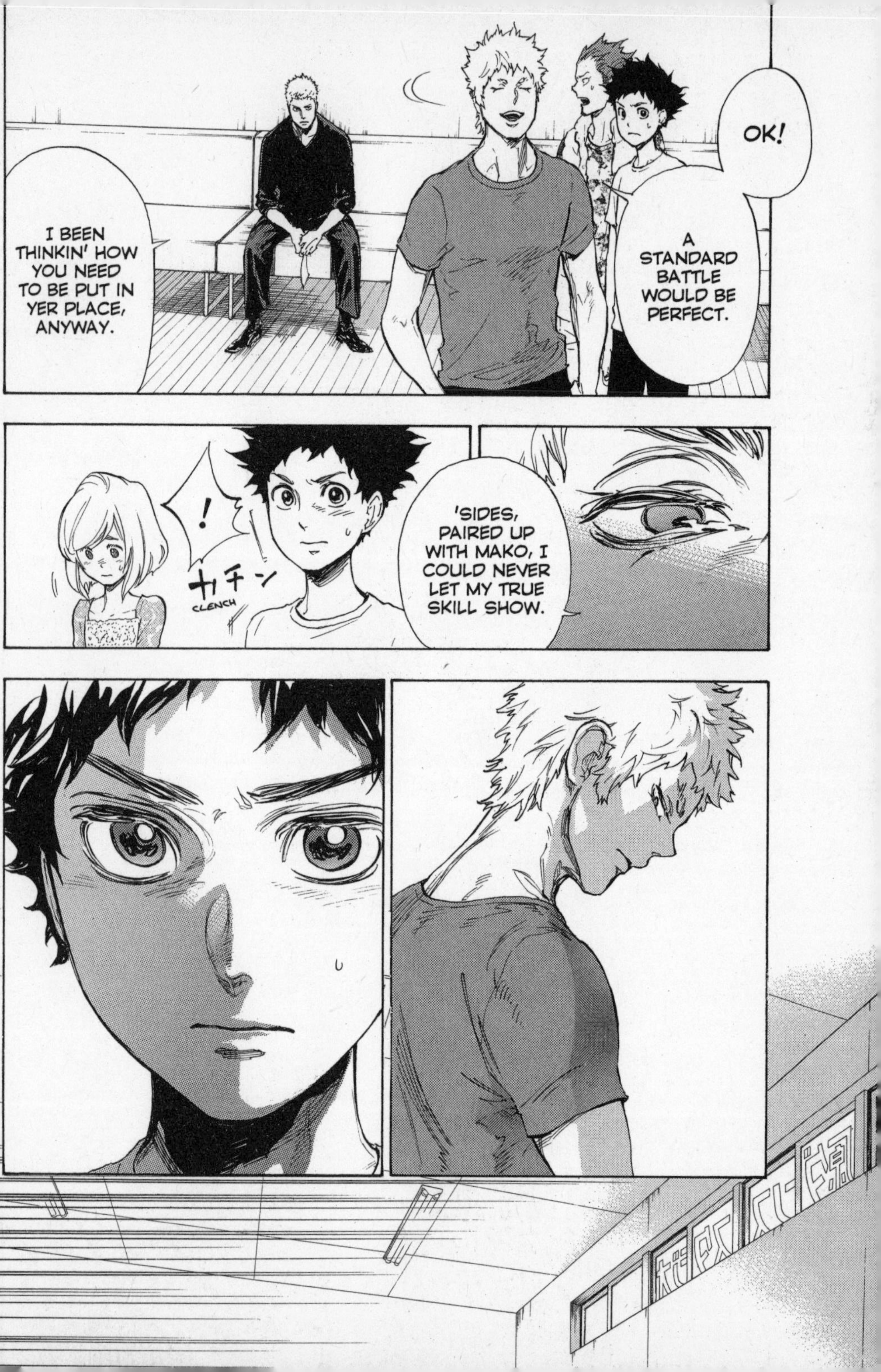
OK!
A STANDARD BATTLE WOULD BE PERFECT.
I BEEN THINKIN' HOW YOU NEED TO BE PUT IN YER PLACE, ANYWAY.
'SIDES, PAIRED UP WITH MAKO, I COULD NEVER LET MY TRUE SKILL SHOW.
!
カチン
CLENCH

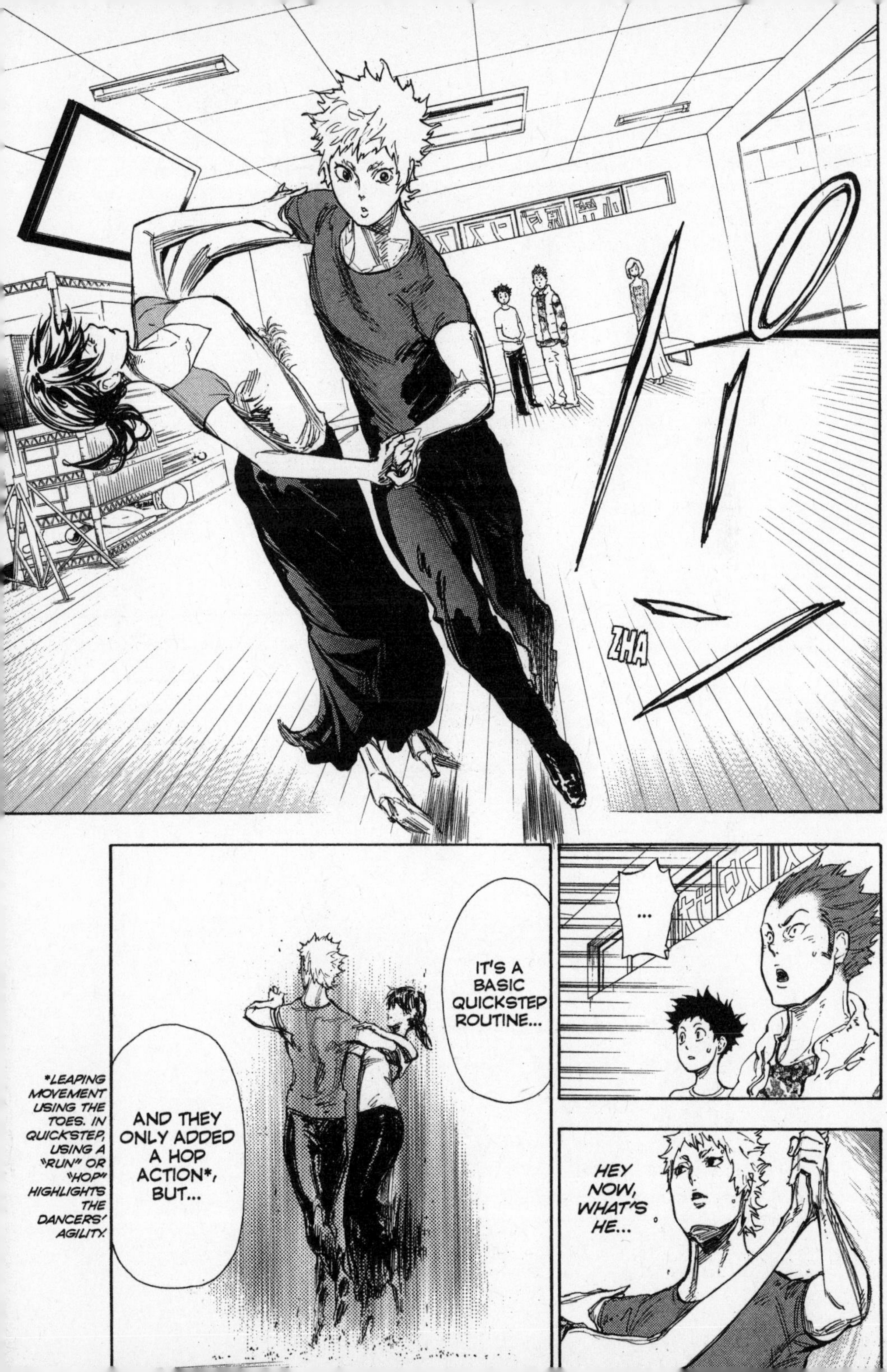
ZHA
...
HEY NOW, WHAT'S HE...
IT'S A BASIC QUICKSTEP ROUTINE...
AND THEY ONLY ADDED A HOP ACTION*, BUT...
*LEAPING MOVEMENT USING THE TOES. IN QUICKSTEP, USING A "RUN" OR "HOP" HIGHLIGHTS THE DANCERS' AGILITY.

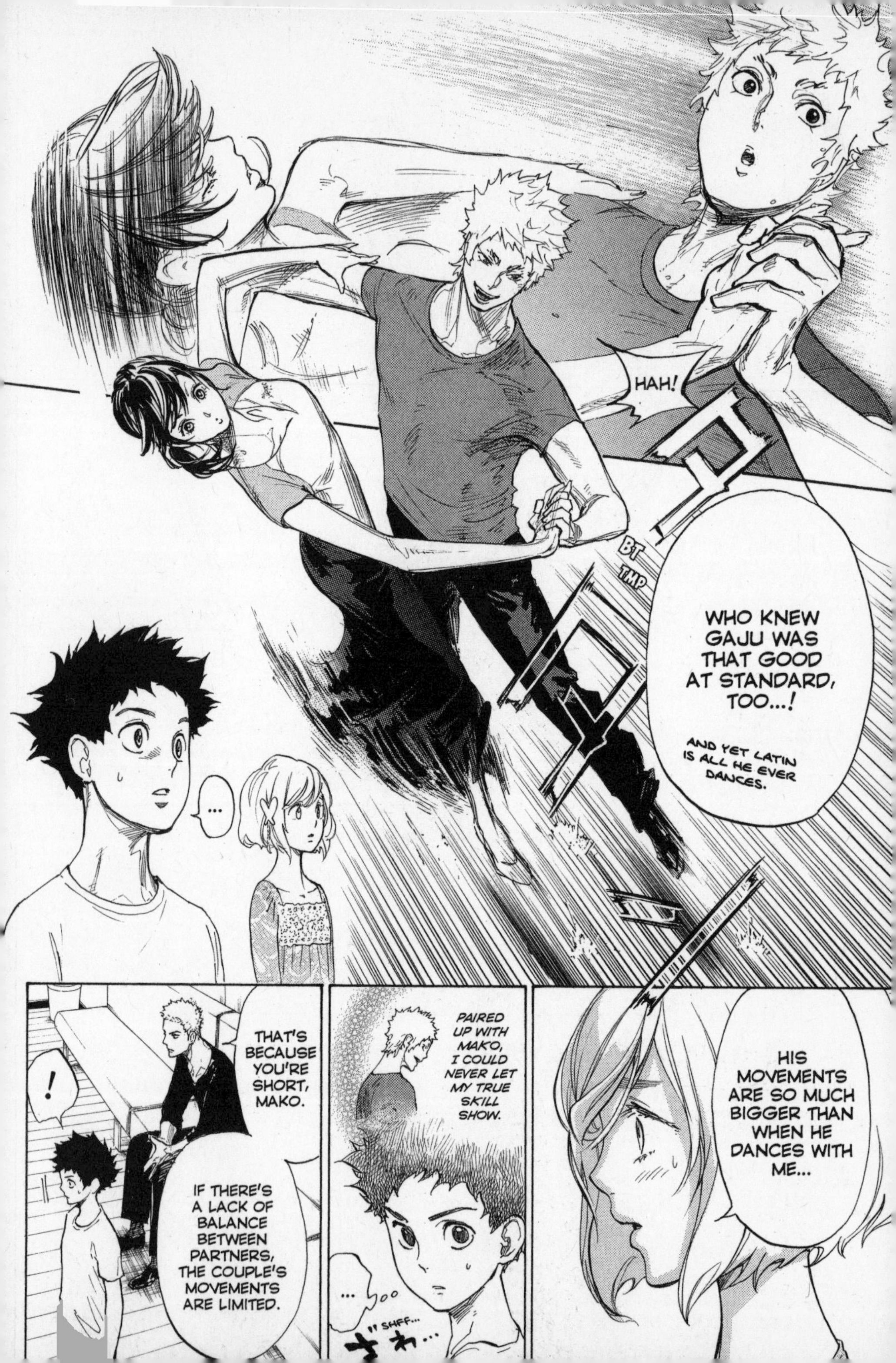
HAH!
BT
TMP
WHO KNEW GAJU WAS THAT GOOD AT STANDARD, TOO...!
AND YET LATIN IS ALL HE EVER DANCES.
...
HIS MOVEMENTS ARE SO MUCH BIGGER THAN WHEN HE DANCES WITH ME...
PAIRED UP WITH MAKO, I COULD NEVER LET MY TRUE SKILL SHOW.
...
SHFF...
THAT'S BECAUSE YOU'RE SHORT, MAKO.
!
IF THERE'S A LACK OF BALANCE BETWEEN PARTNERS, THE COUPLE'S MOVEMENTS ARE LIMITED.

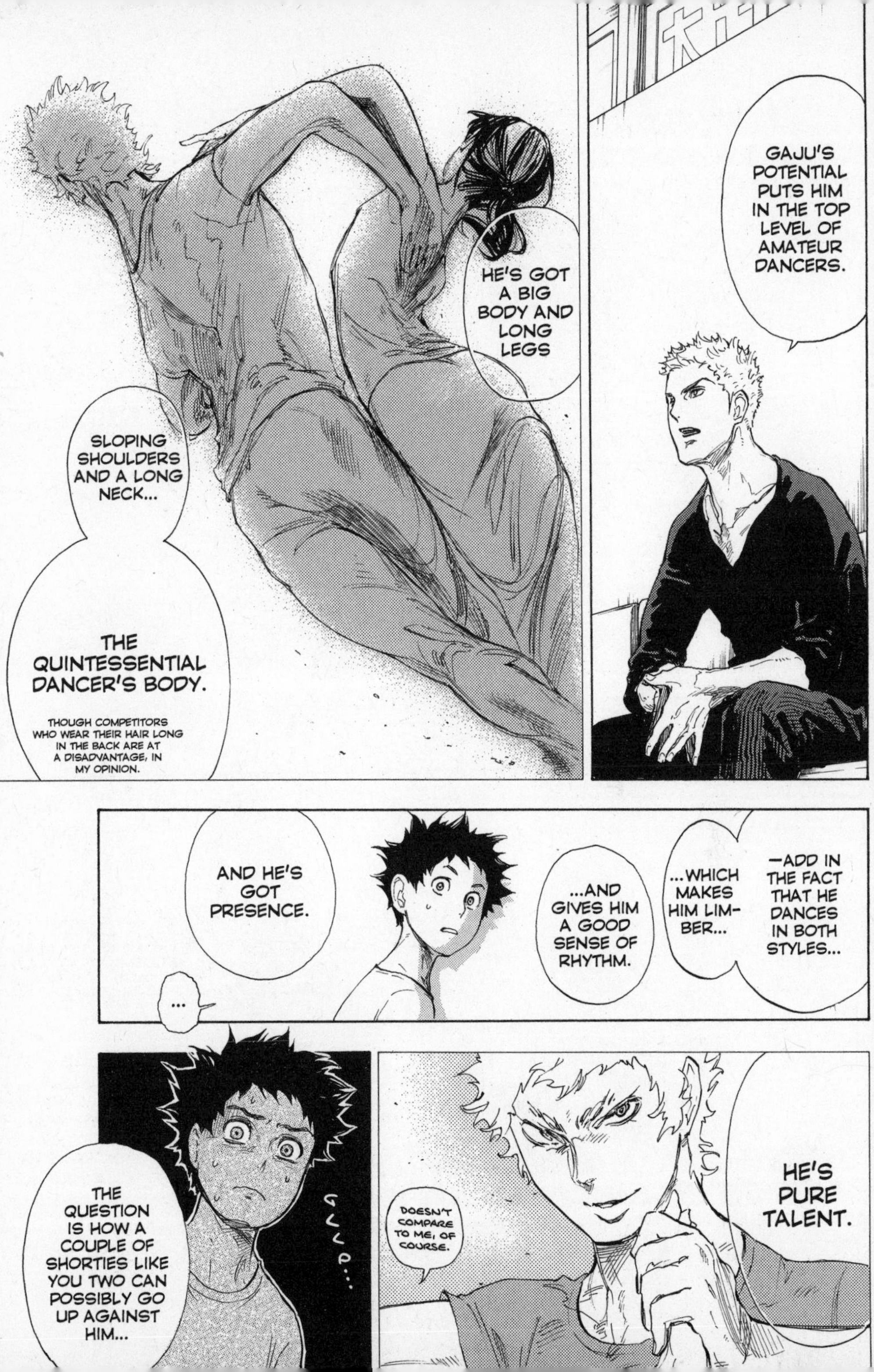
GAJU'S POTENTIAL PUTS HIM IN THE TOP LEVEL OF AMATEUR DANCERS.
HE'S GOT A BIG BODY AND LONG LEGS
SLOPING SHOULDERS AND A LONG NECK...
THE QUINTESSENTIAL DANCER'S BODY.
THOUGH COMPETITORS WHO WEAR THEIR HAIR LONG IN THE BACK ARE AT A DISADVANTAGE, IN MY OPINION.
—ADD IN THE FACT THAT HE DANCES IN BOTH STYLES...
...WHICH MAKES HIM LIMBER...
...AND GIVES HIM A GOOD SENSE OF RHYTHM.
AND HE'S GOT PRESENCE.
...
HE'S PURE TALENT.
DOESN'T COMPARE TO ME, OF COURSE.
GULP...
THE QUESTION IS HOW A COUPLE OF SHORTIES LIKE YOU TWO CAN POSSIBLY GO UP AGAINST HIM...

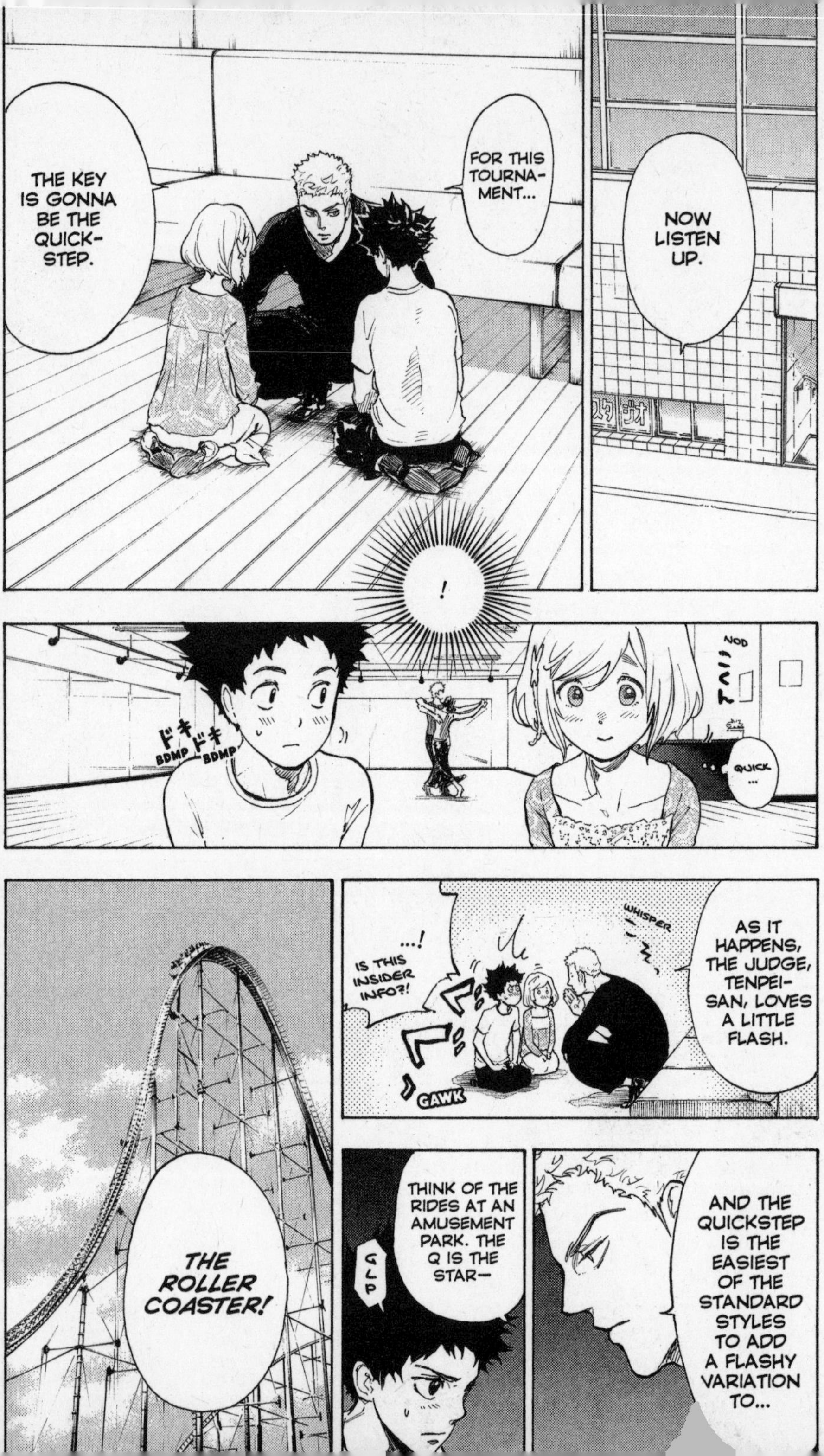
NOW LISTEN UP.
FOR THIS TOURNAMENT...
THE KEY IS GONNA BE THE QUICKSTEP.
!
NOD
QUICK...
ドキドキ
BDMP BDMP
WHISPER
AS IT HAPPENS, THE JUDGE, TENPEI-SAN, LOVES A LITTLE FLASH.
...! IS THIS INSIDER INFO?!
GAWK
AND THE QUICKSTEP IS THE EASIEST OF THE STANDARD STYLES TO ADD A FLASHY VARIATION TO...
THINK OF THE RIDES AT AN AMUSEMENT PARK. THE Q IS THE STAR—
GLP
THE ROLLER COASTER!

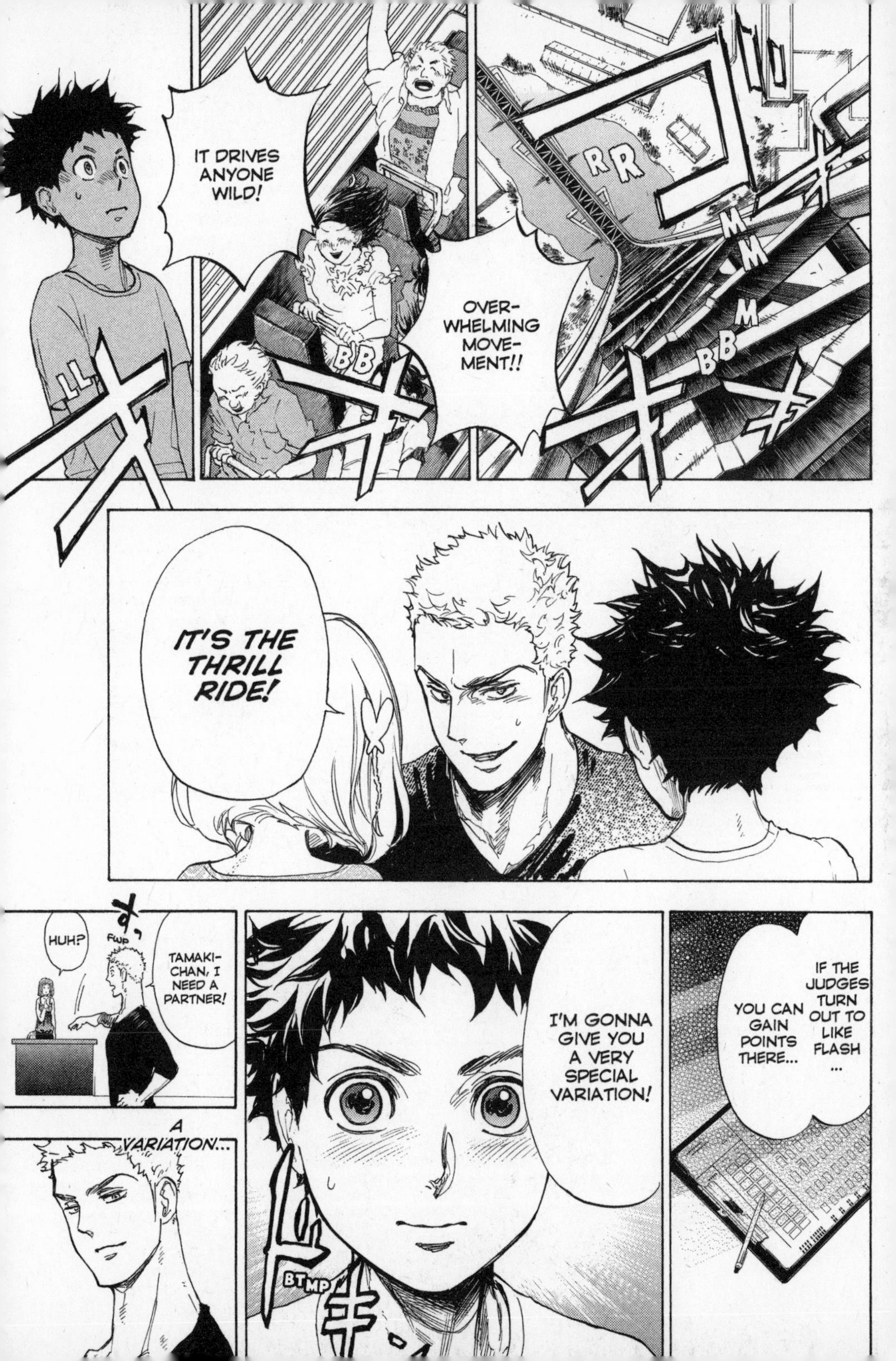
RR
MMM
BB
OVER-WHELMING MOVEMENT!!
BB
IT DRIVES ANYONE WILD!
LL
IT'S THE THRILL RIDE!
IF THE JUDGES TURN OUT TO LIKE FLASH ...
YOU CAN GAIN POINTS THERE...
I'M GONNA GIVE YOU A VERY SPECIAL VARIATION!
BTMP
TAMAKI-CHAN, I NEED A PARTNER!
FWP
HUH?
A VARIATION...

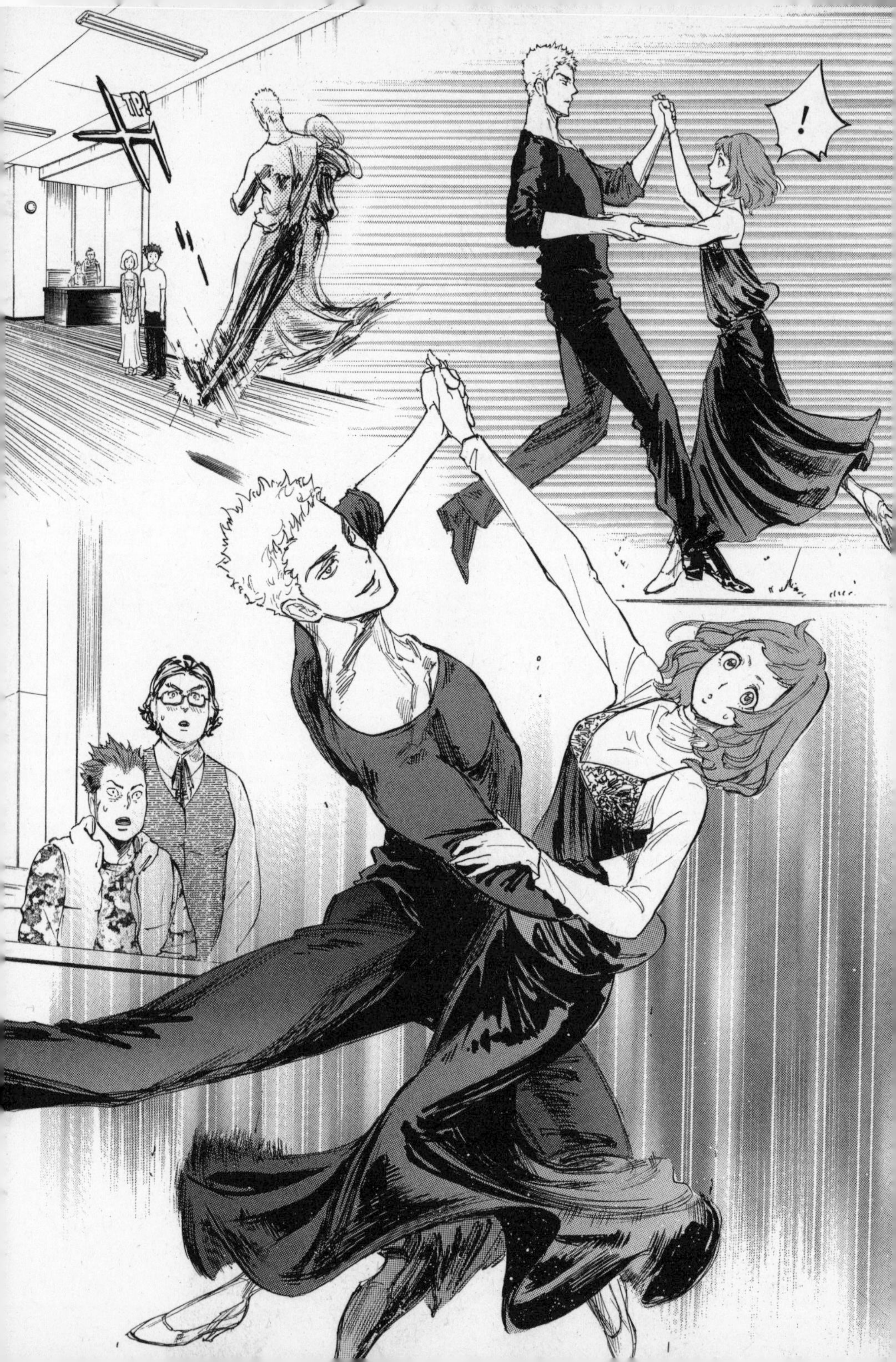
!
TP!

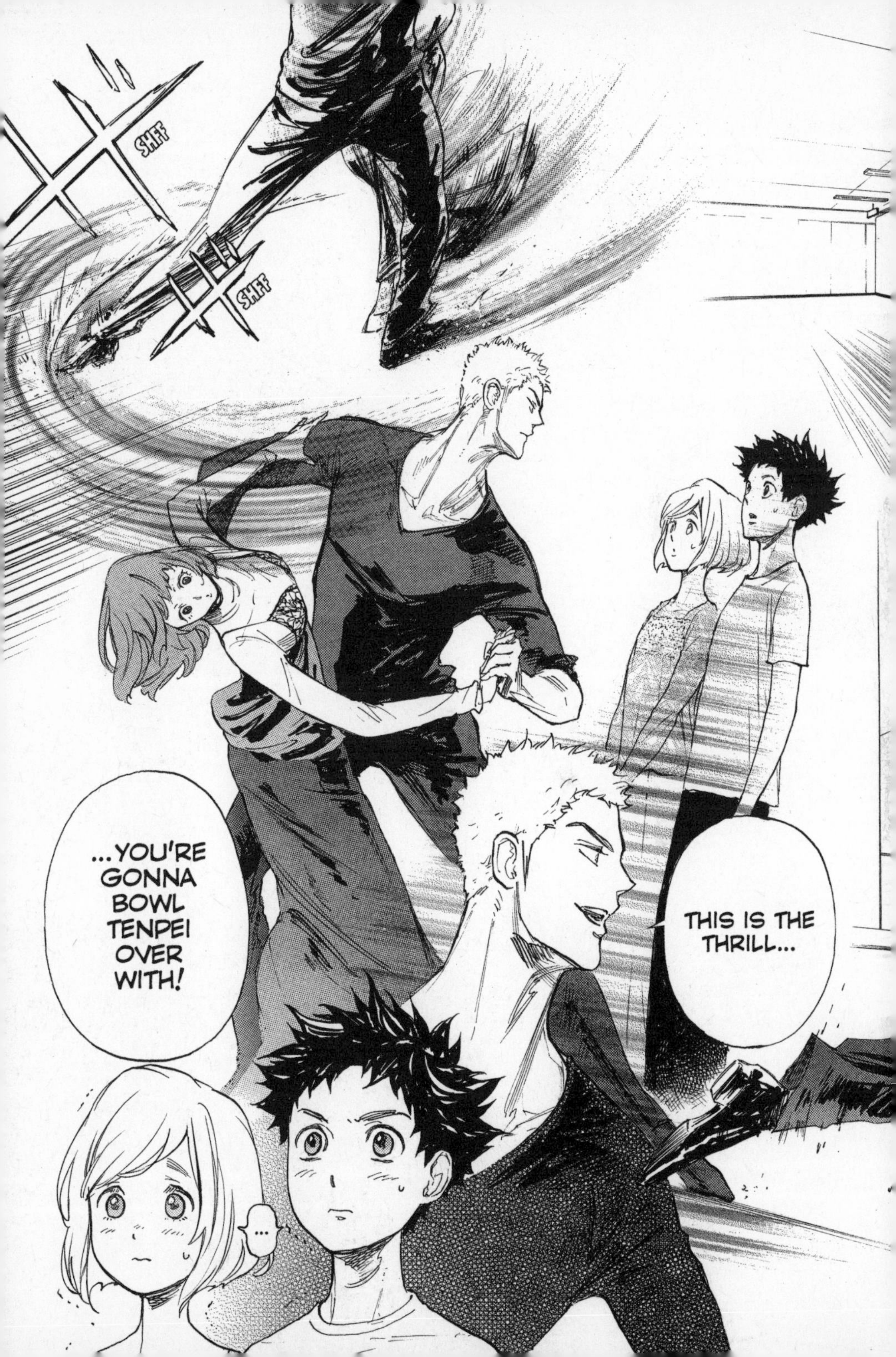
SHFF
SHFF
THIS IS THE THRILL...
...YOU'RE GONNA BOWL TENPEI OVER WITH!
...

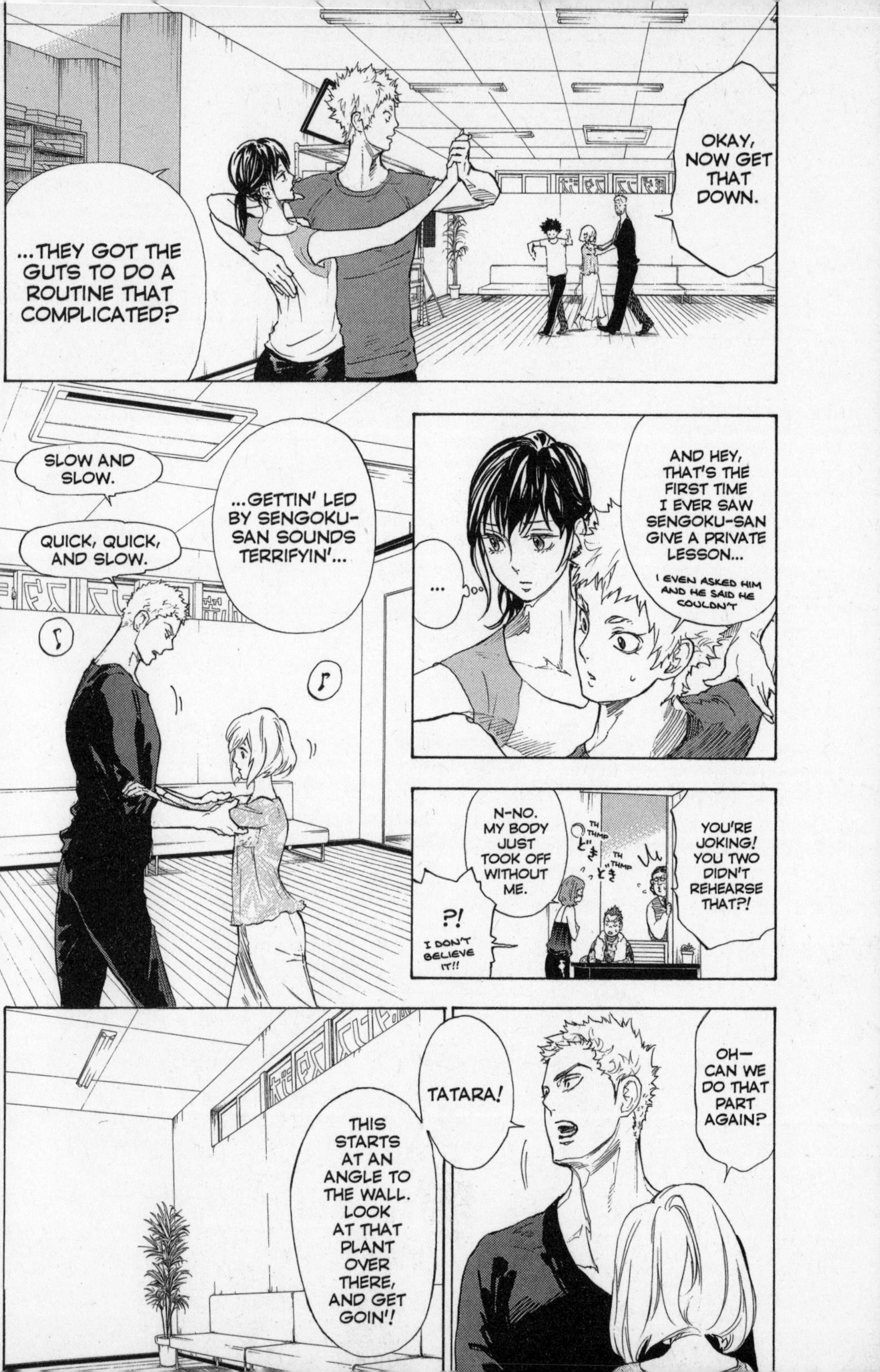
OKAY, NOW GET THAT DOWN.
...THEY GOT THE GUTS TO DO A ROUTINE THAT COMPLICATED?
AND HEY, THAT'S THE FIRST TIME I EVER SAW SENGOKU-SAN GIVE A PRIVATE LESSON...
I EVEN ASKED HIM AND HE SAID HE COULDN'T
...
YOU'RE JOKING! YOU TWO DIDN'T REHEARSE THAT?!
TH THMP
TH THMP
N-NO. MY BODY JUST TOOK OFF WITHOUT ME.
?!
I DON'T BELIEVE IT!!
...GETTIN' LED BY SENGOKU-SAN SOUNDS TERRIFYIN'...
SLOW AND SLOW.
QUICK, QUICK, AND SLOW.
OH— CAN WE DO THAT PART AGAIN?
TATARA!
THIS STARTS AT AN ANGLE TO THE WALL. LOOK AT THAT PLANT OVER THERE, AND GET GOIN'!

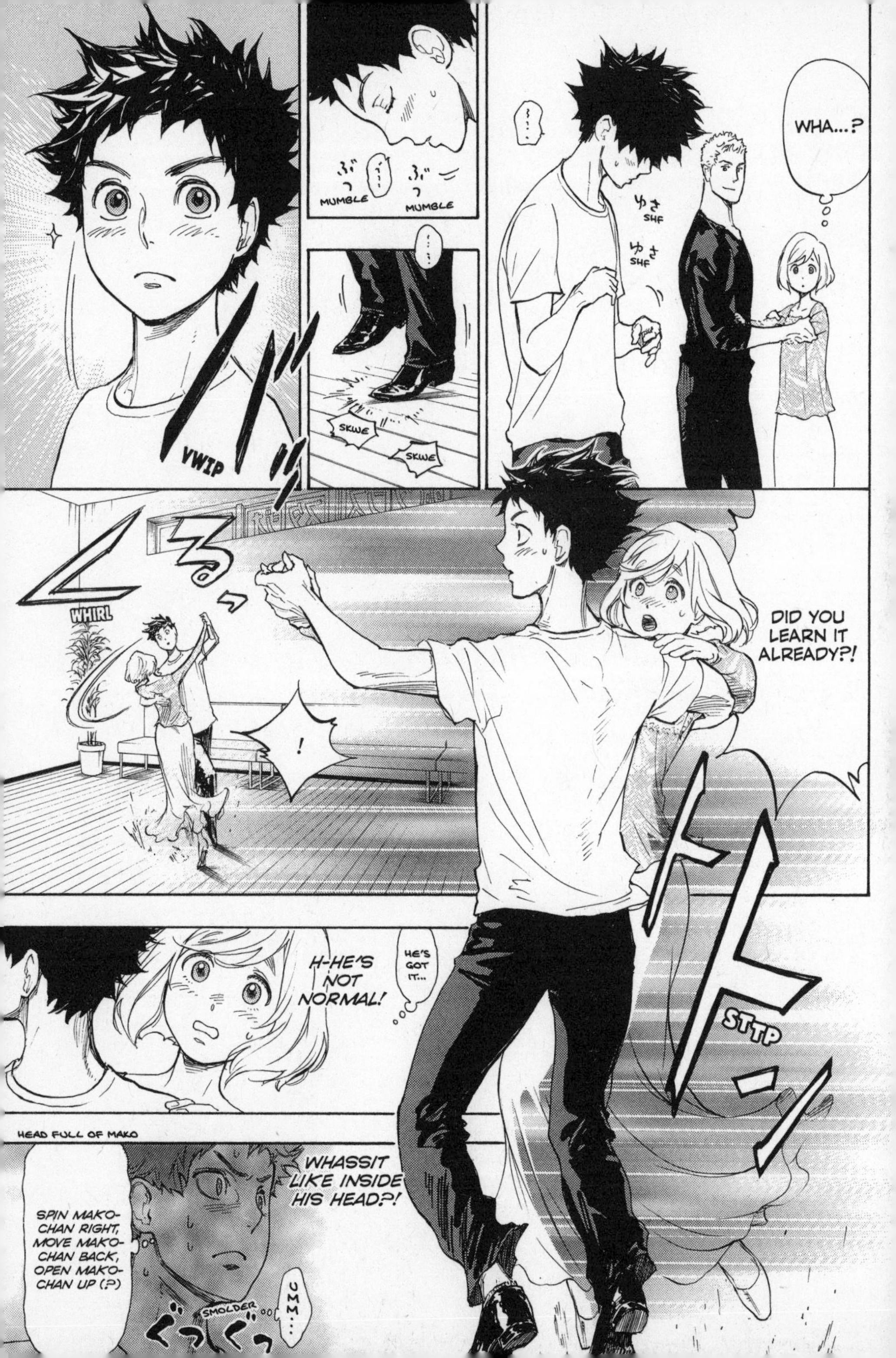

WHA...?
...
ゆさ
SHF
ゆさ
SHF
ぶつ
MUMBLE
...
ぶつ
MUMBLE
...
SKWE
SKWE
VWIP
DID YOU LEARN IT ALREADY?!
!
WHIRL
STTP
HE'S GOT IT...
H-HE'S NOT NORMAL!
HEAD FULL OF MAKO
WHASSIT LIKE INSIDE HIS HEAD?!
SPIN MAKO-CHAN RIGHT, MOVE MAKO-CHAN BACK, OPEN MAKO-CHAN UP (?)
UMM...
ぐつぐつ
SMOLDER

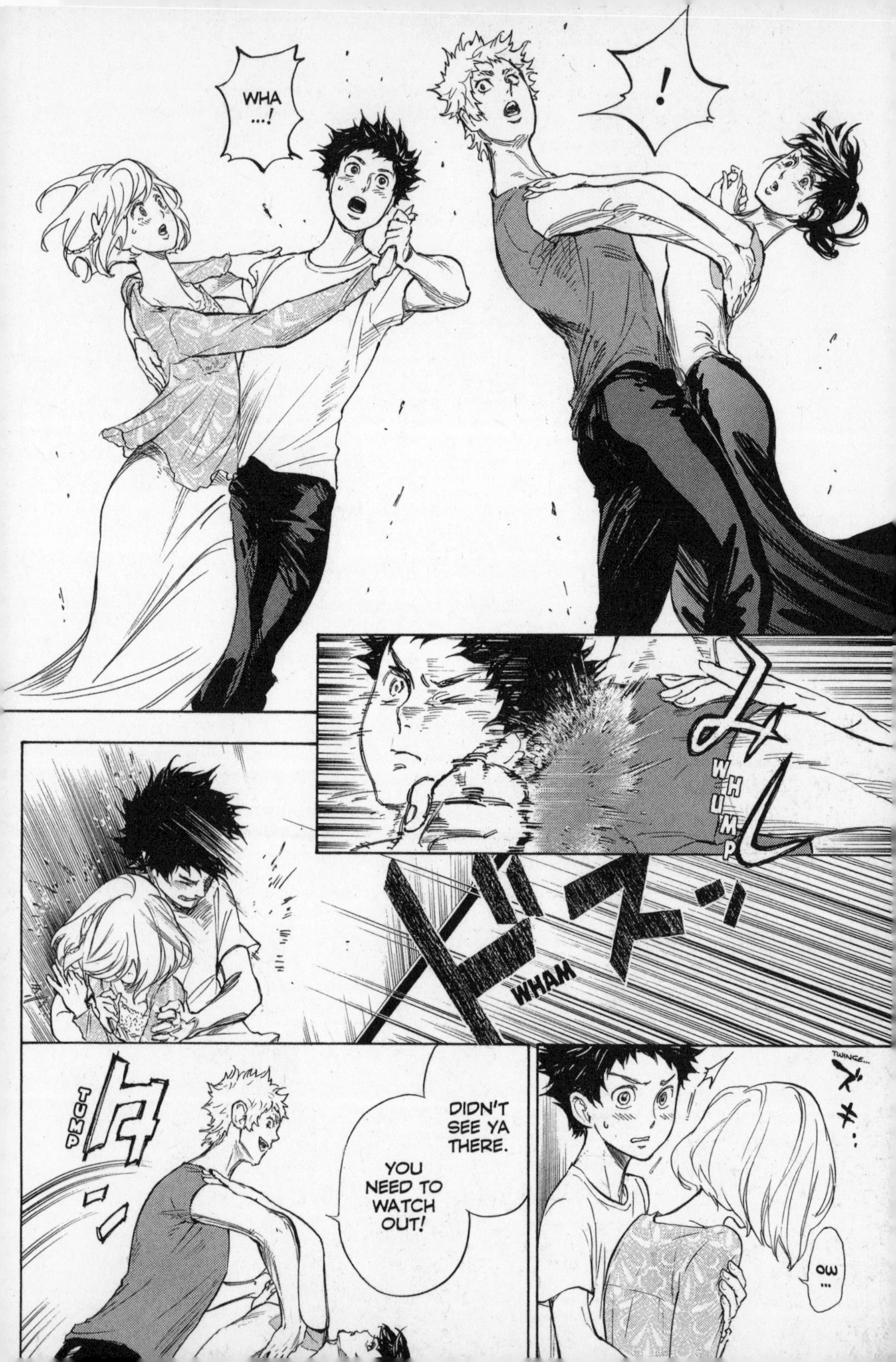
!
WHA ...!
WHUMP
WHAM
TWINGE...
OW ...
DIDN'T SEE YA THERE.
YOU NEED TO WATCH OUT!
TUMP

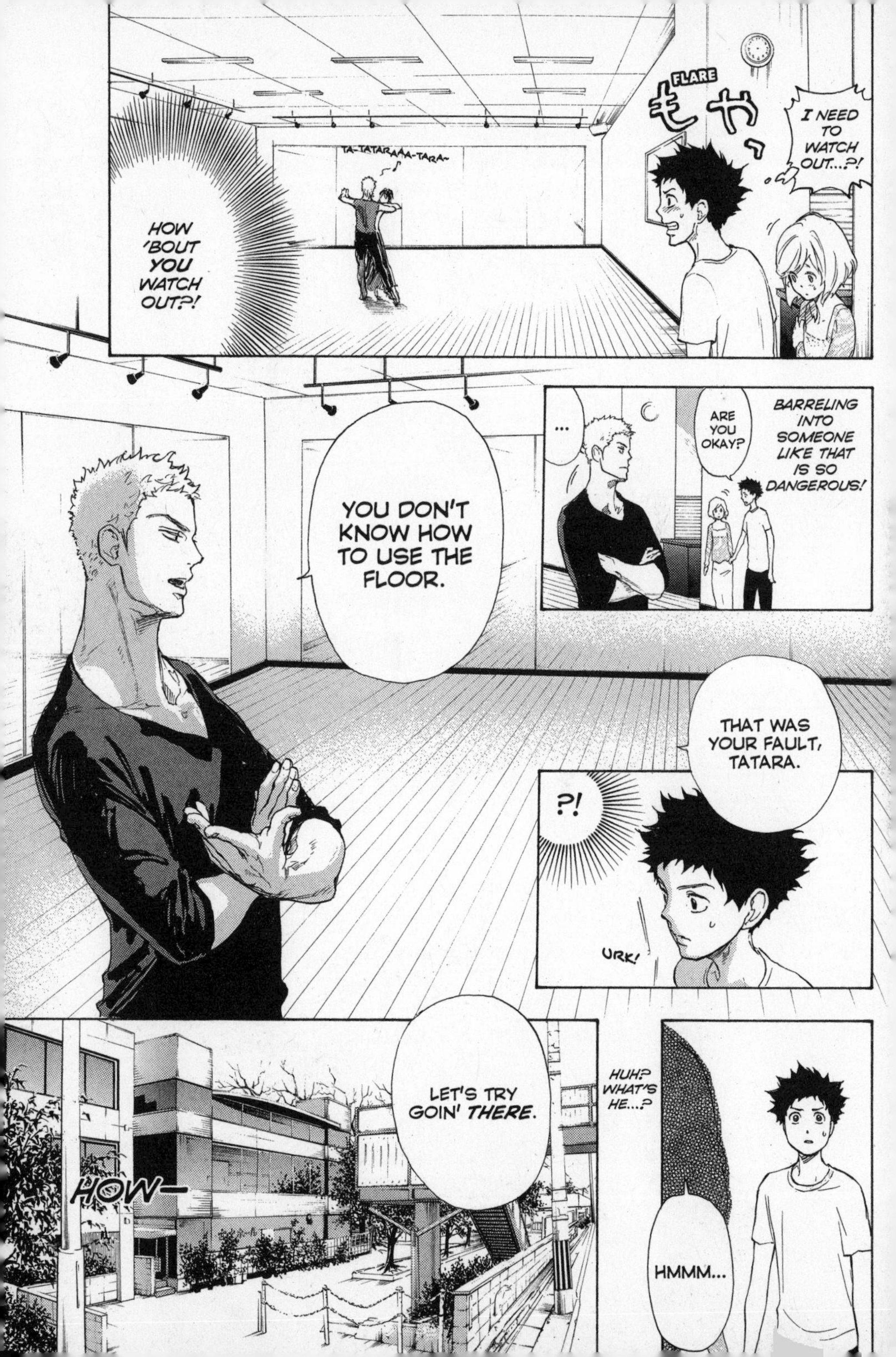
FLARE
もや
I NEED TO WATCH OUT...?!
TA-TATARAAA-TARA~
HOW 'BOUT YOU WATCH OUT?!
BARRELING INTO SOMEONE LIKE THAT IS SO DANGEROUS!
ARE YOU OKAY?
...
THAT WAS YOUR FAULT, TATARA.
?!
URK!
YOU DON'T KNOW HOW TO USE THE FLOOR.
HUH? WHAT'S HE...?
HMMM...
LET'S TRY GOIN' THERE.
HOW—

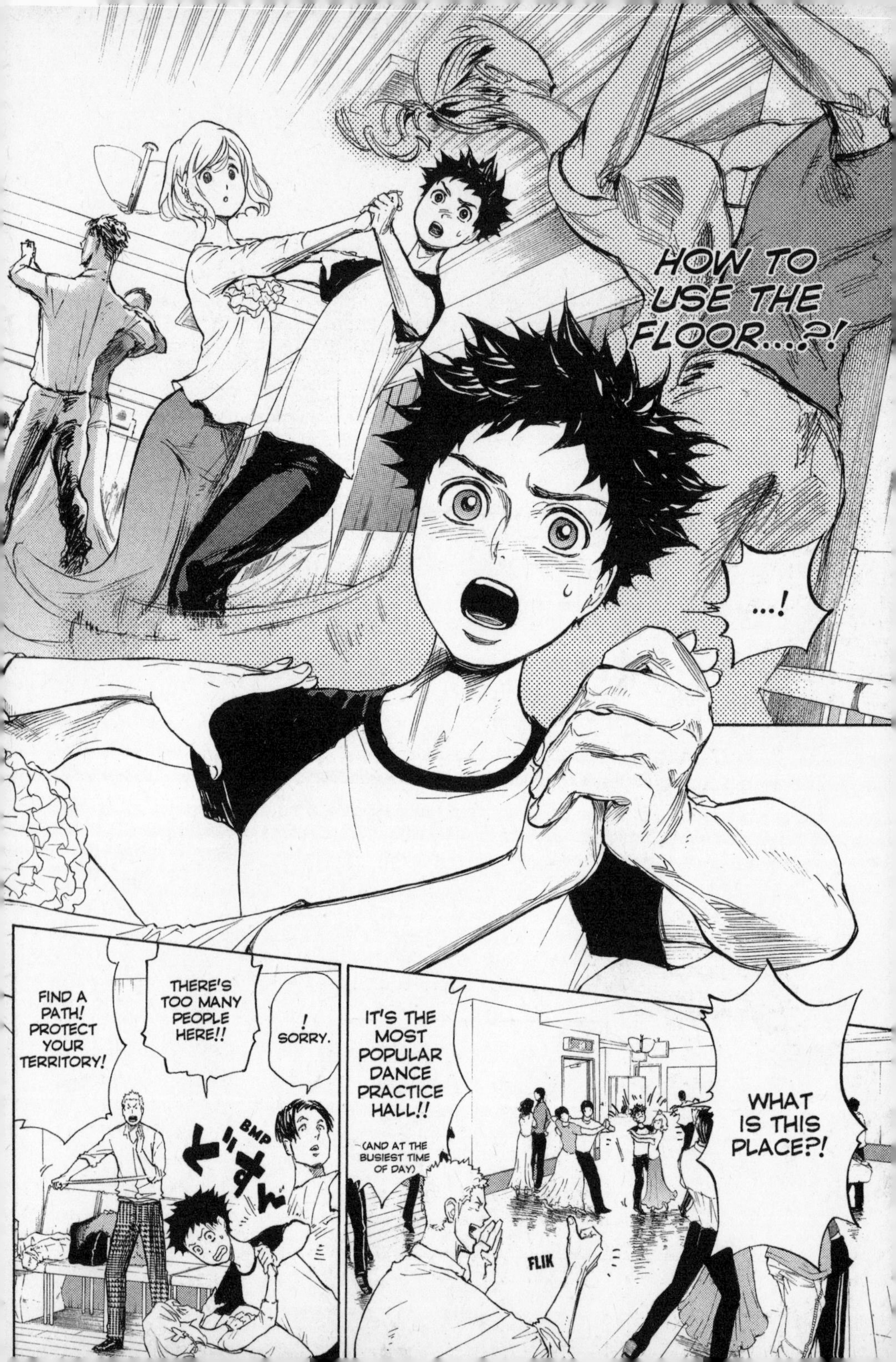
HOW TO USE THE FLOOR...?!
...!
WHAT IS THIS PLACE?!
IT'S THE MOST POPULAR DANCE PRACTICE HALL!!
(AND AT THE BUSIEST TIME OF DAY)
FLIK
! SORRY.
BMP
どすん
THERE'S TOO MANY PEOPLE HERE!!
FIND A PATH! PROTECT YOUR TERRITORY!

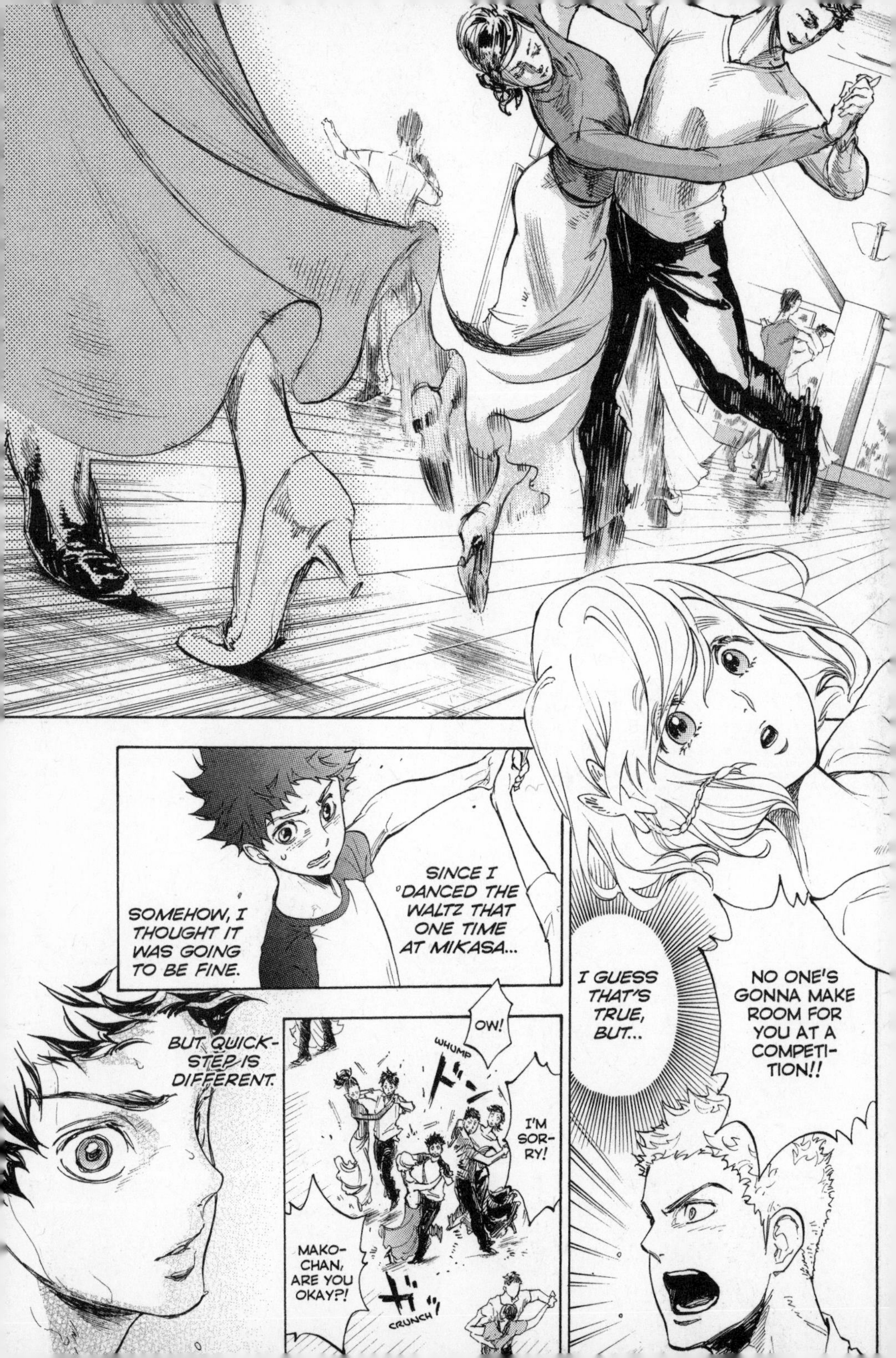
NO ONE'S GONNA MAKE ROOM FOR YOU AT A COMPETITION!!
I GUESS THAT'S TRUE, BUT...
SINCE I DANCED THE WALTZ THAT ONE TIME AT MIKASA...
SOMEHOW, I THOUGHT IT WAS GOING TO BE FINE.
OW!
WHUMP
ドー
I'M SORRY!
MAKO-CHAN, ARE YOU OKAY?!
ド
CRUNCH
BUT QUICK-STEP IS DIFFERENT.

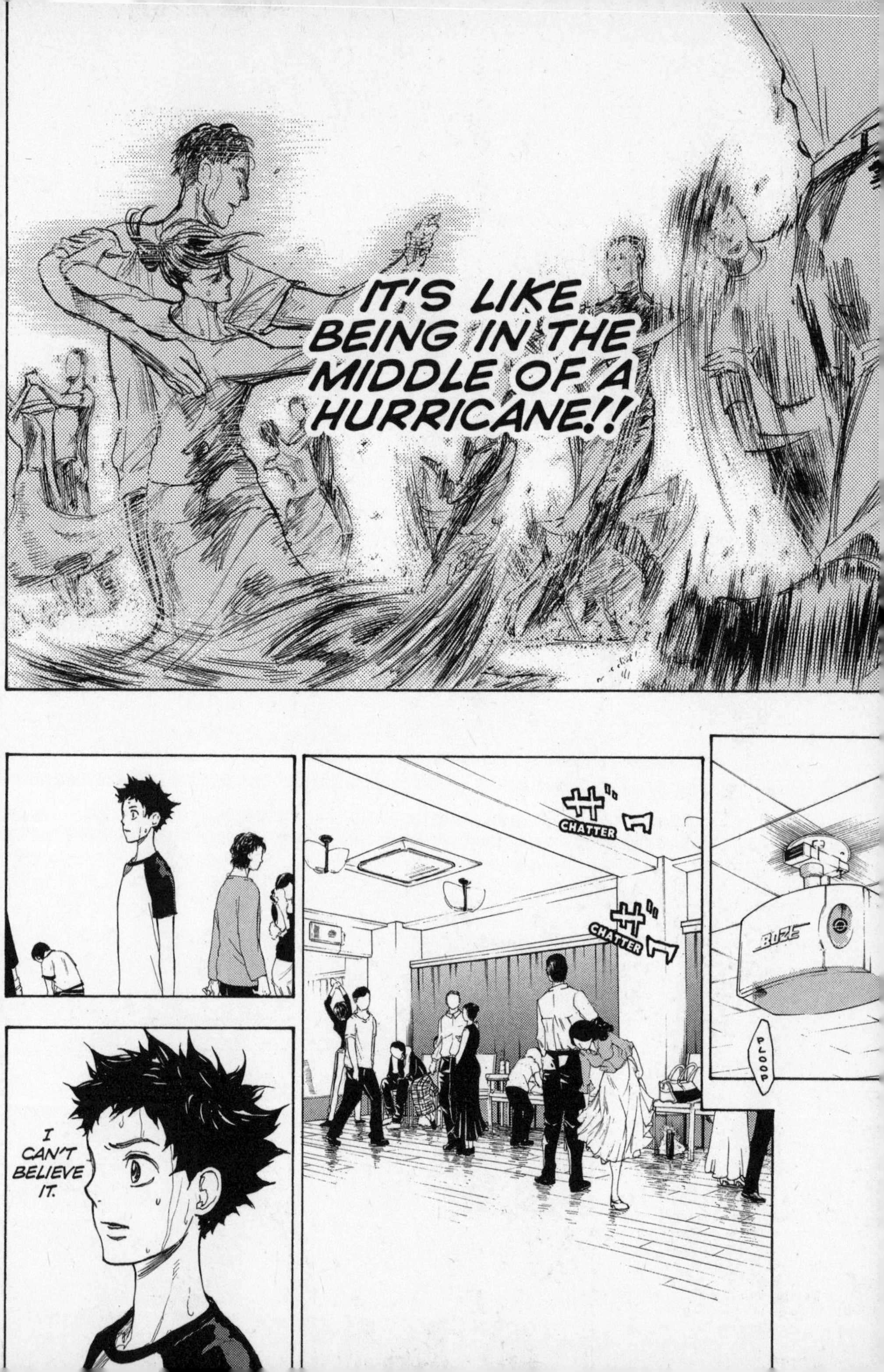
IT'S LIKE BEING IN THE MIDDLE OF A HURRICANE!!
PLOOP
CHATTER
CHATTER
I CAN'T BELIEVE IT.

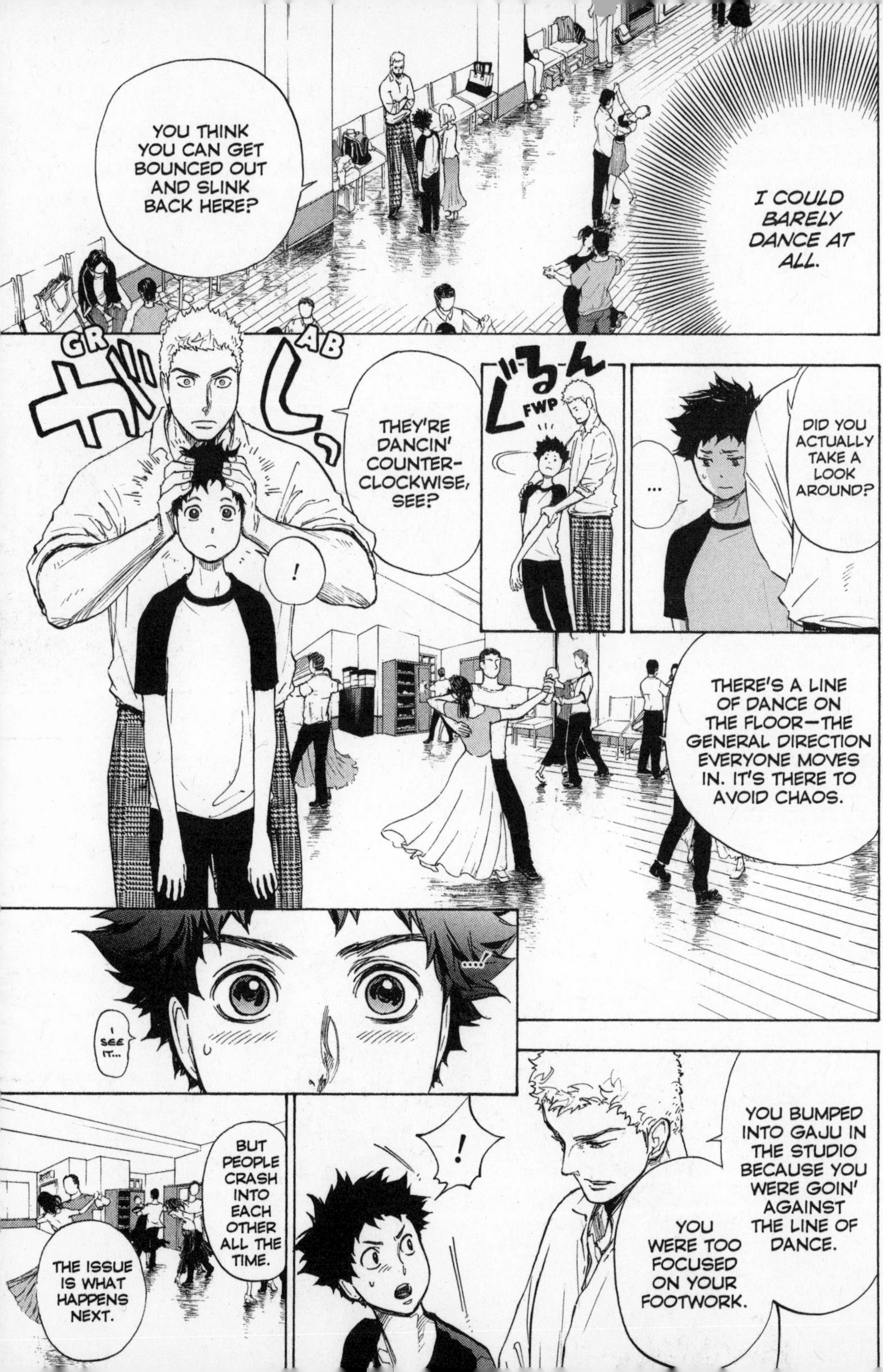
I COULD BARELY DANCE AT ALL.
YOU THINK YOU CAN GET BOUNCED OUT AND SLINK BACK HERE?
DID YOU ACTUALLY TAKE A LOOK AROUND?
...
FWP
THEY'RE DANCIN' COUNTER-CLOCKWISE, SEE?
AB
GR
!
THERE'S A LINE OF DANCE ON THE FLOOR—THE GENERAL DIRECTION EVERYONE MOVES IN. IT'S THERE TO AVOID CHAOS.
I SEE IT...
YOU BUMPED INTO GAJU IN THE STUDIO BECAUSE YOU WERE GOIN' AGAINST THE LINE OF DANCE.
YOU WERE TOO FOCUSED ON YOUR FOOTWORK.
!
BUT PEOPLE CRASH INTO EACH OTHER ALL THE TIME.
THE ISSUE IS WHAT HAPPENS NEXT.

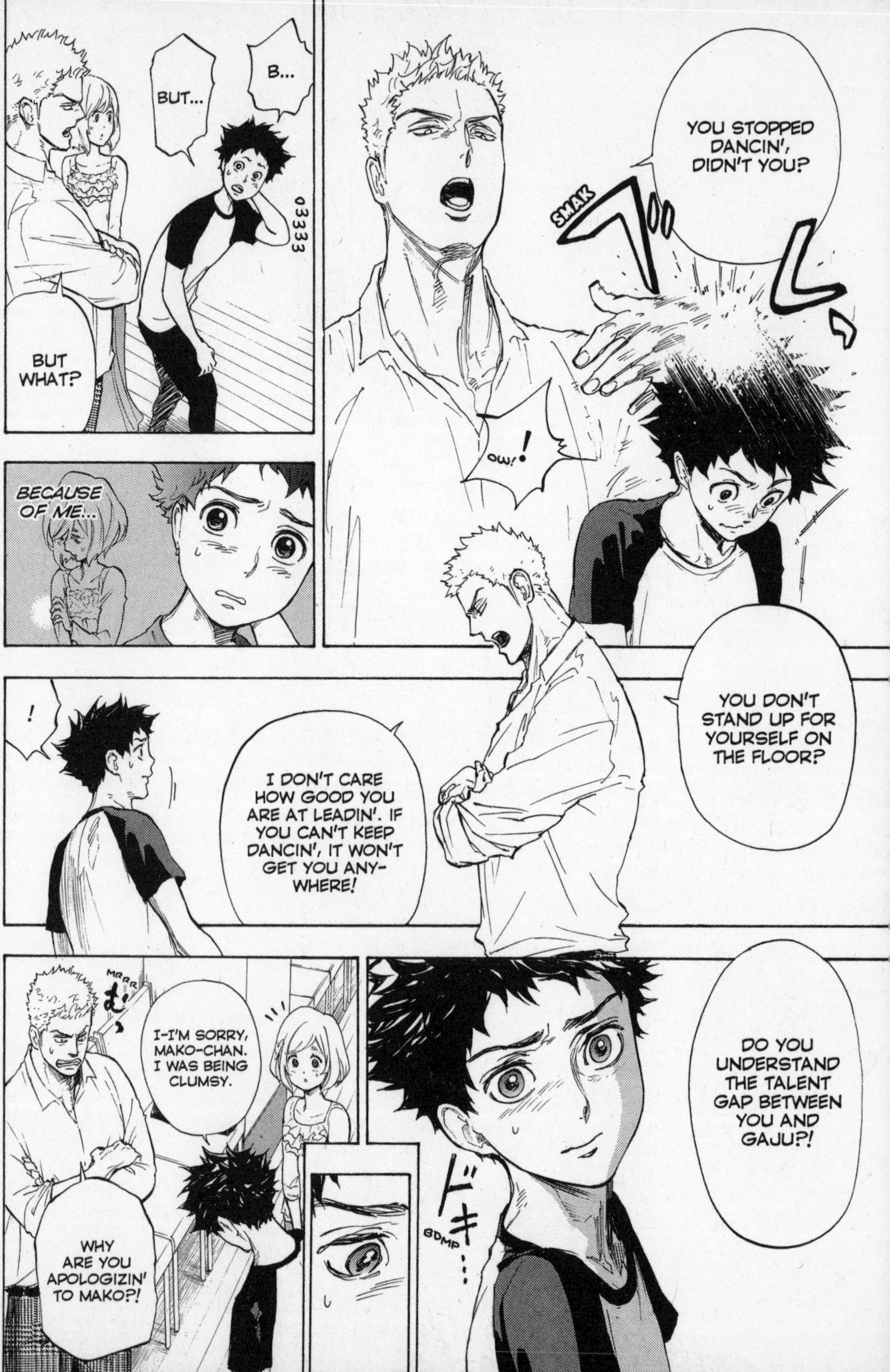
YOU STOPPED DANCIN', DIDN'T YOU?
SMAK
OW!
B...
BUT...
BUT WHAT?
BECAUSE OF ME...
YOU DON'T STAND UP FOR YOURSELF ON THE FLOOR?
I DON'T CARE HOW GOOD YOU ARE AT LEADIN'. IF YOU CAN'T KEEP DANCIN', IT WON'T GET YOU ANYWHERE!
!
DO YOU UNDERSTAND THE TALENT GAP BETWEEN YOU AND GAJU?!
BDMP...
I-I'M SORRY, MAKO-CHAN. I WAS BEING CLUMSY.
MRRR
WHY ARE YOU APOLOGIZIN' TO MAKO?!

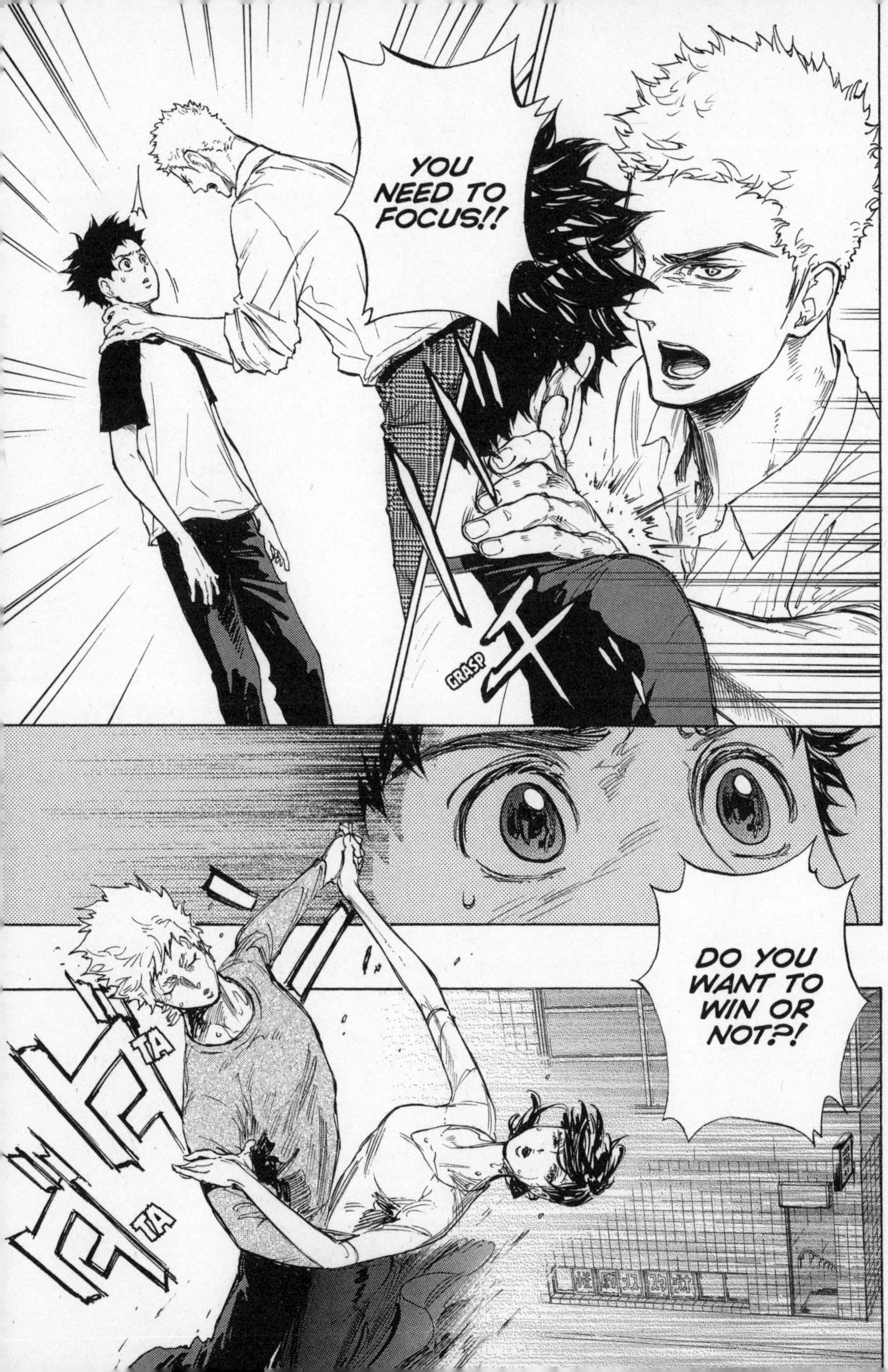
YOU NEED TO FOCUS!!
GRASP
DO YOU WANT TO WIN OR NOT?!
TA
TA

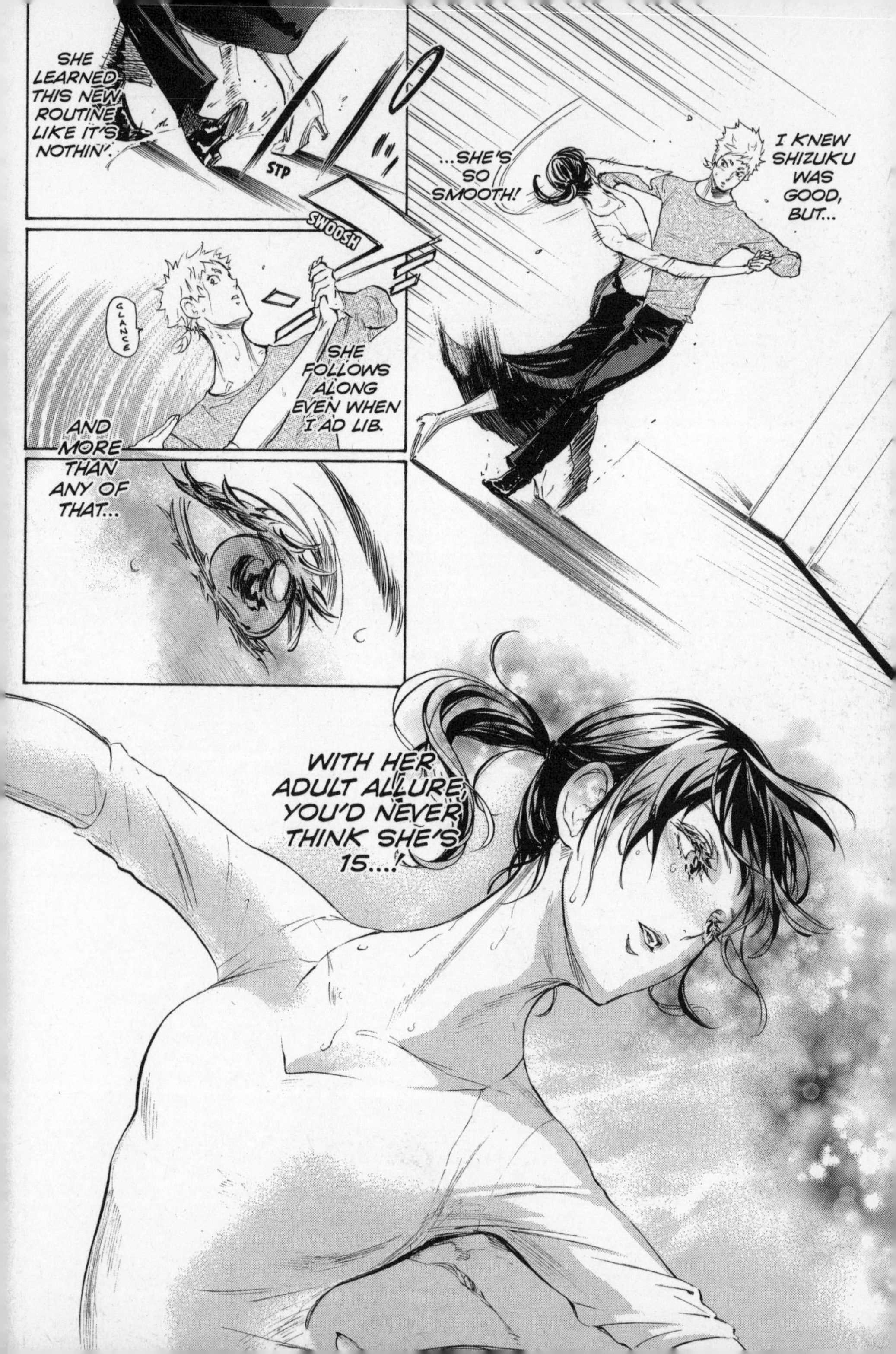
I KNEW SHIZUKU WAS GOOD, BUT...
...SHE'S SO SMOOTH!
SHE LEARNED THIS NEW ROUTINE LIKE IT'S NOTHIN'.
STP
SWOOSH
GLANCE
SHE FOLLOWS ALONG EVEN WHEN I AD LIB.
AND MORE THAN ANY OF THAT...
WITH HER ADULT ALLURE, YOU'D NEVER THINK SHE'S 15...!

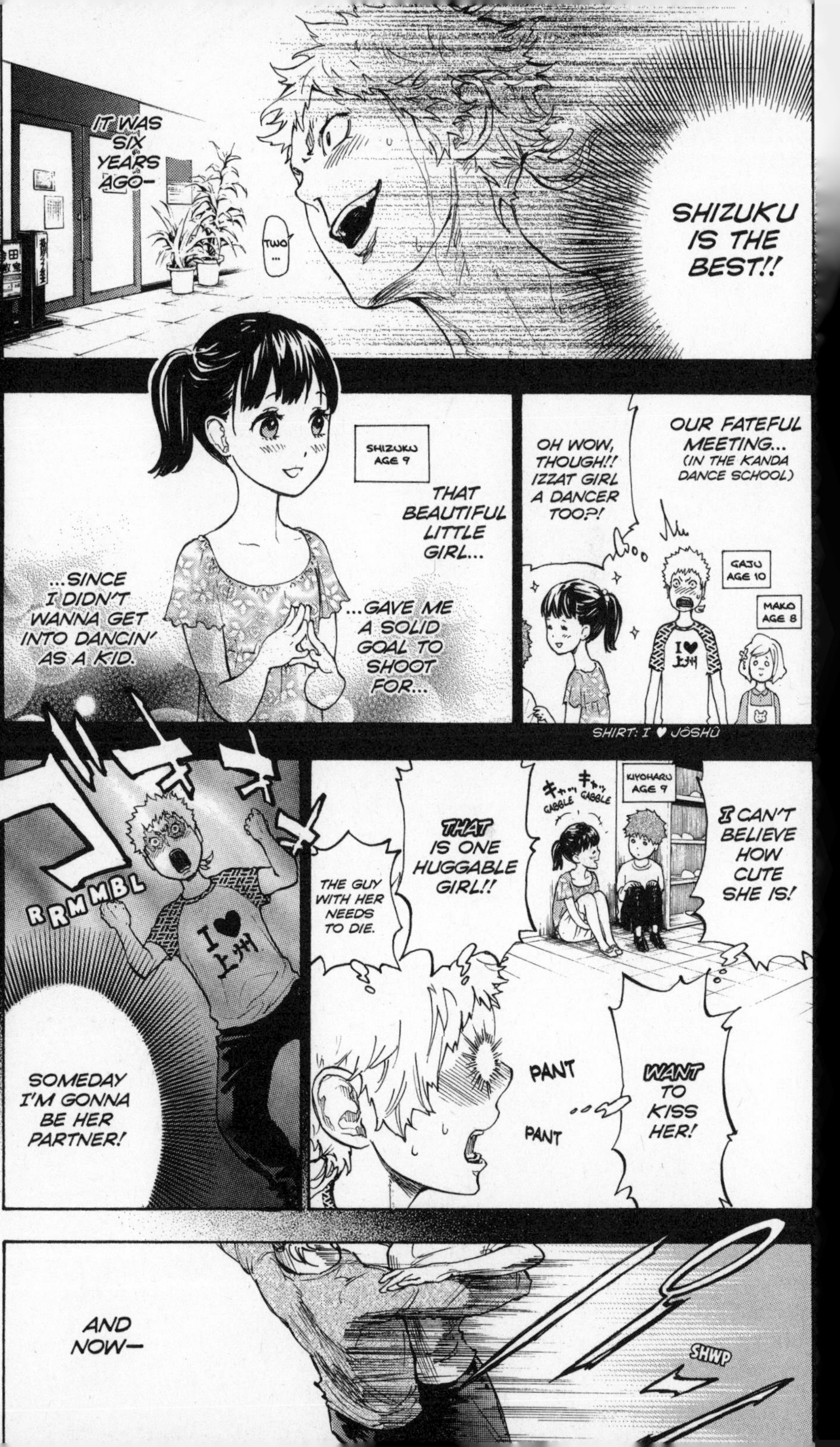
SHIZUKU IS THE BEST!!
TWO ...
IT WAS SIX YEARS AGO–
OUR FATEFUL MEETING... (IN THE KANDA DANCE SCHOOL)
OH WOW, THOUGH!! IZZAT GIRL A DANCER TOO?!
GAJU AGE 10
MAKO AGE 8
SHIZUKU AGE 9
THAT BEAUTIFUL LITTLE GIRL...
...GAVE ME A SOLID GOAL TO SHOOT FOR...
...SINCE I DIDN'T WANNA GET INTO DANCIN' AS A KID.
SHIRT: I ♥ JŌSHŪ
I CAN'T BELIEVE HOW CUTE SHE IS!
KIYOHARU AGE 9
キャッ GABBLE
キャッ GABBLE
THAT IS ONE HUGGABLE GIRL!!
THE GUY WITH HER NEEDS TO DIE.
WANT TO KISS HER!
PANT
PANT
RRMMBL
SOMEDAY I'M GONNA BE HER PARTNER!
AND NOW–
SHWP

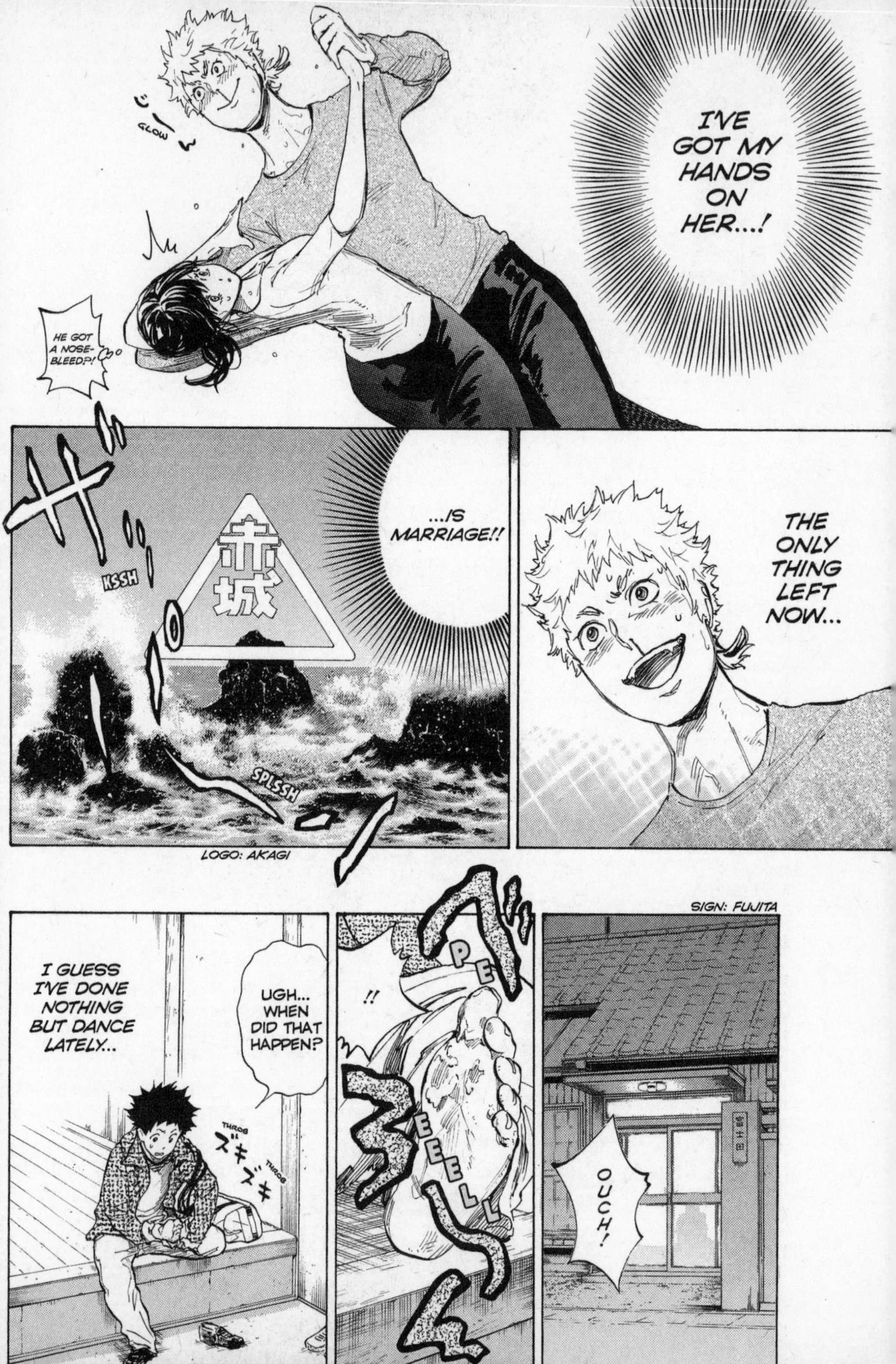
I'VE GOT MY HANDS ON HER...!
GLOW
HE GOT A NOSE-BLEED?!
THE ONLY THING LEFT NOW...
...IS MARRIAGE!!
KSSH
SPLSSH
LOGO: AKAGI
SIGN: FUJITA
OUCH!
PEEEELL
!!
UGH... WHEN DID THAT HAPPEN?
I GUESS I'VE DONE NOTHING BUT DANCE LATELY...
THROB
THROB

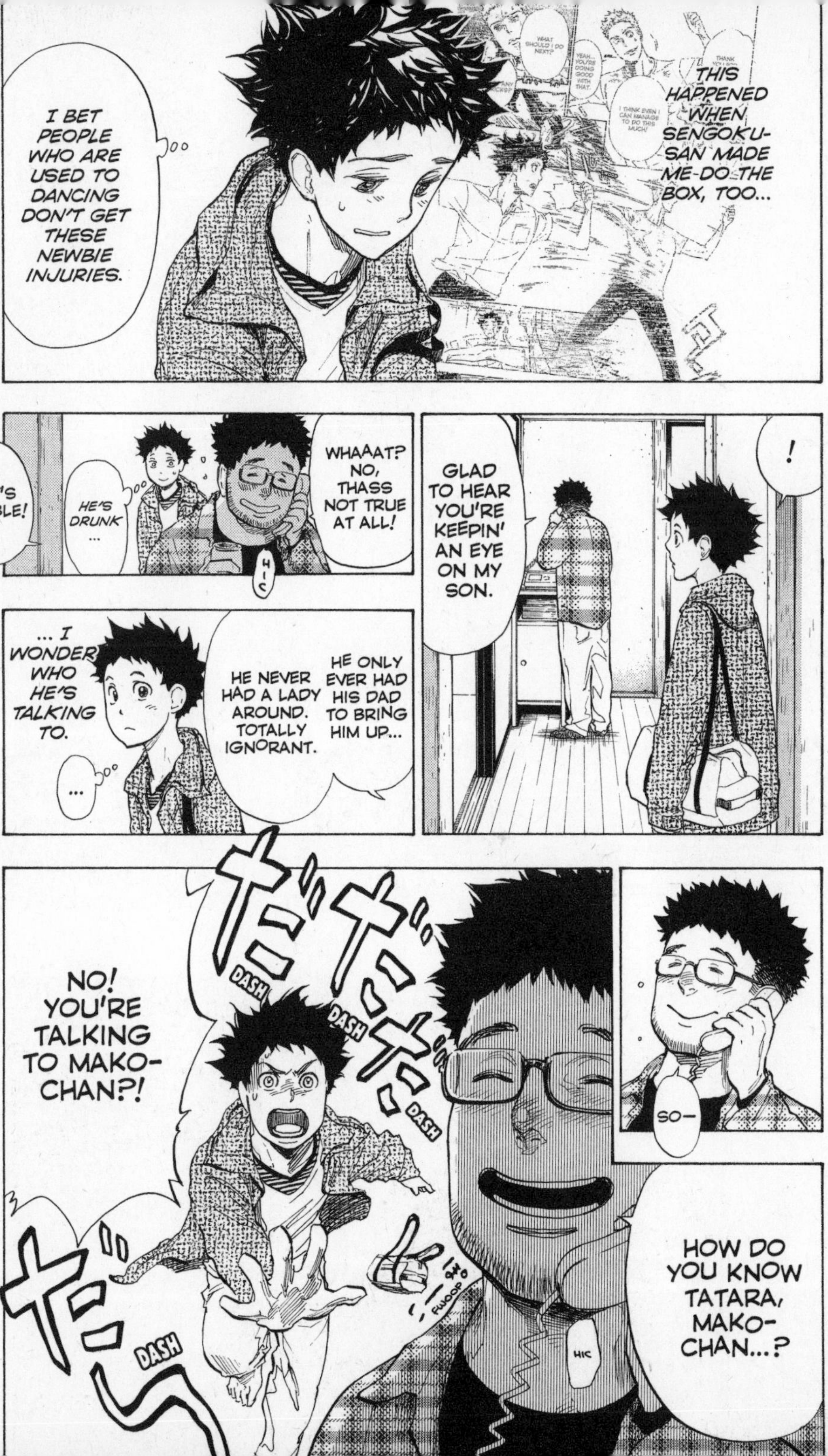
THIS HAPPENED WHEN SENGOKU-SAN MADE ME DO THE BOX, TOO...
I THINK EVEN I CAN MANAGE TO DO THIS MUCH!
YEAH... YOU'RE DOING GOOD WITH THAT.
WHAT SHOULD I DO NEXT?
I BET PEOPLE WHO ARE USED TO DANCING DON'T GET THESE NEWBIE INJURIES.
!
GLAD TO HEAR YOU'RE KEEPIN' AN EYE ON MY SON.
WHAAAT? NO, THASS NOT TRUE AT ALL!
HIC
HE'S DRUNK ...
THAT'S TURRBLE!
HE ONLY EVER HAD HIS DAD TO BRING HIM UP...
HE NEVER HAD A LADY AROUND. TOTALLY IGNORANT.
... I WONDER WHO HE'S TALKING TO.
...
SO—
HOW DO YOU KNOW TATARA, MAKO-CHAN...?
HIC
FWOOP
DASH
DASH
DASH
DASH
NO! YOU'RE TALKING TO MAKO-CHAN?!

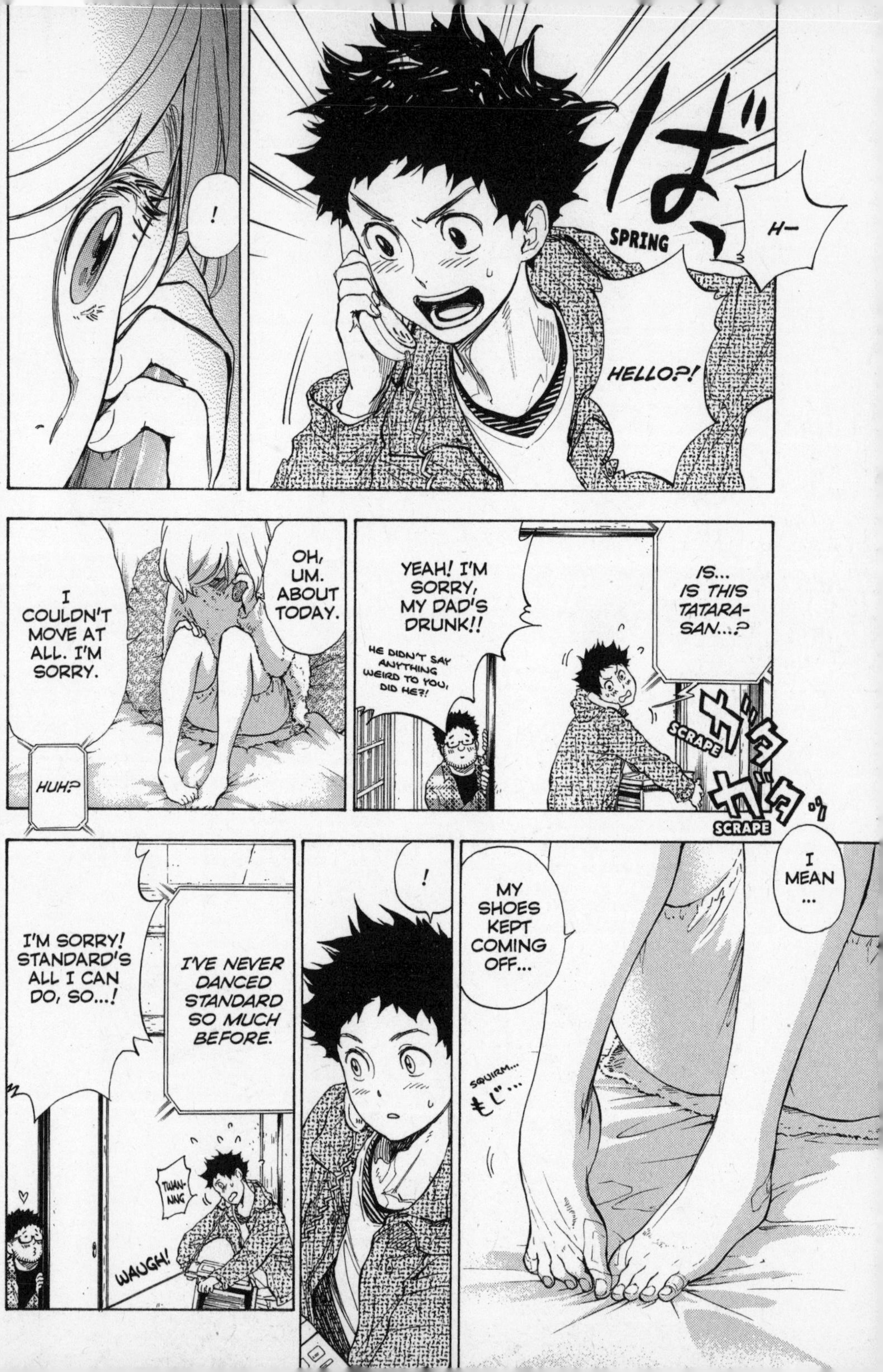
H–
ば
SPRING
HELLO?!
!
IS... IS THIS TATARA-SAN...?
ガタ
SCRAPE
ガタ
SCRAPE
YEAH! I'M SORRY, MY DAD'S DRUNK!!
HE DIDN'T SAY ANYTHING WEIRD TO YOU, DID HE?!
OH, UM. ABOUT TODAY.
I COULDN'T MOVE AT ALL. I'M SORRY.
HUH?
I MEAN ...
MY SHOES KEPT COMING OFF...
SQUIRM...
もじ…
!
I'VE NEVER DANCED STANDARD SO MUCH BEFORE.
I'M SORRY! STANDARD'S ALL I CAN DO, SO...!
TWANNNG
WAUGH!

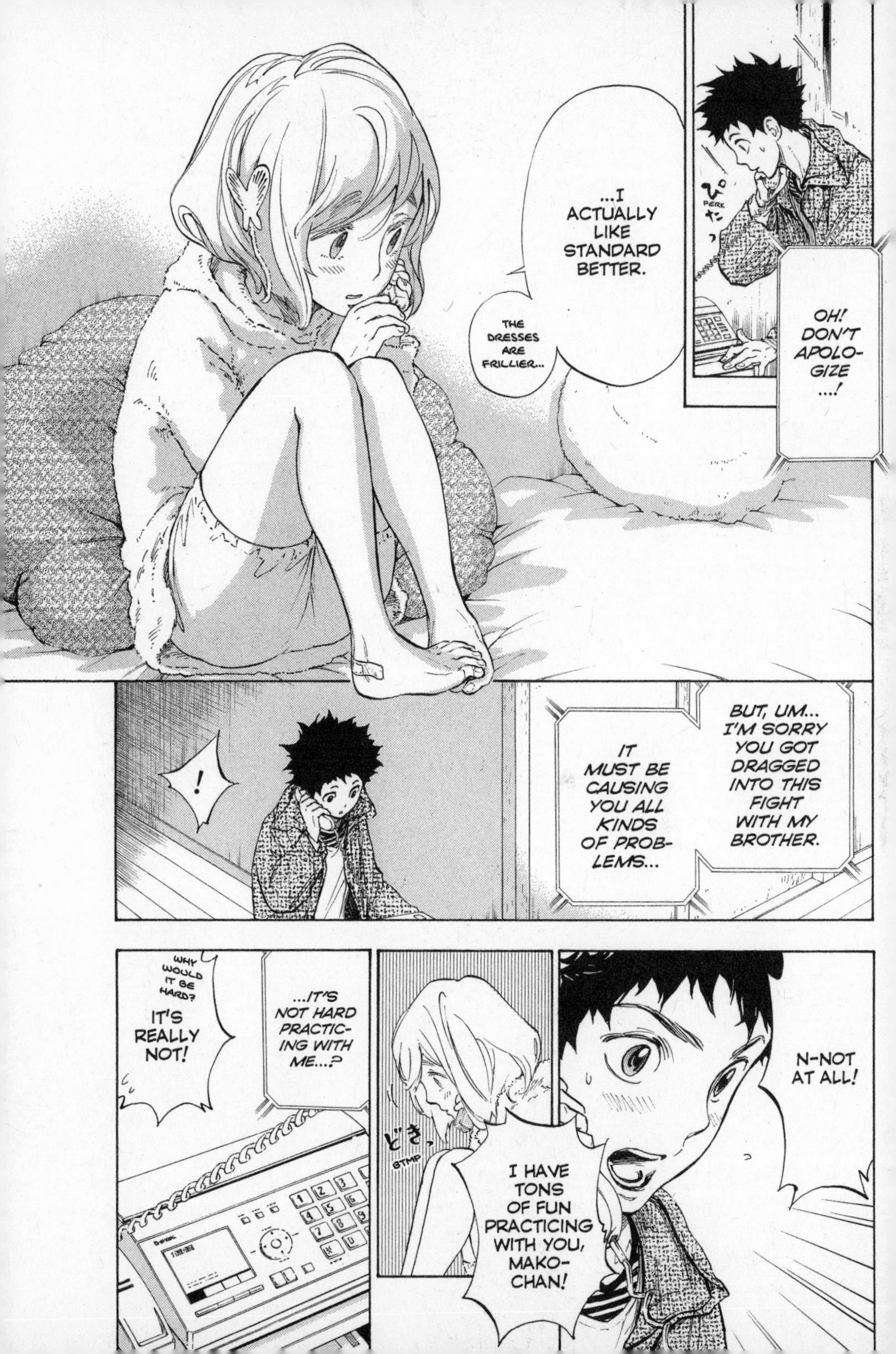
PERK
OH! DON'T APOLOGIZE ...!
...I ACTUALLY LIKE STANDARD BETTER.
THE DRESSES ARE FRILLIER...
BUT, UM... I'M SORRY YOU GOT DRAGGED INTO THIS FIGHT WITH MY BROTHER.
IT MUST BE CAUSING YOU ALL KINDS OF PROBLEMS...
!
N-NOT AT ALL!
I HAVE TONS OF FUN PRACTICING WITH YOU, MAKO-CHAN!
GTMP
...IT'S NOT HARD PRACTICING WITH ME...?
IT'S REALLY NOT!
WHY WOULD IT BE HARD?

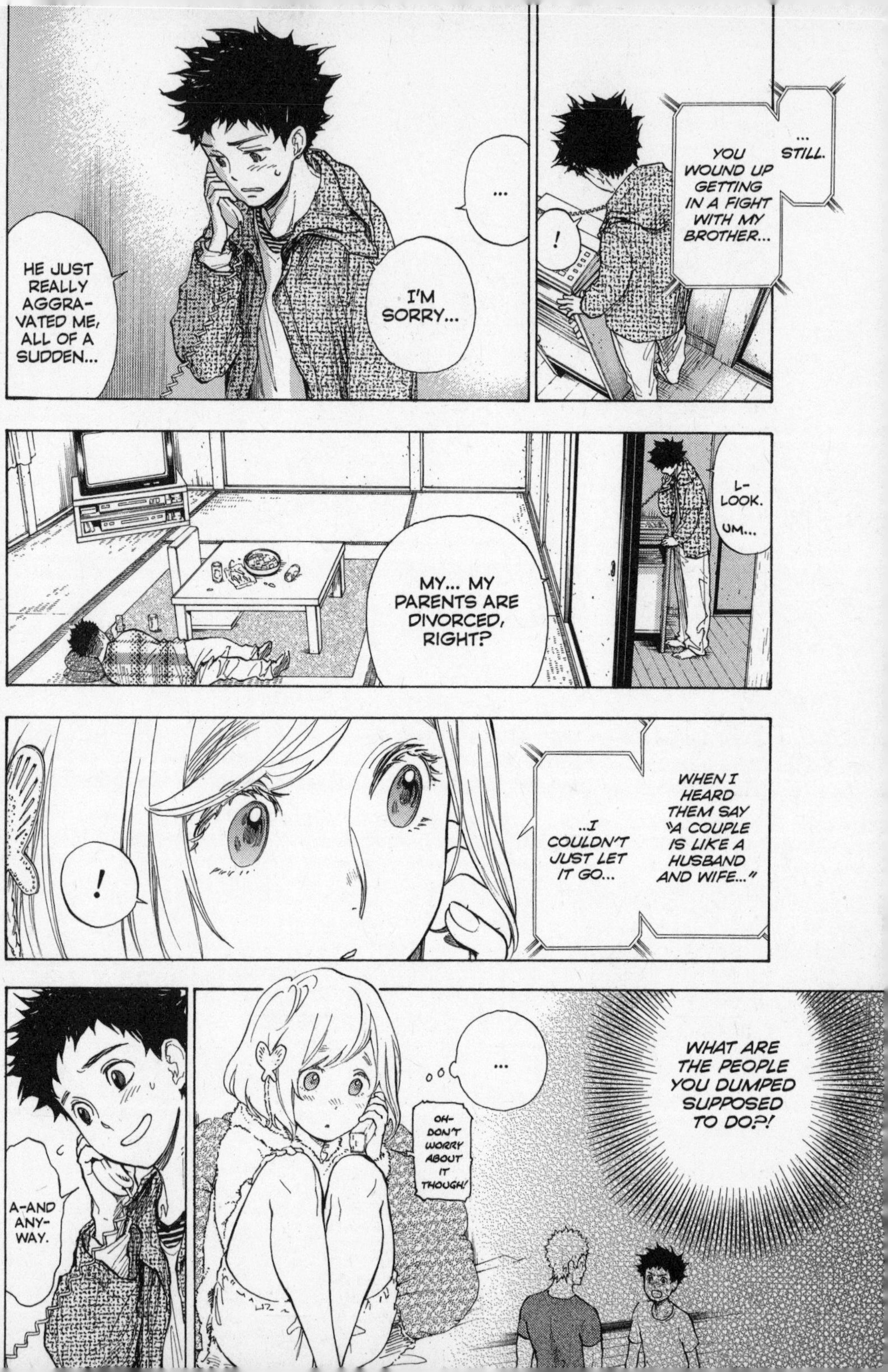

... STILL.
YOU WOUND UP GETTING IN A FIGHT WITH MY BROTHER...
!
...
I'M SORRY...
HE JUST REALLY AGGRAVATED ME, ALL OF A SUDDEN...
L- LOOK. UM...
MY... MY PARENTS ARE DIVORCED, RIGHT?
WHEN I HEARD THEM SAY "A COUPLE IS LIKE A HUSBAND AND WIFE..."
...I COULDN'T JUST LET IT GO...
!
WHAT ARE THE PEOPLE YOU DUMPED SUPPOSED TO DO?!
...
OH- DON'T WORRY ABOUT IT THOUGH!
A-AND ANYWAY.

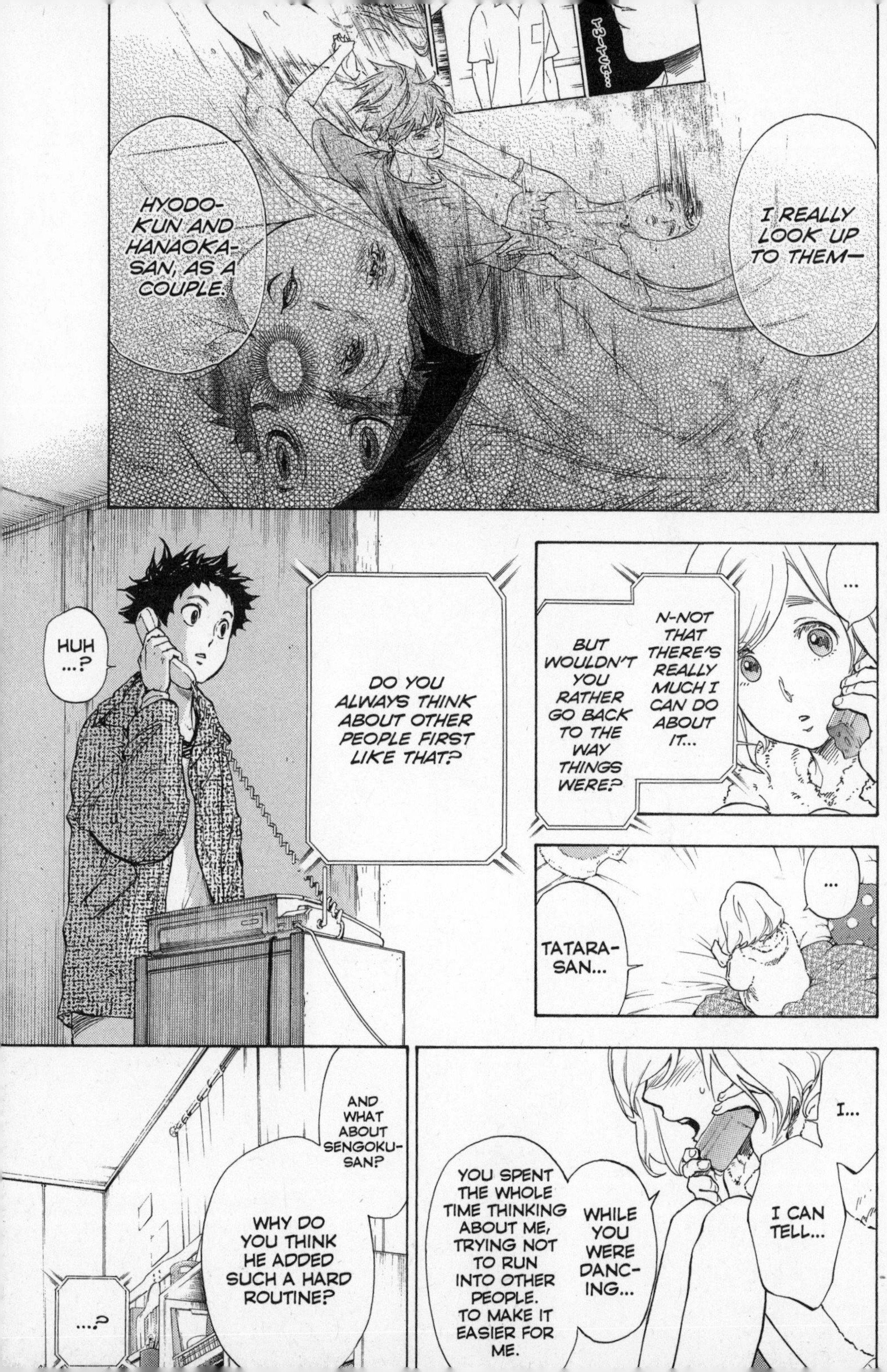

I REALLY LOOK UP TO THEM—
HYODO-KUN AND HANAOKA-SAN, AS A COUPLE.
...
N-NOT THAT THERE'S REALLY MUCH I CAN DO ABOUT IT...
BUT WOULDN'T YOU RATHER GO BACK TO THE WAY THINGS WERE?
...
TATARA-SAN...
DO YOU ALWAYS THINK ABOUT OTHER PEOPLE FIRST LIKE THAT?
HUH ...?
I...
I CAN TELL...
WHILE YOU WERE DANCING...
YOU SPENT THE WHOLE TIME THINKING ABOUT ME, TRYING NOT TO RUN INTO OTHER PEOPLE. TO MAKE IT EASIER FOR ME.
AND WHAT ABOUT SENGOKU-SAN?
WHY DO YOU THINK HE ADDED SUCH A HARD ROUTINE?
...?

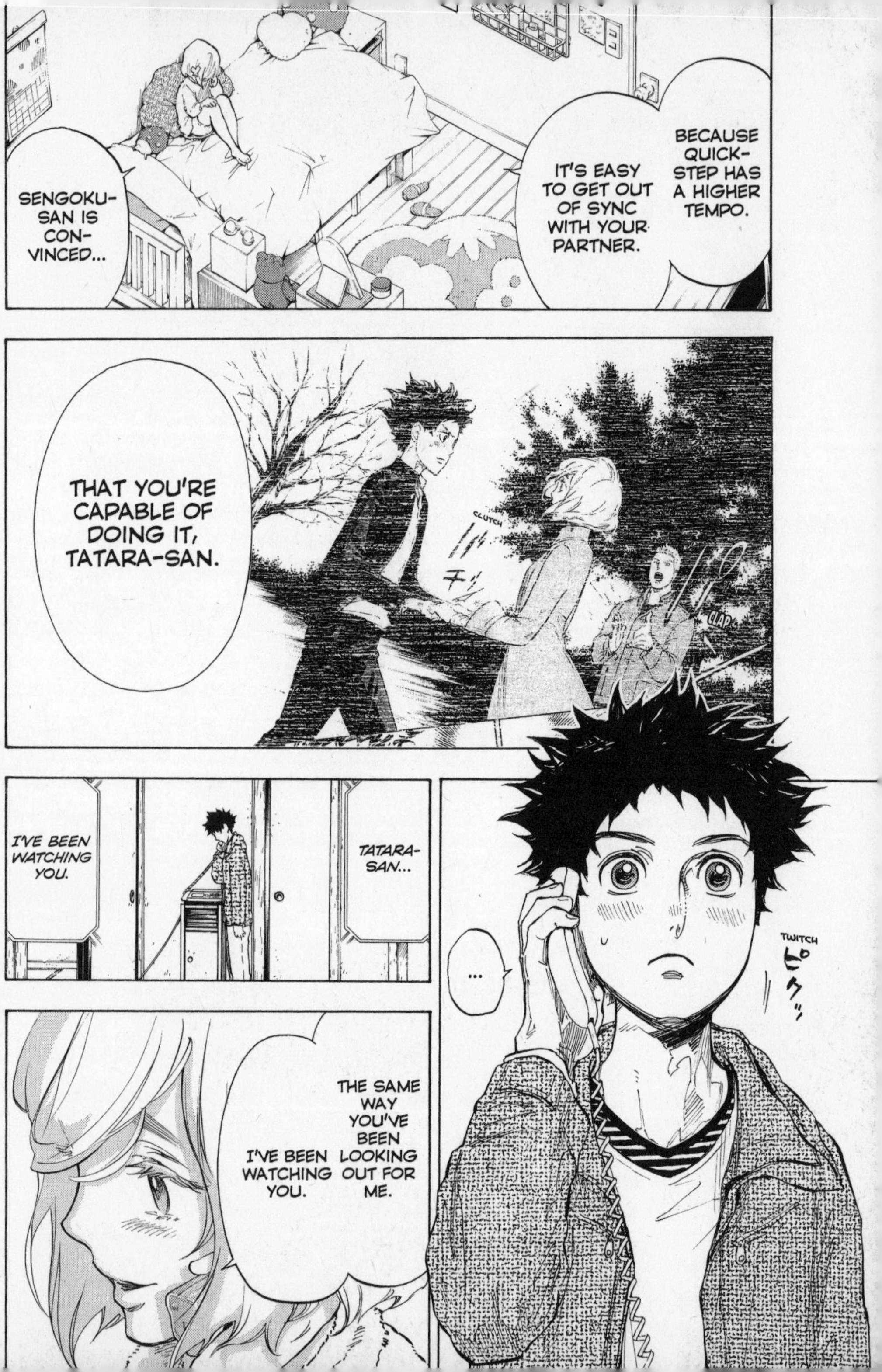
BECAUSE QUICK-STEP HAS A HIGHER TEMPO.
IT'S EASY TO GET OUT OF SYNC WITH YOUR PARTNER.
SENGOKU-SAN IS CON-VINCED...
THAT YOU'RE CAPABLE OF DOING IT, TATARA-SAN.
CLUTCH
CLAP
TWITCH
...
TATARA-SAN...
I'VE BEEN WATCHING YOU.
THE SAME WAY YOU'VE BEEN LOOKING OUT FOR ME.
I'VE BEEN WATCHING YOU.

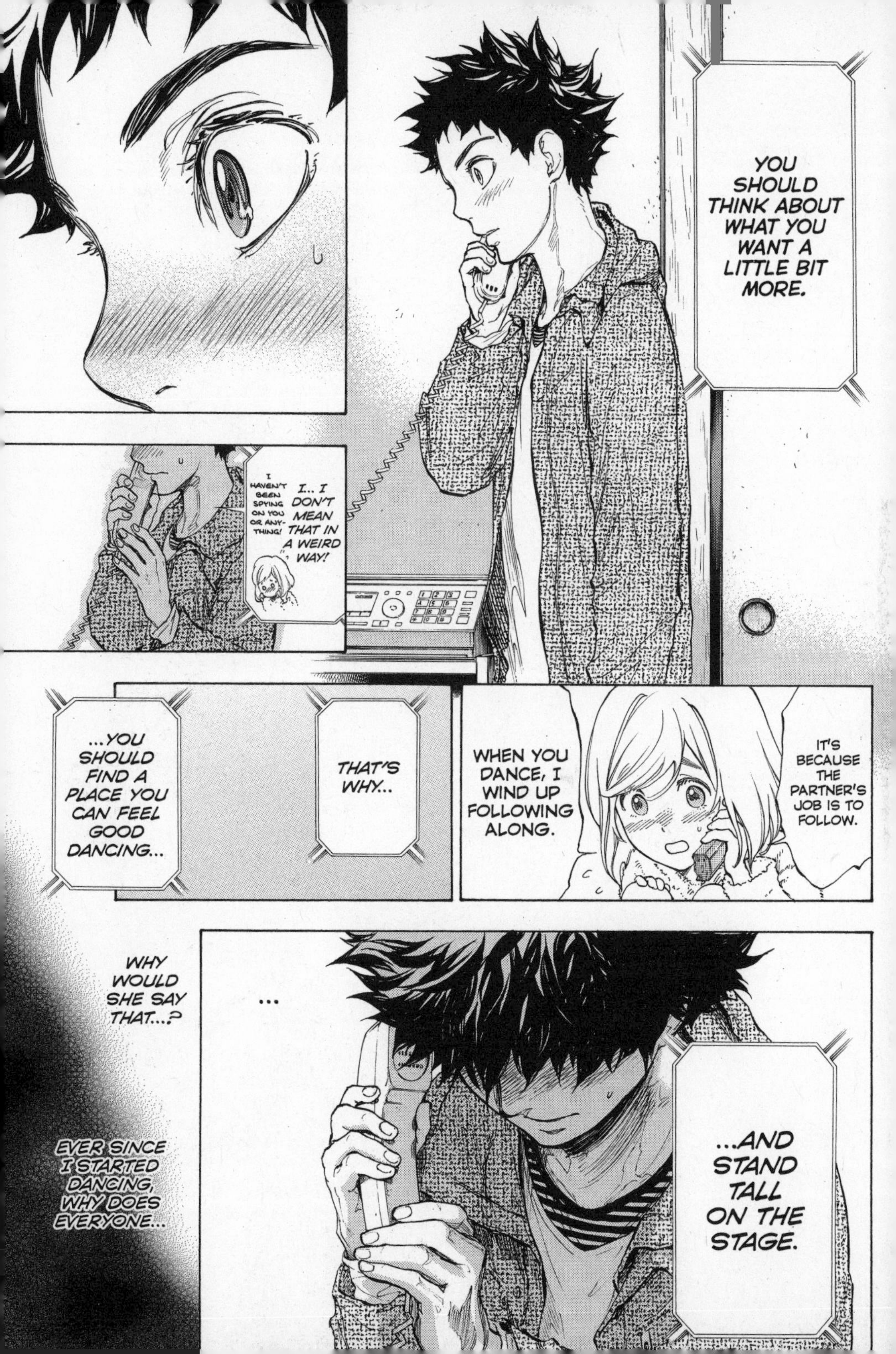
YOU SHOULD THINK ABOUT WHAT YOU WANT A LITTLE BIT MORE.
I... I DON'T MEAN THAT IN A WEIRD WAY!
I HAVEN'T BEEN SPYING ON YOU OR ANY-THING!
IT'S BECAUSE THE PARTNER'S JOB IS TO FOLLOW.
WHEN YOU DANCE, I WIND UP FOLLOWING ALONG.
THAT'S WHY...
...YOU SHOULD FIND A PLACE YOU CAN FEEL GOOD DANCING...
...AND STAND TALL ON THE STAGE.
...
WHY WOULD SHE SAY THAT...?
EVER SINCE I STARTED DANCING, WHY DOES EVERYONE...

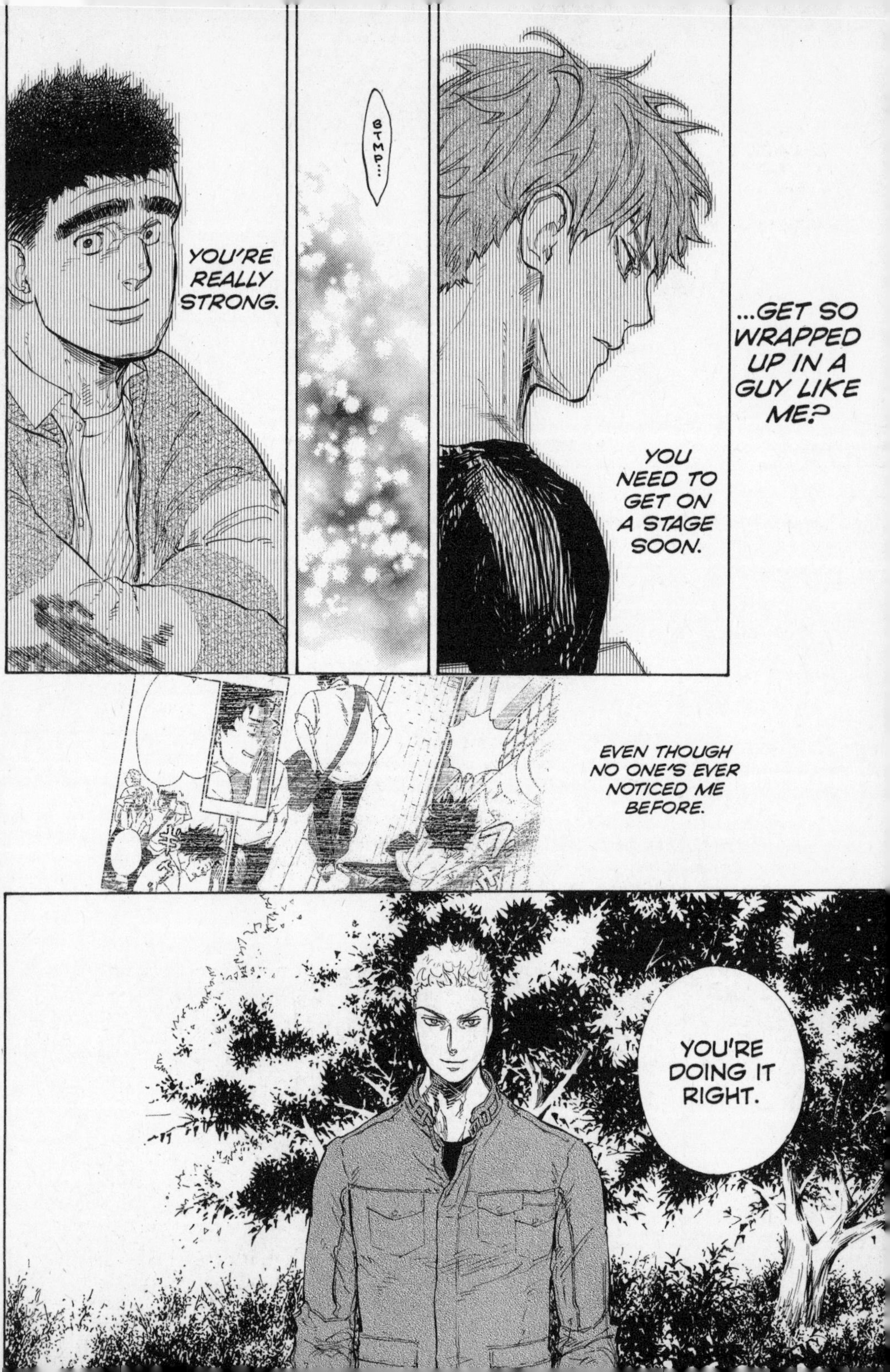
...GET SO WRAPPED UP IN A GUY LIKE ME?
YOU NEED TO GET ON A STAGE SOON.
BTMP...
YOU'RE REALLY STRONG.
EVEN THOUGH NO ONE'S EVER NOTICED ME BEFORE.
YOU'RE DOING IT RIGHT.

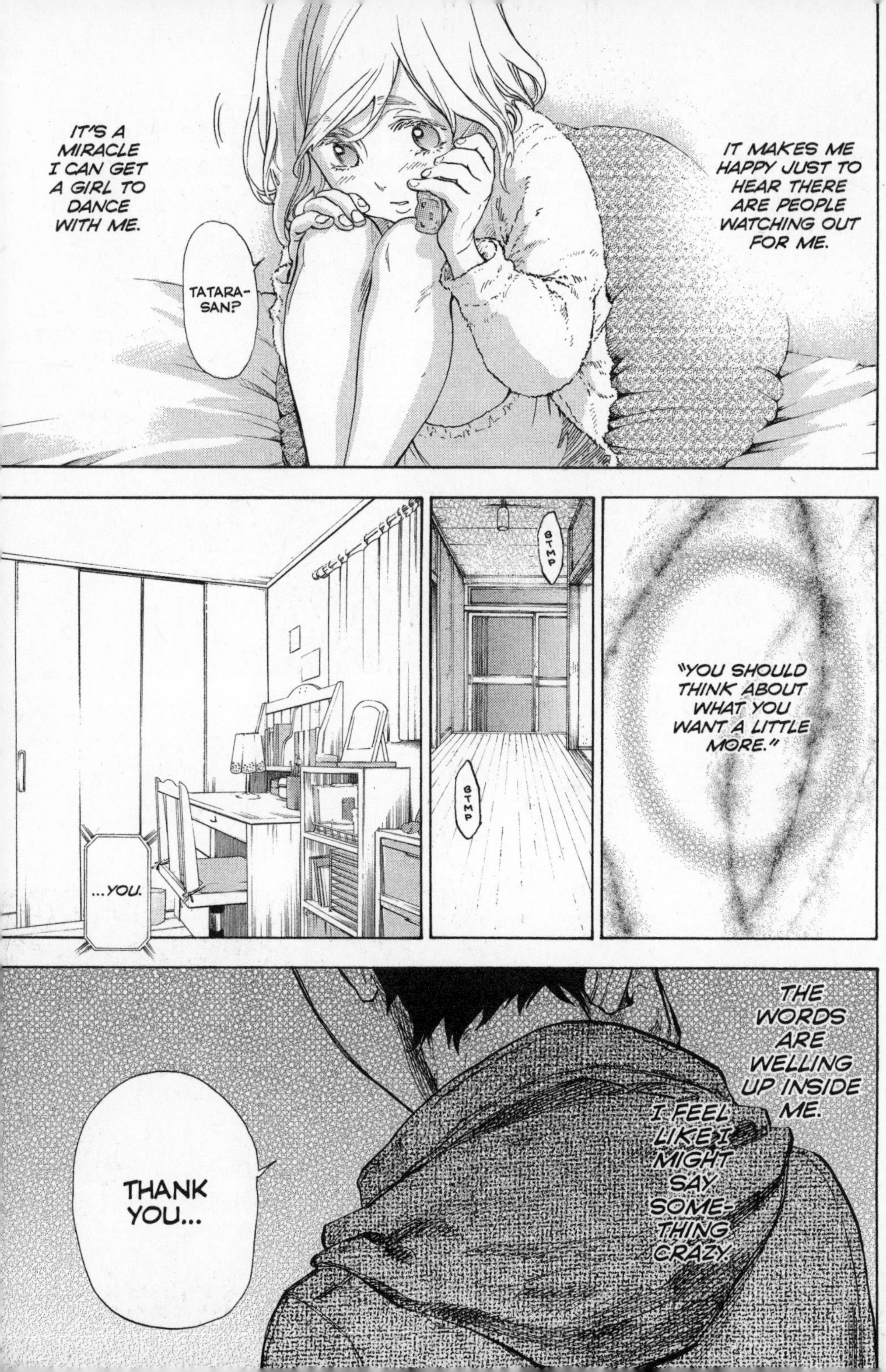
IT MAKES ME HAPPY JUST TO HEAR THERE ARE PEOPLE WATCHING OUT FOR ME.
IT'S A MIRACLE I CAN GET A GIRL TO DANCE WITH ME.
TATARA-SAN?
"YOU SHOULD THINK ABOUT WHAT YOU WANT A LITTLE MORE."
BTMP
BTMP
...YOU.
THE WORDS ARE WELLING UP INSIDE ME.
I FEEL LIKE I MIGHT SAY SOME-THING CRAZY.
THANK YOU...

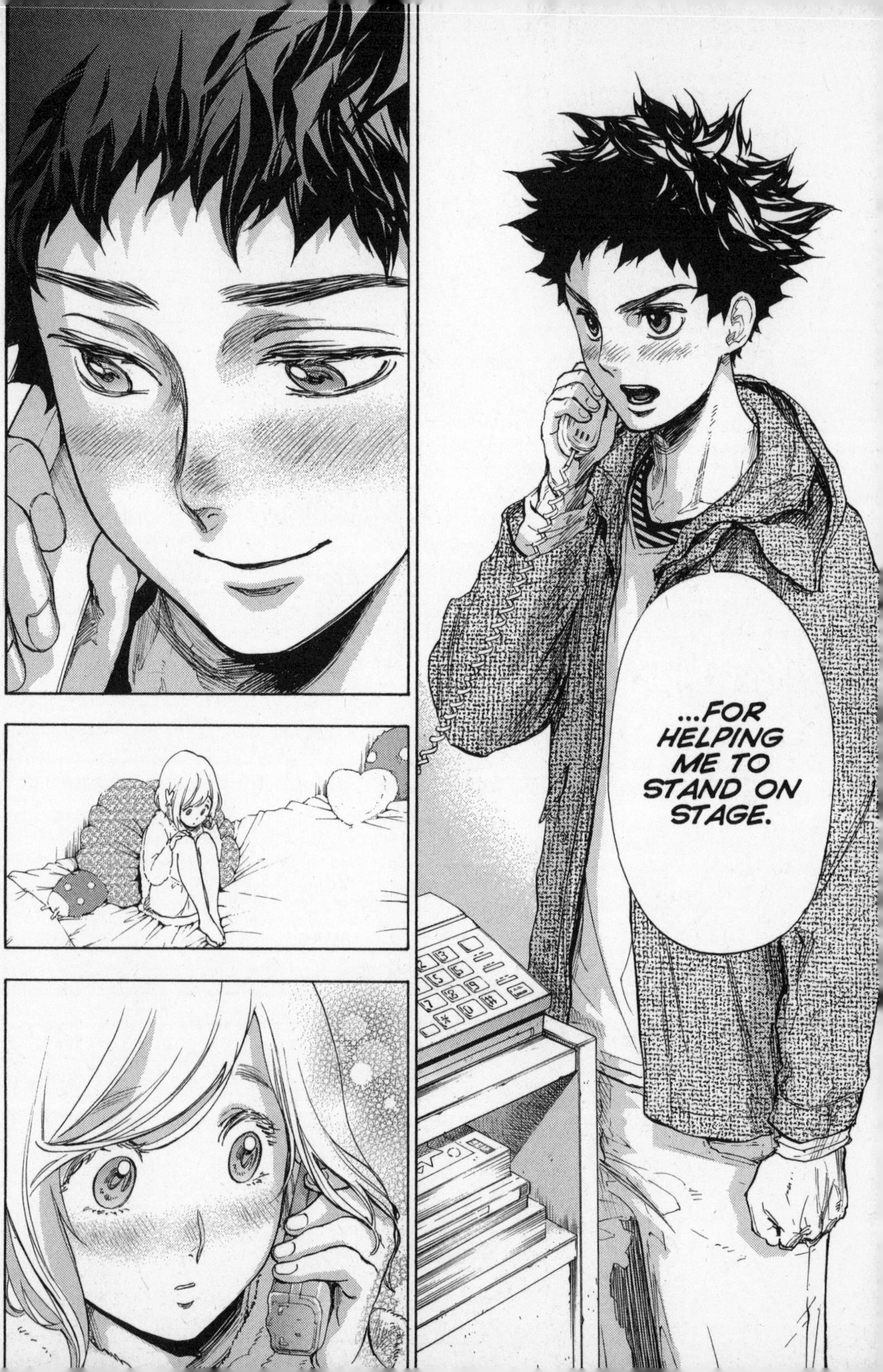
...FOR HELPING ME TO STAND ON STAGE.

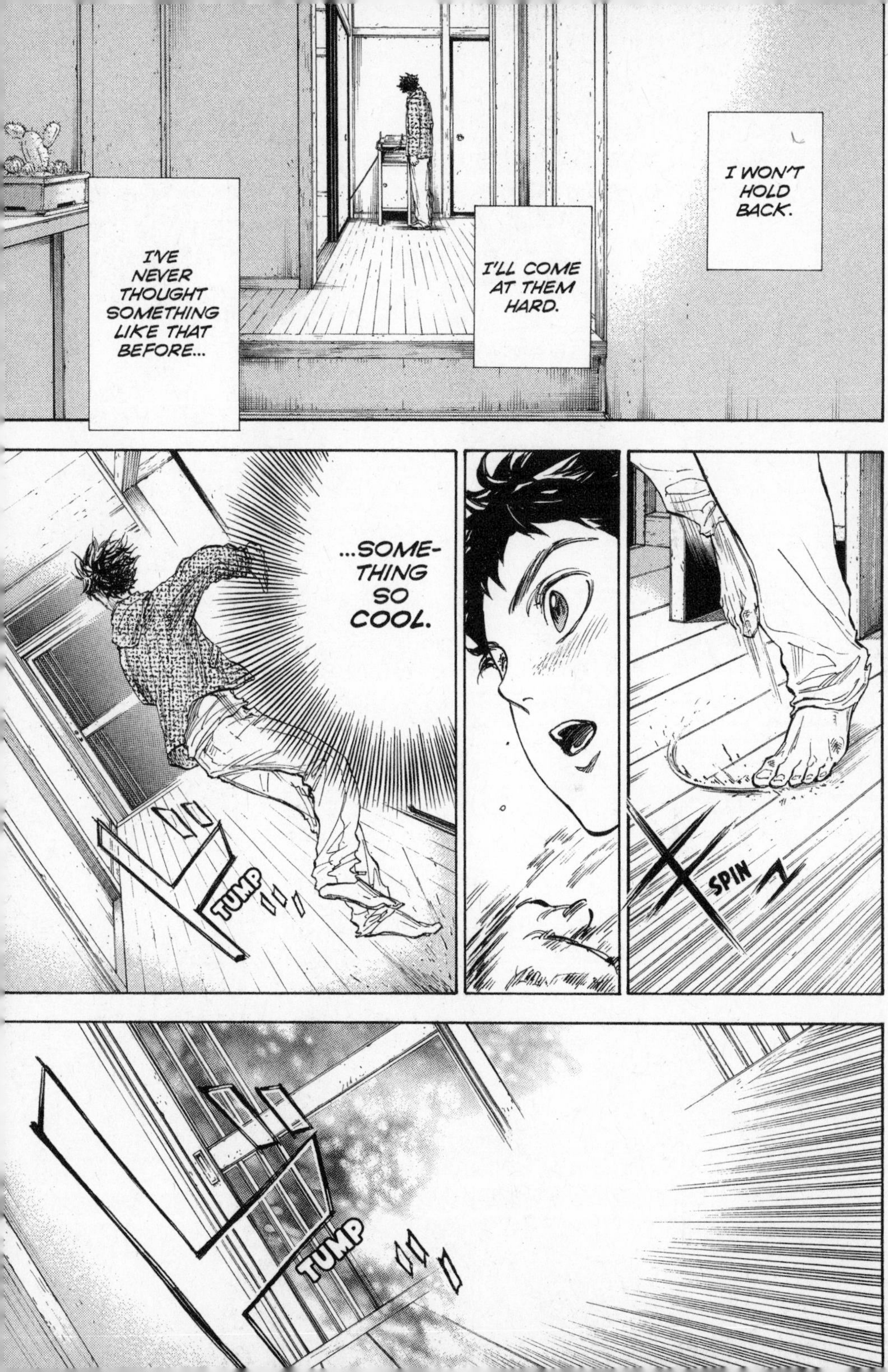
I WON'T HOLD BACK.
I'LL COME AT THEM HARD.
I'VE NEVER THOUGHT SOMETHING LIKE THAT BEFORE...
SPIN
...SOME-THING SO COOL.
TUMP
TUMP

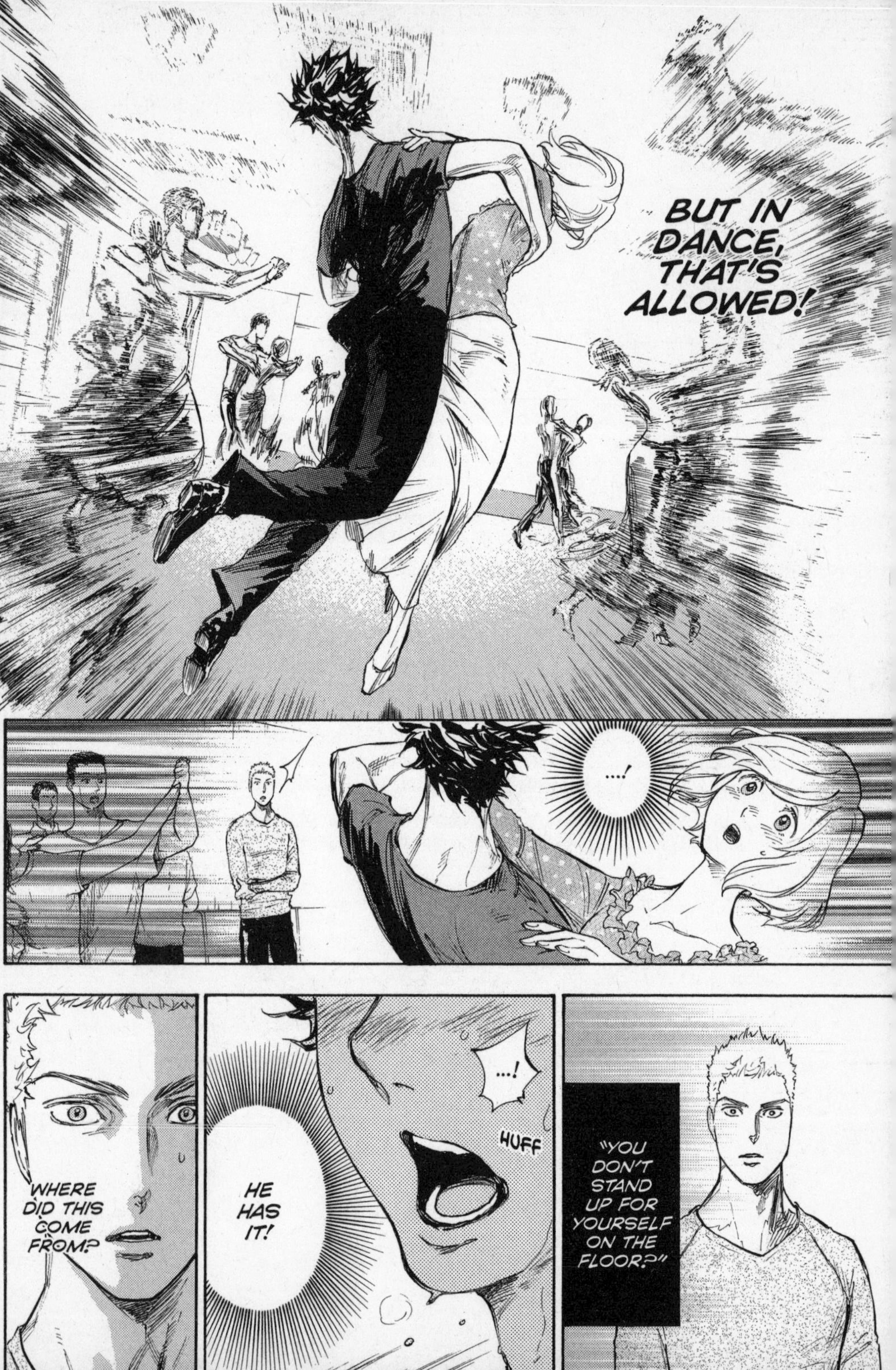
BUT IN DANCE, THAT'S ALLOWED!
...!
"YOU DON'T STAND UP FOR YOURSELF ON THE FLOOR?"
...!
HUFF
HE HAS IT!
WHERE DID THIS COME FROM?

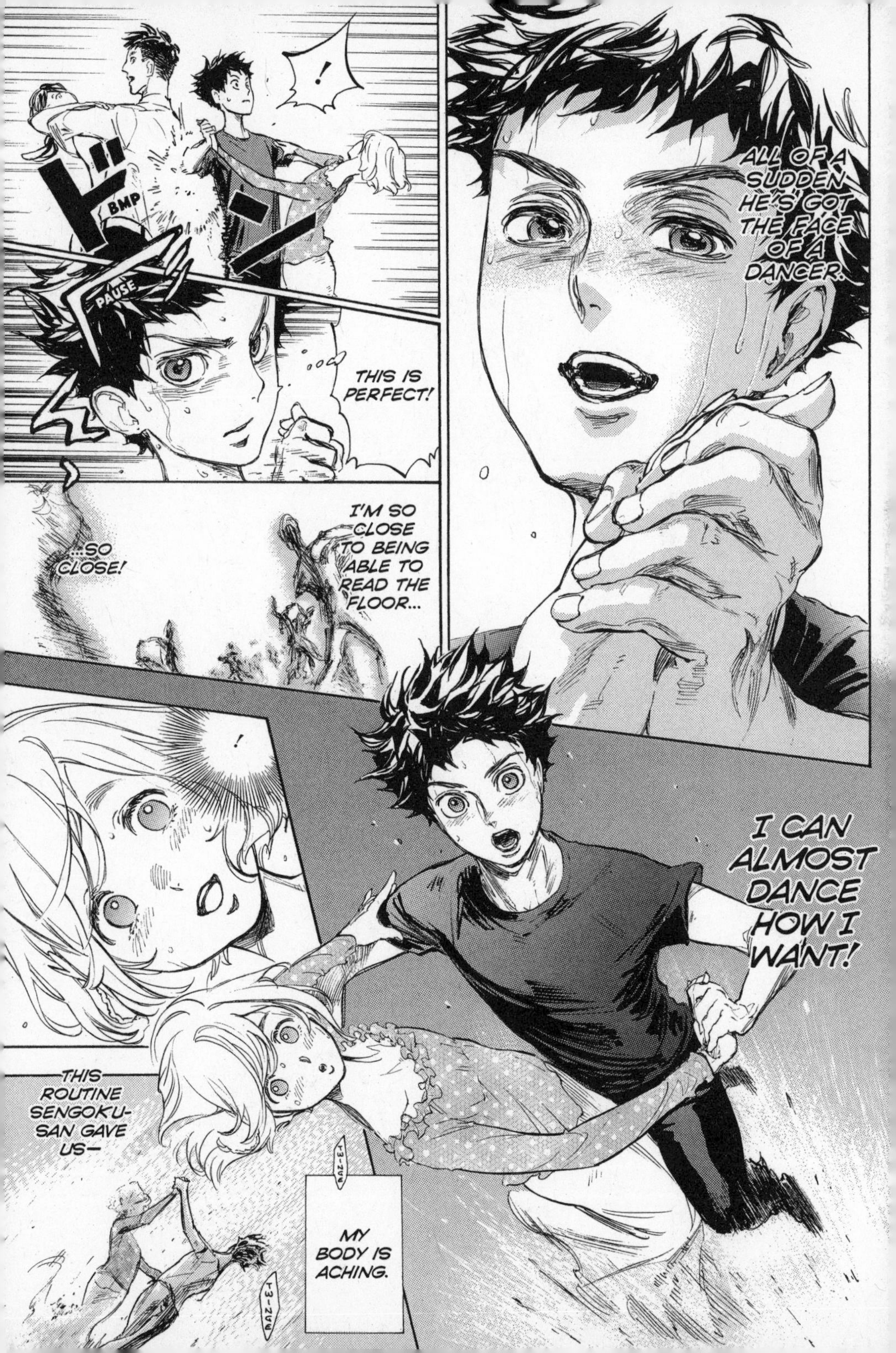
ALL OF A SUDDEN HE'S GOT THE FACE OF A DANCER.
!
BMP
PAUSE
THIS IS PERFECT!
I'M SO CLOSE TO BEING ABLE TO READ THE FLOOR...
...SO CLOSE!
I CAN ALMOST DANCE HOW I WANT!
!
THIS ROUTINE SENGOKU-SAN GAVE US—
TWINGE
MY BODY IS ACHING.
TWINGE

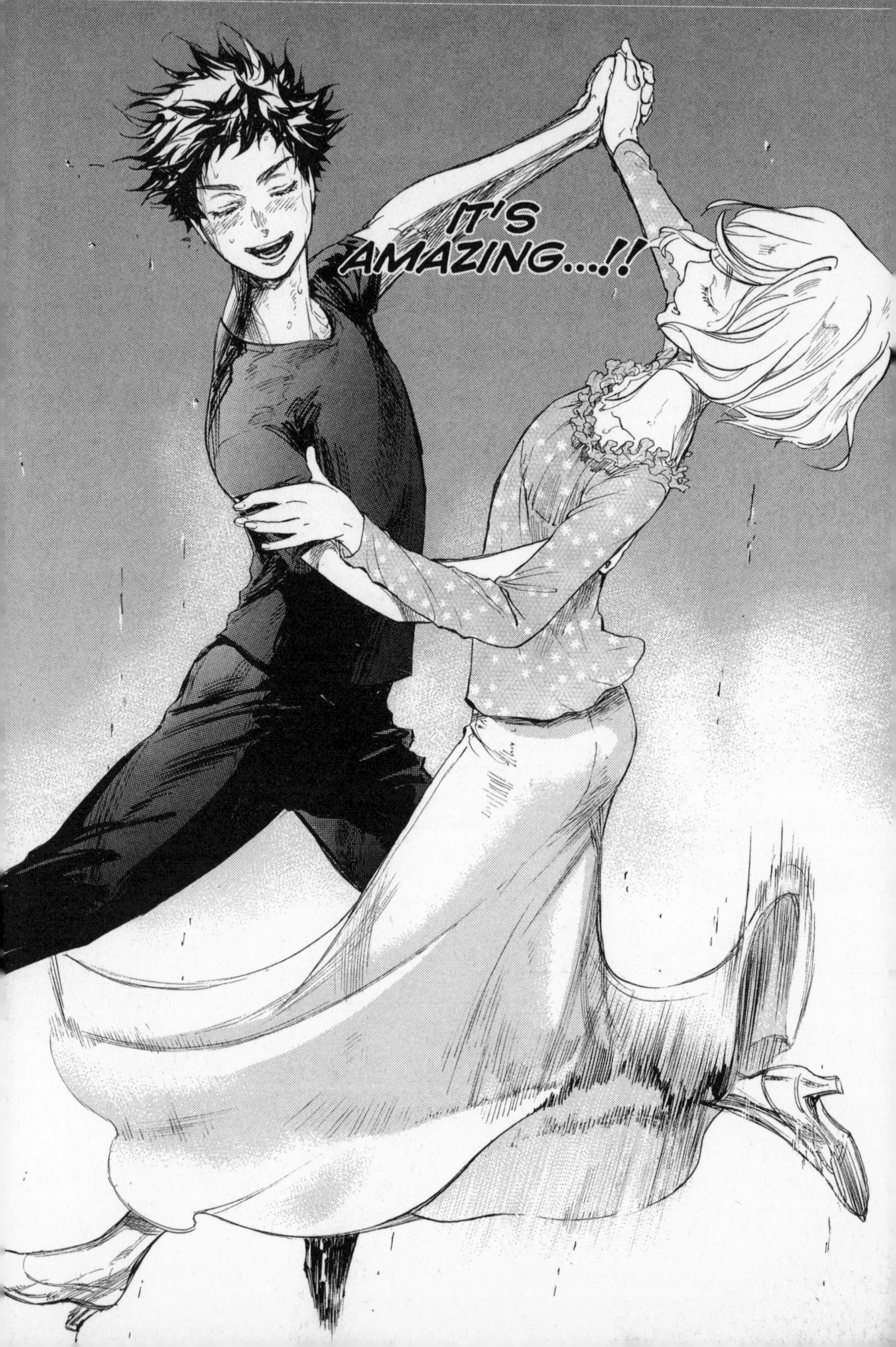
IT'S AMAZING...!!

....!

"CHARM ALWAYS WINS."

IT'S CLEAR WHAT YOU NEED TO WIN.

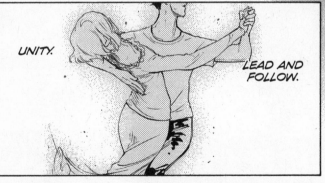

UNITY.

LEAD AND FOLLOW.

AND—

THE ABILITY TO READ THE FLOOR.

STRUCTURAL STRENGTH.

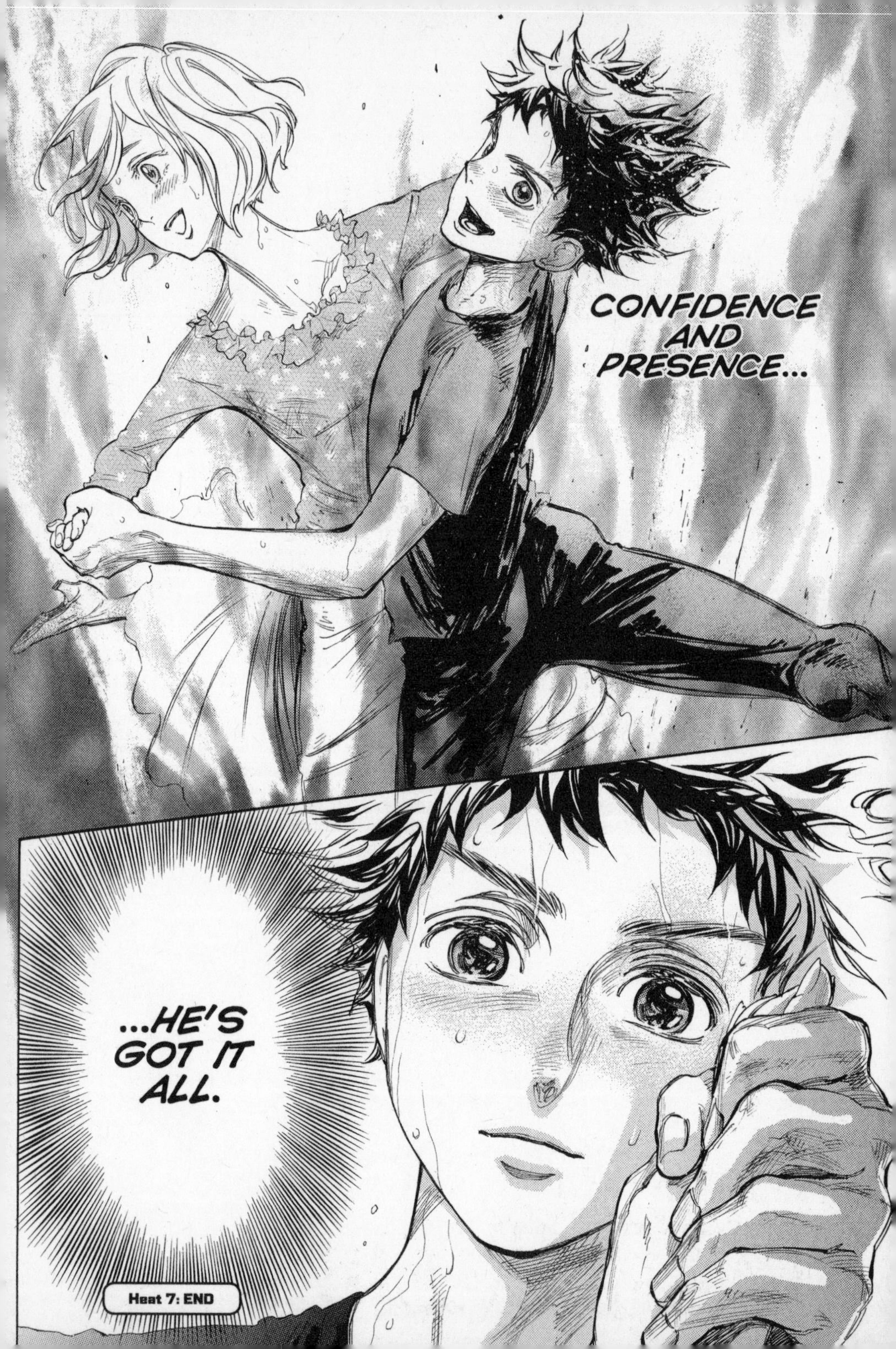
CONFIDENCE AND PRESENCE...
...HE'S GOT IT ALL.
Heat 7: END

WELCOME TO THE BALLROOM

Translation Notes

Garigari-kun, page 90.
"Garigari-kun" is the name of a popular frozen treat and its cheeky mascot. It gets its name from the Japanese onomatopoeia used to describe its crunchy texture: *Gari-gari*, a word that's also used to describe scraping or scratching—which is undoubtedly how the dance studio came to name its shoe-cleaning brush after a popsicle.

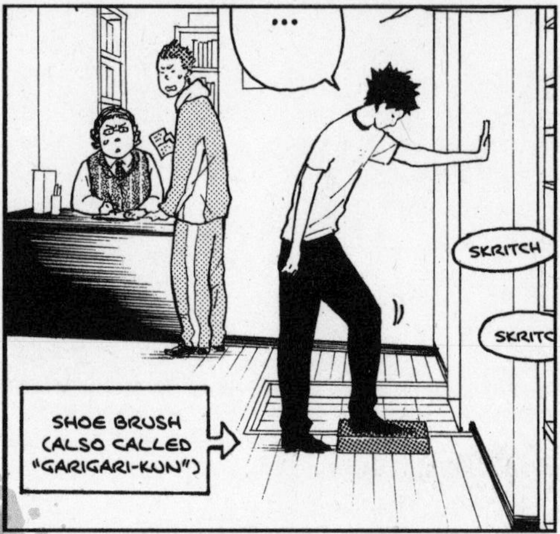
...
SKRITCH
SKRITC
SHOE BRUSH (ALSO CALLED "GARIGARI-KUN")

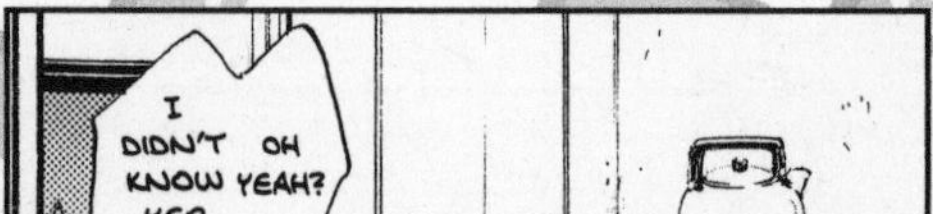
OH YEAH?
I DIDN'T KNOW YER FROM SAITAMA, JINBO-SAN.
I'M FROM GUN-MA.

Gunma and Saitama, p. 98.
As Tatara eavesdrops on Gaju and Jinbo's conversation, he overhears them talking about their hometowns. Jinbo is from Saitama prefecture, while Gaju and his sister Makoto are from Gunma. Saitama is the prefecture immediately north of Tokyo, and Gunma, in turn, is Saitama's northern neighbor. This explains both Jinbo and Gaju's rough-and-tumble speech patterns, which even as they share standard Japanese's origins in the Kanto (as opposed to e.g. Kansai) dialect, are notably more rural and colorful.

A Kodansha Comics Trade Paperback Original.

Published in the United States by Kodansha Comics, an imprint of Kodansha USA Publishing, LLC, New York.

Publication rights for this English edition arranged through Kodansha Ltd., Tokyo.

First published in Japan in 2012 by Kodansha Ltd., Tokyo, as *Ballroom e Yōkoso* volume 2.

ISBN 978-1-63236-377-0

Printed in the United States of America.

www.kodanshacomics.com

9 8 7 6 5 4 3 2 1

Translation: Karen McGillicuddy
Lettering: Brndn Blakeslee
Editing: Paul Starr

Kodansha Comics edition cover design: Phil Balsman

I ♥ Jōshū, p. 171.
In this panel, the ten-year-old Gaju is wearing a t-shirt that uses an archaic term, "Jōshū" (上州) for his home prefecture of Gunma. The province system of geographic reckoning in Japan ended in 1871, when the newly-restored Meiji imperial government established the system of prefectures still in use today.

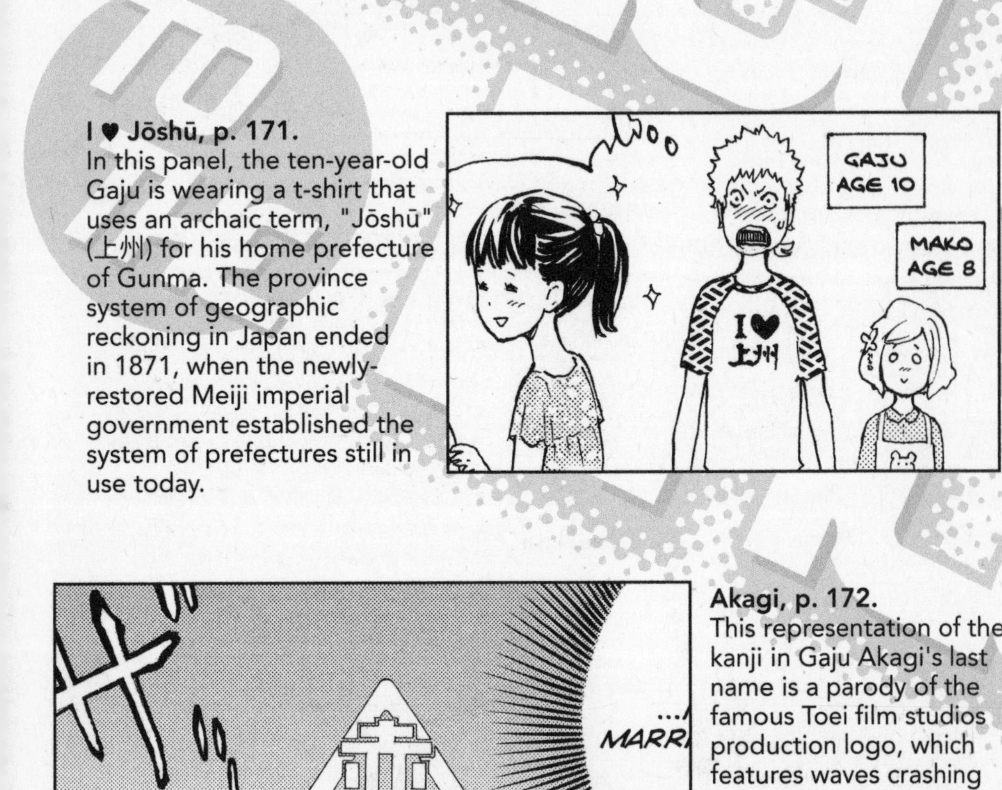
GAJU AGE 10
MAKO AGE 8
I ♥ 上州

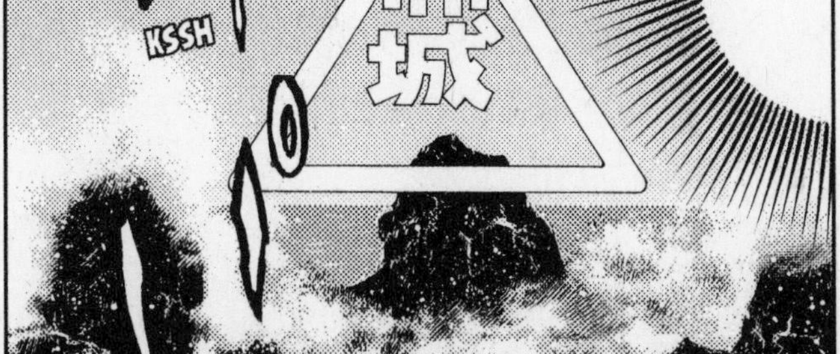
KSSH
赤城

Akagi, p. 172.
This representation of the kanji in Gaju Akagi's last name is a parody of the famous Toei film studios production logo, which features waves crashing over rocks off the coast of Choshi city in Chiba prefecture. The logo appears in front of movies like Battle Royale and TV series like Kamen Rider, to name two examples out of many.